MARKETS, ETHICS, AND BUSINESS ETHICS

STEVEN SCALET

University of Baltimore

Ph.D., Philosophy, University of Arizona
M.A., Economics, University of Arizona

PEARSON

Boston Columbus Indianapolis New York San Francisco Upper Saddle River
Amsterdam Cape Town Dubai London Madrid Milan Munich Paris Montréal Toronto
Delhi Mexico City São Paulo Sydney Hong Kong Seoul Singapore Taipei Tokyo

Editor in Chief: Ashley Dodge
Executive Editor: Nancy Roberts
Editorial Assistant: Molly White
Director of Marketing: Brandy Dawson
Executive Marketing Manager: Kelly May
Marketing Coordinator: Jessica Warren
Managing Editor: Denise Forlow
Program Manager: Reena Dalal
Senior Operations Supervisor: Mary Fischer
Operations Specialist: Eileen Corallo

Art Director: Jayne Conte
Cover Designer: Suzanne Behnke
Cover Image: Postl/F1online/Glow Images
Director of Digital Media: Brian Hyland
Digital Media Project Manager: Tina Gagliostro
Full-Service Project Management and Composition:
Saraswathi Muralidhar/PreMediaGlobal
Printer/Binder: STP/RRD/Harrisonburg
Cover Printer: STP/RRD/Harrisonburg
Text Font: 10/12 Minion Pro

PHOTO CREDITS

page 1: Noam Armonn/Shutterstock; page 18: FOODCOLLECTION/AGE Fotostock; page 29: Alan Myers/Alamy; page 38: Anneka /Shutterstock; page 43: Greg Vaughn/Alamy; page 58: Zurijeta/Shutterstock; page 75: Jim McKinley/Alamy; page 96: ZUMA Press/Newscom; page 115: Aaron Kohr/Fotolia LLC; page 136: PYMCA/Alamy; page 156: Mikko Hyvärinen/Shutterstock; page 172: National Archives and Records Administration; page 191: Roger Hutchings/Alamy; page 209: Corbis Premium/Alamy Limited; page 224: Blend Images/Alamy; page 243: Gino's Premium Images/Alamy

Credits and acknowledgments borrowed from other sources and reproduced, with permission, in this textbook appear on the appropriate page within text.

Library of Congress Control Number: 2013948478

10 9 8 7 6 5 4 3 1

ISBN-10: 0-205-78584-0
ISBN-13: 978-0-205-78584-1

For my Dad
Kenneth G. Scalet

CONTENTS

Preface xiii
Acknowledgements xvi

**INTRODUCTION: THE ETHICS AND VALUES OF BUSINESS
AND ECONOMIC LIFE 1**
I.1 Introduction 1
I.2 The Approach Taken in This Book 2
I.3 The Big Picture 4
   A. Personal and Institutional Points of View 4
   B. The Subject Matter of this Book 5
   C. Three Competing Perspectives about the Role of Ethics in Business and
      Economic Life 8
      Invisible Hand Arguments 8
      Law and Regulation Arguments 8
      Professional Ethics Arguments 9
   D. Organization of Chapters 9
I.4 What You Need to Get Started: A Primer on Ethics 11
   A. Ethics, Norms, and Law 11
   B. Ethical Theories 12
      Assessing the Consequences of Action 12
      Assessing Actions Apart from Their Consequences 13
      The Importance of People's Motives 14
      Character and Virtue 15
      Methods of Ethical Reasoning 16
I.5 Summary 16
Key Terms 17
Discussion Questions 17

PART I BASIC CONCEPTS 18

1. MARKETS 18
1.1 Introduction 18
1.2 What Are Market Exchanges? 19
1.3 Why We Begin with Market Exchanges? 21
1.4 Debates about How to Define Markets 22
1.5 Blocked Exchanges 24
1.6 Background Conditions for Markets to Operate 25
1.7 Three Dialogues That Shape This Book 25

1.8 Summary   27
1.9 Looking Ahead   27
Key Terms   27
Discussion Questions   28

2. THE NATURE OF PROPERTY   29

2.1 Introduction   29
2.2 Property as Relations among People   29
2.3 Hohfeld's Conception of Property Rights   30
2.4 Tips for Learning and Applying Property Relations   33
2.5 Ownership   35
2.6 Further Distinctions   36
2.7 Intellectual Property   38
2.8 The Limits of Property Rights   39
2.9 Summary   41
2.10 Looking Ahead   41
Key Terms   42
Discussion Questions   42

3. PROPERTY RIGHTS, MARKETS, AND LAW   43

3.1 Introduction   43
3.2 Property Rights and Markets   43
3.3 Property Rights and Law   45
Read the Case Study *Property, Law, and Animals* only on MySearchLab   45
3.4 Property Rights and Culture   48
3.5 Understanding Economic Systems   49
3.6 Why Talk about Property Rights?   50
3.7 Relativism   51
3.8 Two Normative Theories of Property Rights   52
3.9 Summary   56
3.10 Looking Ahead   56
Key Terms   56
Discussion Questions   56

PART II   CORPORATE RESPONSIBILITY   58

4. THE STOCKHOLDER THEORY OF CORPORATE RESPONSIBILITY   58

4.1 Introduction   58
4.2 A Debate   60
4.3 Corporate Purpose: Maximize Profits within the Law   62
4.4 Debates about Stockholder Rights and Managerial Duties   63
4.5 Ethical Justifications   65
4.6 Interpreting the CSR Movement from the Stockholder Perspective   67
4.7 Separating the Roles of Business and Government   69
4.8 Self-Interest and Markets   70
Read the Case Study *Madoff Ponzi Scheme* only on MySearchLab   71

4.9 Summary   72
Key Terms   73
Discussion Questions   73

5. THE STAKEHOLDER THEORY OF CORPORATE RESPONSIBILITY   75
5.1 Introduction   75
5.2 A Global Perspective: "All Is Not Well"   76
5.3 Corporate Purpose, Stakeholder Rights, and Managerial Duties   78
5.4 Ethical Justifications   82
5.5 Interpreting the CSR Movement from the Stakeholder Perspective   84
5.6 Corporations and Government   85
　　　Read the Case Study *BP Oil Spill* only on MySearchLab   86
5.7 Ethics, Self-Interest, and Markets   87
　　　Read the Case Study *Patagonia and Profits* only on MySearchLab   87
5.8 Personal and Institutional Points of View Revisited   89
5.9 Corporate Personhood   90
5.10 Summary of Chapters 4 and 5   92
5.11 Book Digest   92
Key Terms   93
Discussion Questions   93

PART III   EFFICIENCY AND WELFARE: THE MOST
COMMON ETHICAL GUIDES IN BUSINESS AND
ECONOMICS   96

6. EFFICIENCY AND WELL-BEING   96
6.1 Introduction   96
6.2 Pareto Efficiency as an Ethical Ideal   97
6.3 How Idealized Markets Create Efficiency Gains   98
6.4 Background Conditions   101
6.5 How Actual Markets Approximate Ideal Markets   103
6.6 How Efficiency Is a Basis for Criticizing Markets   105
　　　Read the Case Study *Potential Extinction* only on MySearchLab   106
6.7 The Ethical and Practical Appeal of the Efficiency Standard   108
6.8 Complications about the Meaning of Efficiency   109
　　A. The Tangled Relationship between Efficiency, Preferences, and
　　　　Well-Being   110
　　B. The Difference between Welfare and Consent   112
6.9 Summary   113
Key Terms   113
Discussion Questions   113

7. PUBLIC GOODS AND THE UTILITARIAN TRADITION   115
7.1 Introduction   115
7.2 Public Goods   116
7.3 Two Neighborhoods and a Park: A Public Goods Problem   118
　　Let's Now Generalize the Problem   122

7.4 The Tragedy of the Commons   124

7.5 Ethical Motives, Government Regulation, Property Rights, and
Corporate Responsibility   125

A. The Personal Point of View: Ethical Motives and Social Norms   125

Read the Case Study *Clean Water Act* only on MySearchLab   125

B. The Institutional Point of View: Government Regulation and Privatizing
Goods   126

C. Corporate Responsibility   127

7.6 Limitations to Pareto Efficiency as a Normative Standard   129

7.7 The Tradition of Utilitarianism   130

7.8 The Attraction and Limitations to Utilitarianism   132

A. Problems with Utilitarianism   132

7.9 Summary   133

Key Terms   134

Discussion Questions   134

8. THE INVISIBLE HAND: ETHICS, INCENTIVES, AND
INSTITUTIONS   136

8.1 Introduction   136

8.2 The Metaphor of the Invisible Hand   138

A. Limited Role for Ethics from a Personal Point of View   139

B. Limited Role for Government and Law from the Institutional Point
of View   141

C. An Adjusted Invisible Hand Model   142

8.3 The Law and Regulation Model   143

8.4 The Professional Ethics Model   144

A. Professional Ethics within an Efficiency Framework   145

B. Noninstitutional Foundations for Professional Ethics   147

C. Mutual Benefit as a Personal Value   148

8.5 Conflicts of Interest   150

Read the Case Study *Blowing the Whistle* only on MySearchLab   152

8.6 Ethics and Values: Moving beyond Efficiency and Welfare Discussions   152

A. The Dance between Ethics, Incentives, and Institutions   152

Read the Case Study *Sarbanes-Oxley* only on MySearchLab   152

8.7 Looking Ahead   153

8.8 Summary   153

Key Terms   154

Discussion Questions   154

PART IV   ETHICS BEYOND EFFICIENCY   156

9. LIBERTY   156

9.1 Introduction   156

9.2 Two Concepts of Liberty   156

A. Negative Freedom   157

B. Positive Freedom   158

9.3 Institutional Implications of Negative Freedom   159
    A. Markets, Property Rights, and an Argument in Support of Markets   159
    B. Property Rights, Poverty, and an Argument Critical of Markets   160
    C. Markets, Voluntary Choice, and Noninterference   161
9.4 Institutional Implications of Positive Freedom   162
    A. Democracy and Markets   162
    B. Democratic Capitalism   163
    C. Two Visions of a Free Society Drawing on both Positive and
       Negative Freedom   164
📖⊢ Read the Case Study *Smoking Laws* only on MySearchLab   166
9.5 Freedom and Ethics   166
    A. Ethics and Business   166
    B. A Tight Conceptual Link between Freedom and Ethics   167
    C. The Disconnect between Freedom and Ethics   169
9.6 A General Model of Ethics and Values   170
9.7 Summary   171
Key Terms   171
Discussion Questions   171

10. RIGHTS   172
10.1 Introduction   172
10.2 Preliminaries   173
    A. Legal, Natural, and Human Rights; and Other Distinctions   173
📖⊢ Read the Case Study *Employee Privacy Rights* only on MySearchLab   173
10.3 Rights as Side-Constraints   175
10.4 Rights and Markets   178
    A. The Entitlement Theory of Justice   178
      A History of Transactions   178
      The Wilt Chamberlain Example   179
      Rectifying Injustice   180
      Applying the Entitlement Theory to Global Capitalism   181
      The Interdependence of Ethics and Justice   183
      Remedies: Invisible Hand, Government Regulation, and Business
      Ethics Models   183
10.5 Criticisms of Nozick's Entitlement Theory of Justice   184
    A. Undeserved Inequalities   184
      Rights to Assistance   186
10.6 Justifying Rights   186
      Trade-offs among Values   188
10.7 Summary   189
Key Terms   189
Discussion Questions   189

11. EQUALITY   191
11.1 Introduction   191
11.2 Fundamental Equality   193

11.3 Implications for Institutions   195
        A. The Tilt toward Institutional Analysis   195
        B. Income and Wealth Inequality Revisited   196
        C. Equal Opportunity   198
☐●└ Read the Case Studies *Hiring Practices* and *Discriminatory Practices*
     only on MySearchLab   200
        D. An Equal Opportunity Society   200
11.4 Professional Ethics and the Personal Point of View   202
        A. The Workplace: Internal Relationships   202
        B. Obligations and Aspirations   203
11.5 Social Contract Theory: Liberty and Equality Joined   204
        A. Business and the Social Contract   205
        B. Professional Ethics and the Social Contract   206
11.6 Summary   206
Key Terms   206
Discussion Questions   206

12. WHAT PEOPLE DESERVE   209
12.1 Introduction   209
12.2 The Concept of Desert   210
12.3 Deserved Wages   212
12.4 Desert and Professional Ethics   214
        A. Entitlements and Desert from a Personal Point of View   214
        B. Entitlements and Desert from an Institutional Point of View   215
☐●└ Read the Case Study *CEO Pay* only on MySearchLab   215
        C. Desert Sometimes Spurs Advocacy for Reform, Sometimes Not   216
12.5 Capitalism and Debates about the Relevance of Desert   217
        A. Challenging the Relevance of Desert   217
        B. The Staying Power of Desert   220
12.6 Deserving Anything at All   221
12.7 Summary   222
Key Terms   222
Discussion Questions   223

13. RELATIONSHIPS AND CHARACTER   224
13.1 Introduction   224
13.2 Relationships   225
13.3 Character: A Criticism of Capitalism   226
        A. Virtue Ethics   229
        B. The Ethics of Care   231
        C. Non-Western Ethical Approaches   233
        D. Relating Chapters 6–12 with Debates about Relationships and
            Character   234
        E. Public Policy Implications from an Institutional Point of View   235
13.4 Relationships and Character: Defending Markets and Capitalism   236
        A Tale of Two Capitalisms and the Pragmatic Point of View   240
☐●└ Read the Case Study *Work-Life Balance* only on MySearchLab   240

13.5 Summary   241
Key Terms   241
Discussion Questions   241

14. COMMUNITY AND THE COMMON GOOD   243

14.1 Introduction   243
14.2 Creative Destruction and Community   244
14.3 The Human Personality: Seeking Change and Tradition   245
14.4 Market Triumphalism versus Concern for the Common Good   246
14.5 Markets That Build Communities   247

Read the Case Study *Life Choices* only on MySearchLab   248

14.6 The Meaning of the Common Good   248
    A. The Common Good as the Shared Interests of Each Person   248
    B. The Common Good as the Aggregated Interests of All Persons   249
    C. The Common Good of Community Derived from the Social Nature of
        Persons   249
14.7 Communitarianism   251
14.8 Justice and the Common Good: Complementary or Conflicting Values?   252
    A. A Progression of Ideas   252
    B. The Relevance of Culture for Ethics and the Common Good   254
14.9 Summary   255
Key Terms   255
Discussion Questions   255

Glossary   258
Index   264

PREFACE

THIS BOOK DEVELOPS a study of ethics as a path toward a deeper understanding of markets, corporations, and the business system. How can ethics guide our interpretation of this world and our choices within it?

This book is designed to help you make ethical decisions and find practical ways to discuss ethics with others. It's written in a conversational tone. In practical settings much of ethics is less about being a lone ranger and more about initiating conversations with others at the right moments. A great practical skill is having the ability to discuss ethical challenges from several angles in dialogue with others. It requires a mix of honesty and humor. The book isn't about giving advice or recommending positions. It's about entering ethical discussions and then clarifying the strongest arguments for and against competing positions. The book aims to increase your comfort and skills for doing two things: (1) interpreting the business and economic system as a whole from an ethical point of view and (2) understanding specific ethical debates for developing your own decision-making within business and economic life.

Consider this puzzle. Some people believe that self-interest alone and free markets create the best business and economic system. In the words of political philosopher David Gauthier, markets ideally are *morally free zones* that allow for the unbridled pursuit of self-interest—and yet all for an ethical result. Others reject this idea, believing that in our professional lives, we must work beyond self-interest and bring ethical reflection directly within our everyday decisions. Both perspectives express a role for ethics but in different ways. Who is right? How do we decide who is right? Which ethical guidelines and self-interested considerations should guide our decision-making in business and economic life? This book addresses these questions, among many others.

The book begins by introducing basic but challenging ideas about ethical theories, markets, property rights, corporations, and law. These discussions lead to a debate about corporate responsibility in Part II. Some say that a corporation's only responsibility is to maximize profits within the law. Others say that this credo misses the *ethics* part. We will examine this debate. Then, in Parts III and IV, the book introduces and applies ethical ideas about efficiency, liberty, rights, equality, what people deserve, character, community, and others. Each of these later chapters offers a central ethical value as a focal point of discussion. Taken together, these chapters integrate a range of values for assessing the moral complexities of business and economic life.

DISTINCTIVE FEATURES OF THIS BOOK

1. *Current business context.* The economic and financial crises of the last several years have motivated a cultural and global debate about the rules of the business system and the choices people make within that system. The book emphasizes a balance between *personal* and *institutional* perspectives, integrating a micro perspective about the

ethics of individual decision-making alongside a macro perspective about evaluating the rules of the system that shape those choices.

2. *Continuity across subjects.* The book examines the role of ethics in business and economic life from the perpsectives of consumers, investors, managers, owners, and employees—basically, all those who participate in the system in one capacity or another. In this sense the book is for all readers who wish to deepen their understanding of markets, corporations, and the business system from an ethical perspective. The book covers all the major topics discussed in texts in business ethics, and the special emphasis is continuity and integration of subjects across business, economics, political philosophy, and ethics.

3. *Engaging chapters.* Each chapter analyzes a central concept with digestible and engaging discussions, and then applies these materials to debates in business and economic life. Students practice ethical reasoning throughout the chapters—including online case studies—to develop skills that are versatile and have many applications beyond the text.

4. *The challenge of ethical debate.* How is productive ethical debate possible? First, it requires mastery of a range of important basic concepts, which are covered throughout the book. Second, there is a fairly well-defined structure to the ideas that lead to competing visions about the role and content of ethics in business and economic life, and this book develops that structure. A study of ethics is more than a balancing of intuitions. An important question is how do those intuitions and debates fit into a more comprehensive understanding of ethics and values? This book focuses on developing this systematic perspective, which reveals intriguing, challenging, and enjoyable intellectual puzzles. Experiencing and responding to these intellectual puzzles can lead to a healthy respect for ethical debate.

5. *Chapter organization.* The goal of each chapter is to integrate and develop important ideas on the chapter topic, analyze provocative ethical puzzles, and indicate how the chapter ideas have versatile applications. The text emphasizes core concepts underlying many ethical debates and how they form building blocks for competing arguments across topics.

   Each chapter includes a listing of skills to be developed in that chapter, an introduction, a summary, a listing of key terms defined within the text, and discussion questions. The discussion questions are especially notable for this text. They are an integral part of the study of each chapter for those who seek a more advanced understanding of the material. These questions can focus your interests on some particular aspect of the reading or indicate additional puzzles beyond the core discussion. The online materials include a brief list of recommended readings that can also be assigned in tandem with the main text. As the chapters progress, the materials become part of an expanding network of ideas for engaging ethical discussions and debates. Taking all of these organizational elements together, each chapter is designed to allow for great flexibility to focus on themes that are of greatest interest.

6. *Practical Applications.* The text includes many applications and examples, and there are accompanying online materials with case studies for analysis, which are indicated by the [insert book icon] symbol within each chapter. In addition, your own online searches can also yield a treasure trove of examples. Many of the best cases and examples happen in real time, and the daily news invariably provides revealing and exciting

applications. By following current events, you can witness the ideas of the text playing out in real time before your eyes.

7. *Background.* This book offers a comprehensive introduction and requires no previous acquaintance with philosophy, business, or economics. The fourteen chapters are designed for a one-semester course of study. The book defines all of its key terms and in that sense is a self-contained study for introductory classes; but the discussions are designed to offer challenges at varied levels of analysis. The writing is appropriate as an introduction for business, philosophy, and general education students; as the main text for business ethics and professional ethics classes; and as a text for interdisciplinary majors that combine philosophy, politics, economics, and law. In addition, the writing is designed for broader and more advanced backgrounds for MBA courses and advanced applied ethics, political philosophy, or ethics and economics courses.

This text is available in a variety of formats—digital and print. To learn more about our programs, pricing options, and customization, visit www.pearsonhighered.com.

Acknowledgments

After a decade of teaching and writing, this book began to take shape through my experience and conviction that many people enjoy and seek discussion of ethical puzzles in business and economics but the opportunities can seem too few. This book responds to the hope of contributing to greater public dialogue about the role of ethics in public life.

There are so many people to thank for all of the discussions, debates, and inspiration—more than I could possibly list. It's a product of many influences and many years.

Let me begin by thanking my Dad to whom this book is dedicated. Over a long career I saw how his undergraduate and MBA students loved his humor, common sense, and humanity about all matters concerning business and economics. Were I to carry forward even in small part his years of inspired teaching, I would feel lucky. I still remember our first conversation about economics—he started by asking me the purpose of businesses—and ever since the two of us have discussed and debated economic issues, always to my enjoyment and profit. I will always cherish the countless conversations through the many drafts of this book, with his probing questions at every step of the way. For everything, Dad, this book is dedicated to you.

I thank my wife Debby and daughter Sophia for their endless encouragement and support, especially in those moments when the work took many times longer than I imagined that it would. Debby always fortified me to take the time that I needed to bring this book to life. My family not only endured innumerable hours that I spirited away on research and writing, but they endured the scintillating conversations that I couldn't help but initiate about topics such as externalities, deontological ethics, and global governance gaps. For this and far more than I could ever write here, I am forever grateful.

At Binghamton University, outstanding students generated dynamic debates year after year, including an introductory class called "Markets, Ethics, and Law" that enrolled more than 2,000 students over a decade. This collective dialogue was a source of great creativity in my thinking and writing. The ideas in this book were also refined through other advanced undergraduate and graduate courses and in my teaching at the University of Baltimore, where I now work. Teaching at a university can keep you young because it provides a continuing antidote to those who think that the younger generation has lost its way. The hard work, intelligence, and passion of young people that I experienced year in and year out is truly remarkable. I have so many students to thank for these years of conversations—too many to mention given the great cumulative impact. Let me especially mention Samuel Itin, Lucas Testoriori, Murray Friedman, and Dustin Frost—their interest in this book project led them to read and offer helpful comments on early versions of this manuscript. These conversations included many alumni interactions as well. I'd like to especially thank Owen Pell, Binghamton University class of 1980, not only for the enriching dialogue on topics related to this book but his inspiring views on education and the role of ethics in business and economic life.

I have special gratitude to David Schmidtz, my advisor at the University of Arizona, where I taught my first course in business ethics and learned new ways to connect philosophy and economics. David created an intellectual community where ideas germinated in an atmosphere of freedom—an idyllic environment. David continues to mentor generations of students into the philosophy profession.

I would like to thank friend and colleague Chris Griffin for years of debate and discussion on topics related to this book. In the tradition of Socrates, Chris will disagree with great zest about anything philosophical that sounds off-base—not just to find better answers but as one friend to another. And in our conversations he's had plenty of opportunity to display this sign of friendship! (Whatever errors remain in this book are probably because I didn't try out the ideas on him first.)

As a senior research scholar at Binghamton University, I thank former Harpur College Deans Peter Mileur and Don Nieman for their support of my research efforts, including research time while employed at Binghamton University for developing early drafts of the book. I have many colleagues to thank at Binghamton for conversations related to this book, including John Arthur, Eric Dietrich, Thomas F. Kelly, Stefan Sciaraffa, and Melissa Zinkin. I thank the University of East Anglia (UEA) in Norwich, England, during my visiting appointments in 2008 and 2010, for office space, time to think and write, and the generous collegiality of its faculty members. I am thankful for those experiences, as well as the study abroad and UEA students who debated the topics of this book. I also thank the University of Baltimore for summer research grants to complete this work as well as my colleagues in the Division of Legal, Ethical, and Historical Studies for their support, and, in particular, Joshua Kassner.

The anonymous reviewers provided incisive comments at various stages of production. I am grateful for their detailed suggestions and ideas. Finally, I would like to thank Barbara Smith Decker for her efforts as development editor, Saraswathi Muralidhar as senior project manager, and the Pearson editorial team for seeing this project through, including production manager Reena Dalal.

INTRODUCTION

THE ETHICS AND VALUES OF BUSINESS AND ECONOMIC LIFE

WHEN YOU FINISH STUDYING THIS CHAPTER, YOU SHOULD BE ABLE TO:

1. *Distinguish between personal and institutional points of view.*

2. *Describe what this book is about and how it's organized.*

3. *Understand several traditional ethical theories.*

4. *Apply a method for critical thinking in ethics.*

I.1 INTRODUCTION

In Victor Hugo's epic novel, *Les Misérables*, the lead character Jean Valjean becomes a force for good, whose decency and selflessness survive the most extreme tests. The story begins with Valjean's release from an unjust prison term and then traces his acts of heroism and sacrifice, both as a mayor and devoted father to an orphan. In short, Hugo portrays an ethical life fully displayed before our eyes.

You perhaps know someone who demonstrates such decency. At some level, everyday values of fairness, generosity, and goodwill are not too hard to understand, even if they can be hard to live by. *All I Really Need to Know I Learned in Kindergarten* is Robert Fulghum's bestselling book that makes this point and, judging by its sales, his idea resonated with lots of people. Share, play fair, don't hit, no biting, clean up your messes. Ethics may have its puzzles but, at some level, ethics is simple.

So why study ethics? Aren't the rules of thumb for personal interactions simple enough? Even when they are, this book is about making decisions and ethical assessments in business and economic life. That's a different ball game—at least this is what I've learned. For example, we need to know something about the nature of markets, property rights, corporations, government, and law to develop a serious understanding of the role of ethics in economic life. These institutions are complex. We also need to examine our roles in this system, and decide which motives we should bring to these interactions. In fact, I have found that studying ethics as it relates to business and economic life a great intellectual challenge, and I hope that you find it as intriguing as I do. Its study requires investigating many factors that simple intuition can't always sort out. Granting our childhood lessons, a commercial context offers special and complicated challenges for applying our sense of ethics and value commitments. And these contexts and others teach us that, at varying levels of depth, ethics isn't always as simple as we might have originally thought.

This book offers a study of ethics and values as a path toward a deeper understanding of markets, corporations, and the business system. How can ethics guide our interpretation of the economic world and our choices within it?

As background for the subjects and debates ahead, this chapter presents the overall approach of the book, introduces a distinction between personal and institutional points of view, describes the organization of the book, and offers a survey of ethical theories.

1.2 THE APPROACH TAKEN IN THIS BOOK

This writing is an invitation to enter a world of people's experiences and interpretations of life. For example, I recall vividly a semester-long study abroad tour that my family and I led with a group of American students in Norwich, England. Just outside our cottage home was the sight of an eleventh-century spire from a cathedral built in another age. Who were those people who created and brought this enormous structure to life? What were their conflicts, their relationships, their everyday lives? It was easy to drift into these reflections during our daily strolls. But the eleventh century is so far away that we were at best outsiders with a few glimpses of what a 1,000 years prior might have been like.

But in the case of this book, we can fully enter the world that we will be studying, as insiders. This is the world of our current business system and the economic life we make for ourselves. It's a world of the ethics and values that we bring into this system. It's not merely about how we describe the institutions and the norms that we experience, like trying to decipher eleventh-century England. Rather, this book invites your direct ethical reflection, interpreting business interactions and economic institutions from within your own ethical perspective, in conversation with others. These discussions can be eye-opening as you consider how to defend ethical positions that you may have long believed but have been rarely pushed to articulate.

Discussing and testing ethical ideas can help you develop your own sense of ethics, and the discussions can be revealing when you experience an exchange of ideas that produces new insights.

It's probably worthwhile to state upfront that the approach of this book is not to advocate particular positions about what is ethical. The writing instead provides arguments that defend competing positions across a range of topics. The word *argument* has a special meaning in this book—it's the activity of giving underlying reasons that support a position. Arguments need not connote argumentativeness. A group of people can reflect on an argument as a team, with the shared hope of trying to assess what to make of the view. In other settings an argument among several people can be heated with tightly held disagreements about a topic. In these cases ethical dialogue can still be productive and revealing, with practice. It's a tremendous practical skill to be able to talk with others who disagree with you about something you care about, all the while maintaining the ability to consider and respond to their ideas and the underlying reasons that drive the differences. Part of a class in ethics is invariably about developing that interpersonal skill. But in the context of this book, the request to give an argument does not connote anything directly about agreement or disagreement. **Arguments** refer simply to the process of giving underlying reasons to support a set of beliefs.

This book presents many arguments in that sense: providing competing reasons to believe one position or another. The writing is designed to take you *inside* these positions by conveying the most persuasive and forceful reasons to support competing points of view. Arguments offer you something: puzzles and challenging lines of reasoning to advance your thinking and help you sort through what you believe. The premise is that studying competing arguments offers the best way to develop and deepen what you believe and why.

This approach suggests how you can get the most out of this book. The tone is conversational, and the writing in one section actively tries to persuade you of a position that the next section actively tries to refute or at least provides a contrasting point of view. And then it's up to you to think about and discuss these positions and determine how to assess their respective insights and shortcomings. The point is to inspire you to deepen your understanding of your own commitments about the ethics and values of business and economic life, whatever you decide they are. Said again, and putting aside all the many details ahead, my commitment in writing the book is to help create a heightened appreciation of the importance of thinking about ethics and values within business and economic contexts. The book doesn't presume the importance of thinking about ethics. It tries to demonstrate it by actively engaging you in the discussions.

These remarks help explain the format of the chapters. The writing at times challenges what you believe. For example, starting especially with the discussion on corporate responsibility, the book makes various arguments and then poses questions that ask you to critically assess those arguments according to your beliefs. Generally, the questions are not rhetorical but indicate a finishing point of some argument or important idea, and you are invited to pause and assess it, before reading onto the next section.

Also, each chapter includes discussion questions that indicate how you can advance the ideas of the chapter according to your interests. The main writing is designed to provide depth regarding the underlying concepts and arguments for a given topic; the discussion questions apply these concepts in versatile ways and push the boundaries of the chapter discussion. Online materials include *extended case studies* indicated by book icons "📖" in the margins of each chapter. On-line resources also include brief biographies of historical and contemporary figures mentioned in the text, as well as a list of complementary readings, most of which are easily accessible through library collections.

Consider also that you can't read a single day of the news without finding something relevant to the discussions in this book. The link to current events is part of what makes the materials ahead so vital. If you commit to following the news carefully as you read this book you will create opportunities to reinforce its ideas and stretch your abilities to analyze business-related news from an ethical point of view.

These are all ways to be proactive about reading the text. One final thought on the overall approach of the book. These ideas have been field-tested for over fifteen years through discussions and debates by thousands of students. I've always noticed that those who pursue conversations outside the class setting are the ones who usually get the most out of studying the ideas, in the form of study groups or even casual exchanges with others who care about these issues and have relevant life experiences. The discussions in this book can create easy conversation starters outside of the class. In this sense the writing is for general readers as much as for the classroom, as the discussions to follow are an invitation for anyone to bring ethical reflection and an active mind to bear on their interpretation of the ethics of business and economic life.

I.3   THE BIG PICTURE

A. PERSONAL AND INSTITUTIONAL POINTS OF VIEW

Let's consider the following case: An overseas manager is authorized to offer a wage that she knows is not nearly enough to support the families of the employees. She knows that the company is making record profits and that these employees have few employment options. She also knows that this option is probably the best that is available to them.

Consider two questions:

a.   Is there anything that the manager should do about this situation? If so, what?

b.   Is there anything wrong with a system that regularly creates this situation? If so, why? If not, why not?

This is a simplified case that abstracts from many details that could be relevant. The point that I want to emphasize is not how you answer these questions with the information given but to note how (a) and (b) are two different kinds of questions. They represent a contrast between addressing ethical questions from a personal or an institutional point of view. Answering questions from a **personal point of view** addresses how people decide what they should do within a given situation. Answering questions from an **institutional point of view** addresses how people assess the activities of institutions.

A comprehensive ethical analysis considers questions from both perspectives. An answer at one level of thinking—what to do now?—often relates to an answer at the other—how do I assess this institution? The **ethics of individual decision-making** is the study of what choices people should make, how people should live, and how people should treat each other. Question (a) pertains to the ethics of individual decision-making from a personal point of view.

Question (b), on the other hand, takes an institutional point of view, asking us to draw on one or more values to ground our assessments. *Values* refer broadly to whatever standards we use to judge situations. **Values** need not directly determine our action. If I describe a situation as good or bad, it can still be an open question about what, if anything, I should do, given this assessment. For example, we may value a friendship but then wonder what to do in the face of a conflict. Similarly, we may value equality or freedom, but then wonder how we should act, given our commitment to these values.

We develop ethical perspective by understanding how our larger vision of values fits into the ethical puzzles of our daily lives—an important thesis of this book. This integration is a practical issue: our ethical motives often depend on how we see our broader value commitments. We draw on these values to interpret the behavior of people and the institutions that surround us. These ideas shape the organization of the book, as described in Section I.5.

This book is written to develop opportunities for you to reflect on both levels of assessment: the ethics of individual decision-making within a scheme of rules *and* the values that guide how you assess the institutional rules that so influence our lives.

For example, let's return for a moment to the case of low overseas wages. Question (a) is about making an individual decision. Question (b) is about assessing global capitalism. What do we need to know to answer each of these questions? If someone disagrees with your response to either question, what constitutes good evidence and reasons to defend what you believe? This book is about studying and developing intellectual building blocks for addressing both types of questions.

A study that integrates personal and institutional perspectives is especially important in today's global environment. When major economic institutions come under strain, as they have in recent years, the ethics and values of business and economic life becomes a conversation that not only addresses what to do in a given situation but evaluates the role and rules of business across the larger society. We will develop this theme throughout the book, especially in Chapters 4, 5, 8, and 10.

Let's introduce one further concept to summarize this discussion. A **normative analysis of business and economic life** is a study of the actions and assessments that we should make within and about business and economic life. Normative reflection is an umbrella concept that includes both ethical judgments about what to do and assessments about what is valuable. Consider this example. My neighbor and I see a car drive by on our block.

> Chapter 1 develops the distinction between normative and descriptive analysis.

It's simply an observation, not a normative judgment. But when I think "slow down" and wave my arms at the driver, or my neighbor thinks "Wow, that's a great looking car," both of us are making normative judgments—we are explicitly or implicitly appealing to some standard or norm to decide how to act (in my case) or how to judge something (in my neighbor's case). Both personal and institutional points of view express a normative perspective. This book is about a normative analysis of business and economic life.

B. THE SUBJECT MATTER OF THIS BOOK

Let's present the big picture of the book prior to its many details. You will find that, with their many arguments, applications, and particular analyses, the chapters ahead develop each piece of this overall picture.

First, consider how we all bring *our beliefs and motives* to make decisions and interact with others in many settings. These beliefs and motives are as varied as the entire human landscape; and they include our sense of ethics. We may be motivated by self-interest or altruism, envy or goodwill, and much else.

Second, consider that *institutions* shape and constrain our decisions. These institutions include markets; corporations and other businesses; the workplace; financial institutions; local, state, and federal government; nations; international organizations; religious and other nonprofit civic associations; family life; schools; and others. We occupy diverse roles in the more narrow sphere or economic life, which may include interactions as consumers, owners, managers, employees, and investors. No matter our roles, we are constrained and guided by property rights, laws, treaties, global and domestic pressures, cultural norms, self-interested drives, and our personal sense of ethics and values. Social, political, and economic institutions coexist and change constantly both within nation-states and across them through a global reach and presence. A global perspective is especially important for our subject, because understanding markets, corporations, and the interactions that define economic life are today rarely self-contained entirely within a nation-state.

Third, when we make decisions within this complicated network of institutions, the cumulative results may or may not *respect or promote various values*. We are not robots;

we see what's happening around us and we bring a value system to assess the institutions that have created a landscape of opportunities and constraints. What do we want out of the institutions that surround us? We may hope that we live in a system that increases human welfare, creates freedom and equality, helps realize good communities, or other values. Values such as these guide our assessments about the way that these institutions should be structured. Further, we sometimes face difficult ethical challenges within these institutions and need to make our choices about what to do. What kind of ethical and self-interested motives and decisions should we make within our roles, given our beliefs about how institutions function or how they should function?

A study of the ethics and values of business and economic life takes up all of these questions and ideas. In particular, this book integrates a study of ethics at the micro level of individual decision-making alongside a broader macro perspective, which includes ethical assessements of the institutions that shape our choices.

This big picture reinforces why, even if ethics has features of simplicity, we need more than kindergarten for studying all of these materials. An important part of the complexity is that the motives that we think are appropriate in economic life depend on what we think business and economic institutions should be doing and the values that we think our joint activities should be promoting or respecting.

FIGURE I.1   The Ethics and Values of Business and Economic Life

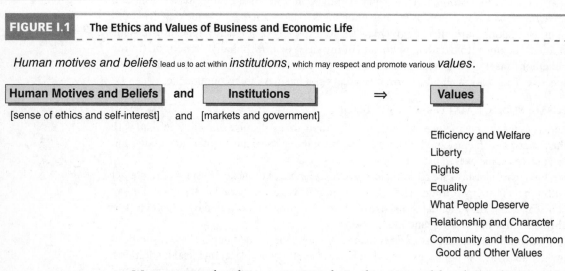

Human motives and beliefs lead us to act within *institutions*, which may respect and promote various *values*.

Human Motives and Beliefs	and	Institutions	⇒	Values
[sense of ethics and self-interest]	and	[markets and government]		

Efficiency and Welfare

Liberty

Rights

Equality

What People Deserve

Relationship and Character

Community and the Common Good and Other Values

We can express these basic normative relationships in a model, as depicted in Figure I.1. This figure offers a broad and systematic perspective for understanding many of the debates to follow.

Consider first how Figure I.1 reproduces the discussion above. Following Figure I.1 from left to right: we bring our motives and beliefs into our interactions with others, within institutions, which may or may not respect or promote various values. Our economic institutions include corporations, financial institutions, nonprofits, and other businesses; and we occupy various roles within these institutions. Of special note in our study ahead is that these institutions include property relationships backed by law and regulated through government. Figure I.1 uses the terms *markets* and *government* to represent the interactions between the economic and political spheres. Whatever our role, we make decisions against the backdrop of institutional structures and the right-hand side of the figure summarizes some of the values that we may hope that the system promotes or respects.

Consider next the *shape* of this diagram. The horizontal line represents the role of ethics for individual decision-making; the vertical line represents the values that we hope social interactions and institutions will achieve. In this respect Figure I.1 depicts the *two levels of normative reflection* that mirror the discussion of personal and institutional points of view earlier in this section.

To explain further, both our *sense of ethics* and *self-interest*, as listed on the horizontal axis in Figure I.1, refer to the broad mix of motives, sentiments, conscience, principles, and beliefs that lead individual decision-makers to act and choose one way or another. Philosophy as a discipline has a long history of considering the nature of our motives and beliefs, and the social sciences offer many insights about how our basic economic and political institutions function, given our choices. Some argue that a sense of ethics aligns with (or always aligns with) our self-interest; others argue that they sometimes or often conflict. Later chapters debate the best way to think about the relationship between the two. The values of efficiency and welfare, liberty, equality, and others, seen on the vertical axis, refer to standards for assessing the institutions that surround us. The values listed in this figure may reflect your values or you may bring a different set of values. In either case, we bring an entire normative worldview to our lives, and a comprehensive study of ethics and its controversies considers how to integrate both personal and institutional points of view. As we will see, disagreements occur in both horizontal and vertical directions, both about the sense of ethics that we should bring to our individual decisions and about the values that matter most for assessing the system.

The general structure of this normative model has relevance for any institutional setting. The special subject of this book, which is also the title of this Introduction and Figure I.1, is the **ethics and values of business and economic life**. We have already initially described the *ethics of individual decision-making* and the nature of *values*. The remaining phrase, **business and economic life** refers to the range of business, financial, and economic institutions that include interactions and decisions by consumers, managers, investors, employees, and owners.[1] In this respect the book has a broader scope that what can be captured by the word *business*. The analysis ahead is relevant both for our roles within a business organization, such as a manager or employee, but also for our other roles in economic life, such as consumers and investors. The chapters ahead sometimes refer to the model of *ethics and values* or the *ethics of economic life*, depending on context, but these shorthand expressions will always imply the fuller meaning.

Finally, consider that Figure I.1 depicts a **normative model**, representing complex normative relationships through a single diagram. The aim is to highlight important parts of a system to suggest how these parts relate to each other. Figure I.1 offers a quick visual summary of ideas that will be elaborated throughout the book. This model is not meant to imply that the normative study ahead is mathematical or particularly formulaic. Understanding the springs of human motivation and the nature of ethics and values is both art and science. Rather, the model depicts a summary of how the parts of this normative system relate together and how we might break down complicated relationships into smaller units of analysis. A challenge for any discipline of thought, including ethics, is how to bring some systematic order to a complicated array of factors. At this early point,

---

[1]This model could generalize further and integrate all of the institutions of society, including education, family, religious institutions, and others, but this book is about relationships in economic life.

it's not important to understand the relationships summarized in this model in any depth. The idea is to introduce a wide-angle view of the book as a whole. Each chapter has its own subject matter that fits into the wide perspective depicted here, as will be explained directly below. We will also return to and deepen these introductory ideas in Chapter 8.

C. THREE COMPETING PERSPECTIVES ABOUT THE ROLE OF ETHICS IN BUSINESS AND ECONOMIC LIFE

Many ethical complexities of business and economic life can be given order and perspective through this model. For example, let's preview three broad arguments about the role of ethics in business and economic life that will be developed in the chapters ahead.

FIGURE I.2   Three Competing Perspectives about how to Integrate Ethics, Self-interest, and Institutions

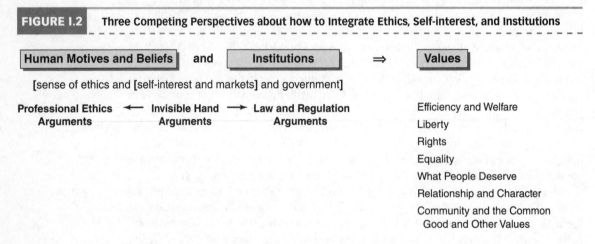

Invisible Hand Arguments

One dominant tradition of economic thought is guided by the metaphor of an *invisible hand*. According to some versions of this argument, markets are like an invisible hand that guide self-interested people to create good outcomes, without the need for any special ethical motives and without the need for individuals to intend this result. For example, I buy clothes for my family in pursuit of my interests, but look what happens: the tailor gets the money to feed *his* family. I didn't intend that result for his family; I was thinking only of my own gain. But both of us are made better off as a result, or so this argument goes. This metaphor will be discussed at length in Chapter 8.

In Figure I.2, the brackets around "self-interest and markets" highlight this *invisible hand argument*. The brackets depict how, according to this view, those two factors (self-interest and markets) are sufficient to create good outcomes, such as improvements in efficiency and welfare. We will examine this fundamental argument closely in Chapters 6–8. This argument captures the worldview of many people today. The argument also shapes how to understand the role of ethics in a business setting—ethics can have a limited scope on this view. Many people find this invisible hand perspective wholly or partially compelling as a basis for exploring the ethics of business and economic life.

Law and Regulation Arguments

But reflections about how the economic system operates lead others to stress a central role for government within business and economics. The right-hand arrow that points from markets to government in Figure I.2 signals an entire class of *law and regulation* arguments that defend the view that the economic system ought to include a significant role for law and government. These arguments deny that self-interest and markets alone will produce good outcomes for society without significant governmental oversight. But like invisible hand arguments, they tend to imply that people are motivated primarily by self-interest, and so any viable system of business and governmental rules is best to presume a limited role for ethics in peoples' decision-making.

Professional Ethics Arguments

Others stress the pervasive and important impact of ethics for shaping and influencing the business and economic system. The left-hand arrow that points from self-interest to a sense of ethics signals a range of perspectives that, in one way or another, defend a heightened sense of social responsibility and business ethics within the economic system. Advocates of this perspective, for example, may support voluntary measures for corporate responsibility or argue that we should be guided by various ethical principles in our daily professional lives.

Both *professional ethics* and *law and regulation* arguments move away from *invisible hand* arguments but in different directions, as represented by the arrows in Figure I.2. Advocates for professional ethics envision human motives and beliefs that can and should go beyond any narrow understanding of self-interest. Advocates for law and regulation focus on an extended governmental role within markets.

To summarize this discussion: the horizontal relationships on the left-side of the model represent a range of competing perspectives about the appropriate balance of *ethics*, *self-interest*, and *institutions* that should define our business and economic lives. As will be developed later, these distinctive perspectives are very useful for understanding current policy debates and for understanding why people disagree about the appropriate role of ethics in economic life. The vertical relationships on the right side of the model represent potential controversies about which values the system should promote. Taken together, these competing perspectives generate debates across topics of corporate responsibility, privacy, consumer protection, environmental protection, employee rights and responsibilities, and many others.

> These three competing perspectives are developed in Chapter 8 and applied throughout the remaining chapters.

D. ORGANIZATION OF CHAPTERS

This model also depicts the organization of the book chapters, as seen in Figure I.3.

The book begins with core institutional ideas about markets (Chapter 1), property rights (Chapter 2), law and government (Chapter 3), and corporations (Chapters 4 and 5).

FIGURE I.3   Organization of Chapters

Human Motives and Beliefs	and	Institutions		⇒	Values	
Sense of Ethics (all chapters)		Markets	(Ch. 1)		Efficiency and Welfare	(Ch. 6–8)
Self-Interest (all chapters)		Property Rights	(Ch. 2)		Liberty	(Ch. 9)
		Law and Government	(Ch. 3)		Rights	(Ch. 10)
		Corporations	(Ch. 4–5)		Equality	(Ch. 11)
					What People Deserve	(Ch. 12)
					Relationships and Character	(Ch. 13)
					Community and the Common Good	(Ch. 14)

One important purpose of these chapters is to motivate a study of ethics and values by making transparent how ethical reflection is a response to what we find happening within these institutions.

We next consider the global debate about the social and ethical responsibilities of corporations (Chapters 4 and 5). In addition to the intrinsic interest of this topic, these chapters debate the serious disagreements about the roles of ethics, incentives, and institutions in economic life, illustrating the three competing perspectives in Figure I.2. These chapters also aim to demonstrate why a systematic normative perspective is so important to fully understand and assess ethical debates in business and economic life, and this systematic perspective requires a study of values, such as those listed in the right side of the model in Figure I.2.

Beginning in Chapter 6, the book focuses on particular values and their importance for ethics. We first consider the value of efficiency and welfare (Chapters 6 and 7) as a normative guide and then explore a range of important values beyond these (Chapters 9–15). In this way, all the major topics in business ethics are covered through this study. Although no specific chapter corresponds to *a sense of ethics* or *self-interest* (see Figure I.3), these ideas are integrated throughout all of the chapters.

To give a flavor of the analysis to come, consider how it's possible to focus on one value at a time. What is the best way to combine personal ethics, self-interest, markets, and government to produce the most efficient system (the exact meaning of which will be discussed in Chapter 6)? There are fascinating challenges and puzzles for addressing this question, ranging from a *stockholder view* of corporate responsibility (that offers a restrictive understanding of ethics and government for achieving efficiency and welfare) to a competing *stakeholder view* (that advocates a heightened sense of ethics and greater government intervention, believing that efficiency and welfare cannot be achieved without these additional elements, given various *market flaws*—an idea to be discussed in Chapter 6).

But efficiency is not the only relevant value. So we can next ask: if we focus on the concept of liberty, what is the best way to combine personal ethics, self-interest, markets, and government to create a system that best promotes freedom? The answers depend on competing ideas about what freedom means, and these differences become important for how you understand your ethical commitments (Chapter 9). We can ask the same questions about the nature of rights (Chapter 10), equality (Chapter 11), what people deserve (Chapter 12), human relationships and character (Chapter 13), community and the common good (Chapter 14), and other values. This book does not consider all relevant values but focuses on those for which people tend to advocate most strongly; the analysis of these values can lead to the development of skills that can also be applied to the study of other values beyond the scope of this text.

In this manner, the text offers a step-by-step approach for developing an increasingly holistic analysis of normative thought as it relates to business and economic life. It begins with an ethical analysis that can be contained within the narrow values of efficiency and welfare; then each chapter expands and incorporates a larger net of values.

This approach to ethics and values is focused both on individual decision-making and also offers a practical guide for understanding current policy debates. To what extent should government intervene in markets to create an efficient and free society? What is the relevance of inequality for evaluating the system? Does this system give us what we deserve? As we ask these questions, we will also address questions at the individual level: if we advocate social change, how do we create that change in a society with powerful institutions? Why do ethical dilemmas occur in economic life? What is our best response? What personal values should we bring to these ethical challenges?

Ethics can create engaging dialogue that uncovers reasons and arguments for reflection, debate, and revision. The figures above represent where people may disagree or find common ground. They suggest how complicated topics can be broken down into smaller and more manageable units. Although the book does not offer a complete set of normative considerations, its level of comprehensiveness and unity across both ethics and values; across moral, social, and political philosophy; and across the humanities and social sciences is one of its distinctive and unique features.

I.4   WHAT YOU NEED TO GET STARTED: A PRIMER ON ETHICS

We have capacities to make judgments about what we observe, to support or criticize what we see. On what basis do we make those judgments and how do we defend them? To engage this question is to enter into conversations about ethics.

On one level you do not need any further primer to start the study of markets in Chapter 1. However, for those who are encountering philosophy for the first time, it may be helpful to consider a few more distinctions and an introduction to some traditional ethical theories.

A. ETHICS, NORMS, AND LAW

You may notice a difference between someone saying "that is ethical" and "people commonly say that this is ethical." The first expression conveys your point of view; the second expression conveys your perception of other people's point of view. We sometimes need to clarify whose point of view we are talking about when we debate ethics. Are we referring to our own ethical commitments, or are we debating the **cultural norms** that we perceive around us, independent from our own commitments? Cultural norms are the beliefs or behaviors that people within a given culture generally endorse about what is appropriate or inappropriate. Among people who are discussing ethics for the first time and sometimes even among those with much experience, it's remarkably easy to shift between these meanings without even realizing it, only later recognizing what the debate was really about.

> Chapter 3 develops this discussion about cultural norms and cultural and ethical relativism.

Thus, it's helpful to be aware that sometimes people use the term *ethics* to refer to people's norms in some general sense, while at other times they use the term to convey their understanding about what ought to happen, regardless of what anyone else might believe. There is no fixed understanding of the term, so this important distinction can be clarified only in context. Both perspectives can matter. For example, this book invites you to develop your own commitments, beyond your perception of the cultural norms around you. Reflecting on cultural norms can bring great insights as well, however. For example, on a global stage, conversations about norms can clarify why people behave as they do—particularly in unfamiliar surroundings. Recognizing our own cultural norms can also clarify our own commitments and prompt us to ask whether we have implicitly accepted some cultural norms without reflecting on those commitments.

Some people distinguish the terms *ethics* and *morality* to indicate the distinction between studying *cultural norms* and studying *what we believe is truly the case about right and wrong*. Thus, one person may say, "I don't like your ethics; if you really understood what morality requires, you would change your views." There is no set usage of these terms, however. In fact, another person is as likely to make the same point by interchanging the words, "I don't like your morality; if you really understood ethics, you would change your views." So for our purposes, we will use the terms *ethics* and *morality* interchangeably. For any given conversation, you can simply ask those with whom you are conversing for clarification as the need arises.

Consider next a common distinction between a study of ethics and law. Here, let's consider the basic idea that law and ethics are not the same subject. Thus, we can examine the rules that the government asks us to live by as a separate question from making judgments about what is right or wrong. Some laws will reflect our understanding of right and wrong, such as laws against murder; but other laws may not, such as those that at one time supported racial segregation. Further, we often make ethical judgments that have nothing to do with law, such as a view about how friends or coworkers should treat each other. The relationship between law and ethics is complex and fascinating, and we will discuss law in greater depth in Chapter 3. But the point here is simply to recognize that a study of ethics in business and economic life is not assumed to be about a study of law.

Ethical ideas are subject to dispute—both in common usage and in professional philosophy, although in philosophy the point is often to develop meanings that are as precise as possible. We will seek more precision as we go along. But to begin the analysis, all we really need to get started is some intuitive idea of making judgments about right and wrong, better and worse, and the refinements will follow.

B. ETHICAL THEORIES

Ethics is a discipline of study within a long history of thought. **Ethical theories** attempt to bring systematic order to ethical reflection. They organize different ways to express our sense of ethics, and they convey a view about what ethics is really about. This section introduces some leading theories. You may already be familiar with these ideas, although you may not have seen them discussed or identified so explicitly before. The point here is not to analyze and critique these theories but simply to present them for your reflection. Later chapters will apply and elaborate on them within a given topic. So as not to lose the forest from the trees in the details below, the most important insight to consider now is the possibility that ethical conversation is not simply unstructured intuitions. The more you engage in these conversations and debates, the more you will notice general patterns of reasoning that occur again and again across topics. Ethical theories try to capture these patterns and explain why they matter.

Assessing the Consequences of Action

Consider the following case: You discover an important error in company records that you know some of your coworkers will use to implicate your management skills to the detriment of your career, even though it's not obviously your fault. There are various ways to bury the problem without anyone discovering it, and there's some chance that if never discovered the error will not adversely impact the company. Do you bring the error to light and deal with it or bury it and move on? What are the issues?

Consider all the possible *effects* of your choice depending on whether you do or do not bring the problem to light: dealing with it will create interoffice conflict and much finger pointing. It even may lead to your demotion if you don't prevail in those conflicts. On the other hand, dealing with it may avert bad publicity for the company, and it's possible that enough people will rally to your side and exonerate you. The other choice is to bury the problem. In this latter case, chances are good that the issue will never become relevant. At the very least, you avoid serious and probably fruitless office conflict that would occur if you make an issue of the error.

Let's say you do not want to make an unethical decision. So you consider the entire range of potential consequences for your own and others' interests in making one choice over the other. You consider both sides of the ledger carefully: the pros and cons of what might happen depending on how you choose.

To think about the potential consequences of a decision is to use a specific kind of reasoning often called **consequentialism**. Ethical consequentialism is a theory that people should choose to do that which produces the best overall consequences. You would weigh the pros and cons of the various interests at stake and make an "on balance" decision about the best action to take. As proponents of an ethical theory about how to act, consequentialists advocate making the choice that produces the best overall consequences (hence its name), taking everyone's interests into account.

The most famous type of consequentialism is called **utilitarianism**. This theory was developed by English philosopher Jeremy Bentham and further refined by Englishman John Stuart Mill. In short, utilitarians believe that people should act to maximize the aggregate utility of everyone involved, where this aggregate *utility* has been variously interpreted historically as "happiness," "well-being," or "pleasure" (as was Bentham's interpretation). One interesting point to note about utilitarianism is that the decision-maker's interests are not the only ones that count in this view of ethics. We must take into account others' interests as well. This impartial perspective can be highly demanding, requiring as it does that we give equal ethical weight to the interests of *all people* who might be affected by that choice.

> Chapter 3 applies consequentialism to discussions of property rights and Chapter 7 develops and applies utilitarianism as an ethical theory.

It's worth noting that we can be consequentialists in a different way. For example, a strictly prudential perspective can be a form of consequentialism if you choose whatever is likely to produce the best consequences for *you*. Most people regard ethics as requiring more than just looking out for yourself—so many would *not* describe this approach as an account of ethics at all. Others defend the focus solely on oneself as perfectly compatible with ethics, however, and so this view has come to have a name: **ethical egoism**, which is the view that people ought to do whatever is in their self-interests.

Assessing Actions Apart from Their Consequences

Let's now return to the original case about finding an error in the company records. Consider a form of reasoning that contrasts against all varieties of consequentialism. Depending on the underlying facts of the case, you might say, "I have a duty to the company to bring this error to light, no matter the fallout." Alternatively, you might say, "If I don't bring this error to light, I am complicit in deceiving people about the situation, and I have an obligation to myself to be honest, no matter what the result is." Still another response might be, "I made an agreement when I took this job that I would reveal such errors if found, so I must keep that promise." Conversely, I may be inclined to conceal the error if I think none of that is true. For example, I may reason, "It was an innocent mistake that was brought about through no one's fault. By letting this information sit, I would violate no ethical principles that I can conceive of." The issue, I might further conclude, raises no legal questions. I may believe that leaving it alone is not actively lying about anything, and my duty to advance the interests of the company argues for concealing this information rather than bringing it to light.

Whatever you think about these reasons, note how they are not about analyzing the consequences of the potential action. Instead, we search for principles or prior conditions that apply to determine the right answer, independent from assessing and weighing the various effects of our choice.

Some people identify such principles as **duties** (or obligations) that constrain their choices. A duty or obligation is a requirement to do something. For example, the nineteenth-century German philosopher Immanuel Kant became famous in part for defending a universal duty of morality that we should always treat people as ends and never merely as means (no matter how costly).

Nonconsequentialist ethical theories identify a whole class of theories that identify ethical reasons for action apart from weighing the consequences of a choice. These theories are sometimes called *deontological theories of ethics* after the Greek word, which means "the study of duty."

It's not the labels that matter but getting a feel for different kinds of reasons that may drive any given conversation or decision. The idea that an agreement in the past may bind me to act is a nonconsequentialist idea, as is the idea that I have a fiduciary duty to the company or other special relationships that constrain how I should act, or that people have rights that dictate how they may or may not treat each other, no matter how the consequences might unfold.

In this context we can distinguish **forward-looking reasons** (about likely consequences that would result from a choice) from **backward-looking reasons** (about constraints or principles that apply prior to making the choice, independent from assessing the consequences of that choice).

Chapter 7 is about the nature of rights.

Recognizing these distinctions helps us line up our reasons, so that we can take each in turn and analyze its significance for making a choice. These reasons may complement each other and support a clear answer, or just as likely, they may conflict with each other and create a puzzle about what to do. Then we must choose which considerations are the most important. For example, we may believe a prior agreement, once brought to light, creates an absolute constraint on our choice, and then our decision is made. Alternatively, we may believe that both consequentialist and nonconsequentialist reasons matter, and so we sort through a range of considerations and make an all-things-considered judgment about the best choice to make. There is no consensus about one correct form of ethical reasoning.

In sum, ethical reasoning often proceeds in two different directions: forward to the potential consequences of choice, and backwards to the way that past actions and other ethical principles constrain and guide our choices, independent of the consequences of that choice. This distinction is highly useful for bringing clarity and order to our ideas within any given ethical conversation. You are likely to encounter this contrast in your conversations about ethics, and it will be developed in the chapters ahead.

The Importance of People's Motives

Consequentialist and nonconsequentialist theories, as presented above, assess actions and behaviors. For many, this focus is well-placed, as many believe that actions, not intentions, matter most. But lots of people believe that motives matter, too. Don't you sometimes place ethical weight on people's intentions independent from the acts themselves? In a legal setting, consider how criminal liability in the United States and elsewhere usually requires not only that someone commits a guilty act (called the *actus reus* in law) but that the person performs the act with a guilty mind (called the *mens rea* in law). The law will then define the relevant guilty mind, such as requiring that the person intended or knew that he or she was doing the act beyond a reasonable doubt. Not all criminal law requires a finding about people's motives; and in those cases, the standard is called *strict liability*. But the point is that holding people accountable in this way is often thought to be so severe as to be legally appropriate only in limited circumstances.

In our ethical reflections, too, we often assess intentions beyond actions. For example, the **ethics of care** is a recent feminist ethical theory that emphasizes the importance of bringing attitudes of sympathy and empathy to decision-making. On this view and others, being ethical means, in part, bringing the right motives to bear on whatever choices we face, beyond our assessment of the actions that result.

> The ethics of care is discussed in greater depth in Chapter 13.

We can distinguish two kinds of motives that help clarify the scope of a study of ethics. First, we may be motivated by a sense of duty or obligation to perform an action. When we are motivated in this way, we perceive that we are morally required to perform that action. At some level, we believe that we *must* do that action and that we have limited or no ethical choice to do otherwise. Protecting rights are typically interpreted as obligations of justice. For example, the Universal Declaration of Human Rights does not specify what we may or may not do but what we must or must not do. People have claims to be treated certain ways, and we all have duties to uphold those rights. *Justice* as a subject tends to be about specifying obligations that in part justify laws to enforce those obligations.

Second, we may be motivated by a sense of ethics to act in certain ways that we also recognize as discretionary or recommended behaviors. We can puzzle about good or admirable ways to act without characterizing them as obligatory. For example, someone who believes in helping the poor may be motivated to donate personal earnings to those who are less fortunate, but that person at the same time may not describe that donation as a moral obligation. To emphasize this distinction, that person may think, for example, that it would be inappropriate to criticize people who do not make that donation. In philosophy, these sorts of actions are sometimes called **supererogatory actions**. They describe ethically good actions that are not morally required.

Ethics as a subject matter is the general inquiry both about obligations and offering exemplars of praiseworthy or heroic behavior without any obligatory implications. We will apply this distinction in various contexts in later chapters (for example, in Chapter 11, on equality), especially as we may want to emulate someone we admire but not conceive of our motive as the following of a duty. This distinction also clarifies how ethics covers very broad ground, including motives that appeal to a sense of ideals, aspirations, requirements, and inclinations.

Character and Virtue

Let's consider one other ethical approach. We may want to focus less on any particular motive or action in the moment and focus instead on the *character* of a person over a lifetime. For example, we may grant a mistaken action with misconceived intentions as a one-off occasion but believe that what matters most is the person's solid character overall, which identifies an important ethical perspective. Character-based ethical theories emphasize an account of the *virtues* to aspire for and *vices* to avoid, which are less about assessing particular actions and more about cultivating a disposition that becomes a defining part of that person's outlook on life. The ancient Greek philosopher Aristotle developed the single most influential expression

> Virtue ethics and discussions of character will be developed in Chapter 13.

of this view, also called *virtue ethics*. Character-based education conceives of ethical cases studies and particular choices primarily as a means for building or maintaining a good character apart from the value of getting the right answer to any particular dilemma.

Methods of Ethical Reasoning

There are many other ethical theories and concepts that we could introduce, but these are enough to provide an initial sense of a practical structure that can guide ethical conversation. We may wonder what to do in a given situation, and the discussion may include at least the following points of analysis:

1. What are the consequences of choosing one way or the other?

2. Are there ethical principles, constraints, or other values relevant for assessing my potential actions in the situation, independent from analyzing the consequences?

3. What are the motives driving the various options and what should motivate my choices?

4. Is the character of those involved, including my own, relevant to the situation at hand? How so?

These four questions offer some practical guidance for making ethical decisions. We can ask these questions in the face of an ethical puzzle to probe the issues. The questions are not designed to offer a definitive or exhaustive list of queries, but they do show how we can apply traditional ethical theories to develop practical methods of ethical reasoning. These ethical theories and questions can help develop our *sense of ethics* (see Figure I.1) and they become part of a comprehensive normative study of business and economic life, as discussed in Section I.4.

I.5   SUMMARY

Many important ethical lessons of life come our way as early as kindergarten. We can learn much by reflecting on those common-sense standards of decency and fairness. But the ethics and values of business and economic life are complex, and simple rules of thumb are not always sufficient intellectual guides. This chapter introduced a distinction between personal and institutional points of view, sketched the plan of the book, and presented a survey of ethical theories as background for the subjects and debates ahead.

This book offers a distinctive systematic approach to the study of *markets, ethics, and business ethics*. The book's contribution to the literature includes a novel way to integrate philosophy and business-oriented approaches to the study of business ethics, synthesizing many disciplines of thought into a unified study, to be both theoretically rich and practically relevant. The author invites comments and suggestions at sscalet@gmail.com.

The assessment of markets and our roles and responsibilities in business and economic life are broad humanistic concerns, eliciting centuries of reflection across generations of thought. This book welcomes you to a conversation whose urgency and importance only increases with the impact and complexity of our economic world today.

KEY TERMS

arguments
personal point of view
institutional point of view
ethics of individual decision-
    making
values
normative analysis of business
    and economic life

ethics and values of business and
    economic life
business and economic life
normative model
cultural norms
ethical theory
consequentialism
utilitarianism

ethical egoism
duty
nonconsequentialist ethical
    theories
forward-looking reasons
backward-looking reasons
ethics of care
supererogatory actions

DISCUSSION QUESTIONS

1. Return to the first example about the manager hiring employees at low wages. Which is the more interesting set of questions from your point of view, (a) or (b)? What are your answers? To what extent does an answer to one set of questions rely on the answer to the other?

2. Consider the following case: You are working late and need some paper supplies tonight for your daughter's school project. You are the manager in charge. A pack of paper sits in the office supply room, everyone is gone, and it's the end of the workday. Do you take it for the project? What are the issues?

3. Is most of what you need to know about ethics learned by kindergarten? Have you learned anything important in the last year?

4. The four general questions about methods of ethical reasoning posed in Section I.5 are meant to be suggestive without claiming to be definitive or exhaustive. Are there any other generic questions that you think are important to ask when addressing ethical situations and puzzles? What might those questions be?

5. Write a two-page essay that answers the question, "What does it mean to be ethical, in your view?"

PART I

BASIC CONCEPTS

Part I introduces the basic concepts of markets, property rights, and law that form the background and subject matter for the chapters ahead.

Chapter 1 • Markets

Chapter 2 • The Nature of Property Rights

Chapter 3 • Property Rights, Markets, and Law

1

MARKETS

WHEN YOU FINISH
STUDYING THIS CHAPTER,
YOU SHOULD BE ABLE TO:

1. Identify and observe market activity.

2. Define the concept of a market exchange and understand why there are challenges for providing a single, clear-cut definition.

3. Notice cultural filters that may affect how you interpret market activity.

4. Reflect on how ethics is relevant for understanding the role of markets in society.

5. Consider several background conditions necessary for markets to operate.

1.1   INTRODUCTION

As captured British officer R. A. Radford entered the gates of a German prisoner of war camp during World War II, he was prepared to adjust to a new world, but not all of it was new. He found a thriving economy, with markets in many goods, and a highly responsive pricing system with a currency measured in cigarettes. It is perhaps the only known currency that people could smoke. "Around D-day," he recalled in an article he wrote after the war, "food and cigarettes were plentiful, business was brisk and the camp in an optimistic mood. Consequently, the Entertainments Committee felt the moment opportune to launch a restaurant, where food and hot drinks were sold while a band and variety tunes performed."[1]

In another case, a group of economists, curious about the limits of rational choice, entered an insane asylum and found thriving markets despite great restrictions placed on inmates' freedom.[2] The basic message of both these studies was the same: that human needs and desires lead people to create markets even in the most unfriendly and seemingly unlikely environments. Not even sanity is required.

Markets are all around us. There are few places to travel in the world today where people live without markets. Even the poorest places on earth typically display a dizzying array of market stalls and trading. Why is this? These activities are not recent either. Evidence of markets date back at least to the

---

[1]"The Economic Organization of a POW Camp," *Economica* 12 (1945), p. 196. As a trained economist, Radford's fascinating story had this point: "the essential interest lies in the universality and the spontaneity of this economic life; it came into existence not by conscious imitation but as a response to the immediate needs and circumstances. Any similarity between prison organization and outside organization arises from similar stimuli evoking similar responses" (p. 190).

[2]Raymond C. Battalio, et al., "A Test of Consumer Demand Theory Using Observations of Individual Consumer Purchases," *Economic Inquiry* 11(4), pp. 411–428.

last Ice Age, and some form of market and commercial life is writ into nearly every stage of human existence.

Consider a typical day: you may start by opening the refrigerator with foods purchased from a local grocery store, run a few errands to several stores, make some Internet purchases from Amazon.com, Craigslist, or other sites through a laptop from the comfort of your sofa (both of which were probably purchased through some market exchange). After a day at work in a job associated with its own labor market, you may choose among dozens of restaurants and go out to eat, or watch the news to hear about the latest on the stock market or international oil prices. You then go to bed in an apartment that is leased through a local rental market or a home purchased through the housing market. For all of us, the more we look into the activities of our lives, the more amazed we become by the impact and extent of the markets that surround us.

This chapter introduces the concept of a market and includes a few background materials in preparation for the study of ethics ahead.

1.2   WHAT ARE MARKET EXCHANGES?

Markets have taken many forms throughout history. Before we consider the modern system, let's start with the basic idea at the core of any particular form. **Markets** *refer to willing buyers and sellers exchanging items that they value*. We will also call this activity *market exchange*. The *items* exchanged may include tangible goods (such as bread, cars, or computers) or intangible services (such as your labor or getting a pedicure). A restaurant experience, with the food served and the surrounding ambience, includes both tangible and intangible goods, as do many other items that we value.

One way to deepen our understanding of the distinctive human activity of markets is to consider at least two important types of nonmarket environments.

First, rather than a system of markets, we may have a system of **takings** through violence. A taking is an unwilling exchange or transfer. The famous English political philosopher Thomas Hobbes, in his *Leviathan* (1651), offers the most spectacular imagery of humans thrown into a state of nature without any formal rules governing behavior. We are to imagine what would happen. He was not optimistic. War, violence, and brutal coercion: these are all human possibilities that would be realized in a state of nature, he hypothesizes, and none of these violent acts would describe markets. They would be takings. To offer another literary example, William Golding's novel *Lord of the Flies* provides a vivid image of a violent human nature, as a group of boys shipwrecked and stranded on a remote island devolve into a primitive and savage state. Both of these allegories, with their dim views of human nature, illustrate the idea that violent takings are different from market exchanges.

But takings do not have to be violent to fall outside the concept of a market exchange. Let's fast forward to a U.S. Supreme Court case, *Kelo v New London*, where the Court found that the City of New London, Connecticut, was constitutionally permitted to exercise eminent domain to seize Susette Kelo's and others' homes. **Eminent domain** refers to the power the government derives from the Fifth Amendment to take property from citizens if the taking is for a public use and includes just compensation. For example, the creation of the 1950s interstate highway system was possible only through the federal government's extensive use of eminent domain to take private land and convert it into an interstate highway. The point of the New London taking was to redevelop the land to

WHAT MOTIVATES GIVING?

Psychological egoism is the view that people are always ultimately motivated by a desire to advance their own self-interests. Hobbes, for example, was a psychological egoist who would explain the motives behind all gift-giving in terms of the self-interest of the giver. **Altruism** is an alternative account of human motivation, stating that people can be motivated to advance others' welfare without any reference to their own self-regarding desires. Discussion Question 3 prompts further debate about this contrast.

Note that *ethical egoism*, introduced in I.4B, differs from the concept of *psychological egoism* introduced here. (How so?) This distinction has a useful application for understanding the stockholder theory of corporations, as discussed in Chapter 4, Section 7.

These ideas raise basic questions: Do we have a basic human nature? What is it like? How malleable is it based on our circumstances and upbringing? In what direction should we mold our nature if we can? These questions have driven much of the pursuit of philosophy and literature for thousands of years; both continue to inspire writing and scholarly research today. To give one example, *New York Times* columnist David Brooks draws on recent brain research to help us understand these questions in his *The Social Animal: The Hidden Sources of Love, Character, and Achievement.*[4]

What motivates our actions is of primary importance to a study of ethics. Arguments that state a position about our motivational capacities and limitations within a market setting are part of many of the discussions to follow, in Chapters 4–14, with an initial exploration through Discussion Question 4 at the end of this chapter.

encourage economic development in that city. On the one side of the case, an older couple did not want to move. They valued memories more than the money offered to relocate. On the other hand, people were out of work and desperately wanted the government to intervene to create economic development and jobs. Justice John Paul Stevens began the opinion of the Court with a description of the conflict. "In assembling the land needed for this project, the city's development agent has purchased property from willing sellers and proposes to use the power of eminent domain to acquire the remainder of the property from unwilling owners in exchange for just compensation."

This excerpt offers an apt contrast for our purposes: the initial purchases from willing sellers are market exchanges; the takings from unwilling owners, using a government power of eminent domain, are nonmarket exchanges. Takings, whether justified or not, violent or peaceful, happen outside of markets. In general, when the government acts by using its coercive powers, the direct activities that result are not market exchanges.

A second major contrast to market exchanges is the huge world of giving. Unlike political philosopher Thomas Hobbes's and novelist William Golding's views of unchecked humanity, a system of *giving* describes another vision of humankind. All over the world, people offer gifts, many times over, with the purpose that they are not intended as a trade. *Nothing in return* is sometimes our guiding principle. **Gifts** occur when a person offers a good or service to someone without an exchange from the other as a condition of the offering. This human activity may seem marginal next to trillions of dollars of global sales and trading in our economic world, but it is not. According to the Giving USA Foundation and the Center on Philanthropy at Indiana University, the amount of philanthropic contributions fueling the U.S. economy in 2010 amounted to $290 billion, including donations by individuals, charitable bequests, foundation grants, and corporate giving. Over 200 billion dollars of this amount, they found, came from individual donations.[3] Philanthropy often creates personal benefits as well, such as tax breaks, so it's not necessarily "nothing in return." Still, those gifts are not typically interpreted as exchanges between a buyer and seller.

---

[3]http://www.givingusareports.org/
[4]Random House, 2011.

The world of gift-giving happens whenever you offer something without an exchange from the other as a condition of the offering. At the personal level, giving goes well beyond gifts in wrapped boxes. Gift-giving governs much of our lives in how we allocate our time (e.g., through charity, volunteer work, family time, and friendships); and none of these activities are market exchanges.

We can summarize the conceptual points so far: Markets are patterns of exchanges between willing buyers and sellers. They are not takings, which can be exchanges but are nonmarket. They are also not gifts, which are not exchanges at all.

1.3   Why We Begin with Market Exchanges?

There are several distinctions, generally recognized, that we can make to avoid potential confusion. First, the term *market* can refer to a specific place, such as the local farmer's market with its many goods for exchange. It can also refer to a class of goods or services independent of a specific location, such as the market for sports cars. Markets can also refer to the financial sector, as when people ask, "How are the markets doing today?" Further, in economics, discussions of markets typically refer to the supply and demand conditions of a particular good or service, where buyers and sellers interact to create a price.

There is no single correct usage of the term *market*; all of these descriptions are common and have their place in context. One primary reason we begin with the concept of exchange is that many complex issues in economics and ethics are variations on relationships based (at least in part) on the fact that an exchange occurs.

There is one further distinction worth discussing at the outset. The terms *business system*, *market system*, and *economic system* typically refer to an entire network of economic and political institutions that surround exchange, though there is no universally accepted way to describe any given *system*. Here, we start with the simple idea of market exchange. In doing so, we are not yet addressing the nature of large and intricate economic systems. We will characterize the broader business and economic system with its many ethical puzzles only after introducing concepts of property rights, law, and corporations in Chapters 2–4. Later chapters will also discuss markets in relation to the wider society and its values, especially relationships among markets, business regulation, and different forms of government. We begin with market exchange as the first building block for the discussions to follow.

> Chapter 13 examines human relationships in economic life, including but going beyond exchange relationships. The discussion of property rights in Chapter 2 also analyzes relationships that are not themselves exchanges but help make exchanges possible.

Another reason that the chapter starts with market exchange is to emphasize a reality that might be otherwise lost: whether we live in the United States or Africa or the Far East, whether we live under one governmental form or another, whether we live today or lived a thousand years ago, almost all people have experienced market activities sometime and somewhere in their lives. Markets are a thread that connects today's complex world with systems of exchange that date back thousands of years. The core idea of exchange is still at the heart of business and economic life today. Markets happen in prisons and insane asylums and many places around the world. Markets exist whenever people are buying and selling. The motives may be many—and we note this point for later ethical analysis—but the outcome of a market is exchange.

Many people celebrate this history of markets, reflecting on the violent alternatives that have defined much of human history. They argue that markets foster honesty and other positive traits, such as the desire to create value for others. Other people criticize markets, reflecting on alternative visions of communal life and human capacities for giving. These people argue that markets encourage baser motives and actions, such as greed and excessive materialism. There are many ethical judgments to make, and such assessments and others will be part of a more detailed analysis in the chapters that follow. But the aim of these first sections is to set an initial context and to be *observational*, to notice a world around us that uses markets. *What do you see when you see markets? What culture filters impact how you observe market activity?* From this core human interaction of exchange, much results.

1.4   DEBATES ABOUT HOW TO DEFINE MARKETS

It may seem that there is little to debate by starting with such a basic idea as a market exchange. But some of the most fundamental ethical disagreements can derive from differences about what we see and observe in social life and how we define or characterize what we see. For example, two people may witness the same event—a decision to increase gasoline taxes, for example—but disagree passionately about the policy. Part of the disagreement may be over specific policy issues, such as "Whom does a gasoline tax affect? Why tax gasoline and not income?" But just as likely—especially in a political climate—adversaries may characterize the very concept of a tax increase differently. One may interpret the idea of taxes as individuals' fair costs for benefiting from the goods of society. Another may define taxes as taking money from individuals that is already theirs. This disagreement may be deep; and it derives from differences in how each characterizes what a tax is.

   This chapter asks you to think about how you *see* markets at a very basic level. As stated earlier, markets are commonly defined as willing exchanges between buyers and sellers. But in this section, let's consider how offering a precise definition can be surprisingly difficult to do, and why such a basic idea as market exchange can elicit controversy.

   Contemporary economist John McMillan wrote that "a definition of a market transaction, then, is an exchange that is voluntary: each party can veto it, and (subject to the rules of the marketplace) each freely agrees to the terms. A market is a forum for carrying out such exchanges."[5] Open an introductory textbook in business or economics and you will probably find a similar definition. McMillan's veto principle has a nice application to the Kelo case: Kelo could not veto the government taking, so intuitively we say that it is not a market transaction. In this sense, McMillan's definition works well and offers a method for distinguishing trading from takings.

The concept of *voluntary action* has intrigued philosophers for generations, including ancient Greek philosopher Aristotle's famous discussion about the nature of voluntary and mixed actions in his *Nicomachean Ethics*. We will examine the concept of *voluntary choice* more closely in Chapter 9.

   McMillan, like most mainstream economists, stipulates that markets are **voluntary exchanges**, and his proposal is quite intriguing: a market exchange is voluntary if both sides can veto it. That covers a lot, although it's not hard to find counterexamples. Suppose X and Y are committed to engaging only in market exchanges. X comes up with a plan. He puts a gun to Y's head and says, "How about we exchange your car for the change in my pocket?" Y says, "I can't veto that deal, this is no market exchange." X says, "Sure you can, it's just that the consequences will be deadly if you veto."

   This situation is not what McMillan has in mind. It is very difficult to figure out a way to rule out these cases on the veto principle,

[5]McMillan, John. 2002. Reinventing The Bazaar—A Natural History of Markets. W. W. Norton & Company, (p. 6).

though. This point is not an idle puzzle. Many people believe that markets allow some individuals or groups to systematically exploit inequalities of bargaining power to the point that there is almost nothing voluntary about the resulting exchanges. They argue that many real market exchanges are morally similar to X putting a gun to Y's head.

We might call these transactions **desperate exchanges**, borrowing the phrase from political theorist Michael Walzer. These are exchanges that we hope we will never have to make. Desperate exchanges are trades of last resort that occur when and because one party to the exchange is in desperate circumstances. Imagine selling your organs to use the earnings to feed your malnourished children, or consider labor market conditions that resemble indentured servitude or enslavement in some parts of the world. Given these extremes, can we veto deals when the alternative is that our child starves? Yet, these exchanges are still subject to conditions of demand and supply and normal economic analysis. We do not need to consider "exotic" examples either to understand the point. Suppose gasoline prices triple, bus fares increase, you need to get to work and there is a long way to travel. There is a sense that you are stuck at paying those prices because you have no viable alternative. This market exchange starts to feel less voluntary. If we adopt a very stringent account of a voluntary action, then nothing would count as a market exchange; if we decide that anything counts as voluntary, then any exchange whatsoever would count as a market exchange. We are left with an important idea: market exchange entails buyers and sellers who are "willing" to engage in the transaction in some sense, but with much disagreement about exactly how to characterize what counts as a voluntary *willing* versus an involuntary *taking*.

Further, some commentators worry that the generally accepted definition of a market, as stated above, primes us (mistakenly) to observe or presume that all markets are voluntary when sometimes they are not. They argue that *defining* markets as voluntary is "ideologically loaded."[6] What do you think?

For our purposes there are three lessons to draw from this discussion.

1. *Defining markets is not clear-cut.* Debates about its definition persist because the underlying activity is not clear-cut. We want our social concepts, like the concept *markets*, to mirror the complexities of our world, and so precise definitions are not always possible or desirable. Instead, theorists often define social concepts with a cluster of common properties, without insisting that each property be present in each case. Thus, we allow for gray areas and boundary cases. As long as we understand the complexities at hand and what we are talking about, we can continue the conversation. We will further illustrate the idea that definitions sometimes express a cluster of common properties through the important discussion of *ownership* in Chapter 2.

2. *We want to identify markets as an interesting object for ethical study, without stacking the deck against competing ethical viewpoints.* The point is to avoid building a presumptive ethical assessment into the very definition of the term. To facilitate conversation and debate, we want to allow for a broad spectrum of opinion about what people see and observe in market activities. In particular, desperate exchanges raise interesting questions about the "voluntary" nature of markets. So, we include all of these boundary cases as part of our study. We can then debate puzzling or interesting

---

[6]Frank Cunningham, "Market Economies and Market Societies," *Journal of Social Philosophy* 36(2) (2005), p. 130.

cases about what counts as market exchanges, and doing this exercise can increase our awareness about how and what we see. Further, we want definitions that allow us to move from terminology to the more important substantive questions that will become part of later chapters: Do we approve of this activity on ethical grounds? Why or why not?

3. *How we choose to characterize the world impacts how and what we see in the world.* This applies across all aspects of life. So, it's worthwhile to pause and examine the most basic concepts of any subject, as we are doing in this chapter. Do your own observations about markets presume any implicit judgments that markets are appropriate or inappropriate? Do others see markets in the same way that you do?

1.5   BLOCKED EXCHANGES

Although we observe markets all around us, we can also observe many situations where law or custom prohibits market exchanges. Why is this? Contemporary political philosopher Michael Walzer calls such situations **blocked exchanges**, which refer to specific market exchanges that are prohibited by law or custom.

Consider the following list. At this early juncture, it's not our purpose to fully assess the reasons behind these prohibitions, but by reviewing this list, you can reflect on how ethics is relevant to understanding the role of market exchange in society.

- In November of 2010, the U.S. Food and Drug Administration (FDA) sent a letter to four manufacturers of caffeinated alcohols (such as Four Loko and similar drinks), urging them to remove their products from the market. All four manufacturers agreed to do so. Several states and cities then enacted bans on the distribution of these beverages, threatening fines for distributors selling the product. Why is this? Is it a good idea?
- We are legally prohibited from selling many of our body parts, even if we want to do so to help others. But we are legally permitted to sell our blood, semen, or eggs. What determines these prohibitions and permissions?
- You are not legally permitted to sell your driver's license and thereby enable someone else to become a valid driver, even if you (the seller) and another (the potential buyer) both voluntarily consent to the exchange.
- People are not legally permitted, in most circumstances, to sell their labor for less than the minimum wage.
- People are not legally permitted to buy and sell many drugs. But of course, an extensive black market exists for these drugs anyway. Why do the laws exist? Should they?
- We can choose to exercise, or refrain from exercising, our right to free speech, but we can't literally buy or sell the right and thereby pile up extra amounts of it. The same goes for most of our political rights. However, we can use our money in markets to try to increase the impact of our speech. As we will see later, a recent Supreme Court decision confirmed that corporations also have free speech rights and that legislation aimed at curtailing the influence of corporate contributions for politics has been ruled unconstitutional.
- When someone invites you to dinner you could convert the invitation into a market exchange by bringing money and paying for it. But you don't. Why not?

- TV audiences hang on judges' decisions about who is the best dancer in *Dancing with the Stars*. The show could be set up as a market, where the winner is determined by the celebrity who is willing to pay the most for the prize. Though no law prohibits this arrangement, many competitions and awards have standards for success that are not decided through buying and selling.
- We may adopt children but no one sells their children on eBay. (I could be wrong. Here's one story of a ten-year-old who tried to sell her grandmother on eBay: http://www.dailymail.co.uk/news/article-1217074/I-grandmother-eBay-joke-says-10-year-old-Zoe-bids-hit-20-000.html)[7]

Some but not all market limitations are driven by law. Are they justified? Although this chapter is about observing markets without making ethical judgments, one important observation that we can make from this section is that people commonly *form* ethical judgments about the legitimacy of markets and impose these judgments *on* markets, not only through laws but as norms in their roles as consumers, investors, managers, or owners. These judgments create interesting subject matter ahead.

1.6 BACKGROUND CONDITIONS FOR MARKETS TO OPERATE

One last thought about markets. What background conditions must exist for markets to operate? Markets develop within a context, which includes the following:

- *Scarcity*—Economists have long taught that without scarcity, markets would seem to have no point. If everything we could ever want were already available in unlimited supply, then why trade?
- *Buyers and Sellers*—We need people who want to trade.
- *Products*—Goods and services need to exist or have the capacity to be produced.
- *Forum*—A place or way to make the exchange.

  And finally

- *Property Rights*—People follow various rules that guide their market behavior. Markets happen within a *social* context. A stable property rights system is one of the most significant background conditions for markets to operate and forms the subject of the next chapter.

1.7 THREE DIALOGUES THAT SHAPE THIS BOOK

This chapter is a good place to introduce three distinctions that help clarify the approach and strategy of this book. Although these distinctions are often implicit in our daily conversations, drawing attention to them here helps make the chapters ahead easier to

---

[7]This list is adapted from contemporary political philosopher and author Michael Walzer's discussion in *Spheres of Justice* (Basic Books, 1983, pp. 100–103). Walzer calls the above situations blocked exchanges and argues that they oppose the idea that "money answereth all things."

assimilate with your own interests. They also provide important context for your own conversations and debates that may be sparked by the topics of this book.

Consider the following three questions that relate to this chapter:

1. *How do markets work?* Sometimes our goal is *to learn how things work.* We search for a good description or explanation of some feature of the world, and we may learn to make predictions based on the explanations. We can call this type of investigation **descriptive** or **explanatory analysis**. Within the social sciences this work is some-times characterized as *positive analysis.*

2. *What ethical attitudes do people have about markets?* This question is *also* part of de-scriptive analysis, but now the object is to describe and explain peoples' values and beliefs. For example, we could take a poll about peoples' attitudes about markets, or commission a study that analyzes the impact of religion in forming the ethical beliefs of a population. We could study evolutionary biology and brain research to consider the biological foundations of our ethical beliefs.

   A dialogue to address this type of question can begin with a simple survey in the classroom regarding how each person responds to some given ethical dilemma. We could catalog the range of responses that people offer and ask what best explains those responses.

3. *What are my ethical beliefs, how do I defend them, and how should they guide the deci-sions that I make in business and economic life?* Sometimes our goal is to figure out where we stand and why, and to live out what we believe. **Normative analysis** is the study of what ought to be, how we ought to value and assess situations, and how we should act and live. In this respect, a **norm** refers to any value or rule designed to in-fluence our judgments or decision-making.

In this chapter, we can see these three distinctions at work. First, we introduced the concept of a market as part of a descriptive analysis. What is a market? What happens in markets? Then we introduced the concept of blocked exchanges at the descriptive level: What ethical attitudes do people bring to market exchanges? What are these attitudes and how do they influence the development of markets? Finally, the text asked more personal questions, such as, What should you (or we) believe about limits on markets and why? This last question is about adding and defending your own point of view rather than attempting only to describe a situation.

Recall the following excerpt from Section 1.5: "People are not legally permitted to buy and sell many drugs. But of course, an extensive black market exists for these drugs any-way. Why do the laws exist? Should they?"

The first question is *descriptive.* It's about giving a plausible explanation for why our laws take the form that they do. The second question—"Should they?"—is *normative.* It's about what you believe the law *should* be, and why you believe that.

As mentioned earlier, the distinction between descriptive and normative is often im-plicit and intuitive in our daily conversations. But paying attention to this distinction is important for any ethical study, such as the one offered in this book. For example, we can look back at Section 1.4 to clarify some of the analysis with these distinctions in hand. Recall how some theorists worry that the very definition of *market exchange* is not merely *descriptive* but contains an implicit *normative* appraisal, by interpreting every exchange as voluntary and, thereby, always a good thing. That debate can be redescribed through the following question: is it possible to provide a definition of a market without implicitly making a normative appraisal?

So, in the conversations prompted by topics in this book, it will be important to clarify whether your dialogue is about (1) how something works, (2) what peoples' ethical beliefs are regarding this topic, or (3) what we, you, or I should endorse as our own position and why. We need not think that one dialogue is more important than another. The important point is to be sensitive to these different conversations. In your own discussions with others, keep in mind which inquiry you most want to pursue, and be sure that you know which line of inquiry the discussants are actually pursuing.

The overall goal of this book is to create a comprehensive normative study, so after some initial descriptive and explanatory groundwork in this and the next two chapters, later discussions will increasingly focus on normative ideas and theories about how to assess situations and what choices to make. That said, all three dialogues are part of every chapter of this book, so throughout the study you will be able to pursue your interests broadly across all three levels of inquiry.

1.8   SUMMARY

Markets happen; they are written into our long human history and they are worthy of ethical study and reflection. This chapter is designed to spark your interest in the subject ahead.

We defined markets and raised several challenges for providing a single, clear-cut definition. We thought about the relationship and distinction between what we *see* in markets and how we *judge* markets. An immediate point of controversy, for example, is whether or not markets are voluntary by definition. Finally, we considered blocked exchanges to show that people often place limits on the reach and scope of markets. Thinking about the reach and limits of markets creates intriguing discussions that can begin to highlight the sense of ethics and values that we bring to this analysis, which will be developed in the chapters ahead.

1.9   LOOKING AHEAD

Part I of this book identifies concepts and institutions for interpreting our social world as they relate to business and economic life. This chapter is about markets; the next chapters are about property rights, law, and corporations. With these fundamental discussions in hand, we will then debate an important topic of applied ethics and public policy: the responsibility of corporations.

KEY TERMS

markets	psychological egoism	blocked exchanges
takings	altruism	descriptive or explanatory analysis
eminent domain	voluntary exchanges	normative analysis
gifts	desperate exchanges	norm

DISCUSSION QUESTIONS

1. What are some interesting markets that you can identify? Which one do you find to be the most interesting? Why?

2. Are markets natural or cultural constructions? Not everyone agrees. What is your view? How does one gather evidence to answer this question? What is at stake in answering this question?

3. Sometimes economists and psychologists, among others, deny that pure gift-giving is humanly possible. Some say that "nothing in return" cloaks the fact that every gift has an implicit return wrapped into it. For example, we donate to a religious institution, not as a gift, but to receive services. We donate to a charity to receive our own psychological rewards. (This is a view only Hobbes could love.) What do you think? Do we have the capacity to give without strings attached, or is there always an implicit condition? For those who believe that there is an implicit condition, does that fact imply that what we thought were pure gifts are really market exchanges?

4. What motivates people to exchange? Take a few examples from what you observe and from current events to dissect. Does *self-interest* capture the idea? greed? reciprocity? concern for the common good? something else? What general answers can you give about the human motives that drive markets? Does your answer color your attitudes about whether markets are commendable or not? We will examine

these questions further in Chapters 13 and 14. For one thought-provoking story about human motives in markets, see http://www.nytimes.com/2011/08/17/us/17land.html?pagewanted=1&_r=1&hp

5. Imagine a world without any markets. What would occur? What would it be like?

6. Just as some commentators object to the presumption that markets are always voluntary by definition, others note that the terminology of *free markets* invites us to presume that markets are always "free." Do you regard the terminology of *free market* as ideologically loaded? What does *ideologically loaded* mean to you? Is there a problem here or not? (Later in Chapter 9 we will examine the nature of freedom in relation to markets.)

7. Some philosophers have tried to differentiate the meaning of *willing* and *unwilling* exchanges—not in terms of *voluntary* and *involuntary*—but in terms of *noncoercive* and *coercive* exchanges. Does this alternative improve the analysis in your view?

8. Do markets encourage or discourage a culture of charity, nonprofit associations, and gift relationships? Your answers to this question may matter a lot for shaping your assessment of market activities. This topic will be explored further in Chapters 13 (Relationships and Character) and 14 (Community and the Common Good).

2

THE NATURE OF PROPERTY

WHEN YOU FINISH
STUDYING THIS CHAPTER,
YOU SHOULD BE ABLE TO:

*1. Describe a wide range of
property examples in terms of
their relevant claims, liberties,
powers, and immunities.*

*2. Describe what ownership
means and apply the idea to
several examples.*

*3. Research how ideas in this
chapter relate to current events
in business.*

*4. Recognize limitations for
applying the idea of property.*

2.1   INTRODUCTION

On top of my desk, I keep a small collection of mementos gathered from trips taken over the years. I am now looking at a seashell with the off-white colors of the sandy beach and grooves that seem very old. I clearly see these markings on the shell and can show them to others. But where do I see that it's my property? I would like to see something that shows that the shell is mine, but where do I look?

The idea of property may seem so commonplace that we can fail to reflect on its full significance. But at the heart of property lies various mysteries of social interaction. Property rights tell us how people relate to each other with respect to all the things in this world. As long as we live in a physical world, we likely will experience not only some form of market activity (Chapter 1) but live with some system of property rights (see Chapter 3 as well). Property rights describe the web of relationships among people and things that guide and constrain our lives. Property rights may be largely invisible, but their importance for understanding our business and economic relationships is tremendous.

The goals of this chapter are to examine and apply the ideas of property, property relations, and ownership. The goal of Chapter 3 is to integrate these topics with discussions of markets, law, culture, and ethics.

2.2   PROPERTY AS RELATIONS AMONG PEOPLE

Although an artist or a marine biologist may study the contours of a seashell, neither can understand the sense in which the shell is my **property** from looking at the shell. Let's consider this point more closely. First, we often use the word *property* to describe *things* of a special kind: that they are *owned* things. But claims to property also tell us about *relations* of a special kind: property relations among people, with respect to things.

> *Definition 1*: Property can refer to special kinds of *things*: owned things, both tangible and intangible—land, clothes, ideas.

> *Definition 2*: Property can refer to special kinds of *relationships*: relationships among people with respect to things.

> *Property* can refer to *owned things* or *relations among people with respect to things.*

While both definitions have their place, and the first definition is more familiar, the second definition has the great advantage of asking us to look at *relations among people* instead of *things*. The second definition underscores how property debates are fundamentally about *us*. When I look at an object, it is difficult to point out the characteristic of it being owned because we are not essentially talking about the *thing* at all. We are talking about what I and others may or may not do with the object. Thus, to say that the seashell is my property is to say something about what I may do with the seashell (for example, exclusively hold it and use it) and what you may not (for example, take it). Furthermore, these relationships are not directly visible.

Take the nature of time. Although it's very important to us, we don't *see* time. Rather, we see a clock that represents time. Similarly, we do not see property relations, although we can see a receipt, a title, or our name written on the object that is ours, each designed to signify what is our property. By understanding the invisible nature of property expressed in the second definition, as relations among persons, we gain insight into the significance of property and begin to comprehend its complexity.

Property is a deep and abiding topic in social philosophy and the history of thought. From the ancient Greek philosopher Aristotle, to medieval theologian St. Thomas Aquinas, through German philosopher Karl Marx in the throes of the Industrial Revolution (and many others), property debates are both highly practical, as they are about what people do with the materials and resources of their daily lives, and highly philosophical, as they are about understanding how and why people relate and should relate to each other.

The first aim of this chapter is to understand property in a new way, not in terms of talking about an object but in terms of talking about our relations to each other. A second goal is to offer details: Which specific relations are we talking about?

2.3   Hohfeld's Conception of Property Rights

In his *Fundamental Legal Conceptions* (1919), legal theorist Wesley Newcomb Hohfeld describes four relationships (see Table 2.1) for making sense of the myriad complexities of property relations in the Western legal tradition. His analysis was prescient and his concepts remain fundamental for understanding the kind of **property relations** relevant to business and economics. Property relations refer to the ways that people relate to each other with respect to things.

Once mastered, these relations provide extensive insight for understanding our social world: they help clarify what *ownership* means (see Section 2.5); help describe economic systems (see Section 3.5); provide background for understanding what a corporation is (Chapters 4 and 5); and clarify the nature of many disputes in business and economic life

TABLE 2.1 Hohfeld's Four Property Relations

Property Relation	Definition	Example
Claim-right ←→ duty	A has a **claim-right** over X means that some B has a **duty** to respect that claim-right	If you have a claim-right to receive a regular paycheck, then some B (your employer) has a duty to pay this money to you.
Liberty-right ←→ *no* claim-right	A has a **liberty-right** or privilege over X means that B has **no claim-right** to block that liberty.	If you have a liberty-right to use some money to buy a car, then no one has a claim-right that you cannot use this money to buy a car.
Power ←→ liability	A has a **power** over X means that some B has a **liability** to A's exercise of that power.	If you have a power to transfer your payment to a willing seller, then some B (such as the auto dealer) has a liability to receive that payment.
Immunity ←→ disability	A may have an **immunity** over X, which means that B has no power to block that immunity, or, in other words, a **disability** from blocking that immunity.)	If you have an immunity from others spending your paycheck, then no B (presumably no one but you) has the power to spend that paycheck.

(Chapters 6–15). The materials in this section form a background that creates more precision to the issues that lie ahead.

Hohfeld noticed that people relate to each other, with respect to things, in some combination of four distinct possibilities. In Table 2.1, A and B stand for different *persons* and X for some *object*.

These property relations—claims/duties, liberties/no claims, power/liabilities, and immunities/disabilities—offer a vocabulary for speaking precisely about the ways in which people relate to each other with respect to things. *Claim-rights* and *duties* are concepts defined in terms of each other to specify one type of relationship that people may have with each other with respect to some item. Similarly, liberties/no claims, powers/liabilities, and immunities/disabilities are paired relationships with each side of the relationship defined in terms of the other side.

People most likely have *some combination* of these relations for any given object. For example, I may have a power to give away a book *and* the claim-right to exclusively possess that very same book. Take any object, tangible or intangible, and we can describe our property relationships to each other and to that particular thing using this vocabulary.

Hohfeld's property relations give further content to the first aim of this chapter, which is to see property as relations among persons. To illustrate this idea, consider another example. If some person A, such as the CEO of a company, has a claim-right to exclusively use a parking space, then this means that some other person B has a duty not to interfere with the use of that space by not parking there (depending on the parking rules, B likely refers not to a single person but anyone and everyone who is not A). The crucial idea here is that property *is specifying a relation between A and B* regarding that parking space. Consider further: if there were *no* duties to keep people from parking there, then no one could have claim-right to use that space, including the CEO, because others having a duty to use that space is part of what it *means* for someone to have the claim-right. You can't have a claim-right without an implied duty on others, or vice versa. Thus, if you admit that I have that claim-right, then you also have just admitted to bearing some type of duty to respect my claim. So, be careful about what you admit!

In that sense property rights are powerful. Explanations for how they evolved, why they exist, and what they should be are complicated and fascinating. These controversies have created wars, court battles, and the rise and fall of business enterprises. They are also at the heart of more pedestrian disputes about who should clean the microwave in the workplace common room or whether a parking space entails a claim-right or a mere liberty-right to use. (If you have a claim-right to use the parking space, then it should sit empty when you're not there because others have the duty to *not* park there. But if you have a mere liberty-right to use it, then you hope that someone hasn't beaten you to it each morning.)

Let's take the parking space example one step further. If I *assert* that I have the claim-right to park there, you might respond by *denying* that I have the claim-right. Who is correct? We sometimes want to know what property rights are in some descriptive sense, but we also sometimes want to know what they *should* be, independent from what they happen to be at the moment. This normative inquiry may arise as a result of a conflict over a given object, or we may

See Chapter 1 Section 7 for a discussion of descriptive and normative analysis.

be led to think broadly about what justifies property rights. In the next chapter, we will introduce two normative theories of property rights that try to answer where property rights come from and what justifies them. But in this chapter, we will focus on the prior step of mastering basic concepts and applying them in practical ways to set up important normative questions in the next chapter.

So let's apply the terminology for one other practical example. When the U.S. government in 2009 exercised its *power* to give $787 billion to the banking industry as a bailout, should the banks at that time have been at *liberty* to spend the money as they saw fit or should citizens have had a *claim-right* that the money could not be spent on bonuses or high executive compensation packages? While the vocabulary of property relations does not allow us to answer this important question, it does permit us to state the question and frame the issues clearly.

PROPERTY RIGHTS APPLICATION: THIS TEXTBOOK

If you purchased the print edition of this book, then you have a claim-right to exclusively read, mark-up, and dispose of this book. (This means that others have a duty not to interfere with these activities. Note that the statement—"you have a claim-right"— is given meaning only by specifying the corresponding duty that someone else has. That fact specifies the relation between you and someone else with respect to that object. Note also that when you have a claim-right, it's always of a specific type, such as *to use* or *to dispose of* the object.)

You also have a power to loan this book to someone else, which means that some other individual interested in this book may be liable to your kind gesture. (Note that liability in this context is not a negative outcome for the recipient. People may be subject to your power in ways that serve their interests.)

Further, you have a liberty to read the book, which means that no one else has a claim-right to prevent you from reading it. (Suppose you lent the book and needed it back in a hurry. Presumably you could reclaim it, but not in all circumstances, as the lender could also say that by lending it you gave up your liberty to read the book for that time period, which means that the borrower now has the claim-right to exclusively read it under that loan agreement. In this instance, you would have used your power to create your own duty, given that the borrower would have short-term claim-rights over anyone's use of the book, including over you.)

2.4 TIPS FOR LEARNING AND APPLYING PROPERTY RELATIONS

Although the only way to master the property relations just discussed is with practice and by applying them across a range of examples, the following pointers can help.

1. *Specify both sides of the relation.* When asked to specify the meaning of a claim-right, liberty-right, power, or immunity that a person or business may have over an object, our natural tendency is to say more about the person's or entity's relation to that object. For example, if a business has a duty to keep the sidewalk clean, we tend to clarify the meaning of that duty by giving more details about *how* the business must keep the sidewalk clean. But to understand property as specifying relations, we must clarify the other side of the relation. That is, for a business to have a duty to clean the sidewalk means that some *other* person or entity has a claim-right to demand that the business keep the sidewalk clean. For example, a city may have this claim-right as part of codes and regulations that were passed through an elected board of city council members.

2. *Specify what the relation is about.* The pairing claim/duty or liberty/no claim and so forth may seem abstract at first. But these property relations describe practical matters when details about the relationship are provided—such as having a liberty-right *to open a business, as long as you comply with federal, state, and local regulations.* That means, in this case, that no one else has a claim *that you cannot open a business if you're in compliance with those governmental rules.* Your actual property rights are not abstract: they are particular, are practical, and can be specified. Thus, a person doesn't merely have some abstract claim-right. For example, I have a claim-right *to read a book* or *to eat this food.* To learn how to use these terms in practice, you need to specify the content of the property right.

3. *Know how claims and liberties are different from powers and immunities.* Claim-rights and liberties specify what we may, may not, or must do. Powers and immunities, on the other hand, specify how and whether we can *alter* our property relations. For example, I may have a *liberty* to drive on the road, which means that no one has a claim-right to prevent me from using that road. But this fact says nothing about who and whether anyone can change that liberty-right. In fact, the government may have the *power* to institute a curfew or create a speed limit, which would then alter my *liberty* and create a *duty* for me to stay off the roads or drive slower, depending on the rule. *He who has the power can change the rules.*

4. *Recognize that the terms introduced here have specific meanings when used in the context of property rights, which may differ from other common meanings of these terms.* The terms *claim, duty, liberty, power, liability,* and *immunity* all have connotations beyond those used here. That is not a problem, as long as we keep in mind the particular meanings relevant to property relations. For example, *liability* can connote a disadvantage in other contexts, but here, a liability doesn't necessarily imply anything negative. B's liability simply means that B is subject to the power of some A, and this fact can be good, bad, or neutral. For example, willing buyers and sellers are constantly creating liabilities for each other by exercising their powers of exchange. This means that they can alter each other's property relations through a voluntary market transaction.

5. *Remember that the meaning of each property pairing is self-contained.* People may also have various claim-rights, liberties, powers, and immunities with respect to the same object, but those are separate assertions. For example, just because you have a claim-right to receive your paycheck does not necessarily mean that you also have a power to transfer funds. You may have this claim-right, but you may also be under bankruptcy proceedings, which would then limit your power of transfer. That claim-right only implies that others have a duty to issue a paycheck; this fact by itself does not determine what your liberties, powers, and immunities might be after you receive it. Your specific combination of property relations will vary depending on the underlying facts of the situation. You may have lots of claim-rights, liberties, powers, and immunities with respect to any given object, or just a few. Note that when we speak of our property rights, we often signify many property relations at once, but we can always sort them out conceptually by specifying each self-contained paired relation that applies to the situation.

Hohfeld wanted the legal profession to adopt the distinctions above to reduce confusions and ambiguities in the law. When a statute grants a "right" for A to do Y, does the law express a liberty-right of some specified content, or is it a claim-right, a power, or some combination of these? With his own dry humor, Hohfeld offered various confused court interpretations when no one involved had a handle on these distinctions. Hohfeld's analysis won the day. Every first-year law student learns these terms. Though Hohfeld is widely credited for his legal analysis of property rights, the concept of property as a relation among persons dates at least to Immanuel Kant, who, in *The Doctrine of Right* argued that property is best understood not as a relation between a person and a thing but a relation between people's wills.

Most importantly for our purposes, we see how—from birth—we are enmeshed in a complex web of interactions among people related to the objects of this world. These property relations form the background through which markets and commerce develop (see Table 2.2).

Table 2.2 summarizes the discussion in this section. Note that any property holder—an individual, business, government, or collective (to be discussed in Section 6)—can have any of the prescribed property relations over any entity, with respect to either tangible or intangible things.

One important question to ask about our property relations is the circumstances under which we *own* the object and what this means. So, let's turn to that topic next.

TABLE 2.2 The Conceptual Terrain of Property Rights

Property holders have	*property relations*	*over others* with respect to	*things*
Individuals	Claims/Duties	Individuals	Tangible
Businesses	Liberties/No claims	Businesses	Intangible
Government	Powers/Liabilities	Governments	
Collectives	Immunities/Disabilities	Collectives	

A PROPERTY RIGHTS APPLICATION: PATENTS

Suppose A invents Y, and it turns out to be something new and useful, such as Harry Thomason's ideas about solar heating and cooling in 1967. The U.S. Patent and Trademark Office (USPTO) exercises a legal power to grant a patent to A, which means that A, and the rest of us, became legally liable to the decision of this office. Having this power means that the USPTO can change citizens' legal relations with respect to that invention. Once a patent has been granted, A has the claim-right to exclude others from making, using, offering for sale, or selling the invention in the United States or importing the invention into the United States. We normally summarize this constellation of property rights by saying that the government has given A monopoly rights over this invention. In the case of Mr. Thomason, he received patent number 3,295,591 for his invention. The purpose of this monopoly right is to give the inventor legal rights to profit exclusively from the innovation. Some argue that the rationale for these monopoly rights is to create incentives for people to make inventions. Others argue that the inventor deserves the monopoly rights as a reward for developing the invention. The Constitutional Framers thought that the rights of inventors were so important that they enshrined it within the U.S. Constitution (Article 1, Section 8, Clause 8).

Note that property rights cannot be fully understood if they are thought to be simply about the invented object, or even about A's relation to the object. Property rights are more significantly about the *inventor's relationship with other people* with respect to that object. Thus, A's claim-right to exclude is simultaneously *others'* duty not to make, use, and sell that object. We may not notice it, but every time the USPTO grants a patent, the exercise of that power affects all U.S. citizens

by changing their legal property relations in some way. The world of property rights is in constant flux around us.

The patent office is careful to note that the patent does not include a power of enforcement by their office. This means that no person is liable to arrest by order of that office, which probably doesn't bother the busy USPTO employees. If inventors believe that their patent claim-rights have been infringed, they must expend their own resources to compel enforcement, through litigation (see Chapter 3 for discussion about law). On the upside, the patent holder is immune from any other agency or office revoking the patent once granted, except under rare instances.

Finally, as a last twist for applying Hohfeld's property relations to patents, consider that the patent grants the inventor a *claim-right* to exclude others from making money from the invention but only a *liberty-right* for the inventor to profit from the invention. In other words, the patent office carefully notes that the inventor has a mere liberty-right but no claim-right to profit from the invention. To have a liberty-right means that no one has a claim-right to prevent these activities. This distinction has an important practical implication: there is no government office that has a duty to help the inventor succeed, as might be the case if the patent actually gave the inventor a claim-right to make, use, and profit (http://www.uspto.gov/). If an inventor does not have the resources to develop a patent, then that's the inventor's problem.

To specify all the property relations relevant to patent law is complex. Please consult a patent attorney! These details are fascinating, as are other examples of intellectual property rights. You might try to describe some of your own examples.

2.5 OWNERSHIP

U.S. patents (see box "A Property Rights Application: Patents") offer an intriguing example of what it means to *own* something. The patent holder owns the invention but note how these rights of ownership differ from the rights associated with my owning a seashell. In the case of the invention, ownership entails a monopoly over the use of the invention for twenty years and then the property right normally expires. In the case of the seashell,

I have a claim-right to exclusively use that shell for as long as I like. It so happened that the seashell that I mentioned at the beginning of this chapter came from a national park that has rules granting me the power to take possession, but barring me from exercising the power to sell the seashell. Apparently, I am legally prohibited from selling this memento. Yet, everyone recognizes that I am the owner—whether or not I have that power to sell it.

How can I be the owner but not be able to use the item anyway I want? Are we misusing the term *ownership* if it has one meaning for patents and another for public seashells? Law theorists often introduce the metaphor of a *bundle of sticks* to guide our understanding. Imagine a single property relation (a particular claim/duty pair) as a stick (as in a piece of kindling). Roam around the world for objects both within our legal system and across legal systems, and you will notice that people—who are recognized as owners of objects—have a bundle of sticks (that is, property relations) that tend to resemble each other. From a great distance, they all look alike but as you get closer, the differences in the size and shapes of these bundles become more apparent.

English jurist A. M. Honore analyzed what ownership typically means in most Western legal systems. Not surprisingly, he found that ownership usually means the following: that a person (or business, government, or collective) has *claim-rights* to exclusively possess, use, manage, and receive income with respect to that thing; *powers* to transfer, waive, exclude, and abandon that item; *liberties* to consume or destroy it; *immunities* from expropriation; *duties* not to use harmfully; and *liabilities* from court judgments.[1] Honore elaborated on these ideas in great detail. These are the typical bundle of sticks that constitute ownership.

But these are just tendencies. For our purposes, the value of the bundle-of-sticks metaphor is to understand how the meaning of ownership can vary. Depending on the circumstances, any single stick can be replaced with some other stick without destroying the integrity of the bundle—that is, without necessarily undoing A's status as the owner. **Ownership** is a good example of a social concept that refers to a cluster of common properties, an idea introduced in Chapter 1 Section 4 when discussing markets. Although Hohfeld's property relations can be stated with some precision, the concept of ownership built from these relationships is far less exact in meaning.

To reflect on the way that the meaning of ownership can vary, try to enumerate the property relations relevant to owning a piece of music, automobile, patented invention, home, business, or some other tangible or intangible item. In each case, the "owner" can be entirely uncontested, yet ownership entails different property relations in each case. We need to go case by case to learn these differences.

SELF-OWNERSHIP

Of particular philosophical and practical interest is the sense in which we own ourselves and our labor, to be discussed directly below in Section 8 and then again in Chapter 3 Section 8 in the context of normative theories of property rights.

2.6 FURTHER DISTINCTIONS

There are several further clarifications and distinctions that can help prevent confusion in any discussions about property.

1. When people talk about their *property*, they are typically identifying what they own, and the implied property relations are generally both advantageous and disadvantageous to the owner. For example, ownership entails liabilities to a court judgment, taxation, and

---

[1] Honore, A.M. (1961) "Ownership." Oxford Essays in Jurisprudence. Oxford University Press, 107–147.

regulation, among other liabilities and duties, which the owner will not usually see as a direct advantage even if the owner supports these arrangements.

Consider how, in many societies, nearly every home owner pays property taxes, many consumer purchases entail sales taxes, and much income is subject to federal and state income taxes. Further, most items that we own can be used only in specific ways, with various legal prohibitions on uses that would directly harm others. As a descriptive analysis, there is no denying that ownership entails these legal liabilities and duties. To satisfy your curiosity, consider researching the legal rules and regulations associated with owning a business or home. These property relations are the source of controversy as well. To what extent and why should business and home owners pay taxes and follow regulations? This normative discussion will be part of later chapters.

2. When people talk about their **property rights**, in contrast to their property, they are typically emphasizing relations of ownership that they value or wish they had, not the ones that they wish they didn't have. This is why it would sound a bit odd to say that being taxed is a property right, though it is one of the property relations entailed by home ownership.

3. When people talk about their property *rights*, they are sometimes referring specifically to their *claim-rights* but they also may be referring more broadly to the entire bundle of claim-rights, liberties, powers, and immunities that serve the person's interests. A primary point of Hohfeld's analysis is that we often need to clarify what we mean when we refer to people's property rights over a specific object. Are we talking about people's claim-rights (and if so, which ones), or are we talking about the larger bundle of claim-rights, liberty-rights, powers, and immunities that regulate people's relationships to some item? There is no one correct usage of this term, so we need to be aware of this potential ambiguity and, therefore, clarify its meaning in any given conversation.

4. **Real property** refers to real estate, or more generally, immovable property. Real property is often contrasted with **personal property**, which refers to tangible or intangible movable property.

5. Although these terms do not have one set of fixed meanings, **private property** usually refers to real or personal property where the owner or owners have claim-rights to exclude others from the use of that property. **Communal property** refers to real or personal property owned by some collective whose members have broad liberty-rights to use (but who may exclude nonmembers from the use of that property); and **public property** refers to real or personal property usually owned by the government and often with broad liberty-rights for citizen use. The contrast between private property and communal property is especially important in the next chapter and will be relevant at various points throughout the text.

The most important clarification for our purposes regarding these distinctions is to realize that the topic of property relations introduced in this chapter does not directly presume or imply the concept of *private* property. Discussions about a society's property relations can help illuminate private, public, or communal property in Western or non-Western societies, as will be emphasized in the next chapter. In this regard, the Hohfeldian relationships will be seen to be highly versatile ideas.

6. What is the purpose of introducing Hohfeld's property relations? On the one hand, people study and debate what our property rights are as a matter of social and legal fact. They seek a descriptive analysis. On the other hand, people also argue about what our property rights ought to be apart from what they are. Hohfeldian terms are useful for these purposes as well. The property applications developed below can be analyzed in descriptive or normative terms.

2.7 INTELLECTUAL PROPERTY

Although we often associate discussions of property with land and buildings, the topic is more eclectic and creative than what discussions of real property might indicate. For

example, one of the most fascinating and controversial areas of property rights related to business concerns the special category of *intellectual property*, often abbreviated as IP. The World Intellectual Property Organization, an agency of the United Nations, defines **intellectual property** as "creations of the mind: inventions, literary and artistic works, and symbols, names, images, and designs used in commerce."[2] **Patents**, as discussed in some detail in the above application, are one form of intellectual property, as are **trademarks** and **copyrights**. Patents are exclusive rights granted by governments to an inventor that creates duties on others not to use or make a profit from a patented invention, without the inventor's permission. Trademarks are signs that identify a distinctive source for the goods or services, enabling its creator to file a lawsuit if someone is using that word, phrase, symbol, or design for purposes unauthorized by the creator of the trademark. Copyrights are legal protections for artistic or literary work.

Who owns ideas?

For example, you could apply for a *patent* to protect your invention, a *trademark* to protect the brand name of that invention, and a *copyright* to protect that one-of-a-kind commercial for advertising your invention.

Although this section does not detail all of the fascinating complications posed by intellectual property, which would be a course all on its own, the following range of cases can spark your imagination about real cases at hand and the creativity of the topic (no pun intended). They also show how conversations about property rights quickly convert into questions of ethics.

- To Joe Quirk's surprise, his novel *Ultimate Rush* seems to be the same story as the movie *Premium Rush*, as reported in a story about his intellectual property case in the *New York Times*.[3] Should a novelist earn proceeds from the profits of a movie when the story is based on that novel?
- It took a fair amount of work for your teacher to put together a class. Should a professor own the curriculum within a given classroom, or should the university?
- Should Google be able to scan books into digital form and make them widely available? Here is Google's explanation of their much publicized and critiqued project: http://www.google.com/googlebooks/library.html
- Domain-name speculators often buy the rights to the names of famous people. They "scoop" the domain name and then try to sell that name to the famous person—for very high fees. Should people be able to make a profit off of other people's names? In what sense is your name *yours*?

---

[2]http://www.wipo.int/about-ip/en/
[3]http://www.nytimes.com/2011/08/21/us/21bcquirk.html

- It's nice to listen to music without paying for it, but the artists who create that music and the companies that sell the music have a slightly different attitude. What rights should artists have over their creations?
- Consider the opening of this article about trademarks from the *New York Times*: "Bite into a Thomas' English muffin and, it turns out, you are about to swallow one of the most closely guarded secrets in the world of baking. The company that owns the Thomas' brand says that only seven people know how the muffins get their trademark tracery of air pockets—marketed as nooks and crannies—and it has gone to court to keep a tight lid on the secret. That leaves one of the seven, Chris Botticella, out of a job—and at the center of a corporate spectacle involving top-secret recipe files, allegations of clandestine computer downloads and an extreme claim of culinary dis- loyalty: dumping English muffins for Twinkies and Ho Hos."[4] Often, when you work for a company, you create and learn information that would be highly valuable to the competition, or to yourself if you started your own business. Suppose you created the information that a company is now using for profits, and then you leave the company. Should you be able to take that information with you? Is it yours? Who owns this information?

Beyond these intriguing examples, another significant context for IP discussions is the tremendous *financial* impact of intellectual property on large businesses. One study estimates that two-thirds of the value of large businesses is found in their intellectual property.[5] In recent years, patents have been at the center of major company buyouts and lawsuits.[6]

2.8   THE LIMITS OF PROPERTY RIGHTS

Let's take a step back to reconsider the broad topic of property. We learned that property is about relationships among persons with respect to things. *All* relationships? Although some theorists do try to describe all of our relationships with respect to things as *property* relations, others argue for the importance of recognizing limits to property terminology for interpreting and understanding our world. As a step into this discussion, let's consider the following question: in what sense do we own our body? We have claim-rights to ex- clusive use of our body and others have general duties not to interfere with how we use our body in most circumstances, without our permission. But we can't sell ourselves or our organs if we want to, or even give them away in many circumstances. And we don't have claim-rights to take our own life, at least not legally, as the state can exercise a liberty to intervene on any suicide attempt. In fact, it's a fascinating line of thought to try to enu- merate all of our property relations over our body. Given various limitations that a little thought will uncover, we will notice that, in some regards, we have less control over what we can do to ourselves than what we can do to our car. For example, we can take apart a

---

[4]William Neuman, "A Man with Muffin Secrets, but No Job with Them," *New York Times* (August 6, 2010), http://www.nytimes.com/2010/08/07/business/07muffin.html?hp

[5]Robert J. Shapiro and Nam D. Pham, "Economic Effects of Intellectual Property-Intensive Manufacturing in the United States," *World Growth* (July 2007).

[6]"Inventive Warfare: Battles over Patents Are Becoming Fiercer and More Expensive," *The Economist* (August 20, 2011).

car engine and sell it for parts anytime we want. Although we may think it obvious that we *own* our bodies (if not, then who does?), another response to this discussion is to say that property is the *wrong concept* to describe these relationships.

Thus, many theories distinguish the category of **personal rights** from property rights to emphasize that some issues should not be understood as property issues at all. Personal rights identify relationships among persons when the subject of these relationships is the persons themselves, not some other thing. We can describe the rights over our car as property rights but we may describe some of the rights over our bodies as personal rights, including rights to speak, assemble, vote, and receive a fair trial. The criminal law can be understood as a set of legal procedures and judgments for determining our personal rights when conflicts arise, independent from interpreting them as a property conflict.

Different theorists identify and justify this distinction in different ways, but the essential idea is that in the universe of "things," persons (what about other animals?) have a value that warrants special legal and ethical distinction apart from what a property rights analysis can provide. In this regard, intellectual property is interesting and controversial because it represents one area where aspects of persons (their ideas and creations) are recognized *within* a property rights framework. But in other cases it seems inappropriate, for example, to interpret a decision about the guilt or innocence of assaulting another person as a property dispute. But where property rights end and personal rights begin is disputed and contested territory. Consider this question: do parents *own* their children until they mature? What is the best way to describe that relationship?

Another highly relevant and contested area for testing this distinction is through debates about corporate rights. Corporations are recognized as persons in the eyes of the law. Does this mean that corporations have *personal* rights like real people do? As a matter of law, the answer is "yes." (We will address the important topic of property rights and corporations in Chapters 4 and 5.)

Finally, let's consider an example to illustrate potential limits to property discussions. Some theorists emphasize a contrast between (private) property rights and collective decision-making. For example, as in the case of *Kelo v New London* discussed in Chapter 1 Section 2, the use of eminent domain generates debates about the primacy of private property rights (for example, individual home owners) versus the collective interests of the large society. In these debates the authority of democratic decision-making is sometimes thought to place limits on the authority and reach of property rights, and *vice versa*. The use of eminent domain becomes a testing ground for identifying those respective limits. We will explore the role of democratic decision-making relevant to business and economic life in later chapters, especially in Chapters 9 and 11 on freedom and equality.

We will examine these potential limits in Chapter 13.

For our purposes in this chapter, there are two primary points that can be drawn from this discussion.

First, no matter how versatile the language and application of property rights, a study in ethics includes debates about the *limits* of understanding personal relationships through the terminology of markets and property.

Second, the Hohfeldian relations of claims, liberties, powers, and immunities can be useful for bringing precision to discussions about our personal rights—outside the context of property. For example, if A has a right to life, then this typically is interpreted to mean that all Bs, under most circumstances, have a duty not to take A's life. We need not be speaking of *property* to see how the concept of a claim-right is still important. *Right to life* is not expressed as a *liberty to life* for a reason: the latter expression does not imply corresponding duties upon others. Consider another example. The United Nations offers a *Universal Declaration of Human Rights*. This declaration is about our personal *claim-rights* and not merely our *liberties*, and the choice of terminology emphasizes the corresponding duties on others that these rights imply (see http://www.un.org/en/documents/udhr/). This chapter helps us see how the United Nations' characterization is not accidental, and why their chosen characterization is a powerful idea. If there *are* human *rights*, then this fact creates significant *duties* to respect these rights. Many people, in fact, regard the idea of protecting human rights as the most widely acknowledged global ethic in the world today.

> We will examine the broader concept of *rights*, apart from discussions of property rights, in Chapter 10.

Let's look at one final example of the versatility of the concepts in this chapter. Perhaps one of the most significant capacities of humans is to alter moral relationships. When A forgives B for some wrong, A exercises a moral *power* of forgiveness, by which we typically mean that B, once forgiven, is now at liberty to reenter a moral relationship with A. A's exercise of a moral power makes a new relationship possible. This example illustrates how we can talk about a range of *powers* that humans can exercise independently from conceiving of them as property relations.

There are many other examples that illustrate the basic point: *claims*, *liberties*, *powers*, and *immunities* can describe relationships among people, apart from the context of property rights and ownership. This fact further illustrates the relevance and practical importance of Hohfeld's ideas.

2.9   SUMMARY

In this chapter, we studied the nature and limits of the concept of property. To understand complex business and economic relationships, we need to know more than the general idea that someone is the owner of an item: we need to know the specific property relations that go into *that* ownership. We can say that owners are typically the agents who have the greatest interests in the property or those who have the most control over the things. But even these conditions are not always true, so the only way to fully understand what ownership entails—for any specific situation—is to enumerate the claims, liberties, powers, and immunities that are associated with that ownership. Sometimes these conditions are provided in a document of legal title, sometimes not, but once they are enumerated as needed, we will know everything that we need to know about our property relationships to that object. Not all of our relationships are defined in terms of property, but the idea of property relations offers a highly versatile set of concepts for understanding and interpreting how our world operates.

2.10   LOOKING AHEAD

A study of ethics in business and economic life is about both the dynamics of exchange and the property rights that create the backdrop of exchange. An important example that will concern us is the idea of corporate ownership and the responsibilities of corporations, the topics of Chapters 4 and 5.

> A study of ethics in business and economic life is about both the *dynamics of exchange* and the *property rights* that create the backdrop of exchange.

KEY TERMS

property	ownership	public property
property relations	property rights	intellectual property
claim-right/duty	real property	patents
liberty-right/no claim-right	personal property	trademarks
power/liability	private property	copyrights
immunity/disability	communal property	personal rights

DISCUSSION QUESTIONS

1. Choose a specific labor market that interests you and describe the property rights relevant to that market.

2. The U.S. Chamber of Commerce estimates that one in every three business failures is directly due to employee theft. Employees steal, but the problem is not only a conflict between employer and employee. Employees have things stolen from them as well. Can you describe theft using the property rights vocabulary of this chapter? Is theft a legal concept, an ethical concept, or both? What makes a taking a *theft*?

3. The Genetic Information Nondiscrimination Act of 2008 prohibits discriminating against persons for employment and health insurance based on genetic information. Does this mean that you own your genetic information? Explain.

4. In the wake of the financial collapse of the late 2000s, the U.S. government offered banks access to large sums of money to keep them from becoming insolvent. The government exercised a power for the banks to have claims over tax monies for the purposes of supporting the banks. What liabilities and duties should the government include in such a deal? Can you explain, based on your own research, how that arrangement worked out in practice, using Hohfeld's terminology?

5. Who owns Wikipedia and the information contained in it?

6. Suppose that a business or the government creates a new life form through its research and development, such as transgenic animals or genetically modified organisms. Do they (should they) own them?

3

PROPERTY RIGHTS, MARKETS, AND LAW

3.1 INTRODUCTION

A simple, yet fundamental, point conveyed in the previous two chapters is that both markets and property rights describe relationships among people. Markets express exchange relationships. They are embedded in culturally and legally diverse systems of property rights, and these property rights also describe a vast network of human relationships. By first establishing this conceptual background, it's easier to see how a study of business and economic life so closely connects to a study of ethics. Business and economic institutions *are* a vast network of human relationships and, as we will see, much of ethics is about assessing the quality and character of human relationships. Thus, there is a very close link between (1) understanding how we conceive of markets and property rights and (2) understanding why we are led to a study of ethics and values. Markets, property rights, and law embed and reflect ethical commitments, and so a study of ethics begins from the ground up by examining the nature of these business and economic institutions.

This chapter, like Chapter 2, continues to develop building blocks for the ethical discussions ahead by examining some connections among property rights, markets, law, and culture.

3.2 PROPERTY RIGHTS AND MARKETS

Markets develop against a background of property rights. This important idea connects materials across Chapters 1–3. It also prompts a question: *which* property rights are necessary for markets to exist? If we're just talking about basic market exchanges, and not the more complicated modern economy, the answer is *not much*.

First, markets require people, or groups of people, who have claim-rights to exclusively possess and use various items. For example, if the world consisted solely of liberty-rights to possess, how could you establish that the item that you or your group wishes to exchange would retain its value to those who happen to possess it? No one would have a duty *not* to interfere with that new possession if the possessor had no claim-rights over the object.

Second, markets also require that individuals have powers to transfer objects to willing buyers. To see this, imagine an all-powerful sovereign distributing all the fruits of the earth and effectively decreeing that no human may transfer any object. People could have property rights to use what they have, but they would be disabled from trading.

Once we have people with claim-rights to use and powers to transfer, then it seems that we have all the property rights we need for markets to develop. But not quite: we still need people who have the ability and desire to exercise these property rights (see Chapter 1 Section 6, "Background Conditions for Markets to Operate"). Still, the conditions are rather minimal, which helps explain why people find ways to create markets in the most varied of circumstances.

One such circumstance is China. We have derived background conditions for markets abstractly but economist John McMillan tested these ideas in practice. He writes, "China's agricultural reform shows the force of property rights. The elementary lesson is that incentives have great force. There is an additional lesson, though, which is less conventional. The productivity gains were achieved without formal legal recognition of the farmers' ownership rights."[1]

Agriculture in China is no minor example. McMillan found that state-owned farms assigned to farmers on short-term leases, with no power to sell the land, no claim-right to indefinite leases, no Western-oriented ownership bundle, could still yield huge productivity gains over the previous communal arrangements. The key was claim-rights to exclusive use of the produce grown on that land and powers to sell that produce and keep at least some fraction of the resulting earnings. In these two respects, farmers had some control over the produce, and the result was that the agricultural market took off.

Studying markets across the globe reveals surprising, spectacular, and implausible market arrangements. They reveal that we may need a set of property rights for markets to exist, but we don't need to presume anything resembling a capitalist economic system or a Western form of ownership. Stable expectations generated by a minimal set of property relations can be sufficient to create flourishing markets.

At this point, we're not assessing the ethics of markets and property rights but reflecting on how the ideas link together conceptually and historically as the first step toward a more comprehensive ethical study. For example, the case of agriculture in China illustrates how a study of markets connects with a study of the property rights that form the background for market exchange. We could continue a *descriptive* study by asking why the agricultural market took off. But we could probe this case *normatively* as well: are those property rights and exchanges a good idea? Section 8 of this chapter introduces two normative theories of property rights as a first step toward developing, in the chapters ahead, a more systematic study of ethics and values in relation to business and economic life.

See Chapter 1 Section 7 for the distinction between the terms *descriptive* and *normative*.

[1]John McMillan, *Reinventing the Bazaar: A Natural History of Markets* (W.W. Norton, 2002), p. 98.

- -

3.3   PROPERTY RIGHTS AND LAW

At the most general level *property rights* are the recognized rules that govern how people relate to each other with respect to things, as discussed in the last chapter. These rules form a background for any market development. They are often defined and enforced by law.

Law, for the purposes of this study, refers to a system of rules that function as the final coercive authority of a geographical region, usually enforced by a set of institutions, such as a government. This definition is by no means the last word on the nature of law. An entire field of study, called the philosophy of law, deals partly with the debate about what counts as law.[2] *Final* conveys the idea that people have no court of appeals outside this system for challenging its decision; *coercive* conveys the idea that those who enforce decisions about law will do so with or without your consent; and *authority* conveys the idea that law commands general assent, though the reasons and motives for people to follow the law can be quite diverse, such as through fear or endorsement. A law can be authoritative even if various people break the law, as long as the law dispenses commands that create a general following of the law.

Read the Case Study *Property, Law, and Animals* only on MySearchLab

Typically, a nation-state enforces law, and particular governments of a given nation-state create and interpret law, through legislation and the courts. At least this is how some states function. The rulings of the U.S. Supreme Court represent the final word in the U.S. judicial system, although the executive branch may fail to enforce the law and the Constitution allows for constitutional amendments that change the law through a carefully choreographed set of procedures. This example illustrates that *final* most often refers to the entire set of governmental institutions, not just one branch. Law is coercive through its enforcement mechanisms, including fines or arrests, or through subtle or not-so-subtle strategies of creating a climate where people fall into line.

This account of law is broad enough so that an effective mafia could be recognized as the law of an area if it's truly the final coercive authority of that region. But it's also narrow enough to have substantive debates about whether areas of the world simply lack any effective law at all.

This discussion of law is useful for another reason as well. When we study the topic of corporate responsibility, we will encounter debates about global corporations that operate across differing—and sometimes competing—systems of law. With some interpretations, this definition may even imply that corporations operate in regions that lack any effective law at all. Such facts raise interesting questions about the responsibilities of corporations in varying legal environments, as will be discussed in Chapters 4 and 5.

Domestic law refers to the law for citizens of a particular nation-state, with varying levels of local and national jurisdiction. Laws arrived at through treaties among nation-states comprise **international law**, which provides rules about relations among states and relations among individuals and states, as well as other organizations. An important and challenging application of the concept of law is whether the nascent judicial and

---

[2]The definition suggested here is drawn from Christopher Morris's analysis in *An Essay on the Modern State*, where he sorted through a variety of definitions of *state* and *law* before settling on the idea of *final coercive authority* as the most useful definition, a conclusion shared by many contemporary legal theorists and which reflects a long tradition of thought. Courtesy of Cambridge University Press, 2002.

arbitration systems of international law really count as *law*. There is no general conceptual agreement about how to characterize international law, though for practical purposes, there is no doubt that businesses adjust their decision-making to property rules created and enforced through both domestic and international legal proceedings.

Although governments and law exert a tremendous impact on property rights, a complete account of the property rights of a people is not *defined* by government or law, either conceptually or in practice. Let's consider this point in some detail. Recall again the economic world of Radford's POW camp experience in Chapter 1. People respected various property rights without governmental enforcement. To appreciate how property rights can exist without reference to law or government, consider life within the home. There are many family norms that develop over time that are not always easy to predict or articulate. But they matter a lot and some influence how family members relate to various objects in the home. We can distinguish **customary property rights**, which are informal and work outside the law, from **legal property rights**, which are interpreted and enforced within the law. Customary property rights are regulated by custom; legal property rights are regulated by government. There are many customary property rights both within and outside the home that have no particular legal backing.

Another striking example of the conceptual and practical distinction between property rights and law is provided by Peruvian economist Hernando De Soto through his work documenting extralegal markets in various countries around the world. Even the casual visitor to the poorest regions of the earth cannot help but notice bustling markets. De Soto argues that many of these markets exist outside the control of any effective legal system. Local social norms determine the evolution and enforcement of the property rights that regulate many of these bazaars and centers of trade. His argument, in fact, is that many of the world's poor are locked out of the formal legal system, which traps them from being able to use their assets to their own advantage. For example, banks require borrowers to offer collateral as a condition of a loan agreement. If the borrower fails to pay back the loan, the bank thereby has the legal power to collect on the collateral and recoup some of its losses. But for many people in developing countries, *nothing* they own, including the shanty that they live in, is formally recognized *by law* as their property. They have no legal papers and no help from the government or courts when property disputes arise. Instead, they have customary rights to ownership, which are stable enough to create bustling local markets but lack the legal backing needed for getting a bank loan. The result, De Soto observes, is that many of the world's poorest people become trapped in a market world, an orderly world without law, but a world in which it can be very difficult to start a small business.

Although many markets are carefully regulated by various laws, De Soto's writings offer a striking example of understanding the idea and importance of customary property rights. Economist and Nobel Peace Prize recipient Muhammad Yunus responded to the problems studied by De Soto by introducing the concept of microcredit or **microlending**—the offering of entrepreneurial loans to the very poor in situations where traditional banks judged these persons not creditworthy. The concept led to Yunus's founding the Grameen bank and initiating a major institutional effort to spread economic growth from the ground up, even in the face of tenuous property holdings. Yunus is one high-profile example of an individual's effort to apply an ethical perspective, not merely in the context of interpersonal relations but through a systemic response. He created institutions that transformed *customary property rights* into more *formalized legal rights*, and because of his lending practices, Yunus has been praised for improving the lives of the extreme poor and received the

Nobel Peace Prize in 2006. The widespread attention given to microlending in the last decade occurs in the context where many of the loans were offered to women who lacked opportunities to start a business. Not everyone has supported Yunus's efforts, as some have critiqued these efforts as attempts to import Western banking practices on the customs of a region. But in this context especially and across many other topics as well, a study of markets and property rights is relevant to a study of gender, as historically women within homes have been shielded from full participation in markets, both through custom and law.

> Chapter 11 on *equality* addresses issues of human equality in relation to the ethics of business and economic life.

We do not need to cast a global net to discuss the distinction between customary and legal property rights. Western economies have many property rights that are customary. The value of a handshake, in terms of various understood agreements, expresses a commitment to customary property rights. The practices of exchange on Craigslist and other online trading systems are often based on a fluid set of customary rights. Social networks present an especially interesting case for stretching the boundaries of customary rights. Further, the way people do things within an industry or within a single corporation often expresses customary rights that can be learned only with experience. The distinction between law and custom is as important for all cultures.

These more informal property rights can be crucial for understanding subtle but important differences *across* corporate and national cultures. International business practices differ across cultures not only in their laws but in their customary property rights as well. These informal property relations are fertile ground for questions of ethics in business, as the norms that develop from custom are often sustained or criticized on ethical rather than legal grounds. As an illustration of this idea, consider the commonplace practice of tipping. Suppose your friends decide that they will no longer tip at restaurants—no matter the quality of service—because they are not legally obligated to tip and they would like to pocket the change. What is your response to your friends? Why do you respond that way? Tipping describes a customary property relation between wait staff and patrons; and a debate regarding tipping depends partly on understanding the relevant social norms and your own sense of ethics, given those norms.

The concept of *fair trade* offers another example of customary rights that influences the development of markets. Businesses that sell coffee, tea, crafts, and foods will advertise their products as certified fair trade to express support for sustainable practices and working conditions. They hope that buyers are willing to pay a premium for products that support more costly sustainable practices. This example can frame a debate about the motives that can and do drive market exchange. It also illustrates how customary property rights can shape and be shaped by peoples' norms and ethical beliefs, such as consumers' sense of a justified wage to a coffee grower.

Let's summarize the key ideas. Property rights presume people who are willing to govern themselves by rules that specify people's claims, liberties, powers, and immunities with respect to the goods and services at issue. Property rights are an intermediary between markets and law, but are distinct from both. On one side, markets develop against the backdrop of some set of property rights. On the other side, governments are often the institutions that regulate and enforce these property rights through their use of law. In this sense, property rights are a glue between markets and government. But the idea of property rights is also distinct from law because these property rights often express, to some degree, property relations not specifically defined by law. Depending on this mix of legal and customary rights, the development of markets and property rights varies by culture,

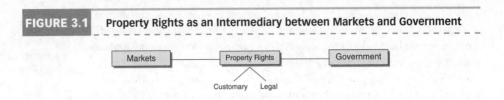

FIGURE 3.1   Property Rights as an Intermediary between Markets and Government

by place, and by organization, and they guide how we relate to each other with respect to things (see Figure 3.1).

3.4   PROPERTY RIGHTS AND CULTURE

The discussion of customary property rights highlights the important role of **culture** in business and economics. *Culture* is defined in many ways depending on context, but most often refers to the shared norms, values, and practices that guide and shape some group or organization. Property relations are often culturally specific and their study can require great sensitivity to the various norms that drive people's behavior. Some of these norms, for example, can be relevant for understanding why markets develop in some circumstances and not in others. The *blocked exchanges* of Chapter 1 Section 5 illustrate this point. These blocked exchanges represent both customary and legal rules that constrain or prohibit powers of transfer regarding specific items.

But there is another point to emphasize about property rights and culture, introduced last chapter: the concept of property relations is separable from culturally specific concepts of ownership and private property. Property relations are useful not only for understanding Western economies but also for understanding societies around the world—including what anthropologists study in places farthest from Western development.

Law professor Stephen Munzer presents the example of canoes among the indigenous Melanasia, who inhabit the islands north and east of Australia. He asks of this society, "Are canoes private or public property in Melanasia?" Here are some observable facts: An individual has claim-rights that others may not damage his canoe, a claim-right to use the canoe, a power to sell or give away the canoe, and an immunity from being forced to sell the canoe. But this same person also has a duty to ferry certain travelers across the water and if he were to renege on this duty, then others have a claim to damages.

If we import Western concepts of *private property* rights or *ownership*, Munzer points out, it is difficult to understand this arrangement. For example, who owns this canoe? There is no clear answer. The concept of ownership is too vague and expresses a specifically Western idea. So that is the wrong question, says Munzer. We could ask instead, "What are the property relations accepted in this community?" Describing these relations tells us what we need to know about how people relate to each other with respect to this thing.

Although ownership may be a foreign idea to various indigenous peoples, understanding what is *not* foreign to them requires, in part, a grasp of their *communal* property system (compare Chapter 2 Section 6 for definitions of *private, communal,* and *public property*). And communal property relations do not directly lead to the concepts of private property or ownership. *Claims*, *liberties*, *powers*, and *immunities* are versatile ideas for interpreting social arrangements across societies and throughout diverse Western and non-Western cultures, without importing market-driven ideas about exchange and ownership into one's interpretation of non-Western societies.

This discussion relates to Chapter 1 Section 4. We characterize the world based on how and what we *see* in the world. Concepts create filters that guide our understanding. For this study, markets and property rights will frame many of our discussions ahead. Given the global environment in which business and whole economies develop, it's important that these concepts be understood from a global standpoint, in the context of both our own culture and that of different cultures around the world. This explains the emphasis on characterizing markets and property relations separately from the concepts of ownership and private property. The China example illustrates how some markets require some minimal property relations but not necessarily Western-type private property. Additionally, the canoe example illustrates the versatility of applying the various property relations without presuming that we're talking about private property and ownership.

Even so, the language of property relations is not neutral, as *any* concept encourages us to focus our observations on one aspect of our experience over another. We may worry about misinterpreting the meanings behind our interactions, as the discussion of *personal rights* illustrated earlier (Chapter 2 Section 8). For many theorists, personal rights identify important limits for interpreting our own relationships over things through the lens of property (when *we* are the things under discussion). We may also consider whether we miss something important by interpreting the value of community in traditional indigenous societies by cataloging their interactions through property relations, even if we do describe them as communal. We may still be seeing their society through our eyes rather than theirs. These points are especially relevant when corporations do business across diverse cultural environments. When a pharmaceutical company wants to patent a traditional indigenous healing practice, it can be difficult even to *characterize* the conflict, beyond knowing how to deal with the conflict. Likewise, when Western ownership practices spread to India, China, and other non-Western societies, it can be difficult (or even tragic) to try to assess the relative gains and losses of these changes without a broader sense of meanings within that culture.

We can acknowledge all of these points while recognizing that the concepts of markets, property relations, private property, and ownership form the background for many of our familiar economic institutions and remain critical for understanding many of the issues that lie ahead. These concepts will provide a filter through which we will pursue an extended treatment of business ethics in Chapters 4 through 13. But the discussion here also suggests that we consider the relevance of *personal relationships* and *community* to business and economic life beyond the concepts of exchange and property, the subject of Chapter 14.

3.5   UNDERSTANDING ECONOMIC SYSTEMS

As economic systems become more complicated, *legal* property rights become more important for understanding the business and financial world. In part, this is the point of Hernando de Soto's study of the poor. Economic globalization is not about the spread of markets—they were already there—but more fundamentally about the spread of specific

ECONOMIC SYSTEMS TODAY

Differences in economic systems today are most clearly expressed by describing their complex property arrangements, which encourage or discourage certain kinds of markets to develop. This study requires understanding the legal property rights system of that nation, the role of business activity within that system, and the interaction with the flow of goods and services around the world.

legal rules that support more complicated forms of market development. We can apply our study of markets and property rights to offer a few preliminary remarks about economic globalization and the nature of economic systems.

First, the idea of an **economic system** through which markets develop is best understood as the entire web of property rights that support and surround markets. The *system* includes not only facts about market exchange but all of the customary and legal property rights that frame how markets develop and connect to one another; how governments regulate, encourage, support, or prohibit various markets; and how people participate in those markets.

Second, not long ago people divided the world largely by referencing two competing economic systems, *capitalism* and *socialism*. A great deal of analysis focused on characterizing the practical and philosophical differences of these two systems, but the environment today is different both practically and intellectually. This doesn't mean that discussion or use of broad ideas about capitalism or socialism is unimportant. But it does mean that differences in economic systems today are most clearly expressed by describing the details of their complex property rights arrangements that encourage or discourage certain kinds of markets to develop. This study requires understanding the legal property rights system of that nation, the role of business activity within that system, and the interaction of the flow of goods and services around the world. No one label can quite capture these details, and these details are where the most important questions take place.

The discussions in this chapter provide especially important context in a global economy, including the huge populations in China and India, with a combined 2.5 *billion* persons, and their extensive business developments in the last thirty years. In Chapters 4 and 5, we will discuss the business system domestically and internationally, including the role of corporations in a modern economy.

3.6   WHY TALK ABOUT PROPERTY RIGHTS?

The first three chapters have introduced various links between property rights, markets, law, and culture. The discussion so far brackets any systematic ethical discussion because we have not yet developed the tools to engage these debates. Consider one further property example to illustrate the fundamental difference between using concepts to *interpret* and *explain* our world from the endeavor to make *ethical assessments*. Economist Amartya Sen won the Nobel Prize in Economics in significant part because of his work on famines. Rich in details, we can readily understand his most central point based on the analysis of this chapter. In his book *Poverty and Famines: An Essay on Entitlements and Deprivation*, he argues, counterintuitively, that famine is not fundamentally caused by a lack of food.

How could this be? Sen's response: famines are about the lack of *claim-rights* to food. Sen found that most famines over the last two centuries occurred when there was enough food to go around, but the starving people had no claim-rights to acquire it. Famine, Sen argues, is a property rights failure. Sen's work offers a principal example of the explanatory insight offered by studying property rights. It is impossible to understand why famines occur, according to Sen, without understanding the details of the property rights systems that were in place at the time of the famines.

This example illustrates how property rights are an important concept that helps interpret and explain our social world. Yet, this explanatory task does not capture our full reaction to Sen's research. If famines are mostly a property rights failure, then this is a preventable human failing not to be blamed on nature, and a world that is able to but does not prevent famines is ethically horrendous. This ethical judgment was part of Sen's moral compass in studying famines. The point here is simply to note that stating and developing an account of the *wrong* of famine is a different intellectual endeavor from explaining *why* famines occur. The first project is normative and part of philosophy, the second is explanatory and part of social science (compare Chapter 1 Section 7, and the discussion in the Introduction related to Figure I.1.).

At the same time, these projects are related endeavors because the basic explanatory concepts frame the ethical questions that we will ask. For example, only by understanding the basic idea of property rights can we formulate the following ethical question, "What kind of property system *should* we live with?" The explanatory and the ethical are also related because ethical arguments typically appeal to concepts in social science to complete the arguments. It's hard to argue for the wrong of famine without having a bare outline of facts about what famines are and what causes them.

This discussion about Sen's work relates to the progression of ideas in this book. These first three chapters introduce basic explanatory concepts prior to—and as a way to frame—the ethical puzzles that lie ahead. As we will soon study, large corporations are tremendously influential institutions that work through markets and are legally defined by a special set of property relationships. We will examine debates about their responsibilities.

3.7   RELATIVISM

Discussions about culture raise anthropological and philosophical questions about the nature of diversity and relativism. We observe that groups and cultures have different histories—they have different property rights arrangements and different ways of life. Others see similarities across cultures, as in the following adage that people are the same wherever you go. These can be contrary or complementary observations; they lead to the question, "To what extent do people and cultures differ and to what extent do they share human commonalities?" More specifically, we may also seek to explain people's ethical beliefs, asking, "Are there common ethical principles that all people endorse across cultures? What best explains the diversity of ethical beliefs?"

These questions, fascinating in their own right, often lead to deeper philosophical questions about the nature of truth and objectivity. **Ethical relativism** is the general thesis that normative standards are relative to the beliefs and practices of a group, culture, or individual. More specifically, a **cultural ethical relativist** believes that ethical standards are relative to a given culture. That is, right and wrong are defined by a given culture, and there is no further truth about what counts as right or wrong. This view is also sometimes called *conventional* relativism to refer to the idea that ethics is always relative to the conventions of a society. By contrast, an **individual ethical relativist** believes that ethical standards are relative to what an individual thinks, with no further valid standard of ethical evaluation. Right and wrong express the relative beliefs and attitudes of *each individual*

CONVENTIONALISM ABOUT PROPERTY RIGHTS

Conventionalism about property rights is the belief that property rights arise from or are determined by the conventions of that particular society. Theorists develop this idea in many different ways. For example, this idea could be understood descriptively as the claim that laws and norms express the property relations defined by that society. But conventionalism may also express a form of cultural relativism, that the conventions of that society supply the only standard to evaluate the legitimacy of those property rights.

with no further truth about what is objectively right or wrong. Some people refer to this view as *subjective* relativism to emphasize their belief that ethics is entirely subjective to the individual. All forms of relativism are skeptical that ethical debates can express absolute or universal ethical standards.

Relativism in all its varieties is the subject of much contemporary and historical philosophical debate. Views that reject relativism go by several names, depending on what an advocate most wants to emphasize. For example, **ethical universalism** is the view that at least some ethical beliefs have validity that applies universally across all individuals and cultures. Similarly, **ethical absolutism** is the view that at least some ethical beliefs apply absolutely and without further qualifications, no matter the cultural framework. Finally, proponents of **ethical objectivity** believe that ethics can yield objective truths that are not merely a function of the subjective beliefs of each individual. All of these forms reject ethical relativism, sharing the common perspective that ethical debate *can* lift us outside our relative perspectives and take us to insights that reveal universal, absolute, or objective understandings about ethics.

The most basic point to note here is that discussions about culture often lead to debates about relativism. Be aware of these distinctions as they arise in your conversations, either in this chapter or at other points throughout this book. Consider also that confusions are rife when people shift from *descriptive* discussions about culture to *normative* discussions without noticing the shift. For example, suppose that someone asserts that "property rights are a convention of society." What is this person saying? Does she mean that property relations of a society are expressed through norms and laws (that is, the conventions) of that society? This is a relatively uncontroversial descriptive claim. Or is this person asserting that the legitimacy of a society's property rights derives solely from its conventions and there is no further basis to critique or ethically assess those arrangements? This assertion would be a controversial form of cultural relativism. One position does not imply or follow from the other. For example, someone could grant that practices differ across cultures as a matter of historical fact but also believe that universal standards apply for assessing those property arrangements.

This section offers a very brief introduction to an intriguing area of philosophical thought. The debates to follow do not presume any settled answers about relativism and objectivity in ethics. They only presume a desire to engage and respond to the specific ethical issues at hand, and it will be an open question throughout this book whether and how we should conceive of the objectivity of ethics, the subject area of **metaethics**.

3.8   TWO NORMATIVE THEORIES OF PROPERTY RIGHTS

We have now considered several links between property rights, markets, law, and culture to set a context for understanding and interpreting our economic world. But as a normative question, what *should* our property rights be?

Scottish enlightenment philosopher David Hume provides an answer. Note in the passage how he applies various concepts discussed throughout these last two chapters:

See the Introduction Section 4 for a general discussion of consequentialism.

> What is man's property? Anything which it is lawful for him, and for him alone, to use. But what rule have we by which we can distinguish these objects? Here we must have recourse to statutes, customs, precedents, analogies, and a hundred other circumstances; some of which are constant and inflexible, some variable and arbitrary. *But the ultimate point, in which they all professedly terminate, is the interest and happiness of human society.* . . . [emphasis mine][3]

David Hume endorses a **consequentialist ethics for property rights**: we ought to support whatever property arrangements create the best consequences among all those affected by those arrangements. As one type of consequentialism, a utilitarian would argue that the most ethical system is the one that produces the most happiness for all those impacted by these rules.

Thus, from this ethical perspective, there is nothing special about systems of *private property* or *communal property* by their very nature. Hume wanted to know what happens when people live under these systems. He (and others) believed that private property and markets are important for creating happiness. Others accept Hume's normative position that people's happiness should be the ultimate metric for making ethical judgments, but they dispute the empirical facts of Hume's argument. This broad consequentialist debate previews more in-depth debates in business and economic life that we will examine in Chapters 6 through 8.

Let's consider a historical predecessor of Hume, English philosopher John Locke. He provided a different answer:

> God . . . has given the earth . . . to mankind in common. But this being supposed, it seems to some a very great difficulty, how any one should ever come to have a property in any thing. . . . I shall endeavor to show, how men might come to have a property in several parts of that which God gave to mankind in common, and that without any express compact of all the commoners. . . .
>
> Though the earth, and all inferior creatures, be common to all men, yet every man has a property in his own person: this no body has any right to but himself. The labour of his body, and the work of his hands, we may say, are properly his. Whatsoever then he removes out of the state that nature hath provided, and left it in, he hath mixed his labour with, and joined to it something that is his own, and thereby makes it his property. It being by him removed from the common state nature hath placed it in, it hath by this labour something annexed to it, that excludes the common right of other men: for this labour being the unquestionable property of the labourer, no man but he can have a right to what that is once joined to, at least where there is enough, and as good, left in common for others.[4]

Locke's theory is a leading example of **deontological (or nonconsequentialist) ethics for property rights**. Independent from whether people are better off based on the results, Locke argues that our natural rights over our bodies can create legitimate claim-rights over items in the world external to our bodies.

The Introduction, Section 4, includes a more general discussion of deontological ethics.

---

[3]David Hume, *An Enquiry Concerning the Principles of Morals* (1751), Section III, Part II.
[4]John Locke, *Second Treatise of Government* (1689), Chapter 5, Sections 25, 27.

American philosopher Robert Nozick is a modern proponent of Locke's approach for justifying property rights. Nozick's "Lockean" ideas will be presented in greater detail in Chapter 10 Section 4.

Locke's ideas were central to the development of the American colonies. They played an important role in crafting the U.S. Constitution and they have influenced many legal systems. Locke was particularly intrigued by the question of how private property could be justified. The answer, he believed, is not found by observing what happens when people have private property (as a consequentialist would argue) but by how people's past actions can create legitimate claim-rights over objects. Locke's key premise is that, by nature, we own our bodies and our labor, and when we mix our labor into an unclaimed object, we can thereby make it our own. As we have learned from our study of property rights, the significance of this proposal lies not only in ideas about what the *owner* can do with the object, but in the corresponding ethical obligation that *others* don't use the item without the owner's permission. Property, as he believed, specifies ethical relationships among people, and a legal system should codify those relationships into law.

Let's take one example to illustrate these theories about property rights. Until 2001, Napster was a company that allowed peer-to-peer sharing of music files. But after some music groups filed suit, including Metallica, the U.S. Court of Appeals for the 9th Circuit ruled that their file-sharing platform infringed copyright law. At its peak, Napster had over twenty-five million users and eighty million songs that users could share without any fees passing between the users. Putting aside specific legal issues, we can ask two questions: (1) As a descriptive matter, what were the property rights of those music files during the period where Napster was legally permitted to operate? (2) As a normative matter, should users be able to share music with one another without the original artist having any claim on income that could derive from that distribution?

The normative theories introduced here offer two competing frameworks for addressing the second question. As an ethical question, we could focus on the *benefits* or *costs* of the peer-to-peer sharing and argue that the best rules are those that yield the greatest benefit overall, taking into account everyone affected, such as the artists, users, and the music industry. Alternatively, we could focus on the *rights* of the artists, applying Locke's ideas, and argue that users should face constraints on how they distribute and share music because the artists legitimately own that music by virtue of having created it. We need not think that Hume's and Locke's theories raise the only relevant ethical issues related to music downloads in a digital age. Rather, the case provides a pointed example for applying these theories and for seeing how those historical ideas are as relevant today as they were then.

Let's consider three features of these two normative theories:

1. *Consequentialist and deontological theories apply across a range of topics in business and economic life.* In this chapter, they apply to answering questions about property, but the theories are not essentially about evaluating property rights. They offer general normative frameworks of thought. At the most general level, as first discussed in the Introduction, a set of ethical beliefs becomes a *theory* when there's an attempt to organize intuitions about right and wrong into a systemic account of why we have those intuitions and how they should fit together.
   - A consequentialist believes that our ethical judgments on any given topic should be guided by assessing the consequences of any particular action or institution. The consequentialist interprets ethics as the challenge of analyzing what might happen, and then doing whatever seems likely to produce the best consequences.

- A deontological theorist, such as Locke, believes that our ethical judgments on any given topic should be guided by assessing any relevant rules or principles that constrain and guide what we should do, apart from analyzing the consequences. The deontologist interprets ethics as the challenge of looking backward to identify prior commitments or rules that should constrain and guide our decisions, such as respecting people's rights.

    Both normative theories command broad allegiances, as do other theories that will be part of discussions in this book. As we will see, the contrast between consequentialist and deontological theories is one of the most useful distinctions across many ethical debates beyond this chapter's application to property rights.

2. *The theories of Hume and Locke can be applied to assess whole property systems or some given property issue within the system.* For example, why have property at all? The theories presented give different answers to this broad question. But we can also ask, "Should home owners be required to pay property taxes?" or other specific questions about property rights, such as music downloads. With respect to the taxing question

    - a consequentialist like Hume would assess the range of available options (for example: no taxes, some taxes, high taxes) and advocate tax rates that bring the most good to the members of society overall;
    - a deontologist like Locke would ask whether the taxing decisions were arrived at through a process that did not violate anyone's rights.

        In sum, these normative theories can be applied to address large institutional questions about the basic structures of society or specific questions in applied ethics about how people should treat and interact with each other.

3. *We can usefully distinguish what someone believes from how they defend those beliefs.* As mentioned earlier, some who share Hume's consequentialism may reach different conclusions about private property depending on their view about the impact of private property systems on people's well-being. Alternatively, some theorists may endorse Locke's deontological perspective and yet reach different conclusions than Locke about the value of business and commerce.

To illustrate this point through a dramatic contrast, consider the German philosopher Karl Marx. Although Marx may seem a long way philosophically from John Locke—and he was—they had one premise in common: self-ownership. But unlike Locke, Marx developed this premise into a radical critique of capitalism. Marx believed that the labor relationship in capitalism violates individuals' ownership over themselves and their labor. He developed concepts of exploitation and alienation to describe what he saw as the wrong that occurs when a company owns what employees produce. If workers own themselves and their labor, a Marxist will ask, then why should companies get to keep the value created through the handiwork of the employees?

Without developing these lines of thought further, these examples serve simply to illustrate the distinction between *what* someone argues and *how* he argues it. Both Hume and Locke argue for the same conclusion but they differ in how they argue. Marx and Locke, by contrast, have competing conclusions about the value of commerce, but they share at least some underlying premises about how to argue for their competing positions.

3.9   SUMMARY

People study markets and property rights because they deeply influence our lives. We can analyze property not merely as things but as social relations among people with respect to things. Paying attention to the vast relations of claims, liberties, powers, and immunities that have authority over us can be an eye-opening exercise. Property rights can intrigue us into a deeper understanding of our social world.

We considered property relations, the meaning of ownership, and several important connections between property rights, markets, law, and culture. Property rights are an intermediary between markets and law. They form the background against which markets operate and they are often, though not always, expressed and enforced through a well-defined legal system. Whether legal or customary, these property relationships can seem invisible, and yet, they are as real as the grooves in a seashell.

3.10   LOOKING AHEAD

This chapter concludes Part I of our study. We will next examine the topic of corporate social responsibility in Part II (Chapters 4 and 5).

KEY TERMS

law	economic system	metaethics
domestic law	ethical relativism	consequentialist ethics for
international law	cultural ethical relativist	property rights
customary property rights	individual ethical relativist	deontological (or
legal property rights	ethical universalism	nonconsequentialist) ethics
microlending	ethical absolutism	for property rights
culture	ethical objectivity	

DISCUSSION QUESTIONS

1. One time when market activities collapse is during a panic and crisis. Massive looting, stealing, and chaos can destroy markets. For example, the devastating floods in New Orleans led to the complete abandonment of markets for a time, as the world witnessed on TV. Why is this?

2. Is Amartya Sen correct in saying that famines are essentially a property rights failure? To what extent does Amartya Sen's analysis apply for understanding the complicated nature of hunger in Western economies? Is hunger and nutrition a serious problem in the United States and Europe? What does your research reveal?

3. There are fundamental reasons why the protection of property rights tends to imply government and law. In his *Second Treatise of Government*, John Locke wrote that "the great and chief end, therefore, of men's uniting into commonwealths, and putting themselves under government, is the preservation of their property." Why would preservation of property imply the need for government? (We will consider this question directly in Chapter 8).

4. Would people respect property rights not enforced or enforceable by law? Under what conditions?

5. To what extent should law settle questions about what property rights should be? On what standards should we assess good and bad law?

6. Read the *Kelo v. New London Supreme Court* case on property rights and eminent domain mentioned in Chapter 1 (For an edited version of this case see Scalet and Arthur *Morality and Moral Controversies*, Pearson, 2014, Chapter 15). What are the arguments as represented in the majority and minority opinions? Which points do you find most persuasive? Why?

7. Consider the following argument: "I need a drink of water; therefore, I have a right to a drink of water." Assess how a consequentialist and a deontologist might analyze this argument.

8. Breathing air exercises liberty-rights to use the atmosphere in a very special way; no one has a claim-right to prevent any of us from breathing. Do we have claim-rights to *clean* air? What is your argument?

9. A business partner in another country makes it clear that she would appreciate a kickback as part of the ongoing business relationship. You ask around and realize that this is quite common and even customary. How do you evaluate the ethics of such a situation?

10. Some proponents of *socialism* advocate what they call *market socialism*, such as John Roemer's *A Future for Socialism* (Harvard University Press 1994) or David Miller's *Market, State, and Community: Theoretical Foundations of Market Socialism* (Oxford University Press, 1991). Without knowing their particular definitions of socialism, can you apply the concepts of this chapter to explain how it could be possible to advocate both markets and socialism?

11. Locke is famous for advocating property rights but, in the passage cited in Section 8, notice how he qualifies his position by stating that appropriation from nature must leave "enough, and as good, left in common for others." This qualification is both intriguing and puzzling. Does this idea imply that Locke is really a consequentialist?

12. Environmental regulations often restrict how owners may use their property. Apply the ideas of these chapters to consider whether and how such restrictions may be justified.

13. Some people endorse relativism because they believe in a principle of toleration. The idea is that we shouldn't judge other people or cultures, as we would wrongly impose our values onto them. Therefore, we should be relativists. What do you think of this argument?

14. For further thought, suppose that you encounter people who are intolerant of others for no other reason than they like to impose their will on others, violently. Would you criticize those persons as unethical? Suppose they say, "All beliefs are relative, so for *you* it's unethical to be intolerant but *for me* I think it's ethical to be intolerant, and there's no further truth about the matter." What is your response? Is it "I'm a relativist, too, so I guess you're right" or is it "Your intolerance is unethical no matter what you believe about it." What does this exchange tell you about whether you think of yourself as a relativist or not?

15. Murder is wrong. It's also illegal. Now consider another case: We normally think that infidelity is wrong, but we probably don't think that it should be illegal. What do these examples tell us, if anything, about the relationship between ethics and law? In what ways do ethics overlap and pull apart from law? (Although the debates ahead take law as important background, this book pursues questions of ethics, not law, as indicated in the Introduction.)

16. Though Locke grounded his theory of property rights in natural rights, he did not believe that conventions were irrelevant for understanding the justification of property rights. How can someone be both a deontologist for justifying (some) property rights but believe that other property rights could be justified by convention?

Part II applies the three basic concepts introduced in Part I - corporations participate in *markets* with specific *property rights* backed by *law*. We now ask, "What are the ethical responsibilities of corporations?" Some argue that beyond maximizing profits within law, there are few (Chapter 4). Others argue that there are many, including commitments to the stakeholders of a corporation (Chapter 5). Part II examines both of these arguments.

Chapter 4 • The Stockholder Theory of Corporate Responsibility

Chapter 5 • The Stakeholder Theory of Corporate Responsibility

4

THE STOCKHOLDER THEORY OF CORPORATE RESPONSIBILITY

WHEN YOU FINISH STUDYING THIS CHAPTER, YOU SHOULD BE ABLE TO:

1. Describe the stockholder theory of corporations, which is a view about the purpose of corporations and the rights and duties of stockholders and management.

2. Characterize how proponents defend this theory and how they interpret the value of corporate social responsibility.

3. Discuss debates about the proper role of government associated with this theory.

4. Consider the relevance of self-interest and broad ideas about human motivation in relation to the stockholder account.

4.1   INTRODUCTION

The contemporary world includes the growth and influence of huge corporations across the globe. In general terms, a **corporation** refers to a legal entity chartered by the state with rights and responsibilities apart from the persons running or working for the corporation. For example, a corporation can be sued in a court of law without the individuals working for the corporation being sued. Business corporations take a variety of forms, but the most common types have **stockholders**, also called shareholders, who own the corporation by purchasing shares in the company. Stockholders typically retain claim-rights to sell their shares and receive returns on the profits of the corporation. Stockholders have very limited control over the firm's operations, apart from a right to nominate and vote for a **board of directors**. The role of the board of directors is to oversee the management of the corporation. An historically important feature of stockholder rights is a legal **principle of limited liability**, which means that stockholders are typically immune from paying any debts of the corporation beyond their initial investment in purchasing the stock. This immunity has helped corporations raise large sums of money from investors whose personal finances are legally protected from corporate debt collectors. The property rights concepts introduced in Chapter 2 (claims, liberties, powers, and immunities) are important for investigating the complex property rights of corporations; the field of corporate law is the study of the financial and governance functions of corporations as defined by the state.

Although we need not investigate the legal structure of corporations beyond this bare outline for the arguments ahead, it's worth noting that businesses take other legal forms as well, such as *sole proprietorships*, *partnerships*, and *cooperatives*. These businesses include one or more owners who are typically liable for any debts incurred by the firm's activities and they generally control the business with extensive claims, liberties, and powers over all aspects of its operations. In the case of a corporation, the top management runs the business but does not own it—that's the role of the stockholders.

> See Chapters 1–3 for discussion of property rights, ownership, and markets.

Most business corporations are small, but some are large—so large that people struggle to understand and characterize the purpose, role, and scope of these enormous institutions. Consider, What is the largest economic entity in the world? In 2009, measured by **gross domestic product** (GDP), the United States was first, followed by Japan, China, and Germany. Any guesses about number 22? It's not a nation-state at all—it's Walmart (see Figure 4.1). If we measure revenues as its own economic unit, then Walmart has more revenues than the combined final sales of most of the nation-states on earth.[1]

Writers Sarah Anderson and John Cavanaugh developed this contrast to critique the power of corporations. When they made their comparisons in 1999, they found that just over 50 percent of the top 100 economic entities in the world were corporations.[2] A decade later, writers Tracey Keys and Thomas W. Malnight found that 44 percent of the top 100 economic entities were corporations, while 59 percent of the top 150 economic entities were corporations.[3] Conceptually speaking, what should we make of these comparisons? The information in Figure 4.1 may lead us to believe that GDP is separate from the sales of corporations. But these corporations are located within nation-states and across nation-states, and GDP is constituted, in part, by the sales of these corporations. It's not at all obvious how to assess this information. States have armies, engage in coercive activities, enforce laws; they have citizens and governments. Corporations have employees and managers and boards of directors and stockholders. They do not have armies (at least not obviously), they do not enforce laws or make them (at least in theory), and they operate within a given stable legal environment (at least in some parts of the world). The parenthetical qualifications are crucial for those who believe that in practice corporations exert power whose influence can be comparable to the power of some governments. Others call this a gross exaggeration.

No one doubts, however, the tremendous influence of corporations on modern life. This data invites us to step back and think about the nature and role of corporations in today's society. To offer an historical analogy, English political philosopher Thomas Hobbes wrote *Leviathan* in 1651, a masterpiece

> We will examine the controversial idea that corporations are persons in Chapter 5 Section 9.

---

[1]Tracey Keys and Thomas W. Malnight, *Corporate Clout 2012: The Influence of the World's Largest 100 Economic Entities* (Strategy Dynamics Global Limited, 2012). For more information about this work, see http://www .globaltrends.com/knowledge-center/features/shapers-and-influencers/66-corporate-clout-the-influence-of-the-worlds-largest-100-economic-entities

[2]Sarah Anderson and John Cavanagh, *The Rise of Corporate Global Power* (Institute for Policy Studies, 2000).

[3]Keys and Malnight found that the most recent data, in 2011, gives Royal Dutch Shell and Exxon Mobil an edge over Walmart as the largest corporate entities, measured by revenues. For more information, see http://www.globaltrends .com/knowledge-center/features/shapers-and-influencers/190-corporate-clout-2013-time-for-responsible-capitalism.

FIGURE 4.1   The Largest Economic Entities*

The World's Largest 100 Economic Entities, 2009

1. United States
2. Japan
3. China
4. Germany
5. France
6. United Kingdom
   ⋮
20. Belgium
21. Poland
22. WAL-MART STORES
23. Sweden
24. Norway
   ⋮
32. Denmark
33. South Africa
34. ROYAL DUTCH SHELL
35. EXXON MOBIL
36. Thailand
37. BP
38. Finland
   ⋮

*This chart is reproduced by permission of Tracey Keys and Thomas W. Malnight, Strategy Dynamics Global, SA.

of political philosophy that is studied to this day. "Since that time," writes Quentin Skinner, a contemporary intellectual historian, "the idea that the confrontation between individuals and states furnishes the central topic of political theory has come to be almost universally accepted."[4] Skinner's primary point, though, is that Hobbes's writing is a case study in the ways that historical events can transform our concepts. The idea of the *state*, which once meant the display and behaviors of the royal person in power, had evolved into the abstract idea of an impersonal institution that persists long beyond any particular transition of power. This change in meaning, which took place in the 1600s, tracked historical changes in medieval Europe. At that time, Hobbes recognized that our conceptual world is not merely given to us. We develop and adapt concepts to understand and interpret the world around us, and these concepts change over time.

Today, people are debating the concept of a corporation, which has led to basic disagreements about how to envision their purposes and responsibilities. These debates are diverse and multifaceted, yet the organizing principles that drive these debates tend to spring from one of two competing perspectives. On one side is the **stockholder theory of corporations**. On the other side is the **stakeholder theory of corporations**. As their names suggest, the stockholder theory places primary emphasis on the interests of the stockholder of a corporation. The stakeholder theory places primary emphasis on a wider vision of the **stakeholders** of a corporation, which refers broadly to all those who are significantly affected by corporate activities, including stockholders but others as well, such as the community, employees, and those who are concerned about the environment. Taken as whole, each theory provides a comprehensive and competing normative and descriptive perspective about the role and responsibilities of corporations in society.

This chapter is about the stockholder theory and the most forceful reasons that proponents offer to support this view. Chapter 5 is about the stakeholder theory and the most forceful reasons to support that competing view. The online resources provide case studies to supplement the aim of the text, which is to provide an in-depth study of the underlying ideas that drive each theory. The English philosopher John Stuart Mill once said, "He who knows only his own side of the case knows little of that." These two chapters are an invitation to deepen your own perspective by studying these competing ideas side by side.

4.2   A DEBATE

Let's begin with an exchange between a prominent supporter of each side of this debate. On the one side is John Mackey, the CEO of Whole Foods; on the other is the late Milton Friedman, Nobel Prize winner in economics. This written exchange took place in *Reason* magazine in 2005. Mackey advocates the stakeholder theory of a corporation, to be developed in Chapter 5, and Friedman advocates the stockholder perspective, to be developed

---

[4]Skinner, Quentin "The State" in Political Innovation and Conceptual Change, edited by T. Ball, J. Farr and R. L. Hanson, Cambridge 1989.

in this chapter. As you read this exchange, ask yourself what you understand the disagreement to be about.

Mackey: From an investor's perspective, the purpose of the business is to maximize profits. But that's not the purpose of other stakeholders—for customers, employees, suppliers, and the community. Each of those groups will define the purpose of the business in terms of its own needs and desires, and each perspective is valid and legitimate. . . . It is the function of company leadership to develop solutions that continually work for the common good. . . . The fact that Whole Foods has responsibilities to our community doesn't mean that we don't have any responsibilities to our investors. It's a question of finding the appropriate balance and trying to create value for all of our stakeholders.

Friedman: The differences between John Mackey and me regarding the social responsibility of business are, for the most part, rhetorical. Strip off the camouflage and, it turns out, we are in essential agreement. Moreover, his company, Whole Foods Market, behaves in accordance with the principles I spelled out in my 1970 *New York Times Magazine* article. With respect to his company, it could hardly be otherwise. It has done well in a highly competitive industry. Had it devoted any significant fraction of its resources to exercising a social responsibility unrelated to the bottom line, it would be out of business by now or would have been taken over. . . .

[Friedman, quoting himself from the 1970 article]: In practice, the doctrine of social responsibility is frequently a cloak for actions that are justified on other grounds rather than a reason for those actions.

To illustrate, it may well be in the long run interest of a corporation that is a major employer in a small community to devote resources to providing amenities to that community or to improving its government. . . .

In each of these . . . cases, there is a strong temptation to rationalize these actions as an exercise of "social responsibility." In the present climate of opinion, with its widespread aversion to "capitalism," "profits," the "soulless corporation" and so on, this is one way for a corporation to generate goodwill as a by-product of expenditures that are entirely justified in its own self-interest.

It would be inconsistent of me to call on corporate executives to refrain from this hypocritical window-dressing because it harms the foundations of a free society. That would be to call on them to exercise a "social responsibility"! If our institutions and the attitudes of the public make it in their self-interest to cloak their actions in this way, I cannot summon much indignation to denounce them.

Mackey: But are we essentially in agreement? I don't think so. . . . In contrast to Friedman, I do not believe maximizing profits for the investors is the only acceptable justification for all corporate actions. The investors are not the only people who matter. Corporations can exist for purposes other than simply maximizing profits. . . . Like individuals living in communities, businesses make valuable social contributions by providing goods and services and employment. But just as individuals can feel a responsibility to provide some philanthropic support for the communities in which they live, so too can a business. The responsibility of business toward the community is not infinite, but neither is it zero. Each enlightened business must find the proper balance between all of its constituencies: customers, employees, investors, suppliers, and communities.

Source: Rethinking the Social Responsibility of Business: A Reason debate featuring Milton Friedman, Whole Foods' John Mackey, and Cypress Semiconductor's T.J. Rodgers." *Reason Magazine* (October, 2005).

Friedman and Mackey seem to agree about little, but one point is clear: part of their disagreement is about the very concept of a corporation. Like Hobbes found in the 1600s, concepts evolve over time; and Mackey and Friedman have joined a public debate of ideas that is taking place across the globe. When Walmart announces that it contributed over $400 million in donations in 2009, or made a $5 million donation to fight hunger as part of its ongoing charitable work, Mackey and Friedman (and many others) disagree about how we should interpret and assess the significance of these activities. When BP's oil rig exploded in the Gulf of Mexico and polluted the sea and air, Mackey and Friedman (and many others) disagreed about how to understand what the oil industry was doing there, and what role and responsibilities these corporations should be playing in society.

Competing worldviews about corporate responsibility underlie widespread globalization protests, countless meetings of political and economic leaders, speeches by CEOs, and continuing intellectual debates in the media and public culture. The world we are living in is changing, both politically and economically, and one of the most basic points of contention is, What is the purpose and responsibilities of corporations? Do they have responsibilities beyond maximizing profits within the law?

In the upcoming sections, we will examine the following features of the stockholder theory:

- Corporate purpose, stockholder rights, and managerial responsibilities (Sections 3 and 4)
- The ethical justifications for these respective positions (Section 5)
- How stockholder proponents interpret corporate social responsibility (CSR) (Section 6)
- The role of government in relation to business (Section 7)
- The role of self-interest in business (Section 8)

| FIGURE 4.2 | Stockholder Corporate Purpose |

Note: The stockholder and stakeholder theories can be represented as a wheel with spokes and a hub. The chapter will progressively develop this image as a visual summary of the discussion. The image also depicts how the ideas combine into one integrated theory.

4.3 CORPORATE PURPOSE: MAXIMIZE PROFITS WITHIN THE LAW

Let us begin by expanding on the views of Milton Friedman and his supporters. These ideas are so woven into societal norms, however, that it would be misleading to say that they are simply his. A venture capitalist invited this author into his office, which had a signed photograph of Milton Friedman hanging on the wall. The businessman spoke at length about the inspiration provided by the ideas that we are about to discuss. Friedman's ideas represent the views of a culture, to be found all around us, in the broad public and in the assumptions that drive conversations in business and economics.

To begin, stockholders become part owners of a corporation by purchasing shares with the expectation that managers will be working on their behalf. These purchases are not gifts to the firm. Shareholders expect to receive returns on their investment. The role and duty of management is to make good on the owners' investment by increasing profits within the law. Figure 4.2 is the first of a series of a visual summaries designed to summarize the development of ideas throughout the chapter.

This first statement of the stockholder view specifies the purpose of corporations in terms of *stockholders' property rights* and *managerial responsibilities*. The position begins with an idea that stockholders are the owners or principals of the corporation and that managers are agents whose duty toward those stockholders is to maximize profits within the law. Figure 4.2 is the first of a series of a visual summaries designed to summarize the development of ideas throughout the chapter.

Let's reflect on this position. Suppose that management decides to donate corporate money to a charity. This may seem to be an exemplary act. But consider this analogy. Suppose you give $100 to a bank to help fund your children's college educa-tion and learn that the bank's charitable contributions resulted in less interest payments back to you. Would you call the bank's charitable gifts generous? In fact, wouldn't you rather say that you invested your money based on trust that they would provide as high an interest rate return as they could? Even if you want your investment to go to the very same charity that the bank chooses, shouldn't *you* be the person to decide what to do with those extra earnings rather than a bank manager?

> See Chapter 1 for the distinc-tions between exchanges, gifts, and takings.

These leading questions help state what proponents believe is obvious about corporations. Managers are hired to run a business and to create returns to the owners. Management has a *duty* to increase profits for owners who are not *on the scene* to control and monitor what happens. This duty guards against the temptation for managers to use their position for self-enrichment at the expense of shareholder interests, a practical con-cern that we will explore further in Section 8 within the discussion of self-interest.

In sum, corporate charitable giving can *seem* like a model of corporate responsibility, but for advocates of the stockholder perspective, broad mandates "to do good" with the profits of a corporations work in just the wrong direction. These demands

1. violate the property rights of the owners of the corporation, the stockholders;

2. presume that managers have moral competencies superior to shareholders' competencies about what to do with the earnings;

3. weaken management's duty to the shareholder and invite opportunities for managerial self-enrichment under the guise of doing good;

4. distract from the corporation's purpose to run a profitable business.

Consider one important caveat to the argument so far: both managers and share-holders are free to devote their *private* resources for charitable giving, an appropriate and admirable activity in a free society, as proponents often emphasize. In this way, the stock-holder position is compatible with a broadly charitable outlook. The problem is when management uses *corporate* monies for these purposes.

What do you make of this position so far?

FIGURE 4.3	Stockholder Rights and Duties

4.4 DEBATES ABOUT STOCKHOLDER RIGHTS AND MANAGERIAL DUTIES

Once we grant the initial premise that the stockholders are the legitimate *owners* of the corporation, almost any other position about corporate responsibility can seem irrelevant. The idea that managers can pursue other goals appears to violate the property rights of the owners.

However, there is much more to say. In fact, for the position to express an ethical argument, the position *needs* to say more. To see this point more clearly, suppose our discussion stopped here. What exactly is the argument so far? In a nutshell, shareholders are the owners of a corporation; therefore, they have claim-rights to all profits within the law.

The lessons on property rights from Chapter 2 offer some insight into this argument. We learned there that ownership doesn't necessarily settle the specific property rights of the owner. For example, even if I own a house, it doesn't follow that I can earn profits on the house by converting it into commercial property or using the home to harm others. Zoning and criminal laws prohibit various activities related to the home. To take another example, even if it's true that I own a musical CD, it does not follow that I can make copies of the CD and sell them. Copyright laws prohibit this.

By extension, the fact that shareholders are the owners of the corporation does not yet establish their specific claim-rights. The assertion of ownership, however true, does not yet constitute an argument for the stockholder theory.

Thus, a central issue is how the stockholder position can further defend its account of shareholder property rights and managerial duties. Do shareholders have a claim-right that managers always try to increase profits within the law? Are managers' sole duties to maximize profits for its shareholders?

These questions can be developed descriptively or normatively, a distinction introduced in Chapters 1–3. For example, one attempt to resolve these questions is to show that existing law settles the matter. Most legal commentators, however, have interpreted the U.S. courts as deliberately avoiding decisive legal answers to these questions. On the one hand, the courts allow that managers do have legal duties to advance shareholder interests in broad terms. On the other hand, Reinhart, Stavins, and Vietor write, "The courts' deference towards the judgment of businesspeople—the 'business judgment rule'—prevents many public-minded managerial actions from being legally challenged."[5] This dual message is an enduring legal ambiguity. In practice, courts have repeatedly deferred to the judgment of businesspeople about how to run the firm's operations, both in how they conceive the purpose of corporations and in what decisions they make. In effect, the courts say, They do not exercise the legal power to settle by law the question of managerial duties at stake in debates about corporate responsibility.[6] The intensity of the public debate between Mackey's vision and the stockholder vision takes place against this legal backdrop.

What more can stockholder proponents say on behalf of their position?

Another thought is to assert that managers are subject to an *economic* mandate to create profits. In competitive markets, there is little choice but to maximize profits. The system simply works this way and the stockholder account reflects this basic reality.

---

[5]Forest L. Reinhart, Robert N. Stavins, and Richard H. K. Vietor "Corporate Social Responsibility through and Economic Lens," *Review of Environmental Economics and Policy* 2(2) (Summer 2008), p. 5.

[6]It may be worth noting that even if the law did settle the legal property rights of shareholders, ethical debates about corporate responsibility would still be relevant, as people would likely debate whether the given law was appropriate and lobby for relevant legislation. But the current debates occur in the context that the courts have avoided settling these issues through law.

Friedman asserts this thesis in part in the opening excerpt, and this argument has its followers.[7]

However true, we cannot understand the energy behind defending the stockholder account if it were interpreted *merely* as a descriptive hypothesis about how the system works. Proponents assert that managers have *duties* to shareholders. That's a strong word—it's a normative idea. Proponents readily recognize that economic systems have been and can be organized in many competing ways around the world; so they want *to make the case* for the stockholder view beyond a purported description of the system (a description that stakeholder proponents will dispute in the next chapter).

We are left with an interesting puzzle about *who* has the authority to resolve what stockholder rights and managerial duties ought to be? We can apply a concept from Chapter 2 to reformulate the question: In today's world, who has the *power* to specify the right and responsibilities of management? It's not the law (or not merely). In fact, the culture at large has the power, worked out by the evolving opinions and actions of millions of people as they (1) form their concepts about what corporations ought to do and (2) make their economic decisions within the pressures of the marketplace and the larger society. The intensity of the debates in this chapter and the next derive from what Hobbes understood in the 1650s: ideas that seep into society change society, including peoples' expectations about corporations. Debates about corporate responsibility are about how *we*, within our various roles in the market system, come to conceive of the purpose of corporations. Drawing on another concept from Chapter 3, this debate is about the *customary* rather than legal rights and duties that we ought to ascribe to stockholders and management.[8]

The issues are no longer as cut and dry as they once seemed. We are left puzzling about the nature of the argument. If exclusive duties to shareholders neither are required by law nor are the only possible economic arrangement, what exactly is the *normative* argument for this understanding of corporate purpose? What makes the stockholder account something we should *believe in*? Stockholder advocates have an answer.

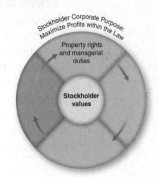

FIGURE 4.4   Stockholder Values

4.5   ETHICAL JUSTIFICATIONS

Consider Friedman's words on this point: "a system based on private property and free markets is a sophisticated means of enabling people to cooperate in their economic activities without compulsion; it enables separated knowledge to assure that each resource is used for its most valued use, and is combined with other resources in the most efficient way."[9] The essence of this argument

---

[7]See, for example, John R. Danley, *The Role of the Modern Corporation in a Free Society* (University of Notre Dame Press, 1994).

[8]Friedman, Milton. The Social Responsibility of Business is to Increase its Profits, *The New York Times Magazine* (September 13, 1970). Over thirty-five years after Friedman wrote his 1970 work "The Social Responsibility of Business Is to Increase Its Profits," he reemphasized this point in the *Reason Magazine* exchange, an excerpt of which began this chapter.

[9]Ibid, p. 33.

is *ethical*, not descriptive. For proponents, a corporate system defined in terms of maximizing profits within the law best protects individual liberty and promotes economic efficiency. Proponents argue that these are important values that we should believe in.[10]

In an article profiling retired U.S. senator and economist Phil Gramm, the *New York Times* writes, "Mr. Gramm would sometimes speak with reverence about the nation's financial markets, the trading and deal making that churn out wealth. 'When I am on Wall Street and I realize that that's the very nerve center of American capitalism and I realize what capitalism has done for the working people of America, to me that's a holy place.'"[11]

Stockholder proponents believe that critics of capitalism typically have a one-sided understanding of the realities of history. Critics observe flaws, but stockholder proponents observe how capitalism pulls people out of poverty generation after generation whereas other systems do not. In addition, the typical poor person today has conveniences and comforts that his cohorts couldn't have imagined a few generations before—comforts that even outstrip the rich of previous generations. Gramm and other advocates believe that being born into capitalism, given its system of liberty, opportunity, and material advancement, can be condemned only against a romanticized understanding of the past.

Efficiency and liberty are the most common values at the core of stockholder theory, although the structure of reasoning is compatible with incorporating a wide range of other values beyond these ideas.

These underlying values are the ideas finally appealed to as the deepest and most important reasons for advocating and believing in the theory. They provide the final answer to the question, "But why should I believe in this view?" They are sometimes implicit in the arguments and often difficult to unpack and analyze. Yet their importance is hard to overestimate. These ideas are the *hub* of the position. If the stockholder theory is represented as a wheel in motion, the hub absorbs the force placed on the spokes and keeps the wheel together as one piece. These values specify the core of the normative argument.

Thus, a full assessment of the stockholder position is possible only with a further study of what these values mean. Since this is the work of coming chapters, let's consider here instead an implication of this argument, if it's correct. The strict duty to the stockholder to maximize profits, in this view, directly fulfills corporations' social responsibilities *because* of the direct benefits that business creates for society. For example, corporate activities create employment and products and services that raise standards of living. This implication is the basis for Friedman's title for his famous essay, "The Social Responsibility of Business Is to Increase Its Profits."[12]

---

[10]Stockholder proponents often claim that efficiency and freedom are mutually reinforcing values but this need not be the case, at least conceptually. We will examine relationships among these values in later chapters.

[11]Eric Lipton and Stephen Labaton, "Deregulator Looks Back, Unswayed," *New York Times*, November 17, 2008.

[12]The term *social responsibility* has competing meanings, depending on which side of the argument you are on. For the stakeholder position to be developed in the next chapter, corporate social responsibility refers to a broad range of responsibilities *beyond* maximizing profits within the law. But stockholder proponents dispute this definition.

THE STRUCTURE OF AN ETHICAL ARGUMENT

Although debates about corporate responsibility often combine many ideas at once or rely on implicit claims that are difficult to dissect, the goal of this chapter is to break down these ideas piece by piece. Consider here how Friedman's and Gramm's ideas illustrate a structure of ethical reasoning, differentiated from descriptive arguments solely about how corporations actually function. As a normative argument about corporations they identify and defend

- one or more *values* that they (and their proponents) believe the corporate system should achieve, such as improved living standards, efficiency gains, or protection of individual liberty;
- how the stockholder account of legal and customary property rights and responsibilities creates the best chance for promoting or respecting these values.

This structure of ethical argument begins with a normative premise (for example, about the value of freedom and efficiency) and ends with a normative conclusion (for example, advocacy for the legal and customary rights associated with stockholder theory). Empirical facts and data become the means to establish that the conclusion is a reasonable inference from the premise. To illustrate this form of argument:

i. we should aspire to live in a world that promotes and respects freedom and equality (normative premise);
ii. as a matter of observable fact, the institutions associated with stockholder theory create or promote freedom and equality (a descriptive premise);
iii. therefore, we should advocate the institutions associated with stockholder theory. Chapter 6 Section 5 expands on and develops this fundamental argument in the context of efficiency discussions.

4.6 INTERPRETING THE CSR MOVEMENT FROM THE STOCKHOLDER PERSPECTIVE

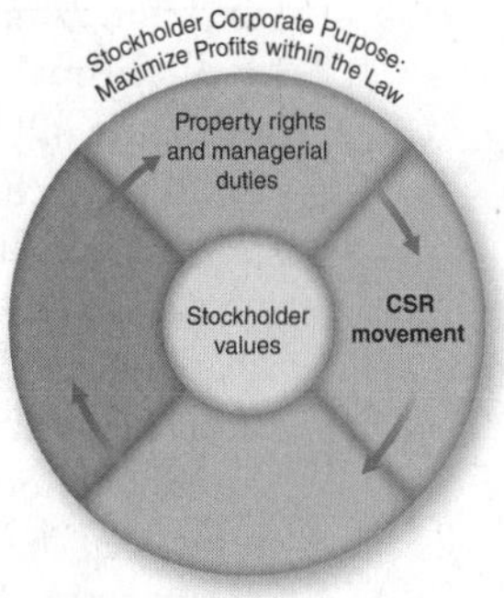

If the stockholder view is so persuasive, then why do corporations devote so much time and resources on community projects and other social initiatives? Consider Mackey's description of Whole Food's responsibilities in the excerpts that began this chapter. He asserts that corporations bear responsibilities beyond increasing profits. This characterization is the norm across many businesses and industries. We can describe the **corporate social responsibility movement** as the entire range of developments and arguments from the past several decades that convey a commitment to corporate actions beyond maximizing profits within the law. These developments include: CSR-related shareholder proposals; a $3 trillion industry of social responsibility investing (SRI); continuing watchdog activities provided by a vast array of international and domestic governmental and non-governmental organizations (NGOs); and extensive media coverage of CSR, including various rating agencies that assess corporate performance based on social contributions beyond maximizing profits.

FIGURE 4.5 Stockholder Account of CSR

At first glance, CSR initiatives seem to violate management's duties to shareholders and the entire spirit of the stockholder position. Thus, the stockholder proponent confronts an important question for developing a coherent account: how are these CSR initiatives to be interpreted?

Stockholder proponents respond that CSR initiatives should not be taken at face value but understood as a financial strategy designed to benefit shareholders. For example, Friedman uses the phrase *hypocritical window-dressing* to describe these activities, conveying his view that corporations are saying one thing (endorsing broad social duties beyond the shareholder) but are driven, and should be driven, to perform solely for the benefit of shareholder returns.[13] This descriptive and normative interpretation of the CSR movement as hypocrisy is alive and well today and explains the cynical response from some quarters regarding any talk about CSR. For example, when technology retailer Best Buy announces a scholarship program that has helped over 15,000 students pay for their college education, a stockholder proponent is quick to note that the point of the program is not to help those students but to improve the image of Best Buy for the purpose of increasing sales.[14] This analysis often paints CSR as a distasteful cloak for profits that should be described for what it is. Any *real* act of social responsibility beyond maximizing profits would conflict with managerial duties to the stockholder. (Stakeholder proponents generally disagree with this interpretation.)

Some stockholder proponents offer a more salutary interpretation of CSR, interpreting these efforts as part of the struggle to balance short-term and long-term investor interests. Acts of social responsibility may conflict with short-term profits, but they are an assessment of the investments necessary to encourage a stable environment for future growth and profitability. For example, even if awarding scholarships is only loosely related to the short-term bottom line of Best Buy, it may facilitate future technology consumption over many years, which will benefit Best Buy in the long run.

This shift in attitude about CSR by stockholder proponents is expressed in *The Economist* magazine, a widely reputed advocate of the stockholder perspective. As recently as 2005, the magazine wrote that "the movement for corporate social responsibility has won the battle of ideas. That is a pity."[15] But by its 2008 Special Report, it acknowledges that times have changed. It says, "Paying attention to CSR can amount to enlightened self-interest, something that over time will help to sustain profits for shareholders." In the eyes of *The Economist*, the only interests that matter for corporations, in the end, are profits to shareholders. But the CSR movement can be interpreted as an ally to encourage corporate strategic thinking over the long run.

How should we interpret activities that fall under the label of *corporate social responsibility*? As we saw in Chapter 1 Section 4, normative disagreements sometimes derive from different interpretations of our social world. In the case at hand, stakeholder advocates believe that the CSR movement shows that society's perception of the purpose of corporations is changing, and for good reason. Stockholder proponents see the world differently. They believe that we should interpret and explain the

---

[13]Rethinking the Social Responsibility of Business: A Reason debate featuring Milton Friedman, Whole Foods' John Mackey, and Cypress Semiconductor's T.J. Rodgers." *Reason Magazine* (October, 2005).
[14]See, for example, http://www.bestbuy-communityrelations.com/our_programs.htm.
[15]"The Good Company" © *The Economist* Newspaper Limited, London 2005.

CSR movement entirely in strategic terms, consistent with their understanding of corporate purpose.

4.7 SEPARATING THE ROLES OF BUSINESS AND GOVERNMENT

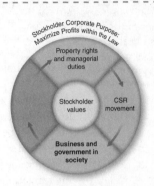

FIGURE 4.6 **Stockholder Account of Institutions**

If corporations have the ability to address major social problems, such as pollution, low wages, impoverished cities, or illiteracy, what's wrong if they solve these problems? Don't opportunities abound for powerful corporations to help society?

Stockholder advocates have a response beyond the duty to the shareholder: it's the role of government to address these social problems, not businesses.

Recall the stockholder statement of corporate purpose: maximizing profits *within the law*. This idea entails a role for government—to create laws that constrain what managers may or may not do in pursuit of profits. Thus, if society sees pollution as harmful, it's the government that has the responsibility to specify rules that limit pollution; it's not the responsibility of businesses to devise strategies that limit pollution. Government should address social concerns through its public policies; management does its fair share for the social good by creating a profitable business and following the law. Thus, stockholder advocates emphasize the role of government for bearing a variety of responsibilities that they believe CSR advocates mistakenly expect businesses to bear.

> See Chapter 1 Section 7 for distinctions among three dialogues that shape this book.

Further, proponents believe that business and government ought to have distinct and separated roles in society. Government creates and enforces coercive laws that are made *legitimate* through democratic procedures. In this usage, **political legitimacy** refers to whatever conditions justify the government's use of coercive power, where democratic procedures would be one leading candidate for creating those conditions. Whatever those conditions are, businesses create goods and services through markets within those legitimately derived legal constraints. For example, if some method for drilling natural gas is likely to pollute the local water supply, then it's the responsibility of government, such as provided by the Environmental Protection Agency, to place limits on how companies drill. The role of the natural gas companies is to find the most effective method of drilling for making profits within whatever laws a democratic society creates for protecting the social welfare.

We may note three observations about this position. First, although some people may be tempted to interpret the stockholder position as maximizing profits without *any* legal constraints, there is not a single leading theoretical defense of the stockholder view that fails to include some role for law and government. The debate is about the extent of that role.

> Chapter 9 Section 4 extends the discussion of legitimacy through an argument about *democratic capitalism*.

Second, stockholder critics note a tension in the way that stockholder advocates often elaborate their view: on the one hand, they admit a governmental role for addressing social problems. On the other hand, they advocate that government should be

An especially important controversy is found in the causes and remedies of the financial crisis that swept the global markets beginning in 2006.

as limited as possible, which drives support for deregulation and limited legal intervention in markets. It's a matter of debate whether this tension expresses a contradiction or not. Some see crass self-interest, without regard to bringing a consistent philosophy to this perspective, such as when corporations lobby for government subsidies at the same time they lobby for deregulation. Others see these actions as part of a broadly coherent philosophy as described by the stockholder theory.

Third, although the stockholder position is often associated with ideals of deregulation and limited government, the latter ideas are not necessarily implied by stockholder theory. For example, in his book *Supercapitalism*, Robert Reich endorses the stockholder perspective but argues for robust market intervention to reign in various corporate harms that would otherwise occur, without those regulations.[16] The dictum *maximize profits within the law* by itself is open-ended about the proper scope and reach of law. On any interpretation of this dictum, government should provide a constraining role on the pursuit of profits; but stockholder proponents themselves disagree about how we should conceive of the activism of that governmental role.

4.8   SELF-INTEREST AND MARKETS

Let's consider one final feature of the stockholder position. What motivates people in business? Here's one answer: self-interest. Advocates of the stockholder view often assert a stronger position: self-interest is the primary if not the only ultimate mover of human behavior. If that is an empirical fact about human motivation, then how should we design an economic system? Answer: we want a system that can create desirable outcomes through the self-interested motives of its participants. If we expect more from people's motives, we will be disappointed.

FIGURE 4.7   **Stockholder Account of Human Nature**

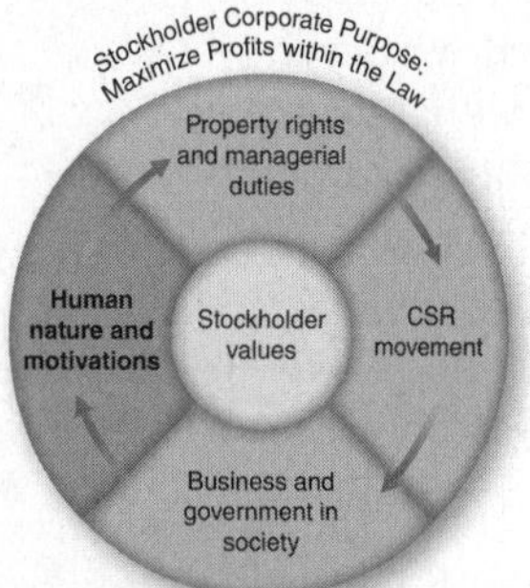

Recall the discussion in Chapter 1. On the one hand markets suggest a willingness to cooperate and follow rules. On the other hand, markets are not about giving gifts. It's a matter for your reflection to identify the motives that you think are most prevalent for explaining market transactions.

Thus, debates about corporate responsibility often lead to broader debates about the types of motives people can and should be expected to bring to their economic lives. For stockholder proponents, an advantage to stockholder theory is that it more realistically characterizes the motives that most people bring to business and economic life. This position has two different shades of meaning. *Psychological egoism* is the descriptive view introduced in Chapter 1 that people are motivated only by their self-interests. *Ethical egoism*, an idea first presented in the Introduction, is the normative view that people *ought* to do whatever is in their self-interests. For example, we may note a difference between saying that people are

---

[16]Robert Reich, *Supercapitalism: The Transformation of Business, Democracy, and Everyday Life* (Knopf, 2007).

greedy from saying that greed is good, which is the infamous line delivered by Gordon Gekko to shareholders in the 1987 movie *Wall Street*. The concept of self-interest need not have a negative connotation of greediness, however. Writer Ayn Rand, for example, argues that self-interest is best interpreted as the interests of the self, and that the best way to respect our individuality is always to pursue these *self-oriented* interests. She is critical of altruism if it's understood as a sacrifice of the self, and so she develops a *normative* defense of self-interest over altruism. Others criticize this argument by emphasizing the ethical importance of trying to get outside of yourself.

Stockholder proponents typically build their case by drawing on a variation of the descriptive claim only—that we are, as an empirical fact, primarily self-interested and so we ought to design an economic system that takes this fact as given.

From this perspective, even specifying a duty as narrowly conceived as advancing shareholder interests is asking a lot, and this demand will predictably lead to scandals and corruption based on the overpowering lure of self-interest. High-profile examples of Bernie Madoff, Enron, Adelphia, Arthur Anderson, and many others highlight the self-interest that underlies human motivation. In light of the dominance of self-interest driving human behavior, the theoretical pursuit of a robust account of *business ethics* or *social responsibility* is met with considerable skepticism.

Rather, stockholder proponents believe that they have the best formula by limiting managements' ethical responsibilities, which are to follow the law and do right by shareholders. The stockholder perspective does not deny *any* ethical responsibilities for management, but believes that wisdom counsels for a set of rules that appeal to self-interested incentives as far as possible. In this light, the great challenge of ethics—as it relates to corporate responsibility—is to understand the separation of ownership and control as part of corporate governance. This topic is explored at length in a classic study by Adolf Berle and Gardiner Means in *The Modern Corporation and Private Property*. The shareholders *own* the corporation but management *controls* the corporation. So how can corporate governance structures be arranged to ensure that those who control the business act as responsible agents for the owners? That is the fundamental question of business ethics and corporate responsibility from the perspective of stockholder theory.

The very topic of corporate responsibility for stockholder proponents is defined as the protection of shareholder interests and reforming corporate governance structures to advance shareholders' interests. One recurring debate in this area is the huge compensation packages of leading executives in the face of poor financial performance.[17] What is the proper role of a board of directors, who fills these board positions, and what are the proper structures in place for board

> Read the Case Study *Madoff Ponzi Scheme* only on MySearchLab

> Chapter 8 examines in greater depth the relationship between ethics, self-interest, and institutions.

SECURITY AND EXCHANGE COMMISSION

The *Security and Exchange Commission* (SEC), is the federal regulatory body with the charge, in its own words, " . . . to protect investors; maintain fair, orderly, and efficient markets; and facilitate capital formation" (http://www.sec.gov/about/whatwedo.shtml). The work of the SEC offers a fruitful case study of the challenges for analyzing governments' role in corporate governance disputes. The SEC is a source of controversy both to those who believe that government is doing too little to avert financial and corporate collapses and to those who believe that government is doing too much.

---

[17]See, for example, Eric Dash, "Big Rewards for Failure among CEOs in America," *New York Times*, January 4, 2007.

members to perform their role effectively? Proponents of stockholder theory focus on these questions insofar as there is concern about weak governance structures.

Let's consider one final nuance to stockholder theory related to discussions of self-interest. On the one hand, stockholder proponents believe that managers bear *duties* to maximize profits within the law. But we also considered that the law does not mandate this duty, at least not in a way that precludes management from exercising discretion to pursue other goals. Not every stockholder advocate is comfortable with this concept of *duty* when given an ethical connotation outside any legal meaning. We can now easily explain this reticence from the discussion in this section: if we're primarily self-interested, then a theory that requires people to draw on moral motivations of duty is a suspect idea, practically speaking. There is another reason for some discomfort: investors can buy and sell their shares. They are not coerced into holding that investment. They can exit the relationship at will. Taking both of these considerations into account, an alternative statement of the stockholder position is to describe a managerial *liberty*, by which managers run their operations as they see fit within the law, and then let investors walk (that is, sell off) if they do not support their managerial decisions. The nuance here in stockholder theory is whether shareholders have (1) claim-rights that managers focus solely on maximizing profits within the law or (2) claim-rights that managers be transparent about their objectives, with a liberty to shape mission as they wish, which allows shareholders to exercise *their* liberties as they wish (to buy and sell shares based on this information).

> See Chapter 2 Section 3 for the important distinctions between claims, liberties, and duties.

Friedman and other stockholder proponents waver on this point. Some may argue that it is *ethically wrong* if management pursues other goals in conflict with profits. Others may argue that it is *unwise* to create an inefficient and misguided use of valuable resources, although it's within management's ethical liberties, with results that the markets will judge.

4.9   SUMMARY

Stockholder theory may be likened to a wheel with four spokes and a hub (see Figure 4.8). One spoke

FIGURE 4.8   **Stockholder Theory as a Whole**

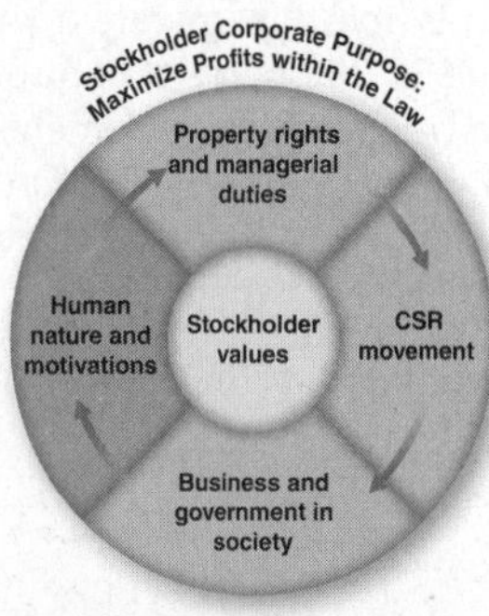

describes stockholder property rights and managerial duties. Another describes how best to interpret the CSR movement; another is about the roles of business and government; and a fourth emphasizes self-interested human motives in economic life. The spokes connect at the hub, and the hub represents the underlying values that give the structure its normative integrity.

In summary, stockholder theorists argue that corporations contribute to the common good of people by focusing on what they do best, which is to convince investors to financially support a firm that will create products that others will buy, thereby giving returns back to investors. From this perspective, corporate responsibility is not about philanthropy or pursuing goals apart from increasing profits. It's about good corporate governance which, when done well, guards against managers padding their own self-interests in conflict with their duties to shareholders. It's an account of corporate purpose and property rights that matches realistic expectations about people's motives in a market system. The system as a whole encompasses a moral vision that emphasizes the value of liberty and efficiency for society. Government performs the separate role of addressing social problems and passing laws that protect the public interest. Managers are welcome to spend their private earnings on charitable contributions as they like, but their duties to increase profits within the law creates a capitalist system worth believing in.

We will next examine the stakeholder theory. Like many ethical debates, we can accept some features of one perspective and some features of another. We can examine the position in pieces apart from viewing the position as a whole. Labels such as *stockholder* and *stakeholder* theory represent a terrain of debate to guide our analysis, but the goal of this chapter and the next is not essentially about choosing sides, but for you to develop your own position, whether or not it can easily map onto one of these labels. A comprehensive defense of either theory depends on a further study of ethics and values, provided in Chapters 6–14. That discussion examines topics beyond corporate responsibility, but its study will continue to deepen your views about the debates of this chapter.

KEY TERMS

corporation	stockholder theory of	corporate social responsibility
stockholders	corporations	movement
board of directors	stakeholder theory of	political legitimacy
principle of limited liability	corporations	
gross domestic product	stakeholder	

DISCUSSION QUESTIONS

1. Suppose that managers of a corporation approve corporate donations to a charity in the local community. How might a stockholder proponent analyze the ethics of this donation?

2. Should managers make decisions based on short-run or long-run considerations? What is your argument? When those perspectives conflict, whom exactly does a manager owe a duty toward? How should a stockholder proponent answer this question?

3. Are short-run competitive pressures so great in competitive capitalism that management is precluded from considering long-term investor interests? Consider how the structure of dual-class common stock, such as found at Google, or the structure of private companies, such as Smucker's, is relevant to this question. What is the best way to characterize management pressures?

4. Consider a CEO who achieves higher-than-expected quarterly earnings for five years but takes on (legal) risks that leave the firm bankrupt by the end of a decade. Did management fulfill its social duties according to the stockholder model of a corporation?

5. What is the most coherent position on lobbying, when argued from the stockholder view of corporate responsibility? Do corporations have responsibilities to refrain from political lobbying? Why or why not? Suppose that government regulations within an industry reflect the lobbying efforts of that industry. How might a stockholder proponent analyze this result? What is your analysis of the ethics of lobbying?

6. Suppose that you are part of the management team of a corporation, and your lawyers regularly advise you about the relevant laws that

constrain the decisions that you could make. Consider the following questions:

- Should you identify ways to push the envelope of legal limits if it will enhance profits?
- Should you identify and pursue all the legal loopholes that can be exploited for advancing the interests of the firm?
- Should you identify the places where enforcement of the law is lax and break the law if you judge that this strategy will increase profits?
- Should you identify the places where breaking the law and paying a fine is less costly than following the law?
- In general, is there an ethical responsibility to follow the "spirit" of the law beyond calculating how to manipulate the law to advance your corporate purposes? What ethical ideas do you draw on to answer these questions? Finally, how should an advocate of the stockholder theory respond to these questions? Why?

7. How important is the role of contracts for understanding the ethics of corporations? We could consider *all* corporate relationships in terms of a nexus of contracts and examine whether and how parties contract with each other. Consider the relationship between costumer and the company of some particular good or service. Is the relevant principle *buyer beware* or does a purchase include an implicit contract that the goods or services do not directly harm the buyer, or at least are delivered as advertised? This question can be debated descriptively (what you perceive the norms to be and what the law says about these questions) or normatively (what the explicit or implicit contracts should be from an ethical point of view). *All* economic relationships can be viewed as implicit or explicit contracts.

What is your descriptive and normative analysis of the expectations in these relationships?

8. Suppose that you take as a premise that corporations are granted a privilege to exist by the state. For example, the legal designation *incorporated* refers to a legal existence granted by the state. Most corporate theorists accept at least some version of this view. Should the conditions of corporate existence thereby be understood as a social contract between the corporation and the state? If so, what is this contract? Legal? Moral? (We will consider the influential social contract tradition further in Chapter 11 through the analysis of equality. See also Chapter 5, Discussion Question 3).

9. What should be the role of the board of directors? How well do boards represent shareholder interests in practice? In a later chapter (Chapter 8 Section 5), we introduce the idea of a *conflict of interest*. One significant ethical concern regarding corporate boards is that its members are often comprised in part by executives of other corporations, who have an interest in large compensation packages, which create upward pressures in the going rates of CEOs across the labor market. To what extent is this a real problem?

10. Some people emphasize that there's nothing unethical about self-interest, and so the sense of ethics and self-interest depicted in Figure I.1 are inherently compatible motivations. It's only when the pursuit of self-interest is at the expense of others' interests that ethical concerns become relevant. But since markets are a system of mutual benefit, the system expresses compatibility of interests. A convincing perspective?

11. Assess the following argument: Self-interest crowds out altruism because self-interest forces others to be self-interested in return, to avoid exploitation. Thus, a few bad apples spoil the lot.

5

THE STAKEHOLDER THEORY OF CORPORATE RESPONSIBILITY

WHEN YOU FINISH STUDYING THIS CHAPTER, YOU SHOULD BE ABLE TO:

1. Describe the stakeholder position about corporate purpose, stockholder property rights, and managerial duties.

2. Characterize how proponents defend stakeholder theory.

3. Discuss stakeholder debates about the role of government in regulating business.

4. Consider stakeholder views about human motivation.

5. Identify the topic of corporate personhood and practical applications.

5.1 INTRODUCTION

What are the ethical responsibilities of corporations? Some say few; others say many. This chapter develops the *stakeholder theory of corporations* in contrast to the stockholder theory developed in Chapter 4. In broad terms, stakeholder theories assign a wider range of ethical responsibilities to corporations beyond the duties to maximize profits within the law. The corporation has responsibilities to its *stakeholders*, who are typically characterized as those entities significantly affected by the firm's activities, such as employees, customers, shareholders, the community or broader society, the environment, and suppliers.[1]

This chapter provides the strongest reasons that proponents offer to support stakeholder theory. In what follows we will examine:

- Stakeholder theory in the context of a global economy (Section 2)
- Stakeholder ideas about corporate purpose, stockholder rights, and managerial responsibilities (Section 3)
- Ethical justifications for stakeholder theory (Section 4)
- How stakeholder proponents interpret corporate social responsibility (Section 5)

---

[1] See R. Edward Freeman, *Strategic Management: A Stakeholder Approach* (Cambridge, 2010) for a seminal development of stakeholder ideas.

- Stakeholder understandings about the roles of government and business (Section 6)
- The role of ethical motives in business (Section 7)

Finally, in Section 9, we will examine debates about corporate personhood with practical applications. Taken together, Chapters 4 and 5 invite you to deepen your own perspective by studying these competing theories side by side.

5.2   A GLOBAL PERSPECTIVE: "ALL IS NOT WELL"

In 2008, Harvard University professor and United Nations Secretary General's Special Representative for Business and Human Rights John Ruggie released a Report to the United Nations Human Rights Council. The Report is about the responsibilities of corporations in a global economy. Ruggie writes,

> [H]istory teaches us that markets pose the greatest risks—to society and business itself—when their scope and power far exceed the reach of the institutional underpinnings that allow them to function smoothly. . . . This is such a time and escalating charges of corporate-related human rights abuses are the canary in the coal mine, signaling that all is not well. The root cause of the business and human rights predicament today lies in the governance gaps created by globalization—between the scope and impact of economic forces and actors, and the capacity of societies to manage their adverse consequences. These governance gaps provide the permissive environment for wrongful acts by companies of all kinds without adequate sanctioning or reparation. How to narrow and ultimately bridge the gaps in relation to human rights is our fundamental challenge.[2]

This Report is one high-profile example of an entire movement of thought that ascribes responsibilities to corporations beyond maximizing profits within the law.

Let's begin this line of thought by reconsidering the core of the *stockholder* theory: managements' duties to maximize profits *within the law*. Consider again what this means: management has at least one duty that is *not* to the shareholder, a duty to follow the law. Why should managers follow the law? Egoism and prudence may play a large part, and we could argue that people follow the law only to protect their self-interests. For example, managers may recognize the potential costs of breaking the law and rationally calculate when it serves their interests to conform. But is following the law also a *duty* beyond rational calculations of self-interest?[3]

---

[2]John Ruggie, "Protect, Respect, and Remedy: A Framework for Business and Human Rights," *Report to the UN Human Rights Council* (April 7, 2008), p. 3. See http://www.reports-and-materials.org/Ruggie-report-7-Apr-2008.pdf

[3]This intriguing question can be pursued along several dimensions. The current context is whether we're obligated to follow the law because it's law. Thus, do corporations have ethical reasons to conform to pollution standards just because it's the law, even when polluting benefits the firm? Are there ethical reasons not to speed even if it gets you there faster? Is one of those reasons simply that you ought to follow the law? Should you follow all laws? If not, what criteria should you use to discriminate which to follow? These questions are only a beginning of the complex relationship between law and ethics, which includes concepts of civil disobedience or conscientious objection. All of these questions reinforce the discussion made in the Introduction that ethics and law are related but distinct subjects.

Most stockholder proponents will readily say "yes," thereby committing to a notable *ethical* underpinning: illegally attained profits should not be part of the legitimate property rights of shareholders. Thus, even if shareholders demand illegal activities as a means to profits, managers should draw a line and say, "We will not be your agent in doing *that*." This position is not to say that, in practice, corporations are not frequently charged with breaking the law. The point here is that breaking the law is not part of any *theory* about the responsibility of corporations. But if this statement is true, then a stakeholder advocate has identified a point of leverage: why believe that legal constraints create the *only* ethical demands on corporations? Why is law the one and only bright line that should constrain the pursuit of profits?

These are leading questions to reframe the debate. The debate is not *whether* management bears ethical responsibilities beyond maximizing profits. It does. The debate, according to stakeholder proponents, is about the *reach and scope* of these responsibilities and whether stockholder or stakeholder theory offers the better analysis.

Further, stakeholder proponents emphasize that law is *not* a bright line. There are many real situations where the law provides hardly any line at all, especially from a global perspective. Consider the entire chain of production from the extraction of resources to the consumer products that we buy. A diamond starts from a mining operation in Africa and ends with a purchase at a local jeweler. A tank of gasoline starts from a drilling operation somewhere in the world and ends in some SUV. A shirt starts with a spool of thread but before it lands in your dresser, a garment factory in Bangladesh that makes the shirt collapses and kills over a 1,000 people (this occurred on April 24, 2013).

Are corporations at liberty to do *anything* in the name of profits in instances where there is little or no effective law anywhere along the change of production? (Can there be any ethical answer that says "yes"?) Stakeholder proponents say "no." They emphasize that, in many circumstances, management must place ethical constraints on their activities apart from any perceived demand to follow the law. If constraints are not placed, their pursuit of profit could cease to be *market* activities altogether, and instead become acquisition by coercion and violence that has marred much of human history.

These reflections represent an important line of argument for stakeholder proponents. It's one of many possible openings into the subject of stakeholder theory, but it may be one of the most forceful arguments aimed at countering the stockholder perspective. If we begin *within* the stockholder account, and then consider the context of a global economy, argue stakeholder proponents, we will be led to endorse the view that corporate responsibilities *must* extend beyond maximizing profits within law.

> See Chapter 1 for the distinction between market and nonmarket activities.

The Ruggie Report offers a prime example of this strategy, describing these legal imperfections as "governance gaps created by globalization." **Global governance gaps** refer to corporate activities that can be conducted subject to no effective law or regulation. The Report draws the following implication: "The corporate responsibility to respect human rights is the baseline expectation for all companies in all situations . . . meaning, in essence, to do no harm." On this analysis, management bears duties not merely to advance stockholder interests and follow the law, but to adhere to ethical constraints to do no harm, whether or not the law permits such harms to take place.

> Chapter 3 Section 3 discusses the nature of law and the distinction between domestic and international law.

We will now develop stakeholder theory along its several dimensions.

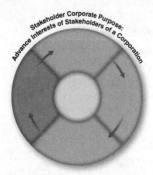

FIGURE 5.1   Stakeholder Corporate Purpose

Stakeholder Corporate Purpose:
Advance Interests of Stakeholders of a Corporation

Note: The stockholder and stakeholder theories can be represented as a wheel with spokes and a hub. The chapter will progressively develop this image as a visual summary of the discussion. The image also depicts how the ideas combine into one integrated theory.

5.3 CORPORATE PURPOSE, STAKEHOLDER RIGHTS, AND MANAGERIAL DUTIES

For stakeholder advocates, the most salient fact about large corporations is that they exert great power that profoundly affects people's lives. Recall from Chapter 4 the comparison of the revenues of corporations against the GDP of entire nation-states. Their sheer size and impact leads most stakeholder advocates to embrace the adage that *with great power comes great responsibility*. What *kind* of responsibility? Stakeholder advocates answer: the purpose of a corporation is to use its resources to advance the interests of all those who are most affected by its corporate activities—that is, its stakeholders. Corporations exist for *all* of these stakeholders. Figure 5.1 is the first of a series of a visual summaries designed to summarize the development of ideas throughout the chapter.

THE STAKEHOLDER IDEA

The concept of *stakeholders* was first elaborated by R. Edward Freeman in his 1986 book *Strategic Management: A Stakeholder Approach* (reprinted by Cambridge University Press in 2010).

This stakeholder position stands in tension to the stockholder theory. First, stakeholder theory offers a contrasting view about corporate purpose. Second, and as a result, stakeholder proponents endorse a different norm for corporate governance and competing ideas about the rights and duties of shareholders and management. For stakeholder proponents, managers should bear responsibilities beyond maximizing profits within law. They have duties to advance the interests of the corporations' stakeholders consistent with making profits. These duties apply to all managerial decisions within a corporation. Shareholders retain claim-rights to profits within law, but only those profits that are consistent with respecting broader stakeholder interests. Stakeholder theorists develop the content of their views in different ways, but they share the perspective that stockholder claim-rights to profits ought to be *limited* by basic ethical constraints or goals independent from law.[4]

THE LIMITS OF LAW

University of Southern California Law Professor Christopher Stone develops a series of arguments about the limits of law and the need for heightened corporate responsibility. See *Where the Law Ends: The Social Control of Corporate Behavior*, Harper & Row (New York, 1975).

---

[4]*Stakeholder* analysis can also refer to a managerial strategy of reducing risks in the context of maximizing profits. In this case the use of stakeholder ideas is a strategy for pursuing stockholder objectives. Milton Friedman, for example, interprets Mackey's stakeholder ideas in this way. This chapter is about stakeholder theory conceived as a *contrast* to stockholder theory. However, there are points when the differences between the theories can seem like a matter of nuance, as we will note later in the chapter.

The Ruggie Report, for example, empha-sizes human rights as one low-hanging fruit for specifying ethical responsibilities of corporations. For example, a series of lawsuits in the 1990s charged that Royal Dutch Shell was complicit with the Nigerian government in human rights abuses against the Ogani people of the Niger Delta, soliciting the help of the Nigerian military to execute, torture, and assault protestors to Shell's operations. The case was settled out of court in 2009. Shell maintains that the settlement repre-sents a humanitarian gesture for family members harmed and killed and not culpability for wrong-doing. Stakeholder advocates assert that human rights impacts are a *minimal* standard associated with the stakeholder perspective. Others ascribe additional responsibilities, and there is great variation in how the content of these responsibilities is elaborated.

FIGURE 5.2 Stakeholder Rights and Duties

BUSINESS IMPACTS ON HUMAN RIGHTS

For extensive information about negative business impacts on human rights, see the Business and Human Rights Resource Center, http://www.business-humanrights.org/, and the United Nations Human Rights Council Report "Corporations and Human Rights: A survey of the Scope and Patterns of Alleged Corporate-Related Human Rights Abuse" This document is at http://daccess-dds-ny.un.org/doc/UNDOC/GEN/G08/136/61/PDF/G0813661.pdf?OpenElement

For example, some stakeholder proponents will emphasize obligations to employees who do the work of the corporation; others emphasize vulnerable populations nearby corporate operations, such as the harm of pollutants on local townspeople or the envi-ronment (Chevron, for example, was ordered by Ecuador's courts to pay $18 billion for environmental damage to the Amazon); still others will emphasize supplier relationships, and the importance of ensuring that so-called sweatshops or other contracted work fulfills minimal labor and regulatory standards.

To take still another case, the global economic downturn has led both activists and CEOs to call on corporations to exercise a social responsibility to create jobs at home. The *Wall Street Journal* offers scant praise for the Occupy Wall Street movement—a global pro-test against the inequities of capitalism and corporate control, "But what about one of the group's chief beefs: business is falling short of its social responsibility, including creating jobs at home? Some politicians have given a nod of legitimacy to the protests."[5] The article notes how Milton Friedman would not be happy with this idea; but it resonates even with the business community, including Starbucks CEO Howard Schultz, who initiated a Cre-ate Jobs for USA program to funnel pooled donations to support small business loans for creating U.S. jobs. And the trend to outsource jobs is a source of continuing political controversy, as some citizens within any given nation-state argue that corporations have a responsibility to keep jobs at home.

---

[5]"Are Companies Responsible for Creating Jobs?" *Wall Street Journal* (October 28, 2011).

ROGER AND ME

Moviemaker Michael Moore become famous for his documentary *Roger and Me*, which looks at what happens to Flint, MI, when Ford shutters its plants for more profitable locations outside the United States. A more recent case is candy maker Hershey Foods' decision to outsource significant aspects of its operations.

Other examples of decision-making in the name of social responsibility include donations to disaster relief or to civic organizations for causes such as literacy, education, or the fine arts. In fact, most major corporations issue annual corporate responsibility reports separate from their financial reporting. These reports are readily available online. Business leaders pool their leading CSR ideas as well. The Committee to Encourage Corporate Philanthropy is a leading example of a network of global CEOs founded by actor Paul Newman to lead "the business community in raising the level and quality of corporate giving."[6]

If we take a broad view of all these stakeholder approaches, we can distinguish two competing perspectives for identifying corporate responsibilities. First, and in keeping with the Ruggie Report, one approach is to focus on the impact of corporate activities on its most direct stakeholders and then to define a set of responsibilities relevant to their sphere of operations. Specifically, the Ruggie Report identifies *constraints on behavior*, such as doing no harm to others. These responsibilities may also include *social goals* related to their core business function, such as paying a livable wage, capping executive salaries, or mitigating environmental damage. The concept is that corporations should be responsible not for solving *general* social problems, but for addressing problems or pursuing social goals tied to their normal business operations.

See Chapter 10 Section 3 for the contrast between ethical constraints and ethical goals.

A second approach is to argue that corporations should promote a more general common good and this responsibility may take them beyond their immediate sphere of operations. On this view, corporations should address social problems such as job creation or literacy or global warming when they have the influence and ability to do so, whether or not they have caused or might cause the social problem, and whether or not it's directly related to their core business. Wholefoods' CEO John Mackey offers this perspective in his statements that began Chapter 4, as do many other CEOs.

ETHICAL OBLIGATIONS AND RECOMMENDATIONS

Some ethicists distinguish the following ideas relevant to variations in the stakeholder theory: corporations may have an *ethical obligation* to respect human rights that would be interpreted as an absolute *constraint* on their conduct. But other activities, such as corporate philanthropy, may imply a different ethical assessment, as admirable *goals* to be *recommended and praised* without creating ethical obligations to carry them out. Chapter 10 Section 3 and Chapter 11 Section 4 expand on these ethical distinctions between *constraints, goals, obligations,* and *recommendations* (sometimes called *supererogatory* acts).

A good starting place for considering leading examples of corporate responsibilities as obligations beyond law is the **United Nations Global Compact** at www.unglobalcompact.org.

---

[6]http://www.corporatephilanthropy.org/

THE UN GLOBAL COMPACT

The UN Global Compact takes stakeholder ideas seriously and describes itself as "the largest corporate citizenship and sustainability initiative in the world—with over 4700 corporate participants and stakeholders from over 130 companies." Founded in July 2000, the UN Global Compact "seeks to embed markets and societies with universal principles and values for the benefit of all," including ten principles about human rights, labor, environment, and anticorruption. These standards specify blocked exchanges (Chapter 1 Section 5), grounded in arguments about *personal* and *human* rights, ideas introduced in Chapter 2 and further developed in Chapter 7.

The goal is to infuse a universally accepted mandate of corporate social responsibility within the business world that specifies ethical constraints on pursuing profits beyond legal mandates. The UN offers an analogy. We now accept, as a matter of principle, that states must respect human rights no matter what their laws may say. Similarly, we should also accept that corporations must respect human rights, no matter what the domestic and international laws permit. The Universal Declaration of Human Rights of 1948 specifies the rights of individuals in relation to states; the UN Global Compact of 2000 specifies the rights of individuals in relation to corporations. Although states and corporations may differ in their form and function, advocates of this analogy justify the comparison by arguing that states and corporations are both huge institutional structures whose organizational chain of command creates decisions and outcomes that could cause great benefits and harms to others. This claim about power and influence underlies the stakeholder movement.

THE UN GLOBAL COMPACT: THE TEN PRINCIPLES

Human Rights

- Principle 1: Businesses should support and respect the protection of internationally proclaimed human rights; and
- Principle 2: make sure that they are not complicit in human rights abuses.

Labour

- Principle 3: Businesses should uphold the freedom of association and the effective recognition of the right to collective bargaining;
- Principle 4: the elimination of all forms of forced and compulsory labour;
- Principle 5: the effective abolition of child labour; and
- Principle 6: the elimination of discrimination in respect of employment and occupation.

Environment

- Principle 7: Businesses should support a precautionary approach to environmental challenges;
- Principle 8: undertake initiatives to promote greater environmental responsibility; and
- Principle 9: encourage the development and diffusion of environmentally friendly technologies.

Anti-Corruption

- Principle 10: Businesses should work against corruption in all its forms, including extortion and bribery.

Source: http://www.unglobalcompact.org/AboutTheGC/TheTenPrinciples/index.html. Courtesy of the United Nations.

The common aim of the stakeholder perspective is to create norms that promote stakeholder interests within daily business operations. In this view, shareholders, boards of directors, and managers should accept that these norms legitimately constrain the decision-making of any corporate profit-making venture, such as protecting human rights, pursuing philanthropy, or safeguarding various employee interests.

Similar to the stockholder theory, stakeholder theory is not essentially a *legal* argument about what the laws are; it's also not essentially an *economic* argument about what corporations need to do to survive and thrive in a competitive environment, although advocates often make the case that a stakeholder approach is strategically advantageous for assessing risk and building reputation. Rather, the argument is *normative*: whatever role we occupy in society, we should all accept that corporations ought to advance stakeholder interests beyond maximizing profits within the law.

What do you think of this position so far?

FIGURE 5.3   **Stakeholder Values**

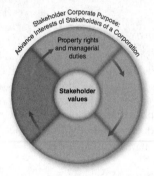

See the box feature The Structure of an Ethical Argument in Chapter 4 Section 5 for more information about the structure of these ethical arguments.

American philosopher John Rawls especially emphasizes how, as a matter of justice, political and economic institutions should recognize and respond to these inequalities, an idea further discussed in Chapter 11.

5.4   ETHICAL JUSTIFICATIONS

Why should we believe in these ideas? Stakeholder arguments take many forms more varied than stockholder arguments, so there is no single dominant argument that represents the normative foundations of the stakeholder perspective. In keeping with this normative diversity, this section illustrates a range of five ethical arguments that stakeholder proponents may variously draw on. These arguments rely on values whose study and application will be the subject of later chapters.

First, stakeholder proponents argue that institutions of great power can help alleviate tremendous global inequalities that plague the hope for a just world. Thus, a commitment to human *equality* in the face of massive global inequalities offers normative grounds to argue for heightened corporate responsibilities. Stated most simply, the argument is as follows: massive global inequalities are unjust; corporations can help alleviate some of these inequalities; and so they should. As we saw in Chapter 4, this argument is insufficient as stated, given that stockholder proponents argue that governments, not businesses, should address these social problems. We will discuss stakeholder views about the role of government in Section 6.

Second, stakeholder proponents sometimes argue that freedom is better promoted through a stakeholder approach, contrary to the claims of stockholder proponents. Consider the freedoms advanced if managers effectively utilized a stakeholder approach, taking into account vulnerable populations from corporate operations, such as working with governments to eliminate human rights violations. One group of stakeholder theorists writes, "There is much at stake in this debate. The shareholder ideologists want us to believe that economic freedom, and therefore political freedom, is threatened by stakeholder theory. Nothing could be further from the truth. The whole idea of seeing business as the creation of value for stakeholders and the trading of that value with free consenting adults is to think about a society where each has freedom compatible with a like liberty for all. . . ."[7]

Third, both stockholder and stakeholder proponents claim that efficiency consideration gives their theory the advantage, and only with concepts introduced in Chapters 6

[7]R. Edward Freeman, Andrew C. Wicks, and Bidhan Parmar, "Stakeholder Theory and 'The Corporate Objective Revisited,'" *Organization Science* 15(3) (May–June 2004), p. 368.

and 7 will we be able to examine these ideas. But let's present here one influential argument that stakeholder proponents sometimes offer. The idea is that capitalism has the potential to improve people's welfare and create long-term efficiencies only if enough people buy into the global economic system. Widespread buy-in by those impacted by the global economy can only occur, however, if corporations take a broad range of stakeholder interests seriously. Therefore, corporations must take stakeholder interests seriously to sustain long-term efficiencies.

Fourth, some stakeholder proponents ask, Who does the *work* of a corporation? It's not the stockholders. It's the employees. Shouldn't the people who do the labor—that is, the employees—deserve recognition that serving their interests be part of the mission of a corporation?[8] And doesn't this leading question apply also to costumers, investors, or the local community that supports the corporation in so many ways? Borrowing from a metaphor introduced by Mackey, just as breathing is *necessary* for human life but not the *purpose* of human life, profits are necessary for corporate survival but not the purpose of corporate activity.

Fifth, some stakeholder proponents especially emphasize the intrinsic value of nature and community. They embrace stakeholder theory because it places people, the environment, and community equally alongside the goal for profits, which allows for alternative or non-Western worldviews about the role of business in society and the nature of property rights. For example, E. F. Schumacher advocated *Buddhist economics* as an alternative to a stockholder model that emphasizes profit maximization. Although Schumacher's ideas have many dimensions, of relevance here is his idea that economic agents should pursue what is sufficient rather than what maximizes profits, and that valuing community and nature implies that corporations should consider a broad conception of stakeholders, including future generations and the natural world in making core business decisions.[9] In this argument concerns such as environmental degradation, deforestation, and global warming can be addressed effectively only through a stakeholder perspective. These proponents may develop their arguments through claims about the common good and the need for incorporate concerns about the common good into their strategic thinking, both locally and globally.

These five ethical arguments serve to illustrate how proponents apply a range of underlying values to support stakeholder theory, including claims about efficiency and welfare (Chapters 6, 7), freedom (Chapter 9), rights (Chapter 10), equality (Chapter 11), what people deserve (Chapter 12), the value of human relationships (Chapter 13), and community and the common good (Chapter 14).

Which normative arguments create, or at least have the potential to create, the more convincing case in your view, stockholder or stakeholder? As you may note, the answer depends in part on what the underlying values mean and which facts and data are most relevant for drawing implications from these values. Both stockholder and stakeholder theories draw from this large range of normative ideas, as do many other debates in the chapters ahead.

---

[8]See, for example, Marjorie Kelly, *The Divine Right of Capital: Dethroning the Corporate Aristocracy* (Berrett-Koehler, 2001).

[9]E. F. Schumacher, *Small Is Beautiful: Economics as if People Mattered* (Harper, 1989).

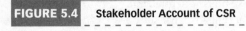

FIGURE 5.4   Stakeholder Account of CSR

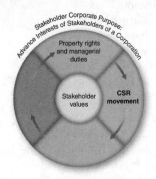

5.5 INTERPRETING THE CSR MOVEMENT FROM THE STAKEHOLDER PERSPECTIVE

Decades in the making, the corporate social responsibility (CSR) movement is now mainstream business. One spoke of stakeholder theory is to support this descriptive thesis and argue that these activities provide evidence on behalf of stakeholder theory.

For stakeholder proponents, **corporate social responsibility** (CSR) refers to the entire range of corporate responsibilities beyond making profits within the law, which is best fulfilled by advancing stakeholder interests. The pursuit of CSR is sometimes called *corporate citizenship, sustainability, social performance* (in contrast to financial performance) or the pursuit of the *triple bottom line* (which refers to *people, planet, profits,* to indicate that corporations should pursue multiple criteria beyond the goal of maximizing profits). There are many labels associated with CSR with no one fixed definition. For stakeholder proponents, the CSR movement is not hypocritical window-dressing, as is a common interpretation among stockholder advocates. Rather, the movement reflects a deeper meaning that the customary norms of society are changing. For stakeholder advocates, CSR initiatives are shaping people's understanding that corporations have heightened responsibilities in a global society.

Stockholder advocates who apply a cynical interpretation of CSR miss this normative point, or so stakeholder proponents claim. When people shop, accept employment, become managers and executives, and invest, they bring their values to the marketplace. **CSR rating agencies** refer to an entire industry of organizations that rate corporations on their social and environmental performance beyond their financial performance.[10] Why do these agencies exist? U.S. law only requires corporations to distribute financial annual reports, and yet most of the largest corporations in the world also produce voluntary **CSR annual reports** to showcase their CSR efforts. Why is this? These reports showcase the nonfinancial social performance of a corporation from the preceding year, including its responsiveness to stakeholder interests. Why do corporations embrace codes of conduct, sustainability objectives, donations to relief efforts around the world, and many other charitable activities? Why do corporations hire **corporate responsibility officers** (CROs) who design and oversee the strategy of social and environmental responsibility for a corporation?

For stakeholder advocates, the obvious answer to all of these questions is that people value CSR. In this sense, the CSR movement provides direct evidence that people do, in fact, apply a wide range of ethical values for informing their business decisions.

Other activities related to the CSR movement include a $3 trillion industry of **socially responsible investing (SRI)**, **CSR-related shareholder proposals**, and a vast array of international and domestic **nongovernmental organizations (NGOs)**. More recently in the United States, **benefit corporations** have begun to take legal root across some states in the United States, which grants a legal status to for-profit businesses that include social responsibility into their core mission.

---

[10]For more information on these agencies, see "Who is Who in Corporate Social Responsibility Rating? A Survey of Internationally Established Rating Systems That Measure Corporate Responsibility" (Bertelsmann Foundation, July 2006).

THE DIFFERENCE BETWEEN MOTIVES AND OUTCOME

How we interpret the CSR movement depends on (1) what we think actually drives corporations to take CSR seriously and (2) whether we think that motives or outcomes matter more for ethically assessing these actions.

Consider the upshot of different interpretations of the CSR movement, from an ethical point of view. Take a first case where corporations are led to consider stakeholder interests only after great resistance—they are forced to take CSR seriously because consumers and investors demand it, and because they are worn down by litigation and public relations debacles orchestrated by NGOs and watchdog groups. Take a second case where corporations draw inspiration from their own management and lead the way in supporting a stakeholder approach. If the *outcomes* are the same in both cases—taking CSR seriously—does it matter what drives the decision-making from an ethical point of view?

In the first case, business decisions are driven by rational self-interest on behalf of shareholders, and those motives lead to CSR efforts, given economic and political pressures. In the second case, business decisions are driven by a moral commitment to the stakeholder approach, with the hope that the market will reward this commitment.

Drawing on the discussion of ethics in the Introduction, those inclined toward a *consequentialist* understanding of ethics tend to lean toward thinking that motivations do not really matter as long as the outcomes are the same. Others believe that the motives that generate action do matter for ethically assessing these actions. Part of the challenge in interpreting the CSR movement is that we often import an ethical assessment into what we observe.

For example, if you are partial to the stakeholder perspective, you may believe that motives should matter, but if you also believe that CSR activities are in fact solely motivated by self-interest, then you may view the CSR movement with as much cynicism as stockholder proponents who see CSR as hypocritical window-dressing. By way of contrast, if you believe that CSR activities are explained in part by managers' sense of ethics, then you will be more inclined to celebrate CSR efforts. Alternatively, stakeholder proponents who do not place much weight on motives may endorse all of these CSR activities, whether or not they were forced by outside pressures. Stockholder proponents will face similar complications about how to interpret CSR depending on their assessment of the importance of motives and outcomes in evaluating CSR efforts.

5.6 CORPORATIONS AND GOVERNMENT

For stakeholder proponents, whenever governments cannot or do not handle major social problems, corporations ought to step up, beyond law, and address these problems, especially when they participate in creating the problem, such as environmental degradation and safe working conditions within their sphere of operations.

Stakeholder proponents argue that stockholder theory is inadequate in a world where governments have limited capacities to fully address social problems. Instead, corporations should act cooperatively with government to mitigate social and environmental problems. In other words, the strict separation of the roles of government and commerce suggested by the stockholder model neither exists in reality nor is a practical model for achieving the moral goals advanced by either perspective.

FIGURE 5.5   **Stakeholder Account of Institutions**

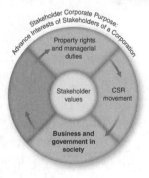

Stockholder proponents defend a strict separation of the roles of business and government in society, arguing that it's the role of government to address social problems. Stakeholder proponents argue that the limited capacities of government and the power and influence of corporations require that corporations address these social problems when they can. Who has the better view? Why?

The goal of business-government cooperation is not a clear-cut stakeholder directive, however, in theory or practice. For example, a democratic government may wish to work with executives from the oil business to negotiate regulations for long-term environmental protection. In theory, stakeholder theorists would argue that these executives should consider a wide set of stakeholder interests within these negotiations, acting as global citizens and pursuing strategies to deal with global warming or other problems that take advantage of their unique position to create positive social change. But, in practice, stakeholder proponents also recognize that businesses might co-opt governments to advance interests at the expense of stakeholders. Corporate largesse can impact the regulatory process: those employed to enforce regulations may serve as an advocate for the industry as much as an independent check on behalf of the citizens.

BP EXPLOSION IN THE GULF OF MEXICO

Consider researching the British Petroleum explosion in the Gulf of Mexico, which provides a compelling study about the relationships between business and government, and the ways that risks can be externalized to vulnerable populations.

Read the Case Study *BP Oil Spill* only on MySearchLab

Chapter 10 considers the chain of production from natural resources to final consumption in the context of examining individual's *rights*.

Not only do potential problems with the business-government relationship occur within democratic states, but corporations that cooperate with dictatorial governments can exacerbate social problems. For example, in 1997 thirteen Burmese villages filed suit against oil company Unical for complicity in human rights violations. Unical sought to create a pipeline across Burma and relied on the Burmese military for help. The military responded by allegedly coercing its population into slave labor to clear the path of development. In 2005, Unical settled and compensated the claims of the villages. The role of large corporations in unstable and undemocratic political environments is the source of much criticism regarding corporate responsibility.

In sum, the practical dynamics between government and business is complicated, and in many situations, it's not clear from within stakeholder theory how and when corporate cooperation with government could and should be appropriate, especially given that multinational corporations face different laws and standards in different nations.

Thus, stakeholder positions vary widely about the role of government intervention in markets. Those advocating limited intervention argue that stakeholder interests are best secured through voluntary market choices. These interests may be pursued through a *top-down process*, whereby international organizations, like the United Nations, specify norms for a global economy that executives endorse, such as the UN Global Compact. Alternatively, voluntary CSR efforts may be spurred by *bottom-up processes*, whereby ethical norms are rewarded by the purchasing decisions of consumer and investors, including the work of grassroots social activists who use media to spotlight corporate behaviors. Both top-down and bottom-up processes can work together to support CSR activities throughout a firm's operations.

Other stakeholder proponents argue for legal requirements, given their skepticism that voluntary measures will be effective. They pursue stakeholder ideas through the patchwork of domestic and international law. This approach is most pronounced in Europe, where corporate social responsibility has become a significant legal mandate. For example, large German corporations require that worker representatives have a role in the management of the corporation (called *codetermination*). Those who support this legal approach may value voluntary initiatives, but they are less optimistic of their impact. They seek to transform customary norms about corporate responsibility into enforceable law.

Despite the variation of stakeholder positions regarding the role of government, proponents press a common set of questions to confront the stockholder premise that business and government should have clearly separated functions in society. These questions are as follows: (1) If corporations can bear social responsibilities beyond the law and there is no practical prospect for governments to effectively address serious social problems, then do not corporations inherit these responsibilities, at least to some degree? (2) Doesn't great power imply heightened responsibility? Stakeholder advocates answer "yes" to both questions.

5.7 ETHICS, SELF-INTEREST, AND MARKETS

FIGURE 5.6 Stakeholder Account of Human Nature

Stakeholder advocates argue that most people want to know that they work for ethical institutions that are vehicles for good. They do not want to be complicit or involved in committing egregious wrongs. Consider this excerpt:

> In data compiled by Business for Social Responsibility, a U.S. employee survey carried out in 2001 by Walker Information found that only 6 percent of employees who thought their senior management was unethical were inclined to stay with their companies, while 40 percent who believed their leaders were ethical wanted to stay.
> Another study of U.S. workers carried out by the Aon Loyalty Institute in 2000 found that when employees do not feel they can trust management, giving them additional benefits has no significant effect on their commitment. Another Aon survey in 2002 showed worker confidence in management had dropped to its lowest level since the survey began in 1997. Extensive anecdotal evidence suggests that employees have more positive feelings about themselves and their work—and demonstrate greater loyalty—when they work for a company they view as having good values and ethical practices.[11]

People want to know, this finding suggests, that ethical motives can have traction in business. This idea may be one of deepest rationales for the CSR movement and for the stakeholder approach to corporations. A system that can support ethical motives not only can curtail harms that markets can cause but also enable people to live with ethical integrity and maintain personal character.

From this perspective a managerial injunction to maximize profits within the law as the *sole* objective of business activity may undermine important facts about human

Read the Case Study *Patagonia and Profits* only on MySearchLab

---

[11]David Gebler, "Recruiting the Best with Ethics in Mind," http://accounting.smartpros.com/x46289.xml

For many ethicists, analyzing the circumstances that enable people to maintain good character is just as important as assessing the ethics of individual actions. This idea was first presented in the Introduction and will be developed in Chapter 13.

psychology. Managers and employees are human, and a system that effectively brackets ethical reflection pulls against our need to integrate our daily decision-making with our ethical beliefs. People expect others to be guided by wide-ranging ethical norms that they routinely can and do follow. Today, these norms include demands for broad corporate social responsibilities. Stakeholder advocates reject both psychological and ethical egoism as descriptive and as a normative account of human motivation.

Debates about corporate responsibility are inevitably about the types of motives people can and should be expected to bring to their economic lives. You might contrast the statements in the preceding paragraphs against our discussion in Chapter 4 Section 8, which is about the primacy of *self-interest* from the stockholder point of view. Taken together, stockholder and stakeholder theories present two very different perspectives about how to interpret human motivation and behavior.

Further, stakeholder proponents often emphasize that the topic of corporate responsibility entails larger questions about the ethical expectations that *we*, as citizens, consumers, investors, owners, and employees, should place on *ourselves*, given the design and purposes of the institutions that surround us. In other words, given the role of ethical motivation in stakeholder theory, proponents often *broaden* the CSR debate to emphasize that the underlying topic is about all of our responsibilities no matter our role in the economic system. In this sense, the topic of CSR becomes a case study for ethical inquiry more broadly, beginning with reflections about markets, property rights, corporations, and law, and leading to reflections about our own individual ethical responsibilities in life.

To illustrate, stakeholder advocates are often activists who are not merely staking out a theoretical position about corporate purpose or managerial duties. They want to convince you to adjust your decision-making as a *consumer*, by buying Green or shunning corporations that behave badly, as an *investor*, by investing to reflect your values, as a *citizen*, by influencing the legislative process on behalf of a stakeholder perspective, as a *stockholder*, by supporting shareholder proposals on behalf of CSR initiatives, as a *board of director*, by demanding that executives take social responsibility seriously, and as an *employee*, *manager*, or *executive*, by bringing ethical beliefs and values to the table.

How does a stockholder theorist react to all of this? The final nuances introduced in Chapter 4, Section 8 explain why the stockholder response is not altogether simple. On the one hand, it's a free society. So if people are misguided enough to support these causes, so be it—markets will adjust. If people are willing to pay for CSR, they will get it. That's the beauty of a market system. On the other hand, shareholders have rights to those profits. Managers have a duty to shareholders that should override all this talk about social responsibility. Moreover, if all these CSR initiatives create burdensome regulatory hurdles, dilute the profit-making mission, and saddle corporations with responsibilities more properly addressed by government, then the economic system will lose its vitality. If CSR must have a place in society, the best option for stockholder proponents is that its impact be felt through the choices of consumers and investors and *not* through managers who think that they actually incur these obligations. Managers should continue to do what they do best, which is to maximize profits within the law, and they will be responsive to what the market will reward, which may (or may not) include marketing and product decisions to reflect consumers' tastes for social responsibility.

Stakeholder advocates, by contrast, say that this stockholder analysis just doesn't *get it* (as Mackey contends in his exchange with Milton Friedman in Chapter 4). Social responsibility is not primarily a marketing campaign premised on the traditional understanding of corporate purpose. It's an entire movement of thought and action that transforms the very concept and purpose of corporations and demonstrates the effective role of ethics in economic life.

5.8   PERSONAL AND INSTITUTIONAL POINTS OF VIEW REVISITED

The preceding paragraphs illustrate how ethical thought integrates both *institutional* and *personal* points of view (see Introduction, Section 3). From an institutional point of view, stakeholder and stockholder theories represent a normative debate about the role and function of corporations in society. From a personal point of view, these theories are about the economic decisions that we all should make in our various roles within the market system, given what we believe the function of corporations ought to be. Consider again the example of the hypothetical manager in Introduction, Section 3. How would you address those questions now? How have the materials in Chapters 1–5 deepened and developed your responses to those questions?

Next, recall the model of the ethics and values of business and economic life (Introduction, Figure I.1). This model can also represent the stockholder-stakeholder debate, as illustrated through Figures 5.7 and 5.8.

Note the following features of Figures 5.7 and 5.8. First, both figures represent only a few schematic ideas about the duties of *managers*. As discussed above, both stockholder and stakeholder theories also express broader views about the responsibilities or liberties of all economic agents in the system. Further, the *sense of ethics* depicted above is not an exhaustive representation, even for the ethics of management. Rather, it focuses on what differentiates stockholder and stakeholder views in relation to the purpose of corporations.

Second, Figures 5.7 and 5.8 suggest further possibilities for probing these two theories. For example, drawing on the materials in the Introduction, if you believe that *personal character* matters, which perspective—stockholder or stakeholder—seems to be more appealing? Why? If you believe that we all have *Kantian duties* to treat people as ends in themselves, what are the implications in this current debate? If you believe that *ethical*

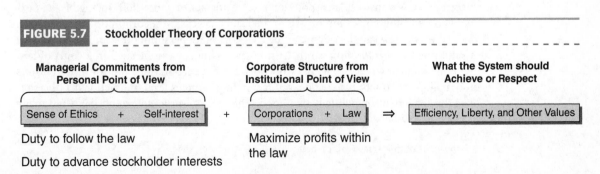

FIGURE 5.7   **Stockholder Theory of Corporations**

Managerial Commitments from Personal Point of View

| Sense of Ethics | + | Self-interest |

Duty to follow the law

Duty to advance stockholder interests

Corporate Structure from Institutional Point of View

| Corporations | + | Law |

Maximize profits within the law

What the System should Achieve or Respect

⇒ | Efficiency, Liberty, and Other Values |

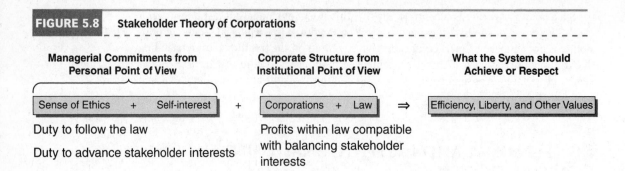

FIGURE 5.8   Stakeholder Theory of Corporations

egoism is a viable ethical perspective, how do you interpret and evaluate the sense of ethics implied by these theories?

Third, Chapters 4 and 5 focus on basic intellectual disagreements, but we needn't lose sight of what we have learned early in life about decent conduct toward others for thinking about professional relationships. Those reflections can be joined to both stockholder and stakeholder theories for a complete account of the sense of ethics that we should bring to economic life. Said again, the debates of Chapters 4 and 5 are a snapshot of an important debate, without attempting discussion of the fuller range of a sense of ethics that may be relevant to our professional or economic lives.

Finally, these figures highlight how stockholder-stakeholder debates make competing claims from both *personal* and *institutional* points of view—claims about how we should make decisions and about how to evaluate the institutional structure of corporations. We could focus the topic of corporate responsibility on *individual* decision-making or on the responsibilities of corporations from a broader *institutional* point of view. Best of all, we could examine both levels of analysis and how they interact, which has been the approach of these two chapters. This distinction, between the personal and the institutional, is also relevant to the last topic of this chapter: corporate personhood.

> Discussions of personal character, Kantian duties, ethical egoism, among other perspectives, are first presented in the Introduction. Later chapters examine these ethical ideas in greater depth.

5.9   CORPORATE PERSONHOOD

Are corporations persons? In 1819, U.S. Chief Justice John Marshall provided what has become a classic answer: "a corporation is an artificial being, invisible, intangible, and existing only in contemplation of law."[12] The legal answer is yes, corporations are persons. Why does the law say this? Some argue that corporate personhood is an important and useful piece of legal fiction, so that the corporate entity can be sued in a court of law, without suing any actual persons who work for the corporation, and for other reasons too (making contracts, collecting taxes, facilitating complex legal transactions). Others reject the concept of corporate personhood. The topic of *corporate responsibility* has many

[12]*Dartmouth College v. Woodward*, 4 Wheat. 518, 636, 4 L.Ed. 629, 659, 1819.

angles, and one of these angles so far unaddressed is the intriguing philosophical and legal challenges about personhood, which create intellectual and practical puzzles for both stockholder and stakeholder proponents.

When we ask "Do corporations have responsibilities?" are we supposing that some artificial entity—the corporation—has the capacity to be an ethical agent and bear ethical responsibilities? Or is that question always shorthand for analyzing the ethical responsibilities of particular persons? At least one philosopher, Peter French, famously argues that corporate personality is more than fiction: because moral agency is action based on decision-making, because corporations have decision-making that yields actions, and because these complex decisions are not reducible to the thoughts of particular individuals, it's appropriate from a philosophical and *metaphysical point of view* to consider corporations as moral persons independent from the people who work for them.[13] **Metaphysics** is an area of philosophy that studies the nature of reality. If French is correct, we can praise or blame corporations independent from praising or blaming any particular persons working for that corporation. We can say that corporations are the kinds of entities that bear ethical responsibilities, given what they are.

Many people on both sides of the stockholder-stakeholder debate will resist French's analysis as an illegitimate personification of corporations. (Do you? Why? Can *any* collective have responsibilities or is it always only individual persons?) This philosophical puzzle creates the background for studying the legal status of corporations, which does indeed impute legal personhood to corporations. Some support this legal position, others are left uneasy, some others oppose it.

If we take legal personhood for granted, putting aside metaphysical puzzles, the most obvious practical implication is to raise this question, "What constitutional rights and responsibilities granted to natural persons should also be granted to corporations?" This question has surfaced at various points in U.S. history, including the recent landmark Supreme Court decision in *Citizens United vs. Federal Election Commission*. In a tightly contested 5–4 decision, the justices found that a law that banned corporate funding for independent political advertisements during election times violated the First Amendment right to free speech. Thus, the Court found that corporations—as persons—have speech rights protected by the U.S. Constitution. This ruling appears to strengthen the ability of corporations in society to influence politics, which has led some groups (see, for example, http://movetoamend.org/) to rally for a constitutional amendment against corporate personhood. The legal designation cuts more than one way, however, as personhood conceptually allows corporations to be held criminally liable among other liabilities. Thus, the topic of corporate personhood creates an amalgam of contrasting views within and across the political spectrum. With personhood come both rights and responsibilities. The question becomes one of the reach of scope of the legal rights and responsibilities that ought to apply to corporations independent from the rights and responsibilities of natural persons. These legal questions will continue to evolve over time, and their legal evolution speaks to a central theme of these two chapters, that the very concept and purpose of a corporation is a matter of continuing dispute and analysis.

---

[13]Peter French, *Collective and Corporate Responsibility* (New York: Columbia University Press, 1984).

5.10   SUMMARY OF CHAPTERS 4 AND 5

Chapters 4 and 5 aim to introduce basic complexities that can guide your further study of a significant ethical topic in business and economic life. Each chapter states the most forceful reasons on behalf of competing sides of a debate about corporate responsibility. A full defense of either position requires a more systematic study of ethics and values, to be provided in the chapters ahead.

It may seem that *debating* corporate responsibility is pointless, for market pressures or law will determine the outcome, regardless of the nature of debate. But history and ideas have a way of working together. Just as Hobbes discovered that ideas about the state influenced history in the seventeenth century, our ideas about corporate purpose, applied to our consumer and investor choices, and our political decisions, will influence the actual purposes they finally serve in ways that we may only barely perceive today.

5.11   BOOK DIGEST

Integrating and applying the basic concepts introduced in Part I will continue to deepen your understanding of corporate responsibility. *Corporations* (Chapter 4) participate in *markets* (Chapter 1) against a background of *property rights* (Chapter 2) backed by *law* (Chapter 3). Debates about corporate *responsibility* (Chapters 4, 5) provide competing interpretations of our current corporate environment and competing accounts of the roles and responsibilities of management and other market participants. Corporate responsibility is more than a technical debate for corporate backrooms. It's part of a larger historical debate about the *role of ethics and values in markets, business, and economic life* (Chapters 6–15).

Your views about corporate responsibility will depend in part on your direct observations about how people interact within business and economic institutions. Your views

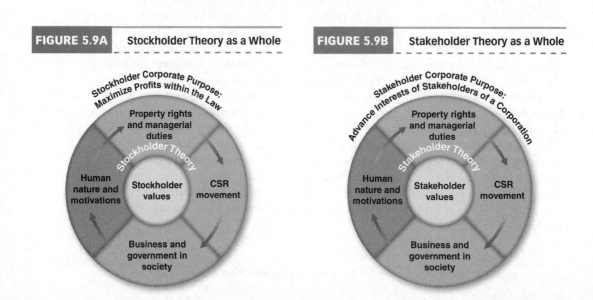

| FIGURE 5.9A | Stockholder Theory as a Whole | FIGURE 5.9B | Stakeholder Theory as a Whole |

will also depend on the underlying values that you believe should guide what a market system does.

Chapters 4 and 5 are a pivot point for studying these values. The next chapter begins with the concept of efficiency as an ethical ideal and proceeds through other values for engaging important debates. These new debates apply and develop basic concepts and arguments in Parts I and II, and introduce new themes and puzzles in business and economic life. You may wish to return to these chapters on CSR to see how later chapters may alter or reinforce your current views. The later chapters continue to balance personal and institutional perspectives; they also break new ground about the nature of self-interest, ethics, and the institutions that impact our choices.

KEY TERMS

global governance gaps
United Nations Global Compact
corporate social responsibility
CSR rating agencies
CSR annual reports

corporate responsibility officers
socially responsible investing
  (SRI)
CSR-related shareholder
  proposals

nongovernmental organizations
  (NGOs)
benefit corporations
metaphysics

DISCUSSION QUESTIONS

1. Introduce at least two ideas relevant to the stockholder and stakeholder debate not discussed in either chapter. Why are those ideas relevant?

2. Corporations are required to follow the law, according to all the positions reviewed in these two chapters. But why? One rationale is based solely on self-interest: that following the law is prudent because the costs of breaking the law are too high. Both the stockholder and stakeholder perspectives reject this justification; they say that following the law is a *duty*. Is it? On what basis?

    Consider this related puzzle: if there is a duty to follow the law, is there a corresponding duty not to exploit loopholes in the law? on what basis? Consider the financial scandals of Enron and Arthur Anderson, and the bailouts of AIG and others in the financial industries. To what extent are these crises explained by a lack of corporate responsibility? Explain.

3. Some commentators observe that because corporations exist by virtue of law, they thereby

enter a contract with society that implies corporate social responsibilities. Former president Theodore Roosevelt sounded this theme at the turn the twentieth century, for example, in one of his State of the Union speeches, in 1903: "Great corporations exist only because they were created and safeguarded by our institutions; and it is therefore our right and duty to see that they work in harmony with these institutions." This oft-heard argument is framed more recently by Charles M. Denny, Jr., a former CEO, in his essay *The Corporation in Modern American Society* (Hubert H. Humphrey Institute of Public Affairs, University of Minnesota, 2008). What is your assessment of this argumentative approach? What social responsibilities could be implied by the argument? To take one example, if a city negotiates significant tax breaks to entice a large corporation to locate its corporate headquarters downtown, does that corporation now have obligations to that city through an implicit social contract? (We will examine social contract theories in Chapter 11.)

4. Stockholder proponents will review the burgeoning list of social responsibilities identified in Section 3 and argue that if all of these ideas are taken seriously, they will (a) pose very significant costs on shareholder revenues, (b) detract from the core function of business, (c) and misalign resources. Which side of the debate has the stronger position?

5. Stockholder proponents will note that any efforts to set product safety standards or employee health and safety standards, above the legal minimum, costs money. They will note that philanthropy is an expense, that attractive wages are costly, that generous retirement benefits and work leave programs beyond legal requirements all cost money. They will note that a stakeholder approach that satisfies a broad range of stakeholders but leads to many lay-offs in an economic downtown may seem much less responsible than a corporation that focuses solely on maximizing profits within law and beats out the competition in lean times. If you are a stakeholder proponent, how do you respond to such criticisms?

6. Consider reading *Citizens United v. Federal Election Commission*, available at http://www .supremecourt.gov/opinions/09pdf/08-205.pdf. If corporations have free speech rights within a democracy, do they then inherit additional ethical responsibilities as well? For a stakeholder proponent, is it better to argue against corporate free speech rights or argue for *additional* responsibilities, or are they unconnected issues?

7. For the stakeholder proponent, what is the primary function of government in relation to business: to *constrain* and *regulate* business or to *cooperate* with business to solve social problems? Can you give examples?

8. Who should have the authority to define the purposes of a corporation? Stockholders? Consumers? Management? Law? Why? Explain how this question—about who has the *power* (in the Hohfeldian sense)—is different from

directly analyzing the claim-rights and liberties of stockholders and management.

9. Can corporate responsibility be addressed sufficiently through corporate law? Harvard economist Edward L. Glaeser ("Can Businesses Do Well and Do Good?" *NYT Economix*, January 6, 2009) recommends creating a legal class of firms that are somewhere in between for-profit corporations and nonprofits. These firms might include investors who receive financial returns attached to a legally recognized division of the firm devoted to other objectives. Glaeser notes how this idea already exists whenever a nonprofit foundation creates a subsidiary for-profit enterprise, such as IKEA. To what extent can disagreements about the nature of corporate responsibilities be addressed through a diverse mix of for-profit, nonprofit, and hybrid firms?

10. If large corporations have responsibilities beyond maximizing profits within the law, what about small business enterprises?

11. Pick a specific industry—such as the newspaper industry, defense contracting, or pharmaceuticals—and examine the specific responsibilities of firms in that industry. To what extent are responsibilities industry specific?

12. Some commentators argue that the stakeholder perspective is hopelessly vague and impractical. Does the UN Global Compact offer an effective response?

13. Professor Keith Davis coined the expression *iron law of social responsibility*, which says in the long run, those who do not use power in ways that society considers responsible will tend to lose it. Is that true? How is this idea relevant to stockholder and stakeholder debates?

14. The U.S. Congress passed the 2002 Sarbanes-Oxley in reaction to corporate accounting scandals, including Enron, Tyco International, Adelphia, and Worldcom. This law requires increased regulations regarding corporate governance and financial reporting and remains a source of controversy today. Some argue that the costs of conforming to

its provisions are excessively bureaucratic. Others argue that the law provided much-needed stability to the financial markets and appropriately heighted ethical and legal requirements. There is an extensive literature readily available online regarding Sarbanes-Oxley. After researching what this law is about, what is its appropriateness from stockholder and stakeholder points of view?

15. What is the appropriate role of nonprofit organizations in society, and how does your answer relate to what you believe should be the appropriate role of for-profit corporations?

16. Some people point out that wars make rich the people who make the weapons of war. To what extent is the profit motive in business involved in the prevalence of war? At a personal level, can someone with a belief-system like a pacifist work for a defense contractor with a sound ethical mind? How so? Finally, what are the responsibilities of businesses in defense industries in your view?

17. Models prompt questions to ask and relationships to examine what might otherwise go unnoticed. Reexamine Figures 5.8 and 5.9. What questions do they prompt and what are some answers?

EFFICIENCY AND
WELFARE: THE
MOST COMMON
ETHICAL
GUIDES IN
BUSINESS AND
ECONOMICS

6

Part III explores the range and structure of ethical thought when efficiency and welfare are taken as grounding values. Part III also integrates Chapters 1–7 by developing the model of ethics and values, first introduced and represented in Figure I.1.

Chapter 6 • Efficiency and
Well-Being

Chapter 7 • Public Goods and the
Utilitarian Tradition

Chapter 8 • The Invisible Hand:
Ethics, Incentives,
and Institutions

**WHEN YOU FINISH
STUDYING THIS CHAPTER,
YOU SHOULD BE ABLE TO:**

1. Define efficiency.

*2. Characterize the argument
that ideal markets are efficient.*

*3. Debate whether or not actual
markets promote efficiency.*

*4. Identify at least two
conceptual complications related
to the ideal of efficiency.*

See Chapter 3 Section 6 for
Sen's ideas about prop-
erty rights and famine.

EFFICIENCY
AND WELL-BEING

6.1 INTRODUCTION

Unlike the ring of freedom, the call for equality, and the love of fraternity, efficiency as an inspiring moral ideal doesn't make many people want to sing and dance. In the words of writer and novelist Aldus Huxley, "The worst enemy of life, freedom and the common decencies is total anarchy; their second worst enemy is total efficiency."[1]

And yet, efficiency plays a tremendous intellectual role in debates about ethics and economic life. Economist and philosopher Amartya Sen goes so far as to say that *all* ethical arguments for markets and capitalism ultimately rely on claims about efficiency. While that may be a little exuberant, it's not an exaggeration to say that judgments about efficiency drive many of these normative arguments.

Is there a way to pump life into what many regard as a dismal concept? That is what this chapter aims to do: to show the great versatility of the concept of efficiency for ethical thought.

The chapter begins with a few brief definitions. Next, we will consider a vision of markets as a great social creation of humanity based on this concept of efficiency. We next examine a contrasting vision by those who criticize or denounce markets based on the very same principle. It's a story that begins with a very simple value but ends as a clash between two worldviews.

---

[1] Aldous Huxley. BrainyQuote.com, Xplore Inc, 2012. http://www.brainyquote.com/quotes/quotes/a/aldoushuxl391055.html, accessed May 1, 2012.

6.2   PARETO EFFICIENCY AS AN ETHICAL IDEAL

Are there any ethical standards that are truly *uncontroversial*? Try this: we should support outcomes that make everyone better off, and let people judge what *better off* means from their own points of view. Consider the immediate appeal and—for some—the brilliance of this simple ethical idea. It's a highly edifying way for people to combine disparate values and be guided by a principle that everyone can believe in. If each person is made better off from his own point of view, then no one has reason to object to the recommended outcome. No matter what else ethics may require, it seems a highly desirable goal to pursue interactions and outcomes that can make everyone better off in this sense.

This basic intuition was made more precise by the nineteenth-and-early-twentieth-century Italian economist Vilfredo Pareto, and the idea has become formalized as *Pareto efficiency*. This standard has been at the core of normative analysis in economics for over a century. Not everyone endorses the normative ideal of efficiency. But proponents of this idea believe that efficiency creates a baseline moral perspective that should be part of anyone's ethical outlook, no matter what else a person might believe.[2]

Consider these definitions. Actions or states of affairs create a **Pareto improvement or efficiency gain** if at least one person is made better off and nobody is made worse off by moving from one situation to the next. A situation is **Pareto optimality** (or **fully efficient**) if and only if there is no feasible alternative state in which at least one person is better off and no one is worse off.

Thus, some situation B can be an efficiency gain over another situation A; but B is not fully efficient unless there is no other way to create any further efficiency gain beyond B. For example, suppose that Adam was planning to go to the movies, Bob was going to spend the day at the park, and Cathy was headed to a concert. But they called each other up to spend the day together. One of them proposes that they go to the beach for the day, and all three immediately agree that this choice is far better than their original plans. Thus, going to the beach is an *efficiency gain* for Adam, Bob, and Cathy. Suppose with further thought, they realize that there is no other option that all three would prefer. For example, someone proposes a day-trip to the mountains as an alternative to the beach, but Adam prefers the beach. Another proposes miniature golf, but Bob doesn't want to do that. In fact, *any* departure from the beach plan is a step in the wrong direction for at least one person. If so, going to the beach is not merely a Pareto improvement from their original plans, but it is *fully efficient* or *optimal* for those three as well. You may wish to devise other examples to reinforce these definitions.

The moral impulse of this view is to celebrate mutually advantageous interactions that make people better off in their own view, without making others worse off. This is efficiency as an *ethical and normative ideal*, a goal that even Aldus Huxley could admire.

Huxley, to his credit, probably had a different concept of efficiency in mind. Efficiency has many varied meanings, in physics, engineering, economics, and other disciplines. For example, a machine that increases production with no change in inputs is more efficient—such as a more fuel-efficient car. A corporation that is especially skilled at maximizing profits is efficient in the pursuit of that goal. In general, the least costly means of reaching any goal increases the efficiency of attaining that goal.

---

[2]Efficiency is an important concept in political philosophy as well, especially due to the writings of philosopher John Rawls, who relied heavily on the Pareto's concept of efficiency to develop and to contrast his own views in *A Theory of Justice* (Harvard University Press, 1971).

Efficiency as a *normative ideal* is about seeking mutually advantageous interactions that make people better off without making anyone worse off.

These ideas may have no relation to ethics or be contrary to ethics. A con artist could be said to work efficiently, as could an engineer, or a totalitarian government. Further, many people argue that a relentless drive to squeeze costs and maximize revenue can crowd out ethics and humanistic concerns. A corporate pursuit of efficiency could mean *whatever it takes to maximize profits*, and Huxley probably had this idea of efficiency in mind. He worried about the total domination of one goal at the expense of other values.

For our purposes in this chapter, *efficiency* refers to the idea as commonly used in economics—the normative Pareto idea defined above about making people better off. It's worth noting, however, one similarity with the amoral concepts of efficiency considered above—which is to try to eliminate "waste." Recall the ethical maxim: create situations that make some better off without making anyone worse off. This outlook improves people's welfare (in a sense to be examined in Section 8) *at no one's expense*. Said again, *not* to pursue efficiency in these situations is to waste welfare gains that have no downside. Many proponents believe that this idea—as an ethical ideal—is a refreshing and inspired thought.

Chapter 14 analyzes the alternative idea of efficiency suggested by Huxley within discussion of the effects of capitalism on community and the common good. For another related discussion, see also Chapter 8 Sections 5 and 6, about the costs of ethical conduct, and whether corporations have responsibilities to ensure that ethical integrity does not require heroic or prohibitively costly decisions at the personal level.

What kind of social organization could facilitate such remarkable results? Are there *any* ways that people can interact to create a world of Pareto efficiency? The economics profession offers an answer to this question: markets! And it offers proof of this result in its study of welfare economics. We will consider the intuitive ideas behind this proof in the next section.

But before we explore these details, keep in mind three basic questions that will reoccur throughout the next three chapters:

- To what extent do markets make us better off?
- What does *better off* mean?
- What do the answers to these questions tell us about our ethical responsibilities?

For many, these three questions are among the most important *ethical* questions to ask about markets, capitalism, and corporations; and they seek a study of efficiency to provide insights for answering these questions.

6.3   HOW IDEALIZED MARKETS CREATE EFFICIENCY GAINS

Let's begin with two people deciding whether to make a trade. We can imagine that they are alone on an island in a *state of nature* (which, in this context, means life without government and laws) and that they face the prospect of trade. The situation is also called a *Robinson Crusoe economy*, derived from Daniel Defoe's novel about Crusoe's shipwrecked experiences on an island.

Consider person A, who possesses two jars of water, and person B, who possesses two baskets of food. These are their endowments. Further, let us suppose that A would like to

FIGURE 6.1   Pareto Efficiency and Trade

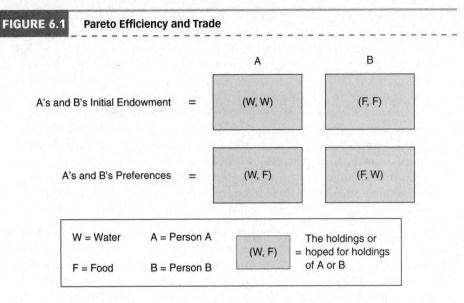

have one jar of water and one basket of food rather than his current bundle of goods, and B would rather one jar of water and one basket of food over her current bundle of goods. These judgments represent A's and B's preferences (see Figure 6.1).

Let's see where this goes. What will they do? Here's one possibility: each may try to take all the possessions of the other person violently and without permission, leaving one or the other, or both, worse off. Here is another possibility: they decide to trade. What is the result of this second option if they both choose to exercise it? Answer: they each perceive themselves to be made better off, relative to their situation prior to the trade. More precisely, the trade creates an efficiency gain in which each person is better off than he or she was before the trade and no one is made worse off.

It is hard to understate this simple yet powerful interpretation of market activity. For market advocates who lean on the idea of efficiency, the moral kernel behind a market system is that mutually advantageous trade creates gains from exchange, and this trading mechanism makes people better off. We could say that A and B are wealthier due to this trade, because from A's own point of view, the worth of his endowment has increased due to this trade. And from B's own point of view, the worth of her endowment has increased due to this trade. This fact also helps explain why they made the trade in the first place: it's in each person's interests to trade because each perceives that his or her welfare improves as a result of the trade.

See Chapter 1 for an overview of the nature of markets.

It is impossible to understand the idea of markets, from an ethical point of view, whether in support or criticism, without reflecting on and assessing these ideas. Their role in arguments about markets is foundational, as made evident, for example, by the words of Nobel Prize–winning economist Vernon Smith:

Markets and how they function constitute the core of any economic system, whether it is highly

For market advocates who lean on the idea of efficiency, the moral kernel behind a market system is that mutually advantageous trade creates gains from exchange, and this trading mechanism makes people better off.

decentralized—popularly a "capitalist" system—or highly centralized—popularly a "planned" system. . . . The ("competitive") market process yields welfare improving (and, under certain limiting ideal conditions, welfare maximizing) outcomes. But is the hypothesis "true," or at least very probably "true"? I think it is "true," but how do I know this? Do you see what I see? A Marxist does not see what I see. . . . The young student studying economics does not see what I see, although if they continue to study economics eventually they (predictably) come to see what I see (or, at least, they say they do). Is this because we have inadvertently brainwashed them? The gasoline consumer does not see what I see. They see themselves in a zero sum game with an oil company: any increase in price merely redistributes wealth from the consumer to the company, which is not "fair" since the company is richer. What I see in a market is a positive sum gain yielding gains from exchange, which constitutes the fundamental mechanism for creating, not merely redistributing wealth.[3]

In this revealing passage, the phrase **positive sum game** means *win-win* situations, where one person's gain is compatible with the other person gaining as well. Trade creates positive sum games, says Smith. This idea contrasts against *zero sum games*, in which one person's gain is possible only if another person loses, such as a sports competition.

Let's consider two other examples from previous chapters to reinforce this idea of positive sum games. First, in Chapter 3 Section 3, we discussed the concept of microlending and the work of economist Muhammad Yunus and the Grameen Bank in extending small business loans to the very poor. For many who admire Yunus and his work, part of the normative appeal of his approach was that he introduced lending practices that yielded Pareto improvements for everyone involved. It was a positive sum game in which Yunus improved people's lives and eliminated the waste of inefficient arrangements that trapped people in poverty. Second, within the CSR debates, some stakeholder proponents argue that *doing good and doing well* go hand in hand, which is to assert that corporate social responsibility is not only the right thing to do but CSR increases the profits of the corporation as well. Whether or not you agree with this rationale for CSR, it's interesting to note that this argument is essentially an efficiency argument: CSR creates win-win situations for all stakeholders, *including* the stockholders, and given this result, *no one* should object to CSR efforts. Many stakeholder arguments rely on this normative appeal. The concepts of efficiency, positive sum gains, and win-win situations have many business applications beyond these two examples.

Before we complicate the island metaphor, can you deny the appeal of a social system that structures interactions so that people make each other better off without worsening the conditions of the other party? That's the ideal of the market system that guides many people's ethical vision. Each time you eat at a restaurant, buy a car, purchase health insurance, you and the seller of that good are engaged in a practice of mutually beneficial exchange.

Chapter 1 Section 4 considers how fundamental ethical disagreements often derive from differences in how we observe our social life.

This is what economist Vernon Smith and many others *see* in a market—a great social invention for improving people's welfare. For advocates, the island scenario conveys much of the ethical essence of our market system and how we should interpret markets.

What is your response to these ideas so far?

---

[3]"Experimental Methods in Economics," *The New Palgrave: A Dictionary of Economic Theory and Doctrine*, J. Eatwell, M. Milgate, and P. Newman eds. (Macmillan Press, October 1987). © The Nobel Foundation 2002.

6.4 BACKGROUND CONDITIONS

Let's analyze the island scenario more deeply. Although spare on detail, the imagery is remarkably useful for guiding our thoughts about the nature of efficiency and its relevance for assessing markets. Consider the assumptions or background conditions that are built into the trading scenario between A and B; and let's ask: *what must be true about the conditions of trade for us to have reason to believe that A and B are really making themselves better off by that trade?*

For example, aren't we taking for granted that A and B know how to advance their own interests, in order to conclude that trade will make each better off? We seem to be assuming that they are the best judges of their own welfare, and that they are rational decision-makers with a coherent set of desires. *Rationality* is a rich idea with many interpretations, but at the very least, we seem to be assuming that people in this trade have the capacity to know their interests and know how to pursue the means to achieve these interests. This relatively minimal understanding of rationality is often called **instrumental rationality**, to emphasize the ability to effectively and instrumentally pursue one's ends, whatever they are.

To clarify the point, suppose that we *didn't* know whether A and B could advance their own interests through their decisions. Then wouldn't that weaken our confidence that trading is really making each person better off?

Let's continue this line of thought in a different direction. What else do we need to presume as a condition of trade to conclude that trading leads to efficiency gains? We also seem to be taking for granted that A and B know what they're getting. If the food is rotten or the water tainted without the parties knowing these facts prior to trade, wouldn't our confidence in judging the trade as an efficiency gain be undermined? They may still trade, but we then might challenge anyone's interpretation that each party was made better off by that trade. (Wouldn't the trading parties eventually discover this fact themselves?)

As we think about this trading scenario more intensely, we can uncover many interesting and implicit background conditions of the trading scenario that we presume in order to be able to draw the conclusion that markets create efficiency gains. Consider a few more. For example, we are assuming that A and B can easily reach each other to trade. Suppose instead that A and B were so far apart that the costs of meeting would be greater than the value that could be gained from the trade. In other words the island scenario assumes away all **transaction costs**, which refer to any costs associated with completing an exchange. High transaction costs could prevent trade from occurring in the first place. In real life, these costs could include a transaction fee (for example, a commission fee for buying stock or extra commission fees for purchasing tickets to musical concerts and sporting events) or the time and energy required to complete the transaction, such as a long drive to the store or the research involved in making the best choice.

THE WEALTH OF NATIONS

Scottish enlightenment philosopher Adam Smith (no relation to contemporary economist Vernon Smith) was the author of the highly influential *The Wealth of Nations* (1776). Smith is widely regarded as the most famous advocate of markets with ideas that have shaped subsequent thought for centuries. We will examine his metaphor of the invisible hand in Chapter 8. Although Smith applied the idea of efficiency throughout his writings (and other values as well), it was not until Pareto formalized the notion of efficiency in the early twentieth century that economic theory became so singularly focused on this carefully defined normative and explanatory concept.

The island scenario also includes the implicit background condition that no one else who may live on the island is negatively affected by the trade. For example, if a third person C lives on this island and experiences pollution as a result of the trade between A and B, then the trade no longer creates a Pareto improvement. Someone has been made worse off by the trade. We may think that this result is especially egregious if A and B intended the pollution, and it may be. Those who emphasize the importance of people's *motives* for understanding ethics will take note of A's and B's intentions. The current point, however, is that C can be made worse off by the actions of A and B, whether or not A and B intended or knew about it. This point underscores a connection to be drawn out in the next chapter: efficiency analysis is a consequentialist ethics, which contrasts against other ethical approaches in later chapters.

Whenever parties external to a trade are made worse off by that trade, the market interaction creates a **negative externality**. Negative externalities are spillover effects on people outside a given transaction that make these third parties worse off. An externality may also be *positive* if the spillover effect makes others better off. If a business pollutes the ground water without the knowledge or agreement of the wider community, the harm on that population is a negative externality. (By contrast, if someone plants a beautiful front yard garden that people enjoy seeing, the garden creates a positive externality for those passersby.) The island scenario depicted above assumes that no negative externalities occur as a result of the trade.

Anything else?

What about the *property rights* of A and B? The island scenario includes the implicit condition that property rights are already clearly assigned and respected. If the parties did not recognize each other's powers to transfer and claim-rights to possess, then what would happen? Violence? The extended discussion of markets and property rights in Chapters 1–3 provides rich context for the analysis in this chapter. Those ideas can be inserted into this discussion: efficiency claims about market exchange presume at least an informal recognition of people's property rights.

Reflections about property rights suggest another implicit condition for trade to create efficiency gains: each party must have property rights over something that the other values. If this condition were absent, then the incentives to trade would be absent, as at least one person would have nothing to offer.

Let's now summarize a running list of some of the background conditions necessary to infer that the trade on the island would be Pareto-improving:

SOME BACKGROUND CONDITIONS FOR TRADE TO CREATE EFFICIENCY GAINS

1. People are rational and have coherent preferences that lead to the trade.
2. People have accurate information about the goods to be traded.
3. The transaction costs of trade are relatively low.
4. The trade creates no negative externalities.
5. Property rights that facilitate trade are clearly assigned and respected.
6. Each person owns something that the other values.

This list is not meant to be exhaustive. But it does get us somewhere. Let's take a step back to see. The value of the island scenario is its imagery, which drives us to answer the following question: what assumptions about people and their circumstances are necessary for it to be true that trade really does make people better off? We can characterize the result as an **ideal market**, which refers to all of the idealized conditions of trade necessary to create efficiency gains. We did not simply stipulate or arbitrarily list these assumptions (items 1–6 above.) Rather, we can intuitively derive the underlying reasons for each element in this list, as we did above, by imagining the simple circumstances of trade on an island. We come to know something that is far from self-evident—that is, this list—from a simple process of intuitive reasoning. The island scenario has become an **epistemic device**, an intellectual tool for developing knowledge in a subject area. *Epistemology* is an area of philosophy about the study of knowledge. The generalized significance of the island scenario is that the image helps us derive and identify the background conditions required for markets to create efficiency gains. In other words, the value of the island scenario is the *method of reasoning* that it suggests, and we will see how it guides much dialogue about ethics and markets.[4]

> ## EQUAL DISTRIBUTIONS
>
> To test your understanding of this discussion, consider the following question: is an equal distribution of goods and services a necessary background condition for creating the conditions of an ideal market? To begin this inquiry, consider the possible range of ownership distributions compatible with condition 6. (The answer to the question is *no*, which has led many to emphasize the important normative limits of the concept of efficiency, especially among those who emphasize the value of equality in economic life.)

6.5   HOW ACTUAL MARKETS APPROXIMATE IDEAL MARKETS

Our world is not an island of two people, so how is this example relevant to us? Proponents who advocate markets based on an ideal of efficiency argue that actual markets with all their complications approximate the conditions of the ideal market.[5] Actual markets create incentives for people to act in ways that continually approximate the background conditions identified above. Competition over time incrementally makes actual markets more like the ideal.

---

[4]A remarkable achievement of modern economic thought is a mathematical proof that formalizes these intuitive ideas. This result is called the first welfare theorem of economics. According to this theorem, given a set of premises not unlike those listed above, markets do not merely create Pareto improvements, as suggested above, but they are fully efficient, creating a social state in which *all* mutually advantageous trades are fully realized. The details of this proof are complicated and not relevant for our purposes, but the island example offers an intuitive account of the reasoning behind the proof. Our example depicts direct barter, which may seem unrealistic in relation to contemporary markets. But we could extend the island scenario to introduce a pricing mechanism to yield the same result (that markets with pricing create Pareto improvements). The intuitive idea is that prices convey information that guides people to realize gains from exchange. It's part of the study of economics to consider these arguments.

[5]Unless otherwise indicated in this and the next two chapters, *proponents* or *supporters* refers to those who advocate market institutions *based* on the ideal of efficiency. *Critics* are those who believe that markets create inefficiencies that undermine support for markets. People support and criticize markets on grounds other than efficiency considerations, and then *proponents* and *critics* will refer to a different dialectical position, as we will see in later chapters. The focus on efficiency in these chapters fits into the larger project of taking one value at a time without indicating that efficiency has a privileged normative position in the overall scheme of the ethics and values of business and economic life.

Proponents who advocate markets based on an ideal of efficiency argue that actual markets with all their complications approximate the conditions of the ideal market.

Let's discuss a few examples to illustrate this argument.

First, supporters will argue that markets create incentives to improve the accuracy of information. For example, *Consumer Reports* magazine is a profit-making business that rates products to give readers information about the quality of consumer goods. If people need or want information about products, incentives create markets to provide that information. Online subscriber–based *Angie's List* is a prime example of this phenomenon. More broadly, the Internet is a treasure trove for this information. Consider how the Internet can create tremendous pressures for organizations to become more transparent. People investigate, ask questions, find information, and publicize this information. Market participants react and respond. Even the businesses selling products commonly allow purchasers to publicly rate the product for better or worse.

Besides, if you think *markets* do a poor job with communicating accurate information, check out www.factcheck.org for one running commentary on the misleading and false claims of elected officials and those running for office. For proponents, it's interesting to compare the accuracy of information in markets relative to politics.

Next consider transaction costs. Markets provide incentives to bring buyers and sellers together, lowering transaction costs. The history of commerce is a history of remarkable innovations to lower transaction costs, from Walmart's efficient supply chain to the seamless purchases on eBay and Amazon, or music and movie downloads that were inconceivable a few decades ago. Corporations relentlessly work to improve efficiencies—where the word *efficiencies* now refers to efforts at delivering a given product at the lowest cost—and part of these efforts is to reduce transaction costs whenever possible. The most significant breakthrough that made the fast-food industry what it is today was the concept of *fast*, and this innovation is all about reducing the transaction costs of how long people wait for their meals. Actual markets drive down transaction costs for the same reason that they provide information: when people want information or want lowered transaction costs, others will have the incentive to offer and sell that service.

Let's now consider the first condition on the list. Should I think that I am basically rational? Do you think that you are? (OK, we may have our moments . . .) Isn't it plausible to assume that I am ultimately the best judge of my welfare, and you are of yours? Advocates of the island scenario argue that the conditions are not as idealized and irrelevant as they might first appear.

These arguments support the thesis that people's rational incentives constantly drive actual markets to approximate the background conditions of ideal markets. For proponents, the island scenario primes our observations about how to *see* markets, and the background conditions help us see the amazing versatility of *actual* markets.

Note how the argument so far has two distinct methods of reasoning.

Step 1: Efficiency is an ethical outcome that any social system should achieve.
Markets, ideally conceived, achieve efficiency, so argue its proponents. (The argument is theoretical in the sense that the conclusion does not rely on claims about actual markets. Rather, given a certain set of premises or idealized *background* conditions, it simply follows logically that markets will create efficient gains. The island scenario motivates and invites you to participate in this deductive reasoning.)

Step 2: Actual markets approximate these background conditions. (This argument is empirical and depends on how markets actually work. The method of proof is to witness actual markets and argue inductively that they often attain the background conditions represented by the island scenario.)

In sum, the overall argument is *normative* and *theoretical* in the first step, and *empirical* in the second. Efficiency is good (normative). Ideal markets are efficient (theoretical). Actual markets are mostly efficient (empirical). That's the argument.

This discussion about efficiency, whether you agree or disagree with the argument, also reinforces and illuminates a general structure of ethical reasoning, introduced in debates about corporate responsibility in Chapter 4 Section 5. A proponent defends an institution or personal interactions within that institution because it promotes a particular value—in this case efficiency.

6.6   HOW EFFICIENCY IS A BASIS FOR CRITICIZING MARKETS

Not everyone sees markets in such benign light. We will now examine counterarguments to the analysis offered above.

Peter Ubel, physician and behavioral economist teaching at Duke University's Fuqua School of Business, writes,

> We humans aren't entirely rational creatures. We decide to roll over and hit the snooze button instead of going to the gym, and then we fret over our health insurance payments. We take out home loans we can't possibly afford. We live hours away from our jobs when free time is clearly our most valued asset. All too often our subconscious causes us to act against our own self-interest. (*http://www.peterubel. com/free-market-madness/*)[6]

These human foibles and bad judgments are everywhere. We often prefer what we later regret and what makes us worse off. Ubel writes, "The combination of human nature and free markets can be downright dangerous for our health and well-being" (http://www.peterubel .com/free-market-madness/). Economist Kenneth Galbraith developed this theme in the 1950s with his influential book *The Affluent Society*, arguing that large corporations systematically induce us—through advertising—to want many things that actually do us no good.

Critics contend that, unlike the observations suggested above, the island scenario provides the grounds for showing just what's wrong with actual markets. The real world is a far cry from the conditions of an ideal market. Actual markets systematically fail to achieve the results that advocates so prize because of massive failures to approximate the background conditions listed above.

Let's be clear about where these criticisms are coming from. Some may respond to the efficiency argument for markets with a surge of objections: this island scenario overlooks how people's rights are often violated through actual markets, how a Pareto improvement is consistent with unfairness, how people are systematically discriminated against and treated unequally, how corporations break laws or are complicit in cooperating with unjust political regimes, and many other potential criticisms. This book takes each of these (and other) ideas in turn rather than assesses them all at once. This chapter and the next are about evaluating markets *solely* through a lens of efficiency. After that, other values take center stage, and in that context we address a widening range of support or criticism of business and market activities based on a more comprehensive range of values. For now,

---

[6]Ubel, Peter. 2009. Free Market Madness: Why Human Nature Is at Odds with Economics—and Why It Matters. *Harvard Business Press.*

HOMO ECONOMICUS

Over the last thirty years, many studies have critiqued the empirical assumptions of *homo economicus* ("economic man") based on rational self-interest. Psychologists, biologists, and economists have chipped away at both sides of this claim (that people are rational and that people are self-interested). For example, the joint writings of Daniel Kahneman and Amos Tversky challenged these assumptions across many books and papers, and earned Kahneman a Nobel Prize in economics in 2002.

the question is relatively focused: if we stay within the value of efficiency, should we accept or reject the conclusion that actual markets create efficiency gains, where efficiency is interpreted as an ethical value?

It is this question that sets the context for the criticisms discussed in this section, which have a limited scope but can be powerful if they convince people who believe in efficiency that the market system *does not*, in fact, promote efficiency in the way that they thought.

How is it possible to develop this counterargument? The answer is to take each background assumption and show how it fails to apply within contemporary society, if you believe that this is true. Ubel, Galbraith, and many others emphasize the widespread irrationalities in human decision-making, and they balk at the heroic idealism of a model that assumes that our lives are governed by rational choice. Their reflections pose a question to consider: How rational do you think you and others really are? Remarkably, your answer to this rather *personal* question has significant and direct implications for how you ethically assess markets from an *institutional point of view*. As is often the case in a study of ethics, how we ethically assess institutions, such as businesses and markets, often depends in part on how we assess ourselves as people. Reflecting on the important connections between personal and institutional points of view is a central and recurring theme of this text, first presented in the Introduction, Section 3.

For critics of markets based on efficiency, each of the background assumptions listed above can be challenged across a range of important interactions (See Figure 6.2).

Read the Case Study *Potential Extinction* only on MySearchLab

Consider problems with information. Information failures are an endemic and sometimes dire problem in the modern economic system. The most recent financial crisis was triggered at least in part by bad information: a financial system that bundled highly complex securities in a way that deliberately and successfully hid information about bad assets. Critics will note that people commonly hide information about products if they can get away with it. Deception and fraud, they argue, are prevalent in market life. Critics will

---

FIGURE 6.2   **Testing the Background Assumptions of Trade**

	Assumption	Reality
• People are rational and have coherent preferences that lead to trade	Yes	No
• People have accurate information about the goods to be traded	Yes	No
• The transaction costs of trade are relatively low	Yes	No
• The trade creates no negative externalities	Yes	No
• Property rights that facilitate trade are clearly assigned and respected	Yes	No
• Each person owns something that at least one other person values	Yes	No

✓ Yes provides evidence that actual markets promote efficiency

✗ No provides evidence that actual markets fails to promote efficiency

note that much of the information we receive about products, from the annual reports of corporations to inspection reports about cars, prescription drugs, toys, and food—even the information on our cereal boxes—are not induced by market incentives alone. They are legal mandates that resulted from a history of markets that failed to provide this information, to the detriment of consumers. For example, law requires that companies provide independently verified annual financial reports based on the judgment that markets would not provide this information effectively without those laws. Areas where law does not mandate information often result in a serious lack of information. Consider the pervasive lack of information about something so simple as the quality of services that we so much rely on: the family doctor, the surgeon, the plumber, our financial advisor. We are largely dependent upon word of mouth. These services matter a lot to us and yet we often have very little information about the choices.

Let's turn to negative externalities. The British Petroleum gulf oil spill provides a devastating negative externality that has made hundreds of millions of people worse off, a market failure of massive proportions. Many devastating examples abound, including pollution in the groundwater, acid rain, smog, and the cumulative effects of global warming. More mundane examples proliferate: the loud noise of the factory next door, the tractor trailers on the highways, the ugly landscape of construction and congestion. Some people look out at the world and see markets not as engines for economic growth but engines for creating negative externalities. They see detritus that corporations leave behind big and small; such as when there are harmful products and environmental impacts with negative effects that may not be fully known for generations.

Many critics identify negative externalities as the single leading ethical problem caused by corporate and market activities. They look at the *effects* of markets on the world, and they see harms foisted on unwitting third parties who are made worse off by market transactions.

Now consider problems with property rights around the globe. Ideally, an impartial court system peacefully arbitrates property disputes and creates judgments based on principles of law and justice. But in reality—critics will emphasize—property rights are often contested, ignored, and resolved by violence. Here is one of many horrifying examples:

> The crisis in Darfur, in western Sudan, has led to some of the worst human rights
> abuses imaginable, including systematic and widespread murder, rape, abduction
> and forced displacement. Hundreds of thousands of civilians have died as a result
> of both deliberate and indiscriminate attacks, and more than 2 million civilians have
> been forced to flee from their homes.[7]

This is not the island scenario. In much of the world today, the assumption of a legitimate and stable property system, let alone stable personal rights, does not match reality, and yet stable property rights are a premise of the island exercise. (Are personal rights?—see discussion in Chapter 2 Section 8. What kind?)

And what about those who have nothing to offer? The island scenario assumes that both parties have goods that the other values. But in a world of the unemployed, the disabled, the elderly, and the infant, many people are not in a position to offer goods for exchange in a market. What does a market have to offer to them?

These debates are the source of deep and fundamental disagreements. Many celebrate markets as positive sum games that improve our welfare. They believe, as does Vernon

---

[7]From http://www.eyesondarfur.org/crisis.html, a site maintained by Amnesty International, USA.

Smith, that markets are among the greatest social institutions that humanity has ever devised, and that each of the criticisms listed above has an effective response. Others see exploitation, harm to others, and abandonment. Their analyses lead them to want to contain the influence and role of markets in social life.

We will not pursue each point and counterpoint further here. These remarks simply begin, rather than decisively portray, all the features of this debate. You may wish to investigate and evaluate each claim beyond the brief remarks made here. The remaining sections of this chapter, as well as Chapters 7 and 8, will introduce materials to deepen the analysis, including discussions about the roles of government and one's personal ethics in response to these positions. But the materials presented so far mark a good place to take stock. Which side in this debate do you believe offers the more revealing perspective about whether markets actually function to promote the value of efficiency?

6.7 THE ETHICAL AND PRACTICAL APPEAL OF THE EFFICIENCY STANDARD

The first aim of this chapter is to introduce the value of efficiency and help you participate in the details of a debate about whether markets promote efficiency or not. This section and the next consider a broader perspective about the nature of this debate— what is common to both points of view, and some philosophical puzzles relevant to both positions.

First, consider the following general features of efficiency debates:

A. *Both sides in this debate endorse the value of efficiency.* They aspire to identify a normative ideal as simple and as uncontroversial as possible. They hope to premise the debate on a value that no one really disputes.

B. *The standard of efficiency expresses ethical commitments that draw many people's allegiance.* When we make judgments about the prosperity of a society, what do we care most about? The answer provided by the efficiency standard is that we care most about the **welfare** (or **well-being**) of individual persons within that society. Individual *welfare* or *well-being* refers broadly to what is good for that person's life. These ideas refer to an individual's *being* and whether that person's life has gone well or not. *Happiness* is one way to characterize the nature of our well-being, and this idea can refer to our well-being in the short term or an assessment of an entire life. It seems intuitive to many that what matters for life and for shaping the institutions of society is people's well-being. Efficiency as an ethical idea is grounded in this welfare notion. Pareto improvements are judgments about good outcomes in virtue of improvements in people's well-being. We will examine the ethical implications of this consequentialist approach in the next chapter.

Further, it seems intuitive to many people that ethics should express an ideal of living that is not at other people's expense. Pareto efficiency, with its concept that interactions must not make anyone worse off, conveys that ideal. Part of the enduring appeal of Pareto efficiency, as studied in this chapter, is that *no one* be made worse off by any particular interaction. Thus, Pareto efficiency does not merely endorse the broad *goal* of improving welfare but does so within an ethical *constraint* that it should be to no one's disadvantage. This idea attracts many people. The next chapter considers alternative accounts of efficiency within a utilitarian tradition that addresses questions about how to make trade-offs in the well-being of persons.

C. *If everyone can accept the same underlying value, then debate can focus on empirical questions, which have determinate answers.* A value that can gain everyone's assent is attractive in its own right. But the additional insight that proponents emphasize is that everyone can then focus on empirical disagreements without muddying the waters over irresolvable value disagreements. Efficiency theorists endorse an approach that allows people to bypass thorny value disagreements and focus on ground-level facts about how markets work—or don't work. Whether these debates can actually be reduced to empirical questions is a matter of dispute, as discussed in Section 8 below; but part of the attraction of the efficiency standard is to encourage focus on questions that empirical methods can address. This line of thought helps explain why an efficiency perspective is so prevalent in public policy analysis.

> See Chapter 10 Section 3 for further discussion about the distinction between *goals* and *constraints*. As we will see, Pareto efficiency, though a welfarist notion, shares one commonality with *rights theories*, by virtue of specifying ethical constraints designed to limit how people can pursue their goals.

D. *The efficiency debate suggests a practical method of ethical inquiry.* We begin by specifying a broad ideal of the good—by introducing a concept of efficiency—and we then launch into a debate about *specific observable conditions* for realizing efficiency. By analogy, consider someone who recommends that we *be happy*. Who could disagree with that? But then we need to know tangible activities that can help us achieve happiness, such as creating good relationships or eating well and getting plenty of rest. Some of these ideas are widely accepted; others are controversial. By considering these details we also refine what we *mean* by happiness. These details are crucial to move from a general concept to practical results. Similarly, if we want markets to be efficient, we need to know the tangible conditions that lead to efficiency, such as ample information, no externalities, low transaction costs, and rational decision-making. In this way the island imagery can help clarify both what efficiency *means* and *whether* actual markets realize efficiency. Ethical thought becomes practical by shifting between abstract values and tangible conditions that realize those values. The island scenario develops this method of critical thinking.

E. *An entire range of seemingly disparate issues becomes unified through this debate.* People's irrational impulses, externality problems, information gaps, property relations, ownership, transaction costs—how are all these disparate ideas related? This chapter shows how. We can understand a remarkable range of topics in public policy and applied ethics through this approach. As later chapters will show, not all ethical debates in business and economic life relate to efficiency, and for some people, *most* do not. For example, this discussion hasn't addressed people's motives, characters, nonconsequentialist moral duties, or the importance of other values. Still, there is much insight in being able to interpret people's judgments about markets or capitalism as an expression of some feature within this analysis.

6.8   COMPLICATIONS ABOUT THE MEANING OF EFFICIENCY

Despite these worthy aspirations, the concept of efficiency raises complications that are unavoidable and instructive, both for those who support markets on standards of efficiency and for those who do not. Let's consider two of these complications.

A. THE TANGLED RELATIONSHIP BETWEEN EFFICIENCY, PREFERENCES, AND WELL-BEING

We will examine additional puzzles and limitations about efficiency within the discussion of utilitarianism in Chapter 7.

What does it really mean to say that someone is made *better off* by a trade? A strictly **subjectivist account** of *better-off* answers that question by saying, It's whatever the subject (the person) prefers. Efficiency gains are defined by whatever standards people express through their **preferences** rather than some external standard as defined by others. *Preferences* refer to a person's attitudes and judgments for making choices. These judgments, for example, depend on people's own assessment of their welfare or well-being or happiness, not anyone else's. There is considerable debate about how best to define these ideas, but all subjectivist accounts define *better off* in terms of the subject's own assessments. Subjectivists believe that the attraction to this view is that it places the assessment of one's welfare in the control of the subject whose welfare is at stake and it avoids moralisms about people's choices.

But what if our preferences lead us away from our welfare and well-being? Can't we observe someone who has super-sized his meal just one too many times?[8] Aren't there at least some objective criteria that allow us to say, "You could be better off if you made better choices"? Reflecting on poverty around the world and especially in India, contemporary philosopher Martha Nussbaum, in her book *Women and Human Development: The Capabilities Approach*,[9] attempts to provide an **objectivist account** of improving people's welfare that is not culturally relative or purely subjective.

These concerns prompt an interpretation of *better off* that defines the idea through objective criteria independent from the subject's own assessment. On this view, markets that satisfy preferences but lower that person's objective welfare are not efficient because they are not making people better off.

WELFARE, WELL-BEING, HAPPINESS

Welfare, well-being, or *happiness* of a person occurs when a person experiences what is good for that person, although people apply many nuances in how they use and distinguish these terms. For example, *happiness* often connotes a subjective state of contentment or joy, whereas improvements to one's welfare need not directly connote feelings of contentment often associated with happiness.

An objective account attempts to address one problem that bedevils subjectivist accounts: why advocate efficiency gains if the outcomes do not advance people's welfare? For example, don't we know that many addicted drug users prefer using drugs but are not making themselves better off? (They may know that themselves at some level.) Some argue that we make a fetish out of preferences if we simply stipulate that our every momentary preference advances our well-being. Objectivists argue that for efficiency to be a normative standard that can attract people's allegiance, efficiency gains must be connected in some objective way to improvements in people's objective well-being.

But an objective interpretation introduces an awkward result: we could end up describing markets as inefficient among people who insist that the interactions are exactly what they want. Who has the ethical right or authority to morally judge that the activity isn't really making that person better off? I see a group of friends playing poker, laughing, and blowing off steam. Perhaps I think gambling is morally objectionable. I then assert:

---

[8]Consider the 2003 documentary *Super Size Me* for a graphic display of whether our eating preferences really do make us better off. The documentary claims that corporations and complicit governments make it difficult for individuals to control their own welfare, which is why, according to this view, what we are led to prefer does not necessarily make us better off.

[9]Cambridge University Press, 2000.

the people playing poker are really making themselves worse off by playing that. Suppose I tell them so. They look at me and say . . . (you fill in the blank). This scenario pushes some people to arc back toward a subjective account of welfare grounded in people's actual preferences.

There is no simple or obvious resolution. It's a puzzle. We could interpret *better off* and *worse off* from a purely subjective point of view (as immediate preferences) or from an objective point of view (in terms of some account of objective well-being). Or we could try to develop some hybrid version of both accounts (see the Discussion Questions for one hybrid idea developed by Scottish philosopher Adam Smith).

Let's illustrate these complications with a market example from the discussion earlier in this chapter. Let's say that A and B want to trade but this trade would hurt the feelings of C. Is that trade a negative externality for C just because it hurts his feelings, no matter the reason? This is the implication of a purely subjective interpretation of *better off* and *worse off*; for in that case, *any* preference against a trade by a third party would imply an inefficiency.

But that would reduce all practical appeal to the concept, as there is very little in life that *someone* won't object to, however slight or off-base. This point seems to create a dead-end for a purely subjectivist interpretation of *better off* and *worse off* for assessing market trades. So let's try a more objective criterion. For example, perhaps a negative externality occurs only if someone is *harmed* or *wronged* by the trade, or if someone's *rights* are violated, independently of what that person prefers. Thus, on this view, an oil spill causes harm and thereby creates a negative externality but someone who merely prefers that a trade be blocked (for no particular reason) does not generate a negative externality.

The implication, however, is that the concept of efficiency now depends on other moral ideas, such as an account of harm or the nature of human rights. These objectivist accounts would make efficiency, like any interesting ethical idea, much more complicated and controversial. This isn't necessarily a problem, but this approach would undermine the original hope of identifying an uncontroversial ethical standard.

We may therefore be tempted to return again to a subjective account to retain the simplicity of the value. But other concerns become apparent: subjective preferences include bizarre, envious, or repulsive preferences. Some people want to harm, torture, and destroy. Should a normative account of efficiency include these preferences and count their satisfaction as an efficiency gain? Many think not. Thus, a subjective interpretation of welfare becomes as controversial as an objective account that builds on other moral ideas.

We have now re-created the original puzzle in the context of analyzing negative externalities: there is no easy way to interpret what *better off* means without introducing counterintuitive implications. Reflecting carefully on the meaning of efficiency inevitably introduces controversies.

The aim of this discussion is not to confuse or undermine the concept of efficiency. Ethical concepts are more like invitations to explore a set of issues than rote definitions to memorize and apply. A concept contains its own logic of analysis that guides people to ask questions without providing all the answers. *At the heart of the concept of efficiency is the need to interpret what it means to make people better off.* This chapter does not stipulate a resolution. There are many interesting attempts, suggested by the remarks above, that are part of a broad philosophical debate about subjective versus objective accounts of well-being and welfare.

The discussion of relativism in Chapter 3 Section 7 can be related to the distinction between subjectivist and objectivist accounts of welfare. In particular, people who are skeptical that an objective account of welfare can be defended often fall back to a subjectivist interpretation of welfare. But subjectivism about welfare need not imply relativism about ethics. Can you explain why?

What does it mean to be made better off from a market exchange? Your own intuitive answers are the place to start. They can be sufficient for answering your questions; or you may find puzzles that require further distinctions and refinement, depending on the kinds of market exchanges that you are assessing.

Gross National Happiness

These philosophical debates are also relevant for understanding the prospects and limits of gross domestic product (GDP) as a measure of a nation's well-being. For example, GDP measures the accumulation of goods and services without attempting to measure the positive and negative impacts that they create. In 1972 Bhutan king Jigme Singye Wangchuck coined an alternative *gross national happiness* (GNH) index based on Buddhist principles, and these ideas maintain a following today. Many commentators question the GDP methods by which most nations measure overall economic improvement in the life of its citizens, although there is no consensus about a workable alternative.

B. The Difference between Welfare and Consent

Suppose we see two people trade and we say, "This is a good outcome." Question: What makes it good? This chapter answers that they were made better off by the trade. But a different answer is, "The trade expresses their *freedom* to decide as they wish." One way to deepen an understanding of efficiency is to contrast the ideal against another. Suppose A is unknowingly hypnotized and induced to trade with B. After A wakes up, he realizes that the trade improves his life dramatically. He objects that the trade was not voluntary and did not express his will but he grants that he is made much better off by the result. An unlikely event, but it serves to illustrate the point that efficiency and consent are not identical concepts. For A, the trade creates an efficiency gain under conditions that lacked consent.

Some people describe desperate exchanges, such as selling one's kidney for money, as an efficiency gain—the trade wouldn't have occurred if the seller didn't believe it would make him better off, and perhaps it does. But this conclusion can be distinct from the further judgment that the trade occurs against the backdrop of compromised freedom, given the desperate circumstances. This discussion offers one insight for future chapters: it's possible to grant that an efficiency gain occurs but still criticize the outcome based on other values. Drawing on ideas first presented in the Introduction, we may believe that the consequentialist analysis of this chapter must be balanced against non-consequentialist considerations as well, including ideas such as our freedom and consent, our motives, and our character. Further, we may wonder whether a focus on efficiency presumes an overly individualistic perspective that undermines an ethics of care or the pursuit of a common good. This is all fair game.

Where do these broader thoughts about competing values leave us? Consider a dialogue about the ethics of the market system. Among those who find the concept of efficiency sufficiently clear and compelling, the structure of the debate will be guided by empirical questions. Where are the externalities and what should be done about them? What are the incentives to increase information and lower transaction costs? Efficiency guides so much public debate about markets and capitalism *because* the analysis tries to keep the arguments ethically uncontroversial with a focus on empirical questions. This approach may lead you to business, economics, and other disciplines in the social sciences. These disciplines pursue empirical questions often against the normative backdrop provided in this and the next two chapters.

The dialogue may take a different direction, however. We may become interested in conceptual and ethical complications at the heart of these disagreements, or we may wish to emphasize other values for ethics. The debates shift away from empirical details and focus on a larger range of values, which, we may believe, better captures our moral perspective. This dialogue may lead you to the philosophy discipline.

We will consider other values and ethical approaches in Chapters 9–15, but there is still much insight to be gained from elaborating an efficiency analysis for ethics, the subject of the next chapter.

6.9   SUMMARY

Do markets and capitalism create efficiency gains? This chapter introduced some tools for answering this question, including the concept of Pareto efficiency, its application to market exchange, and a discussion of the background conditions that either support or undermine efficiency. The next two chapters introduce additional tools to advance the discussion and draw out implications for professional ethics. Two background conditions that greatly influence ethics and public policy are public goods and commons problems, the subjects of the next chapter.

KEY TERMS

Pareto improvement or efficiency gain
Pareto optimality or fully efficient
positive sum game
instrumental rationality

transaction costs
negative externality
ideal markets
epistemic device
welfare / well-being

subjectivist accounts of welfare
preferences
objectivist accounts of welfare

DISCUSSION QUESTIONS

1. Some say that advertising increases the efficiency of markets; others say that it decreases their efficiency. Explain the basis for these conflicting interpretations.
2. Suppose that someone buys an iPad but later learns that it was available for a lower price online. Was the original purchase a Pareto improvement?
3. Which statement offers the greater insight?:
   a. The great flaw of markets is that they leave people behind. Worse, they offer nothing to people who have, often through no fault of their own, nothing to bring to markets.
   b. The great contribution of markets is not merely trade for mutual benefit but that they create positive externalities by raising standards of living for everyone, even those who do not participate in markets.
4. Milton Friedman famously wrote that firms have no responsibilities except to maximize profits within the law, but he also wrote that they must do so without deception or fraud. Use the analysis of this chapter to analyze why he might have qualified his view in this way.
5. Consider two allegories:
   • The first sees a world that begins with unchecked violence and, through a long evolutionary road, markets develop that check people's brutal self-interest to conform to reciprocal moral relations. Human civilization progressed by people seeking mutually beneficial trade through markets.
   • The second sees a world initially populated by familial peace and communal harmony with no private property, the condition of Adam and Eve before the Fall. Then came possessions and ownership, as humanity walked into dissension, inquisitiveness, violence, and alienation from each other and the natural world. With private property

came markets, abetting and stoking the violence and possessiveness that has defined our human history.

On one allegory of humanity, violence comes first and then the pacifying effects of commerce; on the other, communal harmony comes first and then a history of violence abetted by the drive to gain through trade. Which vision has the greater insight?

6. As early as the 1700s, enlightenment philosophers Adam Smith and David Hume wrestled with subjective or objective interpretations of welfare from an ethical perspective. They introduced a concept of an *ideal observer*, which can be applied to the current discussion. In judging whether someone is made better off by an activity, we count the agent's own preferences about the activity—but only those preferences that the individual would have endorsed with a calm and reflective disposition. The hope is to maintain a subjective perspective to some degree but also to introduce a mechanism to discriminate between rash and reasonable preferences. What are the prospects of this approach as a middle way between subjective and objective interpretations of welfare?

7. Consider the blocked exchanges that we discussed in Chapter 1, on markets. Are they blocked because society has judged that those trades do not or would not really make us better off (which implies an objective interpretation of welfare)? Or is it that they *would* make us better off (subjectively or objectively interpreted) but that there are *other* goals beyond welfare that explain and justify these limits? Take a few examples and assess.

8. Corporations can be interpreted to create both negative and positive externalities. In practical terms, which types of externalities are most important for understanding corporate responsibilities?

9. Many people argue that government engages in wasteful spending; and many people argue that the U.S. health care system is inefficient. Use the concepts in this chapter to explain what those ideas could mean.

10. In your view what form(s) of government are compatible with realizing the ideal of efficiency, as introduced in this chapter?

11. Analyze the housing market crisis using the concepts of this chapter. Does the crisis lend more support to one or another side of the debates in this chapter?

7

PUBLIC GOODS AND THE UTILITARIAN TRADITION

WHEN YOU FINISH
STUDYING THIS CHAPTER,
YOU SHOULD BE ABLE TO:

1. Define what a public good is.

2. Characterize public goods and commons problems and apply these ideas across a range of topics in business ethics.

3. Discuss the prospects and limits to utilitarianism as an account of ethics.

7.1 INTRODUCTION

Some human interactions do not work out the way we plan. For example:

> *Police said two burglars struck a Texas store that sells high-end security equipment, and the whole thing was caught on tape by 17 cameras rolling in the store.*[1]

(http://stupidcriminalfile.blogspot.com/)

> *An attempted drive-by shooting was stopped when the shooter forgot to roll down his window. . . .*

(http://www.dumbcriminals.com/; original story at http://blogs .citypages.com/blotter/2009/11/wis_man_attempt.php)

The *News of the Weird* (http://www.newsoftheweird.com/) provides other similar portraits of humanity. Best laid plans of mice and men often go awry.[2] These humorous examples introduce a distinction to clarify the aims of this chapter. Sometimes people make poor choices because they think things through poorly. They may have a dim understanding of their circumstances, pursue their goals counterproductively, or have intentions and

---

[1] © NBC Universal.
[2] This saying is adapted from a poem *To a Mouse* (1785) by Robert Burns and was the inspiration for the title of John Steinbeck's *Of Mice and Men*.

motivations that are odd or destructive. In this chapter, we will not consider these sorts of defects. Rather, we will consider people who are *instrumentally rational*, in the sense that they are good at reasoning and thinking through the best means for achieving their goals (see Chapter 6 Section 4). Here is the puzzle of the chapter: We will study how people like this—people who have no particular defects in reasoning—can nonetheless wind up nowhere, or make themselves and those around them worse off through their interactions with others.

See Chapter 6 Section 2 for an extended discussion of efficiency as an ethical concept.

This distressing outcome can occur within markets. **Market failures** happen when seemingly rational people fail to achieve mutual benefit when they could have or, even worse, when they make their lives worse off along the way. How could this be? It's not difficult to explain how poor decision-making can make people worse off. We've all probably been there at some point in our lives. But, in this chapter, let's consider how bad outcomes can occur when we are at our best: when we are smart, know our best interests, and are very good at pursuing them. It is puzzling and revealing to see how markets and voluntary actions can create **inefficiencies** under these circumstances, which means that people fail to reach mutually beneficial gains when they could have.

This chapter analyzes some amazing and influential puzzles and paradoxes of human interaction. Among the range of potential market failures, we will focus on two situations in some depth: *public goods* and *commons* problems, to be defined below. We will study how these problems unlock mysteries of social interaction and reveal the underlying genesis of a range of challenges and arguments about business ethics, corporate responsibility, and the proper role of markets and government in social life.

The Introduction, Section 4B offers an overview of consequentialist and deontological ethical theories.

The normative ideal of Pareto efficiency studied in the previous chapter is an especially useful concept for understanding these puzzles. But this concept of efficiency has its own limitations as a normative guide. We consider these limitations, beyond those discussed in the last chapter, and then recast efficiency discussions within a broader utilitarian and consequentialist ethical tradition. These last sections reinforce how the ethical focus for Chapters 6–8 is generally a consequentialist ethical perspective, which will be contrasted in later chapters by a focus on deontological perspectives.

7.2 PUBLIC GOODS

We begin with simple ideas to reach a startling conclusion by the end of the next section. *Goods* are typically tangible things that people value, such as cars, and *services* tend to be intangible things that people value, such as babysitting. In the pages that follow, we will call goods and services simply *goods*, although this word will always imply both goods and services.

Many of the goods that I own or could imagine are **private goods**: I can exclude others from their benefits and the benefit I derive from the goods reduces others' ability to benefit. For example, the point of me having my car key is so that I can enforce my exclusive claim-right to operate my car, and when I am driving, no one else can drive my car—unless someone steals it, which underscores the point that legally enforced private property rights most often serve to protect owners' private goods.

A separate class of goods, however, displays interesting characteristics that differ from private goods. When they exist, no one can be excluded from enjoying the benefit of these goods (nonexcludability), and one person benefiting from the good does not reduce anyone else's ability to benefit from that good (nonrivalry). Any goods that have these characteristics are called **public goods**.

Can you identify any public goods? They include streetlights and fire protection, national defense and highways, a noninfectious healthy population, clean air, a great variety of information, weather forecasts, and the Public Broadcasting Station, supported by viewers just like you. There are many more.

The definition of *public* or *private* is often a matter of degree. Actual goods often take on public or private characteristics at some points in time and lose them in others. For example, a local park is typically a public good, although if a festival occurs with an admission fee, the park loses the characteristic of nonexcludability during that festival, as those who do not pay can be excluded from entering. Alternatively, if so many people visit the park that no space remains and there is a waiting line, the park will lose the characteristic of nonrivalry because one person's use of the park reduces the ability of others to enter, until people leave.

> The broader idea about what is good for the public is also typically called the *common good* of society. In Chapter 14, we will examine this idea and consider the relationship between a society's common good and the presence of public goods in that society.

To take another example, roads are usually public goods, because we are rarely excluded from using them and my driving on a road does not typically reduce the ability of someone else to drive on that very same road. But like many real-life examples, roads do not always display public good characteristics. Some roads are toll roads, for example, which implies that drivers can be excluded if they don't pay a toll, and at other times roads can become so congested that rivalry sets in, as highway drivers crawling at five miles per hour on congested beltways can unfortunately attest. There are many further nuances and distinctions that we could make for describing the nature of the goods of a society (but we won't). Instead, we can convey the first key idea of the chapter: public goods are different from private goods and they are all around us.

The point so far is merely to *describe* actual or potential goods. There is no implicit normative claim that public goods by definition are better or worse than private goods. In common speech, we sometimes use the phrase *public good* to convey the broad normative idea of anything that we judge to be good for the public, but in this chapter the phrase does not have this broad meaning. Public goods are simply goods that have the characteristics of nonexcludability and nonrivalry, and they contrast against the characteristics of private goods, which are excludable and rival.

> Property relationships have the capacity to create peace and order if people conduct their daily affairs against a backdrop of stable expectations. A society that creates peace and order creates a public good. See Chapters 2 and 3 for discussion of property relationships.

We rely on so many public goods that their discussion touches on many aspects of social and economic life, including their role in debates about ethics and corporate responsibility. These practical applications explain why we are focusing on the topic.

Work life can be rewarding or miserable depending on the general culture of trust or distrust. Trust is often a type of a public good.

A clean downtown, a violence-free community, an attractive countryside, the state of knowledge in society: the things in life that you value and receive benefit from, that you don't have to pay for, and that you enjoy that doesn't reduce others' ability to enjoy—these are public goods.

We may now notice that the island scenario depicted in the last chapter presumes that the tradable goods on the island are all private goods, an assumption that can easily go unnoticed and can be added to the running list of background conditions described in Chapter 6 Section 4.

We are now ready to pose a leading question: how do various public goods get produced? This question raises a puzzling challenge.

In the last chapter, the island scenario depicted how markets in *private goods* can create gains through trade. A and B trade private goods because rational self-interest provides an incentive for personal gain. Rather than depicting water and food, we could more realistically imagine employees who work for a business that produces food. The logic of interaction is the same: personal incentives drive people to work, they create goods that people buy, and all of this activity could create efficiency gains. Both the labor contract that defines the terms of work and the final sales of the firm's product are exchanges in private goods. Thus, the island scenario can also illustrate how production of private goods is possible.

What special problem could arise if the desire is to produce not a private good but a public good?

Consider: If no one can be excluded from a good once it exists, then the provision of public goods can create a **free-riding problem**. People can enjoy the benefits without paying any costs because no one can be excluded from receiving its benefits. A *free-rider* refers to an individual who enjoys the benefits of an activity without paying the costs. Free-riding can be instrumentally rational: it's better to enjoy the benefits without paying for it, if that is possible, compared to paying for that benefit. If that is true, then how will the public good get produced if everyone wants to free-ride off its benefits rather than pay for its creation?

An example can deepen the analysis, revealing a paradox of human interaction with remarkable application. Many describe the puzzle in these terms: individual rationality can lead people not to contribute to the creation of a public good even when those same individuals know that they would be better off if they did. How can it be rational to make choices that worsen our situation? The puzzles ahead are directly about the limits of markets and our personal interactions for creating efficiency gains, but they are indirectly about the very concept of rational decision-making.

7.3   Two Neighborhoods and a Park: A Public Goods Problem

The following example simplifies a public goods situation but its purpose is to reveal an underlying logic of interaction that occurs in many more complicated real-life scenarios. We will walk through the details of this example step by step. Although simplified, the example is designed to be challenging. The payoff for working through this example carefully is to develop an insider's understanding of the nature of public goods problems.

Suppose two neighborhoods, X and Y, each have an initial pot of $100,000 and a choice to keep the money or contribute this amount to the creation of a park in between the neighborhoods. See Figure 7.1. (You can substitute another public good and different

---

FIGURE 7.1   **Illustrating a Public Goods Problem**

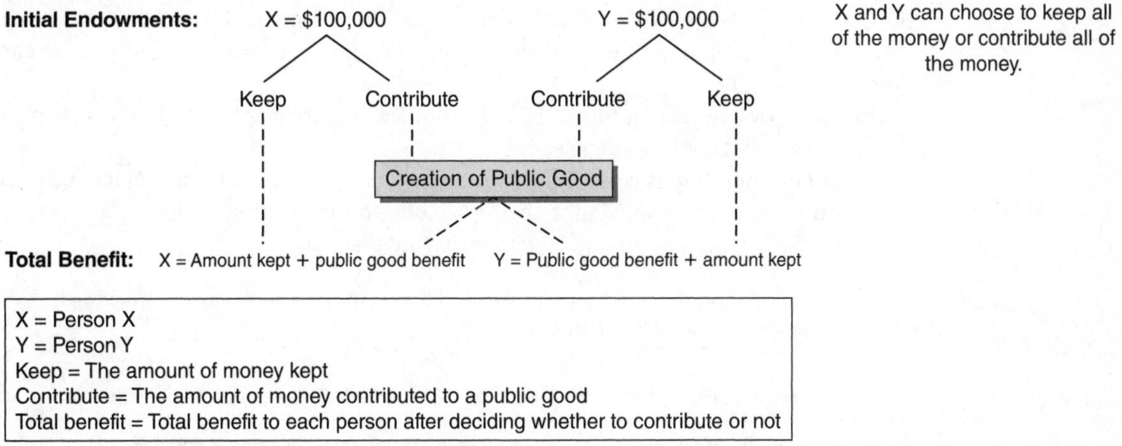

Initial Endowments: X = $100,000   Y = $100,000   X and Y can choose to keep all
of the money or contribute all of
the money.

         Keep   Contribute   Contribute   Keep

                          Creation of Public Good

Total Benefit: X = Amount kept + public good benefit   Y = Public good benefit + amount kept

> X = Person X
> Y = Person Y
> Keep = The amount of money kept
> Contribute = The amount of money contributed to a public good
> Total benefit = Total benefit to each person after deciding whether to contribute or not

numbers into this example if you want, as the exercise does not depend on any specific public good chosen.)

Let's assume that the city stipulates that the park cannot be a private good for either neighborhood. That is, no one from either neighborhood can be excluded from this park if it comes to exist. There are only two relevant parties, neighborhood X and neighborhood Y, and the neighborhoods are similarly situated with nothing else unusual about them. The choice for each neighborhood is to contribute nothing or contribute all $100,000 to build the park. We could increase the number of neighborhoods and vary the levels of contribution to create the same results. These assumptions simply make the exercise in the text easier to follow.

The park will come to exist only if one or both neighborhoods contribute money to the public good. The benefit would be people's experiences playing in the park. To get an idea of the value of the benefit for each neighborhood, we can ask: How much would people be willing to pay to have that park if it existed? In this example, let's assume that the benefit to each neighborhood depends on how nice the park is, and this will depend on the level of contributions. For example, if both neighborhoods contribute their $100,000, let's assume that the resulting park would be worth $150,000 to each neighborhood, summing up its worth for all individuals in the neighborhood. This would mean that the value of the park to each neighborhood is greater than the value of their original endowment. The neighborhoods do not literally receive $150,000 if the park comes to exist. Rather, we imagine that the neighborhood members would experience their well-being improve so much by the park that they report that they would be willing to pay amounts of money that aggregated together add up to $150,000.

Finally, if only one neighborhood contributes to the building of the park, let's suppose that the smaller ill-funded venture creates a benefit to each neighborhood of $75,000. That is, this number conveys the amount of enjoyment that each neighborhood would get from this smaller park, measured by the amount that neighborhood members would be willing to pay in the aggregate for that smaller park.

Recall that if the public good comes to exist, no one can be excluded from its benefits; each neighborhood will experience the benefit whether or not that neighborhood contributes. By contrast, the original sum of $100,000 is a private good, the exclusive possession of each neighborhood.[3] Finally, we can imagine that each neighborhood has a leader who is representing that neighborhood's interests. We are abstracting away from disagreements among neighbors, so we are assuming that no one within either neighborhood objects to the creation of this park. We will consider more realistic scenarios later, but by allowing these ideas for the moment we make the result even more surprising. (Can you see the problem already?)

Let's start by contrasting the decision to contribute to the public good versus keeping the money and not contributing. See Figure 7.2.

If both neighborhoods contribute, then the public good benefit to each neighborhood is $150,000. They each contributed their $100,000 to the creation of the park, and now they are experiencing $150,000 in benefit by having that park.

FIGURE 7.2	Illustrating a Public Goods Problem (continued)

Suppose that X and Y each benefit from the public good by the amount of: ¾ multiplied by the sum of the contributions

If both X and Y contribute their endowment, then
the public good = ¾ ($200,000) = $150,000   ⟹

Therefore, the total benefit to X and Y =
X = Amount kept + public good benefit
   = $0   + $150,000   = $150,000

Y = Amount kept + public good benefit
   = $0   + $150,000   = $150,000

If both X and Y keep their endowment, then
the public good = ¾ (0) = 0   ⟹

X = Amount kept + public good benefit
   = $100,000   + $0   = $100,000

Y = Amount kept + public good benefit
   = $100,000   + $0   = $100,000

POINT: Contributing to the public good project is a Pareto improvement over keeping the endowment.

Question: What will rational self-interested people do?

To answer this question, let's look at the choice situation from X's perspective:

If Y keeps, what is X's best move? X has two options:
→ If X contributes, then the payoff is $0 + ¾ ($100,000) = $75,000
→ If X keeps, then the payoff is $100,000 + ¾ ($0) = $100,000

Thus, X's best move, if Y keeps, is for X to keep.

If Y contributes, what is X's best move? X has two options:
→ If X contributes, then the payoff is $0 + ¾ ($200,000) = $150,000
→ If X keeps, then the payoff is $100,000 + ¾ ($100,000) = $175,000

Thus, X's best move, if Y contributes, is for X to keep.

POINT: No matter what Y does, X's best move is to keep. Y will reason in the exact same way. (You may wish to prove this to yourself.) Therefore, voluntary actions will lead to both X and Y to keep their endowment, which is Pareto inferior to both endowments. Market incentives will fail to promote efficiency.

---

[3]This example is making assertions about the neighborhoods' preferences that, taken together, will lead to a puzzle. Later, we will discuss whether those preferences are realistic and argue that they do represent the types of preferences that create public goods problems across many varied interactions.

- -

If both neighborhoods keep their money, then the public good benefit is $0. The park does not exist. But they each retain their original $100,000.

First result: Contributing to the park makes both neighborhoods better off from their own points of view. They would each receive $150,000 in park benefit once the park exists, which is better than the original $100,000 that each currently holds.

What could be more obvious than the following statement: if they were rational and following their self-interests, they would each contribute to the park. Joint production creates a Pareto improvement.

What will they do?

Argument: They won't contribute to the park and the project will fall through. I am now going to try to prove this to you.

Let's examine X's decision-making. X (or X's representative leader) understands that the other neighborhood, Y, has two options: either keep its money or contribute to the park.

So X asks, "What is our best decision *if Y keeps its money*? In that case, we could either contribute to the park or also keep our money. If we contribute to the park when they don't, then we receive a benefit of $75,000. Disappointing. The public benefit would be the result of our contributions only. The lesser total contribution creates a smaller, less valuable park.

But there is another option. If we do not contribute to the park when Y doesn't, then the park is not created at all. The downside is that we receive no benefit from a park, but we retain our original $100,000.

So what should we do if Y does not contribute to the park? What is our best decision? Answer: Do not contribute to the park either, because $100,000 in hand is better than the lesser park benefit of $75,000 to our neighborhood members.

So now we ask, What is our best decision *if Y contributes to the park*? As before, we could either contribute to the park, or keep our money.

If we contribute to the park when Y does, then we pay our $100,000 and receive a benefit of $150,000. This outcome repeats the calculation above when the relatively larger park is built through both contributions.

However, if we keep the money in the face of Y's contribution, then our total benefit is our original $100,000 *plus* the benefit of a park that Y creates, which would yield us an additional benefit of $75,000. Having the original $100,000 plus the benefit of the smaller park is the best case scenario because it creates a total benefit of $175,000 for X.

Thus, our best decision if Y contributes is not to contribute to the park, as a $175,000 benefit is better than a $150,000 benefit.

Second (paradoxical) result: No matter what Y decides to do, X's best decision is to keep the original $100,000 and not contribute to the park. Y will apply the same logic and make the same decision (you might try to prove this to yourself). Thus, X and Y will choose not to contribute to the park even though they both know that contributing to the park would create an efficiency gain across the neighborhoods. In the face of providing public goods, rational self-interested people will fail to promote efficiency, even when they know that creating the public good will make them both better off.

This result is so astounding that it may seem to be a trick of the example. Let's redescribe the puzzle using a different representation.

| FIGURE 7.3 | Illustrating a Public Goods Problem Using a Game Theoretic Diagram |

Y

		Contribute		Keep	
		Benefit to X	Benefit to Y	Benefit to X	Benefit to Y
X	Contribute	$150,000	$150,000	$75,000	$175,000
	Keep	$175,000	$75,000	$100,000	$100,000

X = Person X
Y = Person Y
Contribute = Amount of money that a person contributes to a public good
Keep = Amount of money that a person keeps

Figure 7.3 summarizes the results of the example. The four boxes represent the range of outcomes that X and Y could choose. If they both contribute and build the park (the upper-left box), then their individual benefit is $150,000 each. The first number in the box represents the benefit to X and the second number the benefit to Y. If both keep the money (the lower-right box), their benefit is $100,000. Thus, contributing is an efficiency gain over keeping their money.

We can now use Figure 7.3 to redescribe the dilemma. This time, let's take Y's point of view and follow the reasoning within the diagram. Y can either contribute or keep, depending on what X chooses. If X keeps, then Y will keep too, because $100,000 is a greater payoff than $75,000. If X contributes, then Y will keep, because $175,000 is a better payoff than $150,000. Thus, no matter what X chooses, Y's best move is to keep, even though Y knows that if they both contribute, they are each better off than if they both keep.

LET'S NOW GENERALIZE THE PROBLEM

Let the numbers in Figure 7.4 represent preferences over outcomes. X and Y represent individual persons. The higher number means that the agent, according to his or her values, prefers this situation to any situation with a lower number. Thus, person X most prefers a situation where person Y foots the entire bill for the public good (represented by the number "4"), and least prefers paying for the entire cost of the public good (represented by the number "1").

People can find themselves seemingly trapped in public goods problems under the following general circumstances. First, the parties realize that cooperating in the provision of a public good is personally advantageous over the public good not existing. But the individual also realizes that if the other person will contribute to create the public good, the very best situation is to let that person contribute and enjoy the benefits without making a contribution. And the very worst situation is to contribute without the other contributing, shouldering the entire burden of contribution with the other person free-riding off this contribution. Whenever these judgments describe the preferences of

| FIGURE 7.4 | Generalizing the Conditions That Create a Public Goods Problem |

	Y			
	Contribute		Keep	
	Benefit to X	Benefit to Y	Benefit to X	Benefit to Y
Contribute	3	3	1	4
X				
Keep	Benefit to X	Benefit to Y	Benefit to X	Benefit to Y
	4	1	2	2

X = Person X
Y = Person Y
Contribute = Amount of money that a person contributes to a public good
Keep = Amount of money that a person keeps

agents in a given choice situation, human interaction can lead to these paradoxical and beguiling results.

Why do dishes build up in the sink among a group of roommates? Here's one intriguing explanation: everyone knows that they are better off with a clean sink than a dirty sink. But what each most wants is a clean sink that someone else cleans, and what each most does not want is a clean sink that only that person cleans! The result: a dirty sink.

Why do common rooms get dirty in the workplace? Why do people break rules that they also rely on others to follow? Why does government provide for national defense, highways, and many other services?

Consider applying the fascinating logic of this section to describe what is happening in these examples. **Public goods problems** occur whenever rational self-interest creates incentives for people not to produce a public good that will make all the parties better off. The general form of the puzzle is often called a *prisoner's dilemma*, named after American mathematician Albert Tucker's famous analysis, which pitted two hypothetical prisoners against each other in a way that illustrated the paradoxical logic of this problem. These problems are also called **collective action problems** or (*social dilemmas*), as they identify unfortunate outcomes that occur through the collective action of what seem to be the rational self-interested actions of individuals. These are situations where multiple persons would each be made better off by some joint action, and yet it's individually rational for each person to choose against this joint action.

In sum, it appears that individual rationality can lead people to make choices that are *collectively irrational* in the sense that people could create a Pareto improvement but they choose not to. The situation is paradoxical because it appears to be rational to interact in ways that directly create an *irrational* outcome.

What do you think? How do you analyze what's going on?

The relevance and application of social dilemmas for understanding business and economic behavior is hard to overestimate. So many ethical puzzles in life and in the business setting relate to human interactions that create social dilemmas. Taking the time to really understand and investigate the logic of this dilemma can unlock what otherwise are mysteries of social interaction.

7.4   THE TRAGEDY OF THE COMMONS

In 1968, ecologist Garret Hardin published an essay called "The Tragedy of the Commons" and the phrase has stuck.[4] Similar to public goods problems, people have long understood that a **commons** can cause problems too, sometimes with tragic consequences. Hardin clarified the analysis and generalized the results to a discussion of population growth and other topics.

Imagine an open pasture—a commons area—that anyone in a village could use to feed their animals. Like a public good, no one is excluded from its benefits, including the grasses that the animals eat. But unlike the characteristic of a public good, the commons area is depletable—one person's consumption can reduce everyone else's consumption. The cows can permanently destroy the grass before it has time to regenerate. This combination of characteristics that define a commons—nonexcludability but depletability—sets a stage for potentially tragic outcomes.

Can you produce the logic of the reasoning? If each person is instrumentally rational and self-interested, he will graze his animals because the animals need to eat. But if everyone grazes their animal in an unrestricted way, it's quite possible that the commons will deplete, the grass will die, and then the animals will starve. Everyone is made tragically worse off. Let's place ourselves in the dilemma. What should I do as a rational self-interested individual? Answer: no matter what my neighbors decide, I am better off grazing my animal. If my neighbors do not graze, then the commons will not deplete and I can take advantage of the good grass for my animals. If my neighbors do let their animals graze, then a little grass for my animals with whatever remains is better than none at all, so I'd better get my animals out there to capture whatever remains of the commons. Everyone applies the same reasoning. As Hardin says, "Freedom in a commons brings ruin to all." Human interaction can lead to the total depletion of the commons.

Some of the greatest corporate environmental challenges today relate to the problems of the commons. Global warming is commonly analyzed as a commons problem. Pollution in the atmosphere and seas, overfishing, and destruction of coral reefs are typically described as commons problems. The extinction of species by hunting is often modeled as a commons problem. Can you explain how these examples can be modeled as commons problems? They are similar to public goods problems by creating the conditions of a social dilemma, but they are even more pernicious, as people can voluntarily choose to worsen their situations by permanently depleting a resource, even when they know that another set of choices—to preserve the resource—would make them all better off.

Public goods and commons problems offer a direct challenge to the island scenario introduced in the last chapter. Here's how. That argument presumed that all relevant goods are private goods. But there are public goods and commons areas that we value. The problem is that markets and their incentives do not appear to encourage an efficient production of these goods. The argument is not that the production of *every* desirable public good or commons area creates a social dilemma or that people do not or cannot find ways to overcome these problems. In fact, a study across cultures and history offers a rich set

---

[4]Hardin, Garrett. "The Tragedy of the Commons" *Science*, 162(1968):1243-1248.

of materials for considering how societies historically and culturally have addressed these potentially difficult interactions.

But even with these qualifications, the argument still has force: In both our personal interactions and in the design of political and commercial institutions, we can find our-selves in the middle of seemingly innocuous interactions that lead to bad social outcomes; and understanding what the problem is can be a first step in solving it. Dealing with goods that are nonexcludable and agents who act in their rational self-interest are core features required to trigger the problem. The examples above can guide your further thinking about additional conditions required to create these dilemmas.

Commons problems, like public goods problems, create *deep* problems of human interaction. They prompt many different responses and many potential solutions. Let's consider a few of these.

7.5 ETHICAL MOTIVES, GOVERNMENT REGULATION, PROPERTY RIGHTS, AND CORPORATE RESPONSIBILITY

A great deal of scholarship and public policy attempts to find remedies to public goods and commons problems as they relate to business.

A. THE PERSONAL POINT OF VIEW: ETHICAL MOTIVES AND SOCIAL NORMS

In her article "Business Ethics in a Competitive Market," scholar Julianne Nelson argues that in the face of market failures, people have a duty of civility to work with others to remedy or avoid these inefficiencies.[5] Nelson joins others who analyze public goods and commons problems fundamentally as ethical failures in people's motivations. People must learn to work better together. For example, in the cattle grazing case above, people should develop rules of fairness to divvy up grazing time so that every cow has her chance (and bulls, too) but in a way that the grasses regenerate. Historically, communities have often figured out how to pre-serve the commons through these social norms. It may seem that public goods and commons problems are easy to analyze: they are the outcomes of selfish attitudes and greed.

On this view, our rationality is not the problem. It's our motives that define our self-interests. We ought to develop social norms that foster cooperation in the face of these dilemmas and disavow the narrow interests that create these dilemmas. People should see exploiting the commons as a *wrong* to be avoided. One of the objectives of the Green movement, for example, is to create ethical norms of preservation that have the effect of protecting a fragile environment that is continually subject to tragedies of the commons.

Critics of this approach point out difficulties in this analysis as an accurate diagnosis or viable solution to the problem. For example, recall the poor peasant facing a commons problem in the cow pasture. Should the peasant refrain from the commons and starve? Is it greedy to want to survive? Peasants need to feed their families. They do not want to contribute to the ensuing tragedy. But they know that if they do not feed their animals in the commons, someone else will, so should they let their family starve by not using the commons at all? It doesn't appear that the motives need to be at all greedy for the tragedy to result. Can't it be unfair to ethically judge people in this dilemma and then recommend that they act against what they know is in their rational self-interests?

Read the
Case Study
Clean Water Act
only on MySearchLab

---

[5]Julianne Nelson, "Business Ethics in a Competitive Market," *Journal of Business Ethics* (1994), p. 13.

In Chapter 14 Community and the Common Good, we will examine alternative approaches to ethics that move away from the individualist premises of this chapter.

Those who emphasize the role of personal motives will respond that the point is about *redefining* what serves our interests. Individual interests must become less individualistic. They can be about serving others' interests. Ironically, people who adapt their individual interests in the face of commons problems wind up serving them better. Think about championship sports teams and the emphasis on playing for the *team*. What's the point of this saying? Isn't it that players are asked to balance their individualistic aims and redefine their very interests in terms of fulfilling their role in the team? Teamwork leads people to work together by identifying interests with others or with the larger collective. Thus, for some, solving commons problems raises fascinating questions of ethics, norms, and the nature of our personal identity. Social dilemmas can help us fine-tune our sense of altruism, self-preservation, self-identity, reciprocity, and fairness. For example, through trial and error, we may learn how kind-hearted people sometimes get exploited when other parties take advantage of them, or, alternatively, we may learn how to cultivate motivations that create a culture of contribution that makes all parties better off.

COLLECTIVE ACTION PROBLEMS

From a personal point of view, we can ask ourselves challenging ethical questions related to collective action problems: Am I creating any public goods by what I do? If not, can I at little cost to myself? Does my conduct create negative externalities on others? Can I curtail these? Am I even aware of those effects?

Are there public goods that I would benefit from and that I could create with others, but they don't happen because of the logic of public goods problems? Is there a way to work together to solve these problems?

Consider next corporate culture and codes of ethics. What is the point of codes and workplace norms? One answer is that they are attempts to solve important collective action problems. Everyone is better off in a work atmosphere where people trust each other and believe that everyone else is following the basic rules. A trustworthy atmosphere is a public good that can lead to increased productivity, less absenteeism, and more job satisfaction. Managers are acutely aware of the fragility of this atmosphere. They intuitively know collective action problems. It's tempting for some employees to free-ride off of a hard-earned culture of trust, to steal from others when it can't be detected, to backbite, to recriminate, to find personal advantage at the expense of cooperative success. And then what had been an invaluable public good becomes depletable. Declining trust becomes a commons problem, as employees circle the wagons and narrow their conception of self-interest and what it requires in the workplace. The atmosphere sours. The resource of trust depletes. It's time to look for a new job. This can describe everyday challenges of work life. Corporations expend enormous resources to instill corporate norms that they believe will help employees work together and succeed. These norms are designed in large measure to solve public goods and commons problems that, absent these norms, will drag down the profitability of a firm.

In sum, one diagnosis of public goods and commons problem is that people's self-interested motives are the root of the problem, and those who support this interpretation argue that changing people's motives is the fundamental solution.

B. THE INSTITUTIONAL POINT OF VIEW: GOVERNMENT REGULATION AND PRIVATIZING GOODS

Ecologist Garret Hardin disagrees. He argues that ethics, from an individual point of view, is impractical in these situations, and worse, collective action problems create a psychological double-bind among those who try. Consider Hardin's reasoning as applied to the commons: On the one hand, if people refrain from using the commons on some ethical principle, they will be made to be fools as others deplete it. The problem will occur anyway, they will be exploited by the actions of others, and they will receive less or no benefit as a result of their choice. On the other hand, if they join others and deplete the resource, they feel guilty for contributing to a problem that they wish would not happen. Hardin argues that a motivational analysis creates a psychological double-bind, and further moral exhortation and arm-twisting will not help solve the problem. Hardin writes, "If you don't refrain [from exploiting the commons], we will condemn you; if you do, we will secretly call you a fool for being shamed into standing by as everyone else exploits the commons."[6] Hardin argues that the call for ethics at a personal level is unsustainable and bound to fail. What we need are different rules that change the choice situation altogether. We should change the *rules of the institution* that create the problem rather than asking people to change their *motives* within the given situation.

Regulation and privatization are two approaches for changing the rules to eliminate commons and public goods problems.

For example, government can create laws to limit access to and regulate a commons. U.S. national parks represent a monumental effort to directly regulate (and create) commons areas. Or, in the face of public goods problems, governments can tax a population and produce these goods directly—which explains roads, parks, police enforcement, and much else. Rather than appeal to individuals' sense of ethics to voluntarily produce the good, the contributions are made mandatory and this action eliminates the collective action problem altogether.

Alternatively, courts can eliminate the collective action problem by assigning private property rights over the good and removing the public nature of the good. We don't have a commons area or a public good if it can be made private so that owners can exclude others from enjoying its benefits. Political efforts to create a market in CO_2 emissions illustrate this policy response. People can then trade in an open market their private property right to pollute. Patents are another attempt to solve a public goods problem by privatizing. Knowledge to cure diseases is a public good, but if a corporation can patent its pharmaceutical breakthrough, then government has privatized this information through claim-rights to profits attained by producing medicines based on this knowledge. Not surprisingly, patents and pharmaceuticals raise complex ethical questions, especially when readily available knowledge (the public good) could be used to create cheap generic drugs but the patent gives the monopoly right to the corporation that discovered this knowledge. The patent provides incentives for innovation but can create ethical puzzles when people in poor health can't afford the price that a corporation charges.

> See Chapter 2 Section 7 for more information on intellectual property, which can now be analyzed again through the concepts of this chapter.

C. CORPORATE RESPONSIBILITY

A good social and community life often depends on the public goods around us—a great downtown, safe and clean streets, the friendly greetings of people around us. People often describe **civil society** as voluntary associations that are not government. These are areas where people volunteer at service organizations, participate in religious traditions, go to local festivals, or enjoy playing volleyball at the beach. A civil society describes the public good

> See Chapters 4 and 5 for debates about corporate responsibility.

---

[6]Garrett Hardin, "The Tragedy of the Commons," *Science* 162 (December 1968), p. 1246.

PUBLIC GOODS, PUBLIC BADS

People can think that they benefit from a public good that others believe actually makes them worse off. See Chapter 6 Section 8 for discussion about objectivist accounts of welfare. This point allows us to clarify some definitions a bit further. A *public good* describes any nonexcludable or nonrival good that people believe that they benefit from; a *public bad* describes any nonexcludable or nonrival good that people believe makes them worse off. We can then bring our own normative perspective for evaluating the various public goods and bads of a society on our own standards.

of creating options for living in voluntary associations with others. Not every feature of civil society is a public good, as much of it is comprised of private goods as well: paying a fee to play in the local baseball league or dance team, paying to enter a museum, buying books and magazines. But even these private goods can create public good benefits, such as a sense of culture and learning that infuses a society and gets passed through the generations. Where would we be, for example, without *Cavemen* and the *Jerry Springer Show*? (These are among the *Chicago Tribune*'s list of the twenty-five worst TV programs of all time. See http://www.chicagotribune.com/entertainment/chi-071024worst_tv,0,3673604.story) These last examples underscore that we don't have to assume that all public goods are high-minded activities. We can bring an ethical assessment to the public goods within a society, and critique them.

To what extent does a business community create public goods for society? To what extent does it have *responsibilities* to create public goods for society?

CAUSE MARKETING

Cause marketing occurs when a consumption purchase is bundled with a small piece of philanthropy. Buy the red Ipod, and $10 goes to a global fund to fight diseases. Buy groceries and donate $1.00 to CHOW at checkout. Public administration professor Angela Eikenberry calls this *consumption philanthropy* and reports that in 2006 almost $1.6 billion in revenues have been raised through cause marketing, up from almost nothing in the early 1980s.[7] What are the pros and cons of this approach for addressing collective action and other social problems? (Professor Eikenberry is critical of this trend; http://www.ssireview.org/articles/entry/the_hidden_costs_of_cause_marketing)

Consider the case of corporate donations. The stakeholder perspective typically describes these donations as an ethical responsibility. It's a responsibility to contribute to public goods that help build communities, and management ought to be motivated by these considerations, beyond the self-interest of the firm.

Stockholder advocates may concede that corporations have liberties to contribute to these community affairs, but they should do so only if they serve stockholder interests for increasing profits. For example, corporations may want to build their reputations and goodwill to mitigate against bad public relations that could occur in the future. Tobacco companies, for example, are among the largest supporters of culture and the arts. Why is this? You may find this industry a particularly good case study for thinking about ethics and corporate responsibility.

Stakeholder proponents not only believe that corporations should contribute to public goods through positive donations, but they see corporate activities as producing a litany of negative externalities and public goods disasters that they are responsible for cleaning up. Michael Moore's movie *Roger and Me* is the documentary about GM's decision to close plants in Flint, Michigan. He documented the negative impact on the community and argued that management should be responsible for the impact of plant closures on the health and life of that community. Moore's thesis was also that employee loyalty to the corporation ought to be reciprocated by corporate loyalty to the community. The idea that corporate responsibility is grounded in an implicit social contract is mentioned in Chapter 5 and developed in Chapter 11 Section 5.

[7]© Angela Eikenberry.

Stockholder proponents, by contrast, argue that corporate activities create public goods merely by doing core business. Commerce creates jobs. Every downtown hopes for a thriving commercial district, not only to pay taxes, but also for the productive life that it brings. Corporations fulfill their social responsibilities because profit-making *creates* public goods.

One set of institutions that address demands for public goods are non-profit and non-governmental organizations (NGOs) across the globe. In the United States alone, non-profit activity includes 1.4 million organizations, paying out over 8 percent of all wages and salaries, and with over $2.6 trillion in total assets (http://nccs.urban.org/statistics/quickfacts.cfm). Non-profits have revenues and costs, they employ and manage people, but the goods that they produce are often public goods, and their charter explicitly identifies a mission other than making profits. They receive tax-exemptions because they are designed to serve this broader public interest. Corporate responsibilities may depend in part on what non-profits can and can't do, and there is frequent collaboration between these sectors.

7.6 LIMITATIONS TO PARETO EFFICIENCY AS A NORMATIVE STANDARD

Pareto efficiency is a normative concept that offers great versatility across a range of problems. But the concept has complications, as initially suggested in the last chapter. The remainder of this chapter examines in greater depth the underlying consequentialist standard.

Many choices in life require trade-offs across people's interests. The Pareto criterion does not recognize trade-offs. No matter how we define *better off* and *worse off, no* social change is recommended if anyone is made worse off by the change. But what are we to do when all the realistic choices require trade-offs between advancing some people's interests at the expense of others'? The Pareto criterion has no answer. These situations limit the practical application of Pareto efficiency. One solution to this problem is to aggregate and compare the overall welfare effects of various options across people, and then choose the most desirable trade-offs. For this reason, economists have developed many efficiency standards beyond the Pareto criterion that lift the requirement that no one can be made worse off by a social choice.

Another limitation of the Pareto idea is that it always takes some situation as given. For example, market efficiency measures mutual gain against a given scheme of property rights. But what if the starting point of exchange is the problem to be assessed? A trade may create an efficiency gain, but if pursued under highly objectionable circumstances, such as great inequality, the judgment that the outcome creates a Pareto improvement can seem to miss the point. If X owns almost everything, and Y owns almost nothing and is at the mercy of X's bargaining advantage, then trading can create an efficiency gain but may miss the underlying moral problem. Recall the example of the manager hiring employees at very low wages (see Introduction, Section 3). How do you analyze the situation now? Recall also the introduction to normative analysis for property arrangements in Chapter 3 Section 8. Whenever we want to assess the underlying property arrangements that may create an efficiency gain, we need a more systematic normative standard beyond Pareto optimality, such as utilitarianism or deontological ethics.

FIGURE 7.5	Calculating Welfare Under Two Scenarios

	Status Quo	Banking Reform
A	1	10
B	3	12
C	2	15
D	5	4
E	10	3
Totals	21	44

A–E = Persons
Status Quo = Keeping banking regulations the same
Banking Reform = Changing banking regulations
1, 3, 2, 5, etc. = Welfare benefit

7.7 THE TRADITION OF UTILITARIANISM

The philosophically rich tradition of utilitarianism provides a response to the limits of Pareto optimality.

Let's imagine how five people (A–E) might be affected by a decision to change the regulations of the banking industry. In Figure 7.5, the numbers represent each person's welfare under two scenarios: if the legal structure maintains the status quo (SQ) and if banking reform (BR) becomes law. The higher the number, the greater the welfare.

The Pareto criterion allows for one judgment: because D and E would be made worse off by BR, the choice is not an efficiency gain.

A utilitarian provides a different analysis. We should consider the total utility in each situation and recommend the outcome that maximizes total utility. BR offers a much higher amount of total utility across all five persons than SQ (44 > 21). Therefore, the prescription is to endorse BR. In other words, a utilitarian would judge that the gains for A, B, and C are so great that BR is desirable even with the trade-off in losses experienced by D and E. The impulse to go beyond Pareto efficiency and toward utilitarianism is this: if you are unwilling to make *any* trade-offs among people's interests, then life will almost always be stuck in the SQ, no matter how bad the SQ, or how important the change. Take something that is to be traded in a market. If you look around enough, you will no doubt find someone somewhere who will object to the trade. You will no doubt find someone who objects to the concept of trading. Should trading be abandoned just for that fact? The utilitarian has a reply. Normative thought requires that we balance interests: we should support markets if, on balance, they do more good than any other alternative, balancing everyone's interests; or abandon them if they do not.

Utilitarianism has many formulations and we will not examine the full range of controversies within this tradition. But we will examine a few. Consider the following statement: act so as to maximize social utility. The standard can apply to the personal point of view for deciding how to make personal choices or to the institutional point of view for deciding what types of institutions we should support. **Act utilitarianism** is the view that an individual action is ethically right if it maximizes social utility. **Rule utilitarianism** is the view that a rule is ethically right if it maximizes social utility. A rule utilitarian, for example, can argue that our institutions can be justified if they enforce a set of rules that have the effect of maximizing social utility. This outcome, however, doesn't require that people behave according to a utilitarian ethics in their individual actions.

What does *utility* mean? Perhaps the most famous utilitarian was English jurist and philosopher Jeremy Bentham, who defended a utilitarian approach for ethics and legislation, and who argued that utility should be interpreted as the absence of pain and experiences of pleasure. A later utilitarian, John Stuart Mill, argued that this interpretation of utility should be given more nuance and definition. He famously wrote that it "is better to be a human being dissatisfied than a pig satisfied; better to be Socrates dissatisfied than a fool satisfied. And if the fool, or the pig, are of a different opinion, it is because they only know their own side of the question."[8] Mill's point was to distinguish between *higher* and *lower* pleasures and to argue that utilitarians, from an ethical point of view, should not count all pleasures on par in the utilitarian calculus.

Philosopher Peter Singer is a prominent contemporary theorist who advocates utilitarianism as a personal ethics. He uses utilitarian reasoning to advocate vegetarianism and significant personal obligations to help the impoverished around the world. Singer's views are especially noteworthy and controversial because he interprets and defends an account of utility to include concern for the interests of all sentient beings, not just the experiences of human beings. These examples illustrate how utilitarians can and do disagree about how to define *utility* and about whose interests count for utilitarian calculations. As a result, their disagreements produce different utilitarian theories.

Although utilitarians vary widely in their views, they all agree that what matters for assessing actions and institutions are the *consequences* of a situation. For this reason, utilitarianism is regarded as the most prominent example of ethical consequentialism, which is the view that all normative assessments depend only on assessing consequences.

Utilitarianism is named for the root idea of *utility*, but most modern utilitarians dispense with that word to describe their views and speak instead of people's happiness, welfare, or well-being. They will argue that actions or institutions should create the best consequences, such as maximizing the happiness of all those that might be affected by some action or institutional arrangement. At the most general level, the consequentialist formula is that *ethical rightness* is defined in terms of maximizing *goodness*, which each theorist may further define in many ways.

Consider one further clarification of this ethical perspective. A utilitarian ethic is not *majority rule*. Rather, the idea is to maximize total goodness by aggregating this good across persons. When we aggregate utility, for example, a social choice where a minority of persons would experience a *dramatic* loss of utility can outweigh a majority of persons who would experience *very modest* increases in utility. Thus, in this case, majority rule could create the wrong result because the net amount would be less than other alternatives. Consider changing the numbers in Figure 7.5 to test these ideas.

To this day, much legislative debate about business regulation and deregulation relies on utilitarian ideas. In particular, **cost/benefit analysis** (CBA) is a decision-making process that weighs the total expected benefits of a decision against the total expected costs, and supports the decision with the greatest expected net benefit. Each CBA analysis has the burden of defining (and justifying) what should properly count as a *benefit* or *cost*.

Let's return to the public goods problems above, as represented in Figure 7.4. If all the participants in a public goods dilemma knew that they were all committed act utilitarians, and they accepted people's appraisals of their own interests, then what choices would they make? It seems clear: they would see contributing as a duty to maximize utility, as 6 is greater than any other outcome. Utilitarianism, at the individual level, if followed and shared in common, can solve social dilemmas. Some people regard the very function of ethics and social norms as the set of normative rules that, once part of people's dispositions, solve many of society's collective action problems that are otherwise intractable. This observation relates to discussions about the importance of character and community in Chapters 13 and 14.

---

[8]John Stuart Mill, *Utilitarianism*, Seventh Edition (Longmans, Green and Co., 1879). See Chapter 2.

Consider next how a rule utilitarian would assess a commons problem. If passing legislation to regulate the commons improves overall welfare more so than leaving it alone or privatizing it, then legislators should support this regulation; if not, they shouldn't. The point is that there is no need to prove that *no one* would be made worse off by that regulation, only that it improves overall welfare more than any other option.

7.8   THE ATTRACTION AND LIMITATIONS TO UTILITARIANISM

Is utilitarianism a morally attractive ethical perspective? A tradition of thought steadily developed over two centuries contains proponents and critics. Consider three points of support.

First, if individual happiness and welfare is what really matters in life, then isn't more of it better than less? If so, then shouldn't we seek to aggregate the amount of it not for one person or several people but across everyone? This is a fundamental intuition that inspires those who hope to develop a workable and intuitive theory.

Second, utilitarians believe that no matter how difficult the technical details of measuring and comparing people's welfare, the approach is far more practical and applicable than other theoretical approaches. Utilitarian reasoning suggests the possibility of *calculating* the ethically correct result.

For proponents, one attraction of utilitarianism as an ethical theory is its commitment to an equal consideration of everyone's interests, which presages the discussion in Chapter 11 about the value of equality.

Third, recall the Pareto concept that prohibits actions that make people worse off. However, in a case in which a million people are benefited by an action but one person's welfare is slightly reduced, then why should that one person's interests dominate the choice? Pareto efficiency can become a dictatorship of one person's interests. Utilitarianism, by contrast, commits to the idea of an equal consideration of everyone's interests. No one person is more valuable than anyone else. The goal is overall welfare, but each person counts equally for determining the best choice. Utilitarians often find this idea intuitive from an ethical point of view.

The contrast between utilitarianism and the veto principle embedded within Pareto efficiency can be applied to examine cases of eminent domain introduced in Chapter 1. You might consider reading *Kelo v New London* as an application of these ideas. On the one hand, some people believe that property owners should be able to veto anyone else's attempt to take that property: my home is my castle. On the other hand, if that property can be put to public use in a way that can advance the welfare of many people, is there a point when that veto should be overridden to support the community? The U.S. Constitution, in fact, enshrines a right of the community to override an individual's veto power under various circumstances, and Supreme Court interpretations have applied utilitarian grounds for deciding these controversial cases of the use of eminent domain.

A. PROBLEMS WITH UTILITARIANISM

Despite these (and other) attractions, utilitarian reasoning has led others to reject the approach altogether or argue for limiting its role within ethical reasoning.

Consider again the process illustrated in Figure 7.5, where the choice now is not about banking reform but, to take one leading example, about the forced donation of your organs to save five people. From an ethical point of view, does it really matter how a decision about your organs affects overall welfare for making the ethical decision? Shouldn't you have an absolute veto over donating your kidney and isn't some utilitarian calculation irrelevant to this judgment? What do you think?

We could discuss a range of other challenging examples. Suppose that the choice was to annul a contract or take away everything that you owned. Many would say that these choices, without your consent, would violate your rights, no matter what aggregate welfare calculation might recommend.

A classic case study of utilitarian reasoning, which is sometimes credited with the growth of business ethics, is a leaked memo from the early 1970s about the internal reasoning of Ford Motor Company regarding the Ford Pinto. This case raised many objections because the memo revealed that, after preparing a cost/benefit calculation that included a measure of the monetary worth of individual lives, Ford decided against recalling defective Pintos that had the minor problem of blowing up on rear impact in limited cases.

These cases and others highlight the intuition that we need an account of people's rights to constrain the scope and relevant application of utilitarian reasoning. Rights may not be the only ethical constraint, as intuitions about people's equality, dignity, character, or what people deserve may also conflict with utilitarian reasoning. In general, whenever we think our ethical decisions should draw from values independent from thinking about the consequences of a situation, we will find utilitarianism lacking as a complete ethical approach to decision-making.

> See Chapter 3 Section 8 for the contrast between consequentialist and non-consequentialist reasoning in the context of property rights.

Rule utilitarians try to address these counterintuitive implications by arguing that a society with rules that enshrine rights will improve social utility more than a society without those rules and rights. Thus, the examples given above need not undermine a utilitarian perspective. Utilitarianism should be understood as the justification for why we have rights in the first place, rather than conflict with a theory of rights. Alternatively, utilitarians may also try to take counterintuitive examples and show how a careful analysis of *all* the consequences of any given choice reveals that the utilitarian result almost always matches our intuitions after all. These utilitarians believe that most criticisms against the theory presume a simplistic or overly formulaic application of utilitarian ideas.

7.9 SUMMARY

A study of public goods and commons problems reminds us of the fragility of our social and economic world. Sometimes we succeed in our social interactions; sometimes we fail. Permanent solutions seem just beyond our grasp. We can make ourselves collectively worse off, sometimes tragically so, even when (or just because) we are individually rational. Both market and nonmarket remedies abound, as do reflections about the point and prospect of ethics and social norms beyond self-interest for solving these problems.

Efficiency analysis and the broader utilitarian framework offer an impressive toolkit of ideas for analyzing business and economic life, including concepts of self-interest, rationality, transparency, transactions costs, negative and positive externalities, public goods and commons problems, property rights, and all the background conditions for market efficiency. These chapters offer insights for analyzing the CSR movement; a range of government functions and court rulings; advertising rules; labeling regulations; taxes for parks, schools, streets, libraries, national defense, and police; consumer protection laws; the Federal Drug Administration, the Security and Exchange Commission; privatizing efforts; deregulation; the non-profit sector; codes of ethics; and much else—many of these activities are in part responses to the ethical analyses introduced in these last two chapters. Even as the book examines new ethical perspectives beyond efficiency and consequentialism, starting with a discussion of liberty in Chapter 9, the concepts of these last two chapters will continue to have versatile applications to those debates.

KEY TERMS

market failure	public goods problems	act utilitarianism
inefficiencies	collective action problems or	rule utilitarianism
private goods	social dilemmas	cost/benefit analysis
public goods	commons	
free-riding problem	civil society	

DISCUSSION QUESTIONS

1. Everyone seems to dislike political campaign tactics that smear the other candidate through misleading negative ads. Aren't we all made worse off by negative advertising? Every political season brings a renewed call for a more positive approach. Yet despite the personal pledges, it rarely happens. Analyze the issue as a public goods problem. (Is it?) Consider different remedies. What is the best way to handle this challenge? Why?

2. Apply utilitarian reasoning to reassess the trading on the island scenario. Reassess the significance of the background assumptions, not in terms of achieving Pareto efficiency, but for maximizing happiness overall. Are the background assumptions different for this normative standard?

3. When a commons problem exists worldwide with no single government to create rules to stop the depletion of a resource, what is the best response? Global ethics? Treaties? Something else? Develop what you believe is an interesting case study for addressing these questions.

4. Identify a public good or a commons problem that you find especially interesting. Why is it interesting from your point of view? Do any of the remedies presented in this chapter apply? Does the example prompt an insight about these problems not discussed in this chapter?

5. In 2003, Craig Newmark, the founder of Craigslist, said in a *New York Times* interview, "We're trying to figure out how to run the site as a commons, yet avoid the tragedy of the commons" (Putnam, Robert. 2003. *Better Together: Restoring the American Community*. Simon & Schuster). Analyze Craigslist as a potential commons problem and research what and how well they are doing at developing a successful commons.

6. Economist Ronald Coase devised the influential *Coase theorem*: as long as a judicial system assigns clear private property rights and there are zero transaction costs for trading, then it doesn't matter how the courts assign those rights to achieve efficiency in the allocation of resources, because the result will always be efficient. Explain the intuition behind this theorem. What is the implication if transaction costs are significant? How would a utilitarian hope that justices resolve disputes about property rights under these circumstances?

7. The public goods problem would dissolve if participants had assurance that others would contribute if they do. Assess.

8. What are some further defenses and critiques of utilitarianism as a normative theory beyond the discussion in this chapter?

9. Is establishing ethical behavior in a market setting a public goods problem? Explain how it might be structured in this way.

10. Much experimental work in economics reveals that in a multi-round game, people tend at first to contribute to public goods projects. But over time, free-riding increases and cooperation collapses. Experimental economics and psychology are two areas that study conditions that tend to increase or decrease cooperation in the face of social dilemmas. Are there real-world conditions where voluntary provision or the maintenance of public goods tends to succeed? What makes that possible?

11. Tit-for-tat is a strategy of human interaction: If others cooperate, then cooperate in turn. If others do not cooperate, then don't cooperate in turn. Is this a good norm of behavior in the face of social dilemmas? What norms of behavior do you endorse? Why?

12. How would a utilitarian analyze debates on corporate social responsibility in Chapter 4?

13. Read the following set of interviews about the oil business, corporate responsibility, and global warming: http://www.pbs.org/wgbh/pages/frontline/heat/themes/corp.html. Analyze the various positions defended by those interviewed by drawing on concepts across Chapters 1–7, including the nature of markets, property rights, corporate responsibility, efficiency, public goods, commons problems, externalities, and utilitarianism. Global warming is also discussed in Chapter 8 Section 6.

14. Find some ethics codes for corporations and assess what they say. What is the point of creating these codes, in your view?

15. Economists often discuss ideas of *moral hazard* and *adverse selection*. What do these terms mean and how are they relevant to the analysis of this chapter? How do these ideas relate to the financial meltdown of recent years?

16. Efficiency analysis ignores questions of distributive justice and utilitarianism mishandles questions of distributive justice. Assess this statement.

17. Should we have to pay for public goods that we enjoy but we didn't ask for? See Robert Nozick's *Anarchy, State, and Utopia* (Basic, 1977) for further discussion.

18. Which normative standard is more appealing: Pareto efficiency or utilitarianism? Why?

8

THE INVISIBLE HAND: ETHICS, INCENTIVES, AND INSTITUTIONS

WHEN YOU FINISH STUDYING THIS CHAPTER, YOU SHOULD BE ABLE TO:

1. Distinguish invisible hand, law and regulation, and professional ethics models of business and economic life.

2. Discuss two approaches for deriving an account of professional ethics.

3. Understand conflicts of interest and responses to these conflicts.

4. Analyze the balance and tension between ethics, self-interested incentives, and institutional constraints and how these forces frame many challenges in business and economic life.

Dancing is just discovery, discovery, discovery.[1]
Martha Graham, American dance choreographer (1894–1991)

8.1 INTRODUCTION

Our **sense of ethics** and values helps us guide our choices and assess the institutions that surround us (see Introduction). These institutions include market exchanges in one form or another. They create some of our most common interactions in life (Chapter 1). Markets develop against a backdrop of property rights, government, and law (Chapters 2 and 3). They are shaped by the tremendous role of corporations driven by incentives for profit (Chapters 4 and 5).

But within a competitive marketplace, what should be the role of ethics and values for consumers, businesses, investors, employees, managers, and owners? The stockholder vision of corporate responsibility sees corporations with few social responsibilities other than maximizing profits within the law (Chapter 4). The stakeholder account, by contrast, argues for a far more robust account of ethics—emphasizing the need to apply our values within a managerial perspective and throughout our economic lives, no matter what our positions in society (Chapter 5).

What more can be said about the role of ethics in business and society? Recall the framework presented in the Introduction (See Figure 8.1).

---

[1]Graham, Martha. "Martha Graham Reflects on Her Art and a Life in Dance". *The New York Times* (31 March 1985).

FIGURE 8.1   The Ethics and Values of Business and Economic Life

---

Ethics from a (personal point of view) and an (institutional point of view)

| Human Beliefs and Motives | Institutions | ⇒ | Values |

A Sense of Ethics   Self-interest   Markets   Government

Efficiency and Welfare

Liberty

Professional Ethics   Invisible Hand   Law and Regulation
Arguments   Arguments   Arguments

Rights

Equality

(These are competing models of the role of ethics in economic life.)

What People Deserve

Relationships and Character

Community and the Common Good

Other Values

We make decisions by bringing our motives—which may include a sense of ethics and self-interested incentives—within institutions that shape our choices. Ethics and personal incentives may harmonize or collide, depending on the roles we occupy and the institutional pressures that we encounter. For example, conflicts of interest represent a collision between ethics and self-interest, one topic of this chapter. More generally, people have different ideas about the best way to balance the pull of ethics, personal incentives, and the institutions that shape our choices. The invisible hand, law and regulation, and professional ethics models present three competing guides for thinking about the role of ethics in business and society. They each form a normative interpretation of business and economic life—but in different directions.

> The invisible hand, law and regulation, and professional ethics models present three competing guides for thinking about the role of ethics in business and society.

Recall the brief description of each model from the Introduction Section 3C. The **invisible hand model** depicts a vision of markets transforming self-interested incentives into a productive society, without the need for extended roles for ethics and government in economic life. The **law and regulation model** suggests that government must exert a far more extensive role in markets, given that self-interested incentives create wide-ranging market failures. The **professional ethics model** suggests that no matter the balance between markets and government, one element is still lacking—the need for a robust sense of ethics and responsibility in business and economic life. On this view, ethics should have a far more extensive impact on business and economic decision-making than the previous models suggest.

The stockholder and stakeholder theories draw from these underlying models, as do many ethical debates in business and economic life. These models are often in the background of policy debates, shaping how people make observations about the business system, how they diagnose its

> See Chapter 1 Section 3 for an introduction to the idea that our observations about markets are impacted by the conceptual and normative filters that we bring to these observations. The models studied in this chapter are examples of conceptual filters that are often in the background of policy debates, shaping how people make observations about the business system, how they diagnose its ethical challenges, and how they suggest remedies.

ethical challenges, and how they suggest remedies. When a dialogue about these issues occur, careful attention to the arguments made provide insight into the fundamental positions of the participants. This chapter will examine the underlying rationale for each of these competing perspectives, integrating all of the materials and building blocks of Chapters 1–7. This chapter also creates a bridge from the materials in these earlier chapters to the continuing study of ethics and values in Chapters 9–14.

> The concept of *integrity* can be understood as a personal value, a topic of discussion in Chapter 13, on character.

Finally, note how Figure 8.1 prompts a question: how do the values that we draw on to assess the system (such as those depicted on the right side of the figure) relate to making individual ethical decisions within the system (depicted by the sense of ethics on the left side of the figure)? How can you join together both personal and institutional points of view? These challenging questions press us to think about the integrity of our incentives, ethical beliefs, and values as one coherent system of thought, the second topic of this chapter.

8.2 THE METAPHOR OF THE INVISIBLE HAND

Let's start with those who most strongly believe in a metaphor of an *invisible hand* that guides a market economy. Consider this brief expression of the view in Figure 8.2, which is also embedded in Figure 8.1.

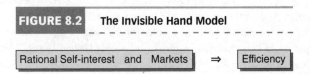

FIGURE 8.2   **The Invisible Hand Model**

Rational Self-interest   and   Markets   ⇒   Efficiency

Introduced by eighteenth-century economist and moral philosopher Adam Smith, the metaphor of the invisible hand exerts a tremendous influence on attitudes about markets. The foundational idea is as follows: people in a market setting intend only their own immediate gain, but like an invisible hand, their individual decisions create a desirable result that was no part of their individual intentions. Smith observed that, in general, people do not trade to improve society. They trade to improve themselves. But the result is an improvement to society, an efficiency gain. The island scenario of Chapter 6 illustrates this idea.

The invisible hand imagery is part of a renowned historical debate about how to create a good society. The ancient Greeks, especially in the writings of Plato and Aristotle, envisioned a tight link between achieving justice in society and the trait of justice in the individual. People must aim for justice—as individuals—for society to achieve justice. Thus, moral education and training in practical wisdom was crucially important for building a good society.

The invisible hand metaphor challenges this tight link between personal and institutional points of view. People tend to be naturally selfish, according to this contrary tradition, and so the beauty of the market is to create the possibility that more immediate incentives of *self-interest*, rather than a refined sense of justice, can be sufficient to create good social outcomes. French aristocrat Alexis De Tocqueville, in his nineteenth-century masterpiece *Democracy in America*, sometimes marveled and sometimes puzzled at the narrow American ambitions for individual self-improvement, reflecting on the contrast against the noble and high-minded aristocratic sentiments infused throughout feudal

Europe.[2] The *idea* of noble and altruistic sentiments is impressive, he thought, but the *results* created by more modest incentives were even more impressive, he found. This sense of self-interest, he concluded, need not imply selfishness when individuals pursue their own gain in recognition that the system improves the livelihood of others as well.

A. LIMITED ROLE FOR ETHICS FROM A PERSONAL POINT OF VIEW

In the context of the invisible hand metaphor, **self-interest** refers to individuals pursuing the satisfaction of their own preferences. Firms can also advance their self-interest in the market by maximizing profits. The invisible hand metaphor, therefore, is the guiding conceptual vision that stockholder proponents (see Chapter 4) use to justify their views about corporate responsibility. Like an invisible hand, markets guide both self-interested people and profit-maximizing corporations to create good outcomes, such as efficiency gains. Although Smith's argument relied on the concept of efficiency, the generalized invisible hand argument is that *good outcomes*, however, defined, can occur without inidividuals' aiming for those outcomes. And this result happens without any individuals aiming to achieve these good outcomes.

What is the role for ethics in economic life in this model? Not much. In fact, Canadian-American philosopher David Gauthier coins the phrase that markets are ideally *morally free* zones.[3] Ethics becomes irrelevant for making economic choices because markets create good outcomes based solely on people's self-interest. Keep in mind two separable ideas. Some look at our economic life and say that ethics is irrelevant as a matter of practice (which they may bemoan). Others look at economic life and say that ethics *ought* to be irrelevant because the best system should not require it. The first statement is descriptive, the second normative. Part of the appeal of the invisible hand model is to link these separable descriptive and normative ideas in the following way: *because* people are primarily motivated by self-gain, attempts to require higher motives are largely futile, and this point argues for a system that relies primarily on people's self-interested incentives to succeed. This argument was part of the stockholder theory of corporate responsibility (Chapter 4 Section 8). Thus, part of the *success* of an institution, on this account, is that it minimizes the need for ethical decision-making at the individual level.

This metaphor exerts a significant hold on our culture and social sciences. So ingrained is this idea, that the modeling process has its own name within the social sciences, **incentive-compatible institutional design**, which is to posit that institutions must be able to produce good outcomes compatible with self-interest alone if they are to work properly. The role for individual ethical requirements approaches zero.

The interpretation that ethics plays *no role* in economic life may be extreme, and supporters of this general model may allow for some role for ethics, as will be discussed below. But it's important, as a first step, to understand the pure vision. First, even if some minor role for ethics can be carved out of this model, the view is that we should minimize ethics in business decision-making, because our goal should be to find rules that align self-interest to promote good outcomes. Second, the invisible hand approach need not deny that we face ethical challenges in economic life. The important response, however,

---

[2]Alexis De Tocqueville (1805–1859) is best known for his two-volume work *Democracy in America* (University of Chicago Press, 2002).

[3]Gauthier, David. 1986. *Morals by Agreement*. Clarendon Press.

is to revise the institution's rules and procedures to eliminate the conditions that lead to ethical dilemmas. The approach is to take an *institutional point of view* to remedy problems of ethics.

The invisible hand model relates to what is sometimes called the **separation thesis**, introduced (but not defended) by American business ethicist R. Edward Freeman, which states that business is business and ethics is ethics: never the twain shall meet. The *separation thesis* refers to the widespread view that "ethics and economics can be neatly and sharply separated. In this context, the challenge of doing business ethics or improving the moral performance of business becomes a Sisyphean task because business ethics is, by definition, an oxymoron" (p. 364).[4] It's illuminating to probe this idea and the invisible hand thesis with a few diverse examples and to consider the prevalence of this market metaphor in a market culture.

For example, recall the opening in Chapter 1 about the development of trade in a World War II prison camp. In writing about the experience, R. A. Radford observed, "Very soon after capture people realized that it was both undesirable and unnecessary, in view of the limited size and equality of supplies, to give away or accept gifts of cigarettes or food. 'Goodwill' developed into trading as a more equitable means of maximizing individual satisfaction."[5] His point was that gift-giving practices prompted various ethical puzzles that were replaced by markets channeling self-interest, and the result (he claims) was even better. It's an intriguing assertion. The value—"equitable means of maximizing individual satisfaction"—did not require people to be motivated to achieve that value. In fact, the ethical motives of gift-giving yielded a *worse* outcome than a system of self-interest and markets, he claims. On this view we should *separate* ethics from business to get the best result.

Here is another example. Suppose you believe that corporate boards of directors should encourage executives to promote stakeholder interests. What is the best way to achieve this outcome? One approach is to appeal to the ethical motives of corporate board members by giving talks and organizing conferences about the ethical prerogatives of board membership. The idea is to appeal to ethical motives from a personal point of view. A second approach is to support legislation that legally requires stakeholder representatives on corporate boards (as is common in Europe). The stakeholder representative can then advocate for the self-interests of those stakeholders. These are different approaches. The first advocates ethical reasoning within the boardroom from a personal point of view. The second advocates changing the rules of the system to realign self-interested incentives to create the desired outcome from an institutional point of view. (Which approach makes more sense to you? Why?) As an example of the second approach, provisions of the 2002 Sarbanes-Oxley law attempt to encourage ethics from the top-down, by holding board members liable for mistakes in financial reporting.

Consider a last example—the U.S. Constitution and its concept of separation of powers. By creating checks and balances, the framers hoped good outcomes could result overall, even if (or just because) participants are motivated by self-interest. They didn't eliminate any role for ethics but their most important focus and concern was about how to structure institutions compatible with the premise that people are primarily self-interested. These are but a

---

[4]R. Edward Freeman, Andrew C. Wicks, Bidham Parmar, "The Stakeholder Theory and 'the Corporate Objective Revisited,'" *Organization Science* 15(3) (2004), pp. 364–369. R. Edward Freeman (b. 1951) is a professor of philosophy and business administration at the University of Virginia.

[5]R. A. Radford, "The Economic Organization of a P.O.W. Camp," *Economica* 12 (1945), pp. 190, 191.

few examples to illustrate why many believe that the invisible hand metaphor, as a prescription about channeling self-interest into good outcomes, is an idea with great insight.

Let's now follow up on the earlier idea that the invisible hand metaphor need not imply a complete separation between ethics and business. First, the fact that ethics at the individual level has a reduced role does not imply an *amoral* understanding of the market system. The model offers the contrary insight: if rational self-interest through markets can create good outcomes, then we have reason to celebrate markets. The system realizes a value—such as the value of making people's lives better off. Thus, the view expresses a *normative* argument that implies a limited role of ethics in business. In this way we can distinguish between those who reject ethics in business because they are psychological egoists or relativists about morality—believing that morality just doesn't matter anywhere—from those who reject ethics in business on the normative argument provided by the invisible hand model. These are different views. Second, this model endorses whatever preferences people bring to the market, which could include ethical preferences, such as buying *Green* products. Ethics, in this sense, is not precluded from the invisible hand model. The role of ethics here is no different than the role of any other preference: a motivational input for a market transaction. Managers, for example, should be highly responsive to marketing products that appeal to consumers' ethical preferences. For these two reasons, the invisible hand argument need not imply the complete absence of ethical reflection from the personal point of view.[6] Still, the argument provides a vision for very few ethical *requirements* within our roles in business and economic life.

B. LIMITED ROLE FOR GOVERNMENT AND LAW FROM THE INSTITUTIONAL POINT OF VIEW

Where is government and law in this model? Nowhere. The model, as stated, has a utopian or allegorical character to it. The idea that humans can organize without government and law has some traction in small-scale religious or intentional communities, some of which exist throughout the world today. But large modern societies rely on government. No one in practical policy debates denies this. Even economist Milton Friedman, who places great emphasis on the value of markets, says, "I do not see how one can avoid the use of the political mechanism altogether."[7]

Why does nearly everyone believe in some form of government and law? An early discussion question posed this question (Chapter 3, Discussion Question 3). We now have the conceptual resources to provide at least one important answer. You may discern the form of one answer from Chapter 6 on efficiency: that without government, it's unlikely or impossible to create the background conditions necessary for markets to achieve good outcomes. Let's apply the concept of a public good from Chapter 7 to develop this argument.

JUSTICE WITHOUT GOVERNMENT?

A theoretical tradition of benign anarchism attempts to envision how humans could be motivated to interact without government and live in peace and justice. Although German philosopher Karl Marx was highly critical of markets and capitalism, he imagined a final communist ideal with no government, a vision that has some similarities with utopian visions of markets with no government. French philosopher Rousseau also envisioned the possibility of a utopian world without government, but he thought markets with private property were incompatible with this vision.

---

[6]Although rightly credited with the metaphor of an invisible hand, Adam Smith also spent a good deal of his career writing about the importance of ethics, including his book *A Theory of Moral Sentiments*.

[7]Milton Friedman, "The Social Responsibility of Business Is to Increase its Profits," *New York Times Magazine* (September 13, 1970), p. 126.

Suppose that there were no government and no laws. What would happen? As noted in Chapter 1, philosopher Thomas Hobbes thought war and violence would result, much like the record of our human history. It's a public goods problem. Public order—the absence of chaos and war and violence—is a good that everyone desires. Further, in a society that has order and peace, no one is excluded from this benefit (it's nonexcludable), and one person benefiting does not reduce anyone else's ability to benefit (it's nonrival). The logic of a public goods problem quickly emerges. Everyone is better off with order relative to chaos. But what people most want is to benefit from the order and break the rules when that is to their advantage. The worst case scenario is paying the costs of respecting order when everyone else is breaking the rules.

If these attitudes accurately depict the preferences of wide swaths of the population, then the predictable result is that maintaining and establishing order will be fragile and liable to break down. All the remedies discussed in the last chapter could apply: demands to be ethical, privatizing the good (creating private security forces), or creating a state with a public police force. Any viable society must unlock this riddle of order. Many argue that the last remedy—a state—is necessary no matter the relevance of the other remedies. Most people find this argument convincing, and they assign the maintenance of order as the *first* function of any viable government.

This point adds a layer of insight to the chapters on markets and property rights. Law is a remedy to a public goods problem. It's not the only remedy; and the fact that markets can sometimes exist without law suggests that other remedies might apply in some circumstances. But this public goods argument explains why property rights are usually backed by law. In fact, we can return to Chapters 1–3 and understand the connections between markets, property rights, and law in a deeper way, bound together by the materials introduced in Chapters 6 and 7. Without government to secure and enforce contracts and property rights, many believe that society will devolve to panic, natural disasters, revolutions, and war. This argument is one important reason why debates about corporate responsibility take for granted at least some government role in economic life (Chapters 5 and 6).

THE COASE THEOREM

Economist Ronald Coase developed the Coasian theorem, which says that clearly assigned property rights are the best method for achieving efficiency when transaction costs are low or nonexistent.[8] This insight impacts many court decisions today. See Chapter 7, discussion questions, for more about the Coase theorem.

Let's revise the invisible hand model to reflect the position that government should play some role in society (see Figure 8.3).

C. AN ADJUSTED INVISIBLE HAND MODEL

Let's take an example. A firm pollutes water and poisons people downriver. On this model, the relevant question is, Who had legitimate property rights to that water? It's the role of a well-functioning judicial system to clarify these rights. If the people poisoned had

FIGURE 8.3   The Revised Invisible Hand Model

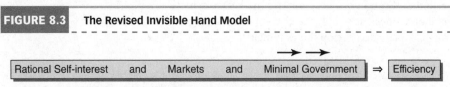

(The arrows above "Minimal Government" represent the direction of analysis of proponents in this model, relative to the previous model.)

---

[8]© Ronald Coase.

legitimate claim-rights to clean water from that river, then the firm violated their property rights. If the firm had claim-rights over the river, then the judicial system should make that fact clear so that people downstream know that they drink that water at their own risk. Suppose now that the water was a commons area with no clear assignment of property rights—a commons problem may loom. In this case, courts should assign private property rights over the water so that people can negotiate usage. Thus, government's primary function in this model is to adjudicate and specify property rights to create an environment where people can trade for efficiency gains.

> Those who see democracy as a foundation for celebrating the role of government in society reject this invisible hand model. They see government as a beacon for securing justice beyond efficiency, a perspective developed ahead.

Government isn't exactly celebrated in this model. The role of government is derivative, to correct for market failures. Chapters 6 and 7 consider a range of market failures when various background conditions are absent, including missing information, externalities, irrational choices, high transaction costs, and others. What are the best responses to this range of market imperfections? Invisible hand proponents argue that markets with clearly assigned property rights and a basic rule of law provide much of the answer. The invisible hand model in Figure 8.3 depicts these relationships: our incentives should spur the development of market institutions against a backdrop of limited government. This model promotes a vision that (a) *ethics* should play a marginal role in business, (b) *incentives* should play a dominating role, and (c) the relevant *institutions* should be markets with limited government in the background to provide for a stable rule of law.

What do you think?

LIBERTARIANS AND LIBERAL EGALITARIANS

The invisible hand model developed in this chapter specifies efficiency as the social goal. But others develop, defend, or criticize this model using other values. For example, proponents of the invisible hand model who place singular weight on liberty are called *libertarians*; critics of the invisible hand model who emphasize both liberty and equality are called *liberal egalitarians*. We will develop these ideas in Chapters 9–11.

8.3 THE LAW AND REGULATION MODEL

Let's now consider a second model, as depicted in Figure 8.4.

The appropriate role of government intervention in markets is a lively debate in our public culture today. The arguments in Chapters 6 and 7 provide many insights for understanding these debates. Currently, government provides labeling regulations, rules on advertising, pollution standards, occupational safety standards, employment laws, food and drug standards; parks, streets, street lights, libraries; banking and financial standards, consumer protection laws; coast guard regulation of waterways; and many, many others. Negative externalities are particularly troubling in markets, and there is a large body of law to constrain how businesses conduct their operations to curtail these externalities.

FIGURE 8.4   The Law and Regulation Model

Law and Regulation Model

| Rational Self-interest and Markets and Minimal Government and Expanded Government | ⇒ | Efficiency |

(The arrows above "Expanded Government" represent the direction of analysis of proponents in this model, distinct from the previous model.)

THE INVISIBLE FOOT

Economists E. K. Hunt and Ralph d'Arge coined the term *invisible foot* to refer to the incentives that lead people to foist negative externalities on others. They turned around the invisible hand argument with the claim that self-interested motives in unregulated markets lead to bad results, even though it is not anyone's intention to create these results. Like the kick of an invisible foot, they argue, unregulated markets lead to misery. Noble Prize–winning economist Joseph Stiglitz also argues for the debilitating effect of negative externalities in market transactions without government regulations.

Each of these government functions can be described as a remedy to problems that occur or supposedly would occur in unregulated markets. Those who support these government functions argue that the benefits of government intervention outweigh its costs in any particular area. Those who criticize the government role argue that markets can and should solve these problems, or that the costs of these regulations are worse than the original problems. Health care is a most challenging case study for debating practical issues differentiating invisible hand and law and regulation approaches. It's an interesting exercise to study government functions and see how many of them can be understood through the analysis discussed in Chapters 6 and 7.

The law and regulation model rejects the limited role of government in the invisible hand model. Proponents of this model believe that markets without careful oversight are ripe for massive failures and harms to the population. There is no exact definition of *minimal* versus *expanded* government in Figure 8.4. These terms refer to a sliding scale that begins with a viable court system for resolving property disputes and expands to many government services and regulations in response to problems that markets do not solve.

Invisible hand and law and regulation proponents often disagree about the *empirical issues*, and so many of these debates depend on evidence-based studies that support government regulation or deregulation within any particular area. However, they also often disagree about what *good outcomes* should mean. Law and regulation proponents may appeal to the values of equality or fairness, for example, as a rationale for regulation, whereas an invisible hand advocate will typically appeal to efficiency considerations (although the invisible hand model need not be premised on this value commitment). Regarding these two types of debates, Chapters 6 and 7 are most relevant when the debate is about the empirical issues; Chapters 9–14 are most relevant when the debate is about the values that should guide business and economic legislation.

One of the more interesting aspects of the law and regulation approach is what is missing: significant weight on the need for a sense of ethics among market participants. The invisible hand and government regulation models share in common the marginal role (or at least a lack of focus) on ethical requirements in economic life. They both examine ethical lapses in markets from *an institutional point of view*, seeking to identify market or government institutions that are compatible with the self-interested motives of participants. The next model challenges this focus on an institutional perspective.

8.4   THE PROFESSIONAL ETHICS MODEL

The model of professional ethics represents a range of arguments that have a common thread, *that our sense of ethics from a personal point of view should play a fundamental role in business and economic life* (see Figure 8.5). This perspective has been present throughout our study, beginning with the idea that *ethical motives* and *personal character* can matter

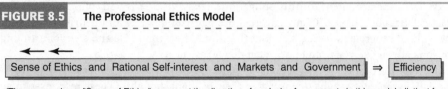

FIGURE 8.5   The Professional Ethics Model

Sense of Ethics and Rational Self-interest and Markets and Government ⇒ Efficiency

(The arrows above "Sense of Ethics" represent the direction of analysis of proponents in this model, distinct from the previous model.)

beyond analyzing the consequences of choice (Introduction) and that we can interpret a range of motives driving market activities (Chapter 1–3). We also surveyed several ethical theories to express and ground what a sense of ethics is about (Introduction), and we examined arguments by stakeholder proponents that a sense of ethics should guide all of our economic decisions, including managerial decisions (Chapter 5).

The previous two models (represented in Figures 8.3 and 8.4) de-emphasize the role of ethics in business and economic decision-making. It's not hard, at least in theory, to conceive of society strictly in egoist and self-interested terms. The point of law enforcement, we could believe, is to instill enough *fear* that people will follow the rules. Law will punish offenders so harshly that each person's self-interested calculation will be to respect law. Likewise, one can (try to) offer narrowly self-interested reasons for *every* human action in a way that might sustain the entire business system. If we believe that people are all *psychological egoists* (see box "What Motivates Giving?" in Chapter 1 Section 2), then our only hope to live together in peace is to find institutional rules that funnel conflicting self-interest into productive interactions.

What then, is a counterargument that supports a significant role for ethics in business and economic life? And what should be the content of those ethical obligations? Part of the appeal of the first two models is that they bracket these difficult questions. But advocates of the model of professional ethics believe that these are the most important questions of all.

A. PROFESSIONAL ETHICS WITHIN AN EFFICIENCY FRAMEWORK

Let's begin with the prior observation that even those market advocates who lean most heavily on self-interest rarely endorse the thesis of psychological egoism. They may advocate a limited role for ethics *in business,* but they rarely wish to deny a role for personal ethics in life generally. For example, the invisible hand and law and regulation arguments are *normative* arguments that *appeal* to our sense of ethics and values even if they de-emphasize the role of ethics in business and economic life. Thus, advocates of the previous models can and usually do grant the importance of a personal sense of ethics but deny the importance of **business ethics** or **professional ethics**, which refers to ethics as they apply to business settings or the professions more generally.

What, then, is the argument for ethics *in business*? There is no *single* argument, but let's begin with the observation that both of the previous models presume at least some role for law. Given this, the proponent for professional ethics poses the following question: do we have an ethical obligation to follow the law in those models? This point is not trivial. Neither stockholder nor stakeholder proponents advocate breaking the law for the pursuit of profits. Economist Milton Friedman, for example, does not advocate that managers conduct a purely self-interested cost/benefit analysis to determine when to break the law, and then break it whenever it's in the firm's interests to do so. Rather, businesses simply *ought* to follow the law.

What is the argument for this obligation? This question is both philosophical and practical. Suppose that a brilliant coworker has figured out a way for the firm to break the law without repercussion. You say, "But that would be wrong." He and everyone around you look at you like you're an idiot. What do you say next?

Perhaps the best thing is to get out of the room. Or you could give reasons why everyone will, in fact, get caught—contrary to their brilliant thoughts. These responses fit an egoist perspective that appeals solely to self-interest.

But there are ways to describe the sense of *ethical wrong* by breaking the law that appeals to ideas in earlier chapters. One revealing description is that lawbreakers free-ride off of those people who respect the law (Chapter 7 Section 2). What makes it possible to commit this crime is that others are living in an orderly world that offenders are choosing to exploit for personal gain. Government can't enforce *every* provision of law, and so society can work only if it counts on people's sense of obligation to follow the law.

Of course, if "it's wrong" does not work as a response, then this answer will probably not help much either. But for those who already believe in the value of market efficiency, it's not a trifling response. Here's what it claims: the invisible hand argument is not a coherent position without including at least one demand of professional ethics—that people must develop a sense of ethics to follow the law. *Given* respect for law, self-interested motivations in markets can create a system that improves people's lives.

Some of the most basic lapses in business ethics are attributable to those who break the law for personal gain. They choose to free-ride to beat the rules of a system and harm others along the way. Purists for the invisible hand model may try to ground *all* motivations in self-interest, but then they face the task of explaining how a society can maintain a rule of law with people who are motivated solely by self-interest. Can *fear* be enough? Advocates for professional ethics argue in return that markets can function effectively only if people trust that most others have a sense of obligation to follow the very same law that binds them all together, or else the system will break down.

> A philosophical question for all the models in this chapter is to explain the sense in which people have an obligation to follow the law.

A notable feature of this reasoning is to consider the connection between (a) a person's belief in some value (in this case, efficiency) and (b) that person identifying some personal ethical obligation (in this case, to follow the law). As a practical matter, the prospect of convincing someone to accept an ethical demand often depends on finding some value that the person already endorses, and then showing that the ethical demand is a consequence of believing in that value. It's a deeply practical way to make progress in ethical dialogue. It's a way to find a point of leverage for advancing an ethical conversation. We are applying this method of ethical argument through the one value that we have so far studied—efficiency. What do you think of this approach in general?

We can now apply all the arguments from Chapters 6 and 7 to consider further implications of this approach, taking the value of efficiency for granted for the moment. Let's focus in particular on the background conditions that create efficiency gains in markets. For example, what sense of professional ethics is necessary for us to live within stable property rights (beyond the stability that government might be able to achieve through its coercive powers)? Advocates of the model of professional ethics have an answer: *engaging in honest dealings and keeping your word*. To take another example: What enables people's choices to be guided by accurate information? Answer: *being transparent*. And the suggestions continue: What minimizes negative externalities? Answer: *not foisting problems on others.*[9] What actions minimize exploiting those who lack coherent and rational preferences? Answer: *not marketing harmful products to the very young*. What can mitigate against debilitating social dilemmas? Answer: *contributing to important public goods and avoiding free-riding*. What actions avoid complicity in creating the most fundamental public goods problem of all (order in society)? Answer: *following the law and not exploiting legal loopholes.*

In this way professional ethics guidelines can be *derived* from an analysis of the value of market efficiency. That's quite remarkable. It's possible to derive fairly detailed substantive ideas about ethical obligations in business and the professions through this approach and then test their viability in various cases. In this view professional ethics isn't an imposed set of rules by outsiders; rather, they describe ethical demands from a personal point of view that derive from that person's value system, such as a belief in market efficiency as an institutional value.

On this derivation, and to summarize the argument in the preceding paragraphs, ethics has an important role in business and economic life because self-interested incentives are insufficient for creating efficiency in a world with market failures.

Should you really believe that the preceding paragraphs identify a compelling list of actual ethical demands in business? Your answer will depend on (1) whether you think efficiency is a worthy goal and (2) whether you think government and markets can achieve efficiency without ethics, as suggested by the previous models.

Let's consider two implications of this approach to professional ethics. First, this argument suggests that norms of professional ethics can have distinctive content apart from family ethics or other areas of personal ethics. Second, on this model of reasoning, the content of our individual ethical demands depends in part on how we understand the point of the institutions that surround us, and what they can and can't accomplish.

Finally, note how this discussion can be interpreted as an *explanatory and descriptive argument* for why the business system has developed standards of ethics as it has; or as a *normative argument* for why, on your own standards, you might endorse an account of ethics in business and economic life. As a normative argument, business ethics becomes the practical expression of your value commitments applied to the roles you occupy in economic life.

B. NONINSTITUTIONAL FOUNDATIONS FOR PROFESSIONAL ETHICS

The previous section does not imply that efficiency is the preeminent value for thinking about ethics or markets. The point was illustrative to show how it's possible to derive an account of professional or business ethics from an institutional value, like efficiency. The method of reasoning can be generalized to values that matter most to you. The previous section also does not imply that professional ethics derives wholly from institutional underpinnings. We can complement the analysis above by considering how professional ethics connects with reflections about the right thing to do, unmediated by our assessment of institutions. For example, the previous section built a case for honesty, transparency, and reciprocity grounded through support of some further value (in that case, the value of efficiency). But consider that many will say that honesty is valuable for its own sake. We may say that being honest is part of being a decent person or that it's an implication

---

[9]See, for example, http://www.baltimoresun.com/news/bs-md-co-derelict-boats-hazard-20100716,0,2664082. story

of following the golden rule, and business ethics is simply an extension of having a basic sense of ethics that applies no matter the context or situation.

Both perspectives have insight. Let's now focus on this second perspective. As first suggested in the Introduction, a large body of psychological research points to early learning about ethics that provides core beliefs that guide us throughout life. It's not uncommon in forums on business ethics to be confronted with simple **ethics tests** to remind us of these lessons. An *ethics test* refers to a quick reference set of principles that guide your decision-making. For example, consider these tests:

> *The golden rule*: Do unto others as you would have them do unto you.
>
> *The New York Times (NYT) test*: Only make decisions that you would not mind finding analyzed on the front page of the *NYT*.
>
> *The dinner table test*: Only make decisions that you could be proud of if your children knew about them.
>
> *The gut test*: After all the reasons get sorted one way or the other, does the decision feel right?

Where do these tests get their force? Perhaps one way to explain their value is simply through the importance of *being an ethical person*. We do not need to understand the nature of markets and capitalism for that. We will develop this idea in Chapter 13 in the context of the value of relationships and personal character in business and economic life.

This section presses us to think about how we sort through our own incentives, ethical beliefs, and values to create a single, coherent belief system—to have ethical integrity. In Chapter 13, we will consider integrity as a value by itself and examine whether markets support or undermine our ability to have and maintain integrity. In later chapters we will examine other non-consequentialist groundings for ethics that may be reflected by the discussion in this section.

We can reconsider the relevance of the survey of ethics in the Introduction in the context of the current discussion. Leading ethical theories suggest somewhat more elaborate tests than those provided above for addressing ethical questions, such as, (1) What are the *consequences* of choosing one way or the other? (2) Are there specific ethical *duties*, constraints, or values relevant for assessing the situation, independent from analyzing the consequences? (3) What are the *motives* driving the various options and what should motivate my choice? (4) Is the *character* of those involved, including my own, relevant to the situation at hand? How so?

You may ground your sense of ethics beyond any of the ways discussed in this book. But no matter whether through ethics tests or your value commitments or through any of the three models discussed above, or through talking about ethics with people you respect, these normative discussions can give you greater control over how you direct your life and help you to see the whole sweep of the market system, and its many details, from an ethical point of view.

C. MUTUAL BENEFIT AS A PERSONAL VALUE

The discussion about efficiency and professional ethics may seem to imply that efficiency is merely an institutional value for understanding markets. But the concept of mutual benefit undergirding efficiency analysis can, by itself, express a code of personal conduct. This code says: always look for opportunities to make others better off as you improve your own situation. Engage life as a series of positive sum games. Confront situations as opportunities for mutual gain. Thus, the seemingly dry concept of efficiency can become highly relevant for a personal belief system or business philosophy. For example, Kip Tindell, the CEO of Container Store, was interviewed about some of his ethical principles. He says, "Maybe the most important one is: 'Fill the other guy's basket to the brim. Making money then becomes an easy proposition.' That's something Andrew Carnegie said on his deathbed that he actually attributed all of his business success to. That's sort of the opposite of a zero-sum game, and it means creating a mutually beneficial relationship with everyone we work with."[10]

We can also note that the principle of mutual benefit has its limits (see Chapter 7 Section 6), which leads some people to a utilitarian perspective for their sense of professional ethics. We might say, Pursue mutual benefit as far as possible, and then manage

ETHICS, NON-PROFITS, AND CORPORATE RESPONSIBILITY

The study of these three models can deepen our understanding of stockholder and stakeholder debates about corporate responsibility studied in Chapters 4 and 5. For example, stockholder advocates believe that self-interest drives the business world and that our legal system must set the basic ground rules to determine what corporations may or may not do. Corporations should maximize profits within those laws. Stockholder proponents, for a variety of reasons discussed in Chapter 4, are skeptical that a robust account of ethics can correct for market failures: that's the job of government and the market itself. Whether stockholder proponents endorse the invisible hand model or the law and regulation model depends on how extensively they believe that government should correct for market failures.

By contrast, stakeholder proponents believe that self-interest alone is insufficient for creating a viable market system. Ethics should be an integral part of doing business and making choices. This picture provides a more complex understanding of human motives beyond the idea of *self-interest* in the invisible hand or law and regulation models. The stakeholder model asks us to reflect about the ethics of our conduct in the business and economic world. What values do we want the system to promote and how are our individual actions supporting those values?

Finally, recall the discussion of non-profits introduced within the discussion of public goods in Chapter 7 Section 5. The non-profit sector is a massive and inspiring effort to provide public goods and infuse a sense of values throughout the economic system. Non-profits combine market institutions with an explicit commitment to values beyond profit. Codes of professional ethics apply to non-profits as much as for-profits in their management practices. A specific account of an institution's organizational ethics—the ethical norms within specific organizations—will depend on many factors, which will include the specific mission of that organization. For example, a hospital will connect the value of being a hospital with an account of its organizational ethics. This is also true of for-profits when they tailor their ethical guidelines to their specific industry.

Non-profits embed themselves in a broader civil society by explicitly serving a societal interest. The existence of these non-profits adds a layer of complexity to debates about corporate responsibility. For-profit corporations, for example, may benefit from and rely on non-profits for carrying out social responsibilities, especially public goods provision. In this way, the responsibilities we attribute to for-profit corporations may depend on our understanding of the reach and scope of society's non-profit sector. The capabilities and limitations of the entire range of institutions in civil society are relevant for developing a full account of the ethics and responsibilities of corporations.

---

[10]Adam Bryant, "Three Good Hires? He'll Pay More for One Who's Great," *The New York Times* (March 13, 2010). See http://www.nytimes.com/2010/03/14/business/14corners.html?pagewanted=all

tradeoffs by producing the most welfare. Here is what Jay Goltz says, in a *New York Times* blog "You're the Boss"[11]:

> About 10 years ago, I was having my annual holiday party and my niece had come with her newly minted M.B.A. boyfriend. As he looked around the room, he noted that my employees seemed happy. I told him that I thought they were. Then, figuring I would take his new degree for a test drive, I asked him how he thought I did that. "I'm sure you treat them well," he replied.
>
> "That's half of it," I said. "Do you know what the other half is?" He didn't have the answer, and neither have the many other people that I have told this story. So what is the answer? I fired the unhappy people. People usually laugh at this point. I wish I were kidding.
>
> I'm not. I have learned the long, hard and frustrating way that as a manager you cannot make everyone happy. You can try, you can listen, you can solve some problems, you can try some more. Good management requires training, counseling and patience, but there comes a point when you are robbing the business of precious time and energy.

Whatever its limitations, utilitarianism recommends an outlook of considering everyone's interests and then doing what creates the most good, rather than focusing on one person's interests. Managerial and ethical leadership often draws on utilitarian reasoning.

What's your reaction to efficiency and utilitarianism as practical guides for professional ethics and personal conduct? Later chapters will present other values that contrast against these discussions.

8.5   CONFLICTS OF INTEREST

You are the chairperson of the board of directors that determines your raise for a corporation. As chair, you have a duty to your shareholders to run the company in their interests. As the person receiving the raise, you have an interest in receiving as high a compensation package as possible.

You are on a hiring committee and one of the applicants is your nephew. You have an interest in hiring him as family member but you have a duty to make the decision without that interest in mind.

You work for a company that audits other companies, but the company also makes profits depending on a positive appraisal. You have a duty to assess the company only on the merits of its fundamentals, but you have an interest in giving a positive appraisal.

Conflicts of interest can develop when a person's duties in a professional role conflict with that person's other interests or duties. More specifically, a conflict of interest refers to situations when someone is expected to be motivated by an impartial judgment in a professional role, but some competing interest potentially or actually interferes with the ability to make an impartial judgment in that situation.[12]

---

[11]Goltz, Jay. "You're the Boss." *The New York Times* (March 9, 2010). See http://boss.blogs.nytimes.com/2010/03/09/the-secret-to-having-happy-employees/

[12]For a more extended discussion of the definition of conflicts of interest, see Michael Davis and Andrew Stark, *Conflict of Interest in the Professions* (Oxford University Press, 2002), pp. 3–19.

Conflicts of interest are important sources of concern for ethics. From an institutional point of view, on the reasoning of the invisible hand and law and regulation models, the best remedy is to change the rules to eliminate the conflict. For example, a company could pass a rule that prohibits anyone on a hiring committee to screen candidates that have any family or personal connections. Professional codes of ethics often specify what counts as a conflict of interest within a particular area and how to handle it if or when it arises. In addition, laws may exist to reduce conflicts of interest, such as accounting laws that require independent verification of financial reports by parties who should have no conflicted interest in supporting deviations from the truth.

An advocate of the model of professional ethics may emphasize an ethical norm of transparency about potential conflicts as the most obvious response when a conflict arises. This idea relates closely to the full information requirement within efficiency discussions (Chapter 6 Section 4). Transparency is also related to the concept of honesty: carrying out your public responsibility without other parties knowing about this potential or actual conflict is to keep them in the dark about factors that affect your ability to carry out your responsibilities as expected. Sometimes transparency is thought to be enough, as with real estate agents who receive the informed consent of both buyer and seller if they are the dual agent for both. Sometimes it is better to remove or recuse oneself from decision-making under such circumstances. The *NYT* ethics test can be especially appropriate to help reason through how to handle conflicts of interest, especially because self-serving rationalizations can be remarkably convincing when conflicts are hidden from public view.

This discussion about conflicts of interest relates to the left-hand side of the model of ethics and values (Figure 8.1). It prompts the question: what is the right balance between ethical motives and the pursuit of self-interested incentives? In general people do not want to be caught within an institutional system that makes ethics *too* costly from a personal point of view. In this sense, conflicts of interest can be like the double-bind in the tragedy of the commons (Chapter 7 Section 5B)—the institutional system is defective if making ethical choices is too heroic for mortals.

Whistleblowing refers to the act of telling others outside of the normal chain of command about some purported unethical or illegal activity occurring within the organization. Whistleblowing may be internal or external, depending on whether the allegations are reported to authorities within the organization or to external constituents, such as newspaper reporters. Whistleblowing often creates a conflict of interest, such as a conflict between a duty to act in the interest of the organization and a duty to act on behalf of the public interest. There is usually a third conflict: the desire to protect one's self-interest and friendships within the organization. Whistleblowers are sometimes celebrated as heroes for exposing some wrong, but they also often experience harsh reprisals from within the organization, such as demotion or firing, and harsh judgments among those who believe that duties toward the organization trump all. The United States currently has a patchwork of laws that attempt to protect whistleblowers to some degree, including legislation to encourage and protect *securities* whistleblowers in the wake of the financial scandals and crises of the last decade. Whistleblower protections are built into the Dodd-Frank Wall Street Reform and Consumer Protection Act (2010). But the fact remains that whistleblowing is often highly costly from a personal point of view.

These reflections capture part of the moral impulse of the invisible hand and law and regulation models: an institutional point of view is important for thinking about the rules that could reduce ethical conflicts in business and economic life. Many people would like to

Read the
Case Study
Blowing the Whistle
only on MySearchLab

work under institutions with rules that create the best chance for ethical outcomes. But the model of professional ethics emphasizes a flip side of this point: ethical challenges will always remain, and so we must bring our sense of ethics for addressing them. This discussion reinforces a central thesis of this chapter: understanding the relationships between ethics incentives, and institutions is of first importance for developing a probing discussion of ethics.

8.6   ETHICS AND VALUES: MOVING BEYOND EFFICIENCY AND WELFARE DISCUSSIONS

A. THE DANCE BETWEEN ETHICS, INCENTIVES, AND INSTITUTIONS

We began this chapter with an excerpt about dancing. It's a metaphor for thinking about ethics, incentives, and institutions. Conflicts of interest and whistleblowing are situations where ethics, incentives, and institutions collide with one another.

Let's consider these three forces as moving together in a three-way dance. For example, consider how some people believe that ethical demands in business are ineffective. They may draw on arguments in Chapter 4 that people are primarily self-interested and to hope for ethical motivations is unrealistic. Or they may argue that competitive pressures in capitalism crowd out ethics and, in effect, make ethical conduct too costly for most people. Suppose this or similar reasoning leads proponents of this argument to advocate greater government action to lead reform without arguing for heightened ethical motives by participants.

But then others will counterargue that government solutions create their own problems: they are often ineffective in stemming unethical or illegal activities; they are often too slow or the political process distorts effective rule-making; or the problems are global without effective legal responses.

Suppose that these shortcomings lead the original debaters to reassess their position. What is the next move in this dance? They may return to the vision of the invisible hand that seeks to create good results without the need for much ethics or government in economic life. But what then about the counterarguments to this position: many see market failures all around. So the debaters may be drawn to consider the professional ethics model that was originally placed in the background. Perhaps the limits of government and the prevalence of market failures means ethics must exert an important role in business. Or they may reconsider the law and regulation model, or return again to the invisible hand model. Who is going to lead this dance for creating a good social system: people's personal sense of ethics, people's personal incentives in a market environment, or the government's active role in defining the playing field?

Herein lies a dynamic of debate that could be plugged into many specific topics in business and economics. The aim is to synchronize the forces of ethical decision-making, self-interested incentives, and the institutional rules that constrain our choices. The value of the dance metaphor is to consider how ethics, incentives, and institutions are moving parts in a business system. The three models surveyed in this chapter are three different choreographies of how to dance.

Consider this example. Carbon dioxide emissions create a commons problem. The commons is our atmosphere and the problem is global warming. If we grant this premise, what are the responsibilities of major oil companies and automakers with respect to their advertising, their lobbying, and their research and development choices for acknowledging and addressing this problem? What are the responsibilities of consumers, shareholders,

Read the
Case Study
Sarbanes-Oxley only
on MySearchLab

and government for addressing this problem? What are the practical impediments for reaching a solution? In debates about how to address global warming, people examine trade-offs between pushing for (a) heightened consumer and corporate *ethics*, (b) the ability or inability of market *incentives* to solve the problem, and (c) the pros and cons for government *institutions* to increase regulation. Remedies and responses range across some combination of ethical demands, aligning market incentives, and advocating new laws. A revealing dialogue among oil executives, activists, and politicians about global warming highlights the tensions between these forces (http://www.pbs.org/wgbh/pages/frontline/heat/interviews/).

In sum the concepts presented in Chapters 1–8 offer versatile normative tools for developing your views (and assessing others' views) on global warming and many other applied topics. The invisible hand, law and regulation, and professional ethics models can help clarify competing ways that forces of ethics, incentives, and institutions can succeed or fail at addressing social and economic problems.

8.7   LOOKING AHEAD

What are the most important values that an economic system should respect or promote? One reference point for exploring this question is the Preamble to the United States Constitution, "We the People of the United States, in Order to form a more perfect Union, establish Justice, insure domestic Tranquility, provide for the common defense, promote the general Welfare, and secure the Blessings of Liberty to ourselves and our Posterity. . . ."

The constitutional framers knew about utilitarian thought, as reflected in their advocacy of the general welfare; they also advocated justice and liberty and other values. This book focuses on the ethics and values of *business and economic life*, and so there is no direct translation to the political values enunciated in the U.S. Constitution. But one basic insight applies: just like the preamble to the U.S. Constitution, a range of values is relevant to business and economic life as well, and Chapters 1–7 have not yet represented this more comprehensive normative terrain.

We will now leave the welfare tradition of Chapters 6–8 and consider other normative standards. These standards offer different insights about how to assess business and economic institutions.

Studying a broader range of normative standards will also bring new insights about the sense of ethics that we should bring to our choices. For example, one argument in this chapter was about deriving a robust sense of professional ethics from a narrow account of efficiency, including duties to keep contracts, be transparent, follow the law, and others. In the chapters ahead we will introduce a wider set of normative values, such as liberty, rights, and equality, and consider the implications of these ideas for our sense of ethics.

8.8   SUMMARY

Models are a summary of ideas. They prompt questions to ask and create a basis to probe the strengths and weaknesses of our own or others' arguments. We examined the invisible hand model, the law and regulation model, and the professional ethics model.

By puzzling through these materials, you will develop the ability to understand a great deal of the arguments that drive public policy debates in the United States today. You will have a greater understanding of the intellectual vision that supports positions that you agree with and disagree with. These chapters are not designed to offer an overall comment about whether efficiency and utilitarianism on balance are values that support or undermine support for capitalism. The goal, rather, is to help you understand the logic of the underlying arguments that propel debate, for developing your own views. Efficiency and utilitarianism may at first seem like dry and uninspiring ideals, and yet these values motivate many debates about markets and ethics, and, for many, they rest on a morally inspiring idea that we want to live in a world that is progressively making people better off through the generations.

The model of ethics and values represents the dynamic between ethics, incentives, and the demands of institutions. There are many different ways to dance. We need to know our values, reflect on the ethics, incentives, and institutions that will get us there, and then join the dance.

KEY TERMS

sense of ethics	self-interest	professional ethics
invisible hand model	incentive-compatible	ethics tests
law and regulation model	institutional design	conflicts of interest
professional ethics model	separation thesis	whistleblowing
	business ethics	

DISCUSSION QUESTIONS

1. Reassess your views on corporate responsibility in light of the ideas in the last three chapters.

2. Some say that business ethics is different from personal ethics and for good reason. Others say that ethics is the same wherever you go. Evaluate these ideas, drawing on the analysis of this chapter.

3. Suppose you know that others are free-riding off of your contributions to a public good that you value. Does this give you reason to stop contributing? Choose some examples and assess.

4. Let P stand for our most important public goods in your judgment. Evaluate the following argument: We need P. We will not get P without government provision. Therefore, the government is justified in providing P.

5. What do you think is the best argument to support the view that we have obligations to follow the law?

6. In your view, is an *explanatory* project or a *normative* project about ethics and values more important? What is that distinction? An explanatory project may take some of the mystery out of the evolution of human norms and ethical standards; but this approach may not offer much assistance for making decisions. In your view, what should be the relationship between explaining and justifying ethical norms?

7. Does working for a cigarette company pose a moral dilemma? How about a weapons manufacturer? Explain your reasoning. If your answer to the preceding questions is "no," is there any type of company such that your employment would create a moral dilemma for you? How so?

8. Find a current headline that draws on several features of the model of ethics and values to deepen your insight of that issue. Apply the model to guide the questions that you ask and the positions that you defend.

9. This chapter suggests how someone who tends toward the stockholder view with limited government may also be a strong believer in corporate honesty and transparency to investors and the general public, with strict support for

following the law and avoiding negative externalities. In this sense, a stockholder proponent
may endorse the professional ethics model as
much as the invisible hand model. Stakeholder
proponents may support the professional
ethics model, but they also might argue their
cause through the law and regulation model.
In these ways and others complex variations
in debates about corporate social responsibility can be mapped onto these three models in
revealing ways. Question: is the demand for
ethics in a business setting a politically con-
servative or politically liberal idea (or both or
neither)? Explain.

10. Business ethicist Albert Carr famously argued
that business is like a game of poker. Just as we
have no problem being deceptive in a poker
game, business has its own set of rules that do
no match our sense of ethics outside of business, but that's OK. Draw on all the concepts
of this course to analyze the analogy between
poker ethics and business ethics.

11. Consider the person who strongly believes that
ethics doesn't apply within the business system
but is also a big supporter of the capitalist system. Is this a consistent position? How so (or
how not)? What is your response?

13. Take water as a commons. Find some current
dispute surrounding water usage and analyze
the issues of that case, drawing on the ideas in
this chapter.

14. Should the government intervene in ecological
crises, such as floods, hurricanes, and torna-
does, to help the economic situation of people
devastated by those natural events? Apply
the ideas of this chapter to analyze different
responses.

15. Is being ethical in business harder to achieve
during a severe economic recession? Are
there any institutional implications for your
answer?

16. Analyze the British Petroleum oil spill by applying a range of concepts introduced in this
book.

ETHICS BEYOND EFFICIENCY

Part IV introduces ethical puzzles in business and economic life that draw on values beyond efficiency and welfare, as well as arguments that support or criticize a range of market activities based on these values. These chapters offer an expanding normative analysis of business and economic life.

Chapter 9 • Freedom

Chapter 10 • Rights

Chapter 11 • Equality

Chapter 12 • What People Deserve

Chapter 13 • Relationships and Character

Chapter 14 • Community and the Common Good

WHEN YOU FINISH STUDYING THIS CHAPTER, YOU SHOULD BE ABLE TO:

1. Distinguish two concepts of freedom.

2. Characterize and explain why some people believe that business and economic life respects and promotes freedom, and others do not.

3. Debate which types of political and economic institutions best uphold and protect freedom.

4. Discuss why some people argue for a tight link between ethics and freedom and others do not, and why this discussion is significant.

9

LIBERTY

9.1 INTRODUCTION

Are you free?

We now turn to a new ideal, with different issues, and a different set of arguments. Freedom is a personal quest, and the rallying cry of people.

Give me your tired, your poor, Your huddled masses yearning to breathe free, the wretched refuse of your teeming shore. Send these, the homeless, tempest-tossed to me, I lift my lamp beside the golden door! (Inscription on the Statue of Liberty, written by poet Emma Lazarus).

This chapter will reflect on the nature of freedom as it relates to the ethics of economic life. We start with two distinct concepts of freedom and then examine competing arguments about the institutional and personal implications of believing in these ideas.

9.2 TWO CONCEPTS OF LIBERTY

Less than fifteen years after the end of World War II, English political philosopher Isaiah Berlin wrote the following in the introduction to his historic essay on liberty:

[W]hen ideas are neglected by those who ought to attend to them— that is to say, those who have been trained to think critically about ideas—they sometimes acquire an unchecked momentum and an irresistible power over multitudes of men that may grow too violent to be affected by rational criticism.[1]

[1]Isaiah Berlin, "Two Concepts of Liberty" in *Four Essays on Liberty* (Oxford University Press, 1990), p. 167.

The story of humanity, Berlin thought, is a story of the ideals and beliefs that move people for good or evil, for peace or war. He echoed the sentiments of his contemporary, John Maynard Keynes, that ideas—more than vested interests—shape and explain the incredible history of humankind.[2] Our lives become mired in a million and one details, and countless small decisions. Yet, even if only in the background, these are large ideas that catch us and frame our worldview.

Chief among these is the idea of freedom.

We often hear it spoken around us or by us, but how often do we think about what freedom really means? Philosopher Isaiah Berlin surveyed over 200 senses of *liberty* across human history. In keeping with common usage, this chapter will use the word *freedom* interchangeably with *liberty*. The distinctions to follow could be expressed through either usage. Berlin came to believe that the meanings of liberty could be broken down into two definitions that are the most revealing. These two conceptions—so deeply rooted within our personal psyches—help explain what drives us to be who we are. They indicate two different visions about how we should organize economic and political order and they each have a long record in human history. Let's consider these two concepts of liberty.

A. NEGATIVE FREEDOM

Living in freedom can mean the lack of interference in doing what we wish. The name *negative* liberty derives from the core idea that freedom can mean the *absence* of something: interference. We discover that we are free when impediments are missing from our path. The greater this area of noninterference, the greater our personal liberty. Berlin called this idea **negative liberty**, also known as *negative freedom*.

Suppose that a labor union is prevented from organizing, some business owners are prevented from selling some product, or some people are so poor that they can't afford to buy enough to eat. Do all these situations have something in common? Yes, each situation included people who were prevented from doing what they wanted.

We all require space in life. With *no* protections against interference, we hardly would be human. Berlin emphasized interferences caused by others, not natural interferences. The fact that the laws of gravity block my wish to jump to the moon may spur innovation, but it does not restrict my personal freedom. For Berlin, a lack of freedom requires a sense in which *others* have prevented me from doing what I wish, whether by intention or as the unintended result of a system that constrains my choices.

Berlin writes, "We cannot remain absolutely free, and must give up some of our liberty to preserve the rest."[3] Why is this? We need laws to protect us. If they are effective, they create a space of noninterference where we can live in peace with others. We are thankful for what they give. But these laws also apply to us and restrict our freedom by preventing us from doing what we want. Society becomes a balancing act. In Chapter 8 Section 2, we analyzed law and order as a public goods problem. But now we can consider a different idea: the creation of law and order is not merely or may not be essentially about increasing

[2] Economist John Maynard Keynes (1883–1846) wrote: "The ideas of economists and political philosophers, both when they are right and when they are wrong, are more powerful than is commonly understood. Indeed the world is ruled by little else. Practical men, who believe themselves to be quite exempt from any intellectual influence, are usually the slaves of some defunct economist" (*The General Theory of Employment, Interest, and Money*, MacMillan, 1936, p. 383). Keynes's economic ideas became so dominant over the next fifty years that his approach to government policy was named after him: Keynesian economics.

[3] Isaiah Berlin, "Two Concepts of Liberty" in *Four Essays on Liberty* (Oxford University Press, 1990), p. 126.

our welfare, however true that is, but also about increasing our personal freedom. For those who focus on the value of freedom, that is the more important point. The relevant freedom at issue is freedom as noninterference. We will discuss institutional implications of this concept of freedom in greater detail below.

The important point now is to understand what this sense of freedom means and to consider its fundamental importance. For Berlin and the many others who try to refine this definition, freedom is a social condition that will exist in society depending on the degree to which people and institutions are not interfering with people's wishes to do what they want.

B. POSITIVE FREEDOM

Negative freedom says something about my circumstances—that my path is clear. But so can the path of a bird or flowing lava. Many people would like to think that human freedom is of a different kind than the bird's freedom or the movement of an object. Positive freedom addresses this intuition. The second concept of liberty is not necessarily in conflict with negative freedom—it's just a different idea.

What is the difference between a person and the bird? The bird, we might say, reacts to the world through stimulus and response. But people are agents who make decisions, exert a will, and change the world in ways for which they are rightfully held responsible. This idea of **positive liberty** is not about people's circumstances but about a *positive* characteristic about *them*. We might say about ourselves: *I am a creative force in control of who I am. I can will changes in the world, and I freely choose my actions.* As Berlin writes, "The desire to be governed by myself, or at any rate to participate in the process by which my life is to be controlled, may be as deep a wish as that of a free area of action, and perhaps historically older."[4] At a personal level, living in freedom can mean self-government.

The ancient Greek philosopher Plato offers the evocative imagery of the charioteer with a team of horses that rage out of control, threatening total destruction to the charioteer and harm to those around them. In this analogy, the charioteer represents our reason and the horses our emotions; control over our lives depends on using reason to direct and guide our emotions. Without the horses, the chariot does not move. But without reason as the charioteer, we will never be able to go where we want to in life. We will not be free.

The greater our self-mastery, the greater our freedom. Advocates of this sense of freedom recognize the distinctive and inspiring capacity of humans to shape and control their lives. Negative freedom is sometimes described as freedom *from* (that is, *from* interference) and positive freedom as freedom *to* (that is, *to* act and be in control).

THE PURSUIT OF HIGHER EDUCATION

What is the value of higher education? A college education can raise our standard of living and, statistically, it is likely to do so. Yet education can have additional ends from the perspective of human development across a person's entire life. We start life through the care of adults. We are infants. Our beliefs are their beliefs. We grow as children into adolescence. When do we become our own person? Can college help in this process? When people say that education is valuable for its own sake, they often mean that it can help us become more in control of our lives with beliefs that we have made our own. We become more free in the positive sense described in this section. This is the root meaning of a *liberal arts* education, to develop capacities of rational thought to increase one's positive freedom of self-mastery.

---

[4]Isaiah Berlin, "Two Concepts of Liberty" in *Four Essays on Liberty* (Oxford University Press, 1990), p. 131.

These two concepts of liberty are personal and are meant to speak to us. The point here is not to judge which is better, but to recognize that people across the ages have valued freedom in both senses, and that they are distinct ideas.

Do you agree? What do you make of these ideas?

9.3   INSTITUTIONAL IMPLICATIONS OF NEGATIVE FREEDOM

These ideas about freedom can be understood as descriptions of what people are, and as prescriptions to help define people's aspirations. In this and the next section, we will consider the institutional implications of freedom as a prescriptive and aspirational value, starting with negative freedom in this section.

A. MARKETS, PROPERTY RIGHTS, AND AN ARGUMENT IN SUPPORT OF MARKETS

Let's return to the island scenario in Chapter 6 Section 3 and look at market trade through a whole new lens. Do you recall that we analyzed jugs of water and parcels of food? Analyzing the *welfare effects of trade* is not the essential point for those who place most weight on ideas of freedom. We do not need to sort through all those background conditions required to establish a welfare increase. The value of trade is elsewhere. We need to know whether people are being interfered with or not.

What should we say about markets? Consider one answer often advocated by proponents of negative freedom: markets rely on people's consent to exchange and this fact captures the basic freedom of the market. It's not the fact of mutual advantage that matters most but that either party can veto the deal that makes the invisible hand model an appealing vision of freedom.

I can block interferences by saying "no" to any trade. Contrast this feature of markets with government: when the city tells a business to follow a certain code and the business says "no," the business gets fined or shut down. When the government takes property through eminent domain and the owner says "no," the government can eventually bring a bulldozer. These are interferences. But the essence of trade, in this view, is that you either consent to a trade or you veto it and maintain your space of noninterference. There is no interference in either case.

Thus, in this argument, the true value of markets is less about efficiency and more about creating a system of noninterference that preserves our negative freedom beyond any other economic organization. In this view, markets realize freedom through trade sustained by a thin set of background rules.

We can dig a little deeper by noticing how these ideas connect with the first lesson of Chapter 2. Property rights are a social concept. The fact that I own property is saying something that's not essentially about a thing but about *my relationships* with others. Recall that negative freedom is also a *social* concept because our freedom depends on noninterfering relationships with others (either directly or indirectly through institutional structures that do not interfere with us).

The insight is this: the grounds of negative freedom are found with the underlying property rights that create relationships of noninterference. *Property rights of noninterference* are the most important social condition that directly protects the value of freedom.

Most proponents of negative freedom support markets because they believe that, given human needs and wants, markets are the likely result of a society that prizes private property rights of noninterference.

It's about privacy and space. With private property rights in the foreground, most proponents of negative freedom are then led, from this commitment, to support for markets, because they believe that—given human needs and wants—markets are the likely result of a society that prizes private property rights of noninterference.

This discussion provides a clean contrast against the discussion in Chapter 6. What do you see most in markets and capitalism: *welfare-improving gains* that result from trade or *property rights* of trade that preserve a sphere of noninterference based on consent? Advocates of negative freedom emphasize the value of the underlying property rights.

B. PROPERTY RIGHTS, POVERTY, AND AN ARGUMENT CRITICAL OF MARKETS

Perhaps you observe neither of these. Political philosopher Gerald Cohen sees a very different picture. "What is the essence of being poor in a free market world?" Cohen asks. It's to live in a property rights scheme that prevents you from getting what you want or need. I want food. I have no money. I go to the grocery store and they say: no money, no food. Is this freedom? Property rights, Cohen observes, cut both ways. Property rights are external rules that often *prevent* rather than enable people from doing what they want. For Cohen and others, market freedom is this: if you have lots of money, you are free. If you do not, you are not free.

Others use the idea of negative freedom to criticize markets. For example, they argue that in a capitalist system if you have lots of money and wealth, you are free. But if you do not, then you are not free—and most people do not.

Thus, Cohen uses the negative conception of freedom, so often at the foundation of arguments on behalf of markets, and argues that markets actually undermine our negative freedom.

Given these contrasting views, we can ask, What combination of markets and government creates the most freedom? For some, it's unregulated markets with minimal government, the invisible hand model. Markets are the flower that bloom from a thin set of rules that protect negative freedom. But others see a world awash in poverty. They see marketplace rules that prevent people from getting what they need. Recall, from Chapter 2, economist Amartya Sen's remarkable finding that most famine-affected regions in the twentieth century had sufficient food in the stricken regions but the people who needed the food were *denied access* to it. In this view, government should regulate markets to ensure that less people are prevented from getting what they need. This is the law and regulation model.

In summary, the value of freedom as noninterference does not by itself dictate a view about the freedom of markets. We saw this result with efficiency analysis. Even if people agree about the meaning and value of efficiency, people will often disagree about the implication of this value for assessing markets. We now see the same dialectic with liberty. We can begin with the same value but reach very different assessments of the market system. These competing conclusions need not suggest that there are no answers or that debates are irresolvable. Rather, your judgment depends significantly on how you interpret what's happening in markets, which depends on your personal experiences and many empirical details. As you gather these details, it helps to be clear about your values—such as whether efficiency or freedom is the more important debating point, in your view.

If your choice is negative freedom, then the policy question is this: What combination of government and markets creates the greatest sphere of noninterference, the most freedom? Is it the capitalist system that we currently experience? The model of ethics and value depicts this debate.

C. MARKETS, VOLUNTARY CHOICE, AND NONINTERFERENCE

Let's examine the concepts of **voluntary choice** and noninterference a bit further. Suppose that I live in grinding poverty and I am offered a very low wage in horrid working conditions. Is taking that job a voluntary choice? Let's consider a second example: Suppose that a natural disaster cuts through my region and the prices for the goods that I need skyrocket. I have no other options at the moment. Is my choice to buy these goods voluntary? (Note that many states have anti-price-gouging laws.)

FREE MARKETS

The concept of *free markets* has different connotations depending on who is using this phrase. For many, the concept refers to markets that lack any government regulation apart from court decisions about property rights. Advocates of nonregulated markets will typically call these *free markets*. Those who criticize nonregulated markets will be less inclined to describe them in these terms, as they tend to believe that externality effects create interferences that contradict this expression.

More generally, *free markets* can also refer to markets that promote negative or positive freedom (or both), with much controversy over whether actual markets realize either sense of freedom, as discussed throughout this chapter.

Professor Serena Olsaretti writes, "I would like to suggest that a choice is voluntary if and only if it is not made because there is no acceptable alternative to it."[5] In her view, if the only explanation for choice is that there were no acceptable options, it's not a voluntary choice. There must be acceptable options, or the only option must be good enough that it's chosen for reasons beyond the fact that it's the only option. The key insight is that the voluntariness of the choice depends on the circumstances that frame the choice.

This section connects with a discussion in Chapter 1 Section 4 about the nature of voluntariness and now extends that discussion in the context of freedom.

Thus, Olsaretti believes that some people in desperate circumstances do not really choose their jobs or other market activities voluntarily, even if they made those particular choices. This position suggests that *choosing* in a market is compatible with being interfered with. This idea differs from Cohen's point that property rights in markets can prevent us from doing many things when we do not have money. The idea here is that, even market activities that we *do* choose can create unwanted interferences when they are chosen within a system that creates unacceptable options.

It's a puzzling idea: do markets interfere with our lives when our options are so limited that we feel that the choices we "consent to" aren't really voluntary? Is that a valid perspective? Consider this analogy: the common practice of parents who frame the choice options for their children, so that the dinner options are broccoli or cauliflower (the candy bar is not an option). Are they thereby interfering with the child's freedom? Let's apply this situation to economic choices: I have two unappealing job options: work at firm A or B, or not work at all and suffer the consequences. I choose A. By making this choice, does the system interfere with me? Or is this view just sour grapes? Whatever your response to these questions, the value of this discussion is to investigate your intuitive understanding of what *noninterference* means. It's the key idea behind the first concept of liberty.

---

[5]Serena Olsaretti, "Freedom, Force, and Choice: Against the Rights-Based Definition of Voluntariness," *Journal of Political Philosophy* 6(1) (1998), p. 71.

Let's describe this puzzle about noninterference in one other way. Recall the Pareto principle in Chapter 6. On this standard, each person has, in essence, a veto against any welfare improvement if it would make that person worse off. In the context of this chapter, the Pareto idea could be interpreted as a *veto principle for freedom*. Thus, those who support markets on negative freedom argue that markets preserve a sphere of noninterference because people can accept or veto any proposed market exchange. We can consent or veto high gas prices by buying or not buying gas, that iPad, the apartment rental, and so forth. No one is forcing that option on us. On the other hand, even if we suppose that this is true, can we veto the *system* of property rights that frames the options and terms of trade? Where and how can we consent to or veto the system as a whole? Emigrate?

Consider another answer: many argue that we need to be able to *control* the most basic rules and institutions of society. Particularly those who see a *lack* of negative freedom in markets want to know how it is possible to dissent from the rules of the system that frame and define our market choices. Having control over these ground rules introduces a different concept of freedom—*positive* freedom. For many, we are not truly free without this control, whether or not we grant that market choices are voluntary and preserve a space of noninterference.

In sum, we can distinguish two challenges introduced in this section: (1) understanding the meaning of voluntary choice and noninterference relevant to the first concept of (negative) freedom and (2) understanding why some people who start with a negative concept of freedom are led to study the positive concept of freedom.

9.4   INSTITUTIONAL IMPLICATIONS OF POSITIVE FREEDOM

A. DEMOCRACY AND MARKETS

Imagine a world in which the broad population ultimately controls the rules of society. This is the celebration of democracy. As Abraham Lincoln spoke on the battlefield at Gettysburg on November 19, 1863,

> It is rather for us to be here dedicated to the great task remaining before us—that from these honored dead we take increased devotion to that cause for which they gave the last full measure of devotion—that we here highly resolve that these dead shall not have died in vain—that this nation, under God, shall have a new birth of freedom—and that government of the people, by the people, for the people, shall not perish from the earth.

Consent becomes a principle of positive freedom and **institutional legitimacy**, which is relevant not only for market trade but for affirming the ground rules of society that make markets possible. *Institutional legitimacy* refers to the conditions under which political and economic institutions are acceptable and justified. Legitimacy can be understood descriptively in terms of people's perception of the legitimacy of its institutions; or it can be understood normatively, as the conditions that ultimately justify those institutions. Unlike the laws of nature, such as gravity, the laws of business and politics are not inevitable background features of life. They can be altered by human decision. This idea is at the heart of the Enlightenment values of the seventeenth century, which challenged the divine right of kings and the inevitability of social arrangements.

For advocates of the concept of positive freedom, the focus on noninterference is misplaced. We are free only when we are the source of control. At the most human level, we gain control of ourselves when we are in control of our mind, our thoughts, and our desires. At a social and institutional level, we gain control over human laws by participating in a democratic process that creates those laws. The laws become *our* system of laws when we have the democratic voice to support, criticize, and alter those laws, and when we endorse the democratic processes that yield the decisions that bind us. This is what Abraham Lincoln was talking about.

Thus, for advocates of positive freedom, support for markets is not the primary institutional implication of freedom. It's about support for democracy. The colonists argued: no taxation without representation. *Representation* is about authority and control. Consider: "I pledge allegiance to the flag of the United States of America, and to the Republic for which it stands. . . ." If you have ever recited this pledge, what are you pledging allegiance *to*? To live in a space of noninterference? Not quite, or not merely, it seems—it's a pledge to a form of *government*, a *republic*, which creates the rules of society by the authority of the people, creating free citizens.

But positive freedom applied to politics has an underside too. Rules bind. That is part of the rub of democracy. Just as property rights limit choice, democracy often forces people to do what they do not want to do. Laws restrict our choices, even if we voted against them. Thus, when we are compelled to follow a law that we reject, we experience a loss in (negative) freedom. On the other hand, when we participate in the democratic process that creates those laws, we experience an increase in (positive) freedom. Therefore, democracy can create a conflict in freedoms.[6]

In summary, we want to be free to control our own lives and the rules of society through democracy—this summarizes the value of positive freedom. But at the same time, we want spaces of noninterference—including noninterference from democratic control. For example, most people do not want our personal freedoms to be decided by democratic vote. We can understand the Constitution and Bill of Rights and debates about government intervention in markets as attempts to balance both concepts of liberty.

B. DEMOCRATIC CAPITALISM

For some, part of the appeal of **democratic capitalism** as a social system is the attempt to join a political structure and a business system in a way that balances both conceptions of freedom at the same time. *Democratic capitalism* refers to a political, economic, and social system that combines a democratic political system with a capitalist economic system. Proponents argue that democratic capitalism creates the most freedom possible because people both choose the ground rules of society, and their actual choice is for a property rights system friendly to markets that minimizes interferences.

Some argue further that the freedom of the one system (the politics of democracy) encourages the freedom of the other (economics of capitalism). Here, democracy refers to the political system and capitalism the economic system. This hypothesis is a question of political science that some accept and others deny, although few deny that democracy

---

[6]The issues are not quite as straightforward as this. For example, if democracy is majority rule, and you find yourself persistently in the minority on every voting issue, then it's debatable (to say the least) that democracy gives you control over the ground rules of society. Connecting positive freedom with democracy is an aspiration that may be more or less true, and it may depend on how a particular democracy works.

and capitalism can separate from each other, both in theory and practice. For example, democracies can exist without developed markets if people do not want capitalism, and they successfully convey this attitude through the democratic process. The ancient Athenians, for example, prized a limited form of democracy but they knew nothing about modern capitalism. In the other direction, markets can exist without democracy, if a dictator enforces a property rights scheme conducive to markets and industrial growth. Many look at Hitler's Germany and the explosive growth of markets in China as prime examples. We can debate the extent to which markets and democracy merge in practice, but democracy and capitalism are not the same ideas. Democratic capitalism is a vision that brings two separable systems together.

Suppose that we do separate them, at least conceptually. Which institutional arrangement, political or economic, is the more fundamental for a free society in your view?

This question has deep historical roots and great current significance. Nineteenth-century French philosopher and politician Benjamin Constant distinguished the freedom of the ancients from the freedom of the moderns. Ancient societies emphasized democracy as the source of freedom, with limited recognition of the value of individual rights of non-interference. This was Athenian democracy, where citizens could make group decisions that might interfere with just about any aspect of life. Modern societies, Constant argued, place increasing emphasis on the rights of the individual and the limits of democracies or any form of government to interfere with those rights. These rights of noninterference, he argued, are the basis for building commercial societies.

To this day we often see much disagreement about the relative balance between democracy and capitalism. Democracies often pass laws that restrict markets. A grocer must follow many regulations about how to process and display food. There is hardly a sphere of market life where some democratically passed regulation does not apply. Even yard sales can require permits and limitations. How do we judge government interference in markets on a standard of freedom? It depends on which concept of freedom you are talking about and how you see markets actually functioning. Arguments on behalf of the invisible hand and law and regulation models of Chapter 8 can now be redeveloped based on the discussions in this chapter. The difference between these models can now be interpreted as the difference between those who believe that freedom should imply more focus and support for capitalist institutions (the invisible hand approach) or democratic institutions (the law and regulation approach) for creating a good society. In the United States, most of the debate presumes that the best political and economic system will express some form of democratic capitalism, with different emphases about the proper role of government for constraining the influence of markets. In Europe and other parts of the democratic world, the spectrum of debate is wider, including support for *democratic socialism* and other economic arrangements that reject capitalism.

C. TWO VISIONS OF A FREE SOCIETY DRAWING ON BOTH POSITIVE AND NEGATIVE FREEDOM

In Section 2, we defined positive freedom from two points of view. From the personal point of view, freedom is self-mastery. From an institutional point of view, freedom is having control over the ground rules of society through democratic participation. We can join together these perspectives. For example, many people associate the value of democracy with expressing one's views in deliberation and debate with others. In this sense, democracy requires having an educated population with a free press and a free exchange of ideas so that people's reflective and rational wills join together in a national conversation. In this view, freedom in democracy is more than the exercise of voting and political power; it is the practice of an educated citizenry collectively deliberating about the bases of social life.

This connection brings added insight to debates about freedom, markets, and democracy. An account of positive freedom can imply the curtailment of markets and expansion of government wherever one limits and the other expands the sense of control people have over their lives. Thus, education is a public good for democracy; it is also a potential public goods problem. Most societies today provide education through government, at least in part. Support for head start programs, restrictions on advertising to children, welfare payments, food stamps, zoning restrictions on businesses: all of these government functions can be interpreted as efforts for individuals to have greater control over their lives—either by the fact of participating in democratic decision-making, such as through zoning disputes, or by the government providing a function that enhances the development of personal control, such as early education.

Thus, those who lean on positive liberty tend to place government in the foreground for freedom and markets in the background. This perspective most closely resembles the law and regulation model of Chapter 8. Those who lean on negative liberty tend to place markets in the foreground for freedom and government in the background. This perspective most closely resembles the invisible hand model of Chapter 8.

These are important contrasts, and yet the discussion of this chapter has tried not to oversimplify these contrasts. For example, markets may create many interferences, as discussed above, contrary to the supposed tight link between markets and negative freedom. One irony of a "free" market system is that most people spend most of their time in a job with many hierarchical rules that severely constrain choice. We may even have our bathroom breaks regulated. Work can imply an astonishing reduction in our negative freedom. (Of course we *accepted* the job, so that is an act of positive freedom. And we get paid, which probably increases our negative freedom. But under what conditions did we choose this job? Hence, the considerations can be complicated.)

Consider another example. Markets may enhance positive freedom far more than suggested so far, by creating wealth, raising standards of living, and fostering a higher level of education. It's not merely that money makes us more free because we can buy more of what we want, but that extra wealth provides grounds to develop ourselves. We can control our lives better and have more opportunity to become who we want to be. Trading not only preserves a space of noninterference but it shapes us. We can experience the dynamics of capitalism, a world of business activity with a dizzying array of products and entrepreneurial spirit. Proponents interpret this economic world as providing the opportunities to create the cumulative expression of great feats of individual will—to make, to create, to be entrepreneurial—to live in freedom. (In Chapter 11, we will study arguments about *equal* opportunities.) Further, stakeholder advocates may also support a strong connection between markets and positive freedom. The stakeholder movement can be interpreted as the effort for individuals and groups to apply their values by using market pressures to control and influence market outcomes.

In sum, neither markets nor government exert a monopoly over one form of freedom. The market system contains many different worlds. Corporate executives fly to meetings in their personal jets; a small business owner with dogged determination and slim chances opens a new café in a location that has failed five times before; a struggling family of four goes shopping at the grocery store for the best deals, eking out a stressful economic life; an employee receives a big paycheck and celebrates with a splendid shopping spree; sharecroppers work in the field under blistering heat, with no health care benefit, no retirement benefits, no worker compensation, and few other options. People experience varying levels of freedom or lack of freedom in both senses of the word throughout the market system—these experiences are so varied and so different that no single expression could possibly capture the kaleidoscope of the experiences of billions of people.

This chapter offers no singular analysis of a sense of freedom that everyone experiences in economic life. These sections introduce you to a range of thought about how you may support or criticize political and economic institutions based on what you take freedom to mean.

Read the Case Study *Smoking Laws* only on MySearchLab

9.5   FREEDOM AND ETHICS

The discussion to this point has been mostly about institutions. This section considers liberty as it relates to our sense of ethics from a personal point of view. First, we will consider how freedom connects with business ethics, and then how it connects with our sense of ethics more broadly.

A. ETHICS AND BUSINESS

Both accounts of freedom are relevant for thinking about demands of business ethics. Let's consider a few examples.

Negative externalities not only reduce welfare but they often interfere with people's lives. From the perspective of freedom, it's the interference without our consent rather than the welfare loss that identifies the wrong of a negative externality. When someone drinks polluted water caused by a corporation upstream, the sense of wrong is not merely that it makes a person worse off, but that the person had no choice but to experience this result. Consider next demands for honesty—should markets operate on a *buyer beware* principle or should buyers and sellers expect accurate information about the nature of the products for sale? A simple answer is not so obvious based on a standard of negative freedom, but far clearer on the standard of positive freedom. Hiding information is a primary means for taking control away from other people's choices. We can't make rational choices if we don't have the relevant information. Within hospital settings, *informed consent* is often an overriding ethical concern. Advocates of positive freedom will emphasize informed consent across the business system as a whole. In markets, we often associate information as a requirement to create efficiency gains, but information is also important for putting people in control of their choices. Businesses and people who deliberately manipulate information to consumers and investors are undermining their freedom to make informed decisions.

Consider more broadly all of the background conditions necessary for trade to be *free*. This task differs from analyzing the background conditions for trade to be *welfare improving*, but we can still return to the island scenario to draw out the argument. Should government be charged with providing those conditions of freedom, and to what extent do we need a sense of professional ethics to pick up the slack where governments or markets fall short? The structure of these arguments follows the same form of reasoning provided in the efficiency chapters, divided as they are among invisible hand, law and regulation, and professional ethics models. We can now apply this analysis as it relates to liberty and efficiency.

For example, consider the invisible hand model of self-interested incentives, markets, private property rights, and a limited government that provides necessary public goods.

What values support this understanding of business and economic life? Drawing on the discussions in this chapter, proponents often argue that this system expresses a scheme of negative liberty, and if accompanied by the view that markets are efficient, then liberty and efficiency combine to reinforce each other in support of limited professional ethics, self-interest, and free markets.

A second vision sees a vibrant participatory democracy that creates the enabling conditions for people to take control of their lives. Public education, a welfare system to improve people's options, other government programs, and limited markets can support this civic life. What values support this view? In general, proponents of the law and regulation or professional ethics models will draw on positive liberty, and if accompanied by the view that markets create great inefficiencies, then these values combine to support a heightened role for business ethics, government regulation, or both.

Because we carried out this method of argument and debate in Chapter 8, we will not pursue these details further here. Note, however, how it's possible to *combine* discussions of efficiency and liberty. We can apply these values for making decisions at the personal level or for evaluating the institutions around us. These chapters introduce discussions at both levels for clarifying our own and others' beliefs about markets and government, and the sense of ethics that people should bring to their interactions.

B. A Tight Conceptual Link between Freedom and Ethics

Let's consider next a topic that is unique to the study of freedom. What is the conceptual link between freedom and ethics? Philosophers often argue that freedom is a precondition for ethics and both go hand in hand; others argue the opposite—that the most important point about freedom and ethics is how they pull apart in practice without other values as anchors. Let's consider both of these points of view.

First, place yourself in a professional role, such as a teacher, and consider some difficult decision that you need to make. For example, a student arrives fifty minutes after a final exam has ended to say that he slept through from late night studying and asks for the opportunity to take the exam now. The exam is 40 percent of the final grade and the syllabus says no makeups except for deceased relatives or serious illness. A friend could have shown the test to this student, there is no way to tell. Rewriting an exam would take a long time and throw off fair grading standards based on a common test. There is no expectation of a makeup, and other students made their plans on the presumption that the stated rule applied to them and everyone else. But the student has been planning on law school for three years, and the result of an F on this single exam would be very detrimental. He is an excellent student. He is honest about what happened (let's assume), rather than making a claim about a deceased great uncle.

What should you do, as the teacher? If you have time, you may talk with colleagues you trust and ask them to offer their opinions, based on their experiences and reflections. Eventually you decide. You must decide one way or the other—that is the role that you occupy.

This example illustrates that ethical decisions are not simply about ethics—they also express our *will*. Whether decided alone or through discussion with others, ethics is an exercise of positive freedom. What is the difference between a computer that processes information and a human who makes decisions? One answer is that we are the author and agent of our decisions, holding ourselves and others responsible for choices. Further, ethical choices tell us something fundamental about who we are—about the values that we endorse. Among all of our choices in life, ethical decision-making is often the preeminent exercise of our freedom, the *sine qua non* of being a free person. Thus, freedom and ethics, many believe, have the following tight link: freedom is an enabling condition for being ethical, and the ethical choices we make are the preeminent display of our freedom.

Let's now ask, Does professional ethics make us free? It's a peculiar question. Consider the following analogy, based on a revealing study of surgical procedures by Dr. Atul A. Gawande of the Harvard School of Public Health.

> A checklist for surgical teams that includes steps as basic as having the doctors and nurses introduce themselves can significantly lower the number of deaths and complications, researchers reported Wednesday.
>
> [A] year after surgical teams at eight hospitals adopted a 19-item checklist, the average patient death rate fell more than 40 percent and the rate of complications fell by about a third, the researchers reported.[7]

A report on the organization's Web site states that surgeon checklists are "currently in active use in operating rooms around the world" (http://www.safesurg.org/).

The surgeon is a hero—saving our lives after years of training to make complex decisions, drawing on great experience and using a refined sense of the special circumstances of every surgery. And surgeons rely on a checklist?

Fione Godlee, the editor of the *British Journal of Medicine*, says:

> There will be resistance to adopting something as prosaic as a checklist. Early adopters will already be using them. Others will be convinced by the New England Journal study. Yet others will want data from their own practice. But some will see checklists as an affront to their professionalism and will never be convinced. At some stage, perhaps sooner rather than later, they will have to go. We shouldn't be conned by Hollywood's version of the hero—the maverick loner who saves the day by breaking all the rules. Instead let's look to the hero of the Hudson River. He and his crew had skill and experience as well as luck on their side, but they had also trained teams for this extremely rare scenario, and they knew exactly what to do.[8]

In the excerpt above, Godlee is referring to the actions of pilot Chelsey B. Sullenberger, as he brought his commercial jet to a safe landing in the Hudson River, effectively saving many lives. For weeks, the media was riveted with images of the passengers standing on the wings of the plane as they awaited rescue boats. But the media also told the story of a pilot well-versed in following standard procedures required to handle an emergency.

A checklist is an external constraint on decision-making. It creates an imposition. To use a checklist reduces our freedom. But then, as suggested by the excerpts above, we discover that it reduces errors and makes us better at what we do. We come to endorse a checklist and accept its guidance so that we can concentrate on other tasks. What had been a *constraint* now becomes an *exercise of our will*. What had been an imposition on our freedom now makes us more free than before.

The point of this analogy is not to suggest that ethics reduces to a checklist. Rather, it's to pose this question: Is ethics simply a set of rules imposed on us from the outside? If so, then

---

[7]Eric Nagourney, *New York Times* (January 14, 2009). See http://www.nytimes.com/2009/01/20/health/20surgery.html.

[8]*British Journal of Medicine* (January 22, 2009). See http://www.bmj.com/content/338/bmj.b238.

ethics reduces our (negative) freedom. But if we come to see the value of ethics and endorse its use, then ethics increases our (positive) freedom because ethics expresses our own will.

German philosopher Immanuel Kant wrote at great length about the connection between ethics and freedom. He derived a *categorical imperative* that he formulated in various ways, including the following: act so as to treat people always as ends and never merely as means. For Kant, ethics as freedom requires that we both recognize the authority of this imperative as binding on us but that we also endorse it as our own at the same time. Ethics must be both binding and self-endorsed.

The point of studying ethics can be about increasing your freedom—your positive freedom to endorse ethics as your own, if you are convinced by its arguments, or to endorse some alternative beliefs, if you are convinced by those. This book presents a conversation, posing questions rather than listing rules, to reflect a commitment to making ideas your own. In a most fundamental sense, your study of ethics can be an exercise in your freedom, developing your own ethical authority through your reason and reflection.

Professional ethics in a work setting may seem far away from this elevated conception of human choice. Ethics can appear to be the prosaic process of applying external rules about what to do and what not to do. So interpreted, ethics is a constraint on behavior that reduces our freedom. But the analogy of the surgeons allows us to close the gap between ethics as *imposition* and ethics as *self-chosen*. We can come to endorse the place of ethics in the professions if we believe that it will reduce our chances of ethical mistakes, based on our own values and perspectives. We can develop the content of ethics in conversation with others, challenging its details with our arguments and reflections. This author, for example, asked a CEO of a large corporation about ethics in business, and he replied that he talks constantly about the importance of establishing a *culture* among the employees of his organization. He went on to describe an ethical culture as the constant tending of standards that come from within, not imposed from the outside by rules and regulations.

> In Chapter 13, we will consider a perennial debate about whether working in business facilitates or undercuts the ability to be an ethical person.

Consider a last example. If you take classes at a university, you find, in one sense, that they constrain you; you become less free. But hopefully they develop who you are and what you believe, which increases your positive freedom. Activities that improve self-mastery increase your (positive) freedom, which can include a self-chosen ethical life.

C. THE DISCONNECT BETWEEN FREEDOM AND ETHICS

Freedom is compatible with choosing badly. *Greed is good* can be the mantra of the free. Even if freedom is a precondition for ethics, others emphasize that we need *other* values to know how to use freedom, or our condition of freedom can disconnect from making ethical choices. For those who emphasize this point, freedom is a blank slate—it doesn't give us the content for knowing how to act ethically; instead, we must draw on other values to know what an ethical life requires.

Isaiah Berlin believed that understanding our current world requires that we understand how ideas, like currents that run through history, sustain and inspire visions about how to organize social and economic life. As a process in deepening our own understanding, we can study one value in isolation from other values (as we have in this book)—such as efficiency, welfare, and rights, each on its own terms, and then combine and integrate them for addressing whatever applied topic is at hand. For those who see how bare freedom can disconnect from ethical choices, a comprehensive ethical study especially demands that we integrate a fuller range of values beyond freedom.

FIGURE 9.1   The Ethics and Values of Economic Life: A General Model

Human Motives and Beliefs	and	Institutions	⇒	Values	
[sense of ethics and self-interest]	and	[markets and government]			

	Values	
	Efficiency and Welfare	(Ch. 6–8)
	Liberty	(Ch. 9)
	Rights	(Ch. 10)
	Equality	(Ch. 11)
	What People Deserve	(Ch. 12)
	Relationships and Character	(Ch. 13)
	Community and the Common Good	(Ch. 14)

9.6   A GENERAL MODEL OF ETHICS AND VALUES

Let's return to the overall framework of the book to place this and the remaining chapters in context. Note first how Figure 9.1 represents the integration of applied ethics and political philosophy for a study of business and economic life. Applied ethicists study how and whether ethical beliefs and motivations should shape individual decision-making, as represented by the "sense of ethics" depicted in Figure 9.1. Our sense of ethics in turn may be shaped by a range of values that are often the subject of political philosophy, such as utilitarian thinking (Chapters 6–8), freedom (Chapter 9), rights (Chapter 10), equality (Chapter 11), what people deserve (Chapter 12), relationships and character (Chapter 13), and the good community (Chapter 14). In short, this model depicts how a normative study of business and economic life requires the integration of both ethics and political philosophy.

> The primer on ethics in the Introduction surveyed ethical theories that attempt to organize and clarify our ethical perspectives.

Second, this model also suggests the importance of integrating the social sciences and the humanities. Along the horizontal axis, the social and behavioral sciences seek to explain why people behave as they do and how we might expect institutions to work, given people's motivations.[9] Along the vertical axis, philosophy and the humanities are relevant for understanding which values we should support at the moral foundations of a good society. In this sense Figure 9.1 combines both descriptive and normative analyses, by framing a study of which institutions and motivations are most likely to create certain results descriptively, such as outcomes of efficiency, or liberty, or other results; *and* by framing normative arguments about how we ought to act and which institutions we ought to support, given our convictions about which values and ethical principles matter most.

> Chapter 1.7 introduced the distinction between descriptive and normative analysis.

In sum, a comprehensive study of the ethics and values of business and economic life is interdisciplinary in the best sense. Each chapter in Part IV focuses on a specific value for clarity of presentation but the discussions ahead address all the parts of Figure 9.1 with an increasingly comprehensive normative perspective for integrating all these values.

---

[9]Figure 9.1 could be depicted in functional terms, as in welfare = f (sense of the ethics, self-interest, institutions); liberty = f (sense of the ethics, self-interest, institutions), and so forth. This modeling could draw on methods in economics for further development.

9.7   SUMMARY

We are free when others do not interfere with us (negative freedom) and when we control ourselves and the environment that surrounds us (positive freedom). The most basic lesson of this chapter is that we often have more than one idea in mind when we talk about freedom. Further, some people see great freedom in business and economic life; others do not. Some people see a tight link between ethics and freedom; others do not. This chapter introduced you to materials to deepen your understanding of these competing perspectives.

KEY TERMS

negative liberty
positive liberty

voluntary choice
institutional legitimacy

democratic capitalism

DISCUSSION QUESTIONS

1. Not everyone agrees about what freedom means. This chapter introduced two concepts. Are there others?

2. What is a college education for? Are you becoming more free through the experience?

3. We now live in a globalized world where human relationships regularly crisscross national boundaries. Just consider all the hands that touched the production of the goods and services that we consume. And yet there is no systematic democratic control over the ground rules that define global capitalism. For many, this is a serious problem of legitimacy, addressed imperfectly through treaties and various international institutions. Does positive freedom imply global democracy?

4. When a corporation donates resources to an elementary school and then includes advertisements within the school, should its actions be interpreted as CSR efforts to support education and more positive freedom, or the manipulation of information that reduces our freedom? More generally, does advertising make us more or less free?

5. What type of workplace environment would create freedom in your view? What type of freedom is this? Is it possible or desirable? What are the challenges?

6. You are middle age. You work five days a week, fifty weeks a year. You have many obligations: a home, a family, obligations of community service, and a thick web of relationships. You think wistfully about your younger years—oh, the freedom of youth! Are you really less free or more free than you were when you were younger? Explain.

7. Pope John Paul II often said, "Freedom consists not in doing what we like, but in having the right to do what we ought." Assess this idea in relation to the concepts of positive and negative freedom.

8. Do markets and democracy realize two different types of freedom? Explain. Which is the better freedom in your view?

9. Some people see freedom in neither markets nor democracy. What are those arguments? Do they have insight?

10. Consider how a systematic study of *political* ethics contrasts against this book's study of *markets* and ethics. A core normative idea in political ethics is making sense of collective decisions that bind us as individuals. How can the resulting political authority and its coercion be justified? A core normative idea in markets and ethics is making sense of individual consent through market exchange. In your view, what establishes the legitimacy of each of these institutions? Does the legitimacy of market institutions derive solely from the legitimacy of democratic political institutions that control those markets, or do markets have their own legitimacy independent from their association with political institutions?

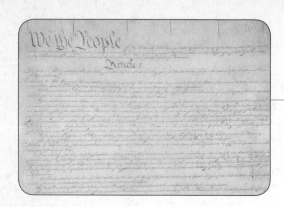

10

RIGHTS

WHEN YOU FINISH
STUDYING THIS CHAPTER,
YOU SHOULD BE ABLE TO:

1. Contrast utilitarian and rights-based approaches to ethics.

2. Analyze the entitlement theory of justice and apply this account to case studies, including an argument about global capitalism.

3. Develop examples that illustrate the interdependency between personal and institutional points of view.

4. Consider several competing justifications for rights.

10.1 INTRODUCTION

English philosopher John Stuart Mill wrote *On Liberty* in 1859, nearly a century before fellow-countryman Isaiah Berlin wrote his famous essay on liberty, which formed the basis of discussion in Chapter 9. "There is no equivalent in our [American] literature to John Stuart Mill's *On Liberty* or the essay, 'Two Concepts of Liberty,' by Isaiah Berlin," writes contemporary historian Eric Foner, reflecting on two of the most significant philosophy writings about liberty ever written.[1]

But Berlin had a quarrel with Mill's position, and the issue is as relevant today as it was then. Why does liberty matter? John Stuart Mill placed the highest value on a free society, and his writings constitute some of the most eloquent defenses of liberty ever written. But ultimately, he defended freedom as a means to improve individual welfare. Mill was a utilitarian in the tradition of ideas presented in Chapters 6–8. Liberty brings great benefits to those who experience it, and that's why it matters.

Berlin was dissatisfied with this defense. If we derive the value of liberty from the value of its benefits, then the argument for a free society is instrumental and subject to a utilitarian calculation: if less freedom turns out to bring more happiness, then we should sacrifice freedom. Berlin argued that this defense creates an insecure foundation. Liberty matters, he proposed instead, so as not to degrade our nature. That is, freedom is a condition of who we are, not just a condition of our welfare.

Let's return to the island scenario to illustrate this debate. Let's suppose that two people are trading under conditions of freedom on a remote island. What they make of their lives with this freedom, Berlin might say, is their business. In other words, for Berlin, the *outcomes* of trade do not identify the most important ethical perspective, or at least they do not tell us why a free society matters. It may be desirable to increase our material conditions, our happiness, and our overall welfare, but freedom matters because of who we are, the exercise of which may often but not always increase our welfare.

---

[1] *The Story of American Freedom* (Norton, 1998), p. xiv.

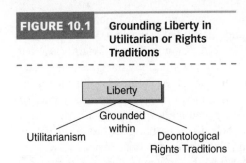

FIGURE 10.1 Grounding Liberty in Utilitarian or Rights Traditions

A utilitarian like Mill, however, will ask, If liberty makes me worse off, both in the short and long run, then what is it good for? This was a compelling question for Mill, and so he argued that liberty in fact makes us better off, which explains why we should value it.

For those, like Berlin, who reject grounding liberty within utilitarian thought, what account of ethics and values provides the clearest contrast to utilitarian reasoning? The answer is often found by giving an account of people's *rights* grounded through a deontological tradition. According to this alternative tradition, ethics is not only, or most fundamentally, about a concern for people's welfare but a commitment to protect people's rights (see Figure 10.1).

This chapter introduces the concept and vocabulary of moral rights, especially in contrast to utilitarian approaches to ethics (Sections 2 and 3). We will then consider one influential account of rights especially relevant to markets and business—American philosopher Robert Nozick's entitlement theory of justice. We will apply this account to an argument about global capitalism, consider the interaction between personal and institutional points of view (Section 4), and examine criticisms of Nozick's entitlement theory (Section 5). Finally, we consider underlying justifications for rights and address questions about handling trade-offs among values (Section 6). Taken together, these topics introduce a range of ideas and puzzles about the nature of rights relevant to business and economic life.

10.2 PRELIMINARIES

In this section, we consider several distinctions about the concept of rights and how people use the language of rights.

A. LEGAL, NATURAL, AND HUMAN RIGHTS; AND OTHER DISTINCTIONS

Rights are powerful tools in society, ranging across the Magna Charta of 1215, the Bill of Rights in the U.S. Constitution in 1791, the Universal Declaration of Human Rights in 1948, and the many current laws that specify our legal rights within various contexts. Debates about rights are often intense, especially when we believe that someone's rights have been violated.

Many practical disputes about our rights are most immediately about our **legal rights**. For example, do corporations have the legal right to free speech? People may dispute what the First Amendment means, and U.S. citizens may then rely on the U.S. Supreme Court's interpretation for settling the question as a matter of public policy.

No matter what our role in society, it seems that some set of rights applies: consumer rights, employer rights, employee rights, patient rights, student rights, and so forth. When we complain that our rights have been violated, we often mean that we believe our *legal* rights have been violated, and we can hire an attorney to represent our claims before the law.

Read the Case Study *Employee Privacy Rights* only on MySearchLab

See Chapter 3 Section 3 for a discussion of the distinction between legal and customary rights.

Chapters 2 and 3 are especially relevant here, as the Hohfeldian vocabulary of claims, liberties, powers, and immunities can help us with a practical study of our legal rights. Most of the discussion in those chapters was about *property rights*, but we also considered how the study of rights generalizes beyond property issues. This chapter is about the nature of rights more generally and provides further normative underpinnings for the ideas developed in Chapters 2 and 3. The discussion in this chapter is about how we *justify* the rights that we claim for ourselves or others, including and beyond property rights. Just as the debate between Mill and Berlin is about underlying justifications (of the value of liberty), we now ask, What are the underlying justifications for the legal and customary rights that any particular society enforces?

There are many interesting and complex responses to this question, but one of these answers is to assert that we have **natural rights**, and these rights should guide the legal and customary rights that we ought to support. Natural rights are rights that human beings have by virtue of their nature as persons. People debate whether we have natural rights. A related concept is **human rights**, which refer to rights that apply to all humans no matter their cultural or other differences. People also debate whether we have human rights, or whether rights are entirely relative to a culture or convention of society. We will discuss natural and human rights in Section 5. The important point now is to clarify the scope of the discussion ahead: this chapter introduces rights theories that are designed to justify and ground the legal rights and customs of society, rather than provide a descriptive account of what our legal rights currently are. This study is normative rather than descriptive.

Another relevant distinction before we apply these ideas to markets is the contrast between **negative rights** and **positive rights**. Suppose you walk by a child who is drowning and you could extend your hand to save this child with little effort. Do you have a duty to do so? More to the point, Does the child have a right to your help? If people only have rights of noninterference, then it appears that the child does not have a right to your help. On an account of *negative* rights, you violate my rights only if you interfere with me, without my consent. Since you are not interfering with the child, you can't be violating his rights. This account of rights relates closely to the concept of negative liberty introduced in Chapter 9. Proponents of negative rights do not believe that people shouldn't help drowning children. They simply argue that the reason you should help that child has nothing to do with that child's rights. Others assert, however, that people do have *positive* rights of assistance—we have duties to help others in desperate need because they have a right to that help. On this view of rights the drowning child can legitimately claim a right for your help. Another controversial example is taxation. Some people argue that certain forms of taxation violate people's (negative) rights. Others argue that taxation is important to uphold people's (positive) rights. At this point, this distinction serves to avoid confusions in what people mean by *rights*. Later we will consider reasons that proponents offer to believe one or the other view.

Finally, rights theorists often distinguish between **individual rights** and **group rights**, depending on whether the right applies to persons or collectives. For example, the Declaration of Independence specifies individual rights for each person: life, liberty, and the pursuit of happiness. But a group of people may also claim rights as a group: such as a political right to self-determination, the cultural right to have a language and culture respected, or the religious right that a religious group be respected.

10.3   RIGHTS AS SIDE-CONSTRAINTS

With these distinctions in mind, let's consider how one prominent rights-theorist expresses the uniqueness of rights as a vocabulary and as an ethical theory. For political philosopher Robert Nozick (and for many others), rights are **moral side-constraints** on action. They say, Do not violate constraint C, where C stands for the rights that cannot be violated.[2]

What if I have a goal that requires me to violate someone's right? If it is a *right*, says Nozick, then I may not violate it, no matter how worthy the goal. That is the point and strength of calling it a right. A utilitarian approach, by contrast, specifies a goal to be achieved, and then advocates pursuing the means to achieve that goal. **Goal-oriented ethical reasoning** takes the following form: pursue actions that achieve G. For the utilitarian, G is the maximization of welfare in society. G could be any goal that we want society to realize.

The distinction between whether rules should be interpreted as side-constraints or goals is very useful *practically*, *personally*, and *legally*, in addition to its *ethical* significance.

Consider some *practical* insights behind these ideas. How do you interpret the work rules that surround you? If your superiors mean that a deadline is a side-constraint on action, then you meet the deadline. But if the deadline is part of a larger workplace goal to increase productivity, then missing a deadline may not be a problem as long as the result

SIDE-CONSTRAINTS, GOALS, AND ETHICAL THEORY

The ethical theories presented in the Introduction relate to this distinction between side-constraints and goals. Consequentialism is a type of goal-oriented morality because it advocates choosing actions or institutions whose consequences best achieve some specified goal. Goal-oriented ethical traditions are called **teleological theories of ethics**, from the Greek "telos," which means end or goal. Not all teleological theories are consequentialist, however. For example, virtue ethics (first presented in the Introduction) is also a teleological theory that specifies the goal in terms of developing one's personal character. We will further discuss this ethical tradition in Chapter 13.

Nozick's account of rights as side-constraints specifies duties that we must follow independent from the consequences of following those duties. In this view we carry out these duties because people have rights, and we should respect these rights as an absolute constraint on any further goals that anyone may wish to pursue. Non-consequentialist moralities specify what we may or may not do, at least in part, without considering the consequences of that choice. These theories are typically developed as *deontological* theories, from the Greek "deon," which means duty.

---

[2]This section and the next draws from Robert Nozick's influential discussion of rights in *Anarchy, State, and Utopia* (Basic, 1974).

is more productivity. Consider the employer-employee relationship more generally. An important management principle is that if the employees grasp the goals of the organization, then it's up to the individual to figure out the rest. Managers generally want people who do not need to ask for direction every step of the way, or else the manager becomes the assistant to the employee. When we can grasp the goals behind the stated rules, then we can apply our common sense rather than memorize a list of rules. Figuring out what to do, given an understanding of the goals, can be a step toward good decision-making. The deeper one's understanding of a goal, the greater can be one's flexibility and latitude for achieving it.

On the other hand, our common sense may require some constraints. As you think about the goal of the university degree that you pursue, do you think that cheating is an acceptable means? Are rules against plagiarism appropriately regulated as a side-constraint on action? Why?

These concepts are also important for life at a *personal* level beyond the professional setting. With experience comes a deeper understanding of our goals in life and the side-constraints that we ought to follow in pursuit of those goals. Happiness is often not merely the unbridled pursuit of our goals but the recognition of where and when to draw a line and say, here lies a constraint. Many regard this reasoning as a path toward integrity that becomes a surer route to a happy life (Chapter 14 develops this idea).

This distinction has important *legal* ramifications as well. If a regulatory agency specifies targets for pollution standards, these targets may be adjustable depending on how the goal of reducing pollution is specified. But if there is a legal rule that lists the specific actions that are not permitted, then the company must follow the letter of that rule, or potentially face fines and litigation. Judicial discretion in sentencing and many aspects of the legal profession wrestle with the pros and cons of rules as goals or side-constraints.

Consider finally how these ideas apply to your *ethical* beliefs. Suppose we could convict an innocent person to avoid a mob. Wouldn't you say that this is unjust, violating the rights of that individual? If so, you might say that judges must recognize and be guided by a variety of side-constraints—that conviction or innocence must be decided independently from weighting the societal consequences of that choice. Is that correct? Try another example to challenge this distinction. The U.S. war in Afghanistan has led to the killing of innocent children. Did those military actions violate the rights of those children? Are those killings justifiable as part of the unfortunate consequences of war? Or can *no* violation of a right be justified in pursuit of a further goal? Wrestling with the distinction between side-constraints and goals is far from theoretical. It's important for understanding your own sense of ethics.

Utilitarianism is a form of reasoning that requires the *weighing of outcomes* to determine the best result, balancing the benefits and costs associated with any choice. Rights theories offer the specification of people's rights, and then an ethic that says don't violate them.

Recall from Chapters 6–8 that we puzzled over the meaning of welfare as part of the analysis of utilitarianism, contrasting objective and subjective interpretations of welfare. For rights proponents, the essential flaw of utilitarianism is elsewhere: it's the goal-oriented account of moral reasoning.

To clarify this point, let's extend the mob case to introduce a puzzle. Imagine that the judge rejects utilitarianism but endorses a different goal-oriented morality.

The judge decides to convict or not depending on which decision would minimize the violation of rights. The judge imagines two possible outcomes: a world with conviction and a world with acquittal. The judge says, "If I'm really committed to rights, then let me make the choice that produces the least number of rights violations, taking into account the loss of life and other rights violations that would occur from an ensuing riot." Advocates of rights as *side-constraints* reject this form of reasoning. We cannot violate the defendant's rights no matter what, even for the goal of minimizing the overall level of rights violations in society. This example, discussed by Nozick, serves to clarify the sharp contrast between the ethics of side-constraints versus goal-oriented moralities.

Why should we believe in a theory of side-constraints on action? Many deontologists lean on the Kantian idea first presented in the Introduction and mentioned in Chapter 9 Section 5: we ought to regard people as ends in themselves. Consider a tool, such as a hammer or wheelbarrow. Tools imply no side-constraints on how we use them. We may use them however we like to repair the house, make a toy, or whatever. If we do not like the tool or it does not suit our purposes, we can throw it away or do with it whatever we like.

On a deontological view, people are not tools. They are separate and morally distinct persons who must always be treated as ends, never merely as tools. What could it mean to treat people as ends, in practical terms? An account of people's rights, say its proponents, provides the answer to that question. Side-constraints express how we may or may not treat people, independently of how they may service some further ends of society. Specifying rights as side-constraints commit us to the principle that people are always ends in themselves and never merely tools for someone else's goals.

For many deontological rights theorists, part of being ethical is to recognize our duties to other human beings and to be motivated to act from these moral duties to respect people's rights. In other words, motives matter for morality. And the relevant motives are to act from moral duty independent from analyzing the costs and benefits of a situation for making a decision. This motivational emphasis contrasts against proponents of utilitarianism, who typically emphasize the importance of outcomes independently from what motivated the results.

According to this deontological tradition of rights, what is the content of our specific rights? The Declaration of Independence tells us that all human beings have the rights of life, liberty, and the pursuit of happiness. They come from our Creator, writes Thomas Jefferson. He then argued that they were being violated, which justified secession from England. English philosopher John Locke, whose writings inspired Jefferson's perspective, specified that humans have natural rights to life, liberty, and property. Locke, Jefferson, and Nozick were all intensely interested in a puzzle. Each argued in his own way that we need law and government to protect and secure our natural rights, but the raw power of law and government is also a primary source through which people have their rights violated. Much study of political philosophy is about making sense of that tension and providing a view of government that tries to resolve that tension. Thus, rights theorists often specify a theory about the proper relation between government and civil society, including its market institutions.

With this background, we will now focus on the nature of rights as they relate to markets and business activities.

The *entitlement theory of justice* refers to a theory that specifies what must be true for private property holdings to be legitimate. In relation to the last chapter, one interesting feature of this theory is that democratic institutions are not a necessary condition for establishing the legitimacy of market institutions. See Chapter 9, Discussion Question 10.

10.4   RIGHTS AND MARKETS

A. THE ENTITLEMENT THEORY OF JUSTICE

Markets develop through property rights that specify who owns what. How do we determine whether what we own is justly held? We will now focus on the non-consequentialist account that derives from John Locke's discussions (see Chapter 3 Section 8).[3] The most well-known contemporary advocate is Robert Nozick, whose strategy is not to list our rights in a roll call but to offer the *form* of an argument that any acceptable theory must follow. He calls the argument the **entitlement theory of justice**.

The argument is intuitive and influential, and its impact goes well beyond its association with any particular author, just as the impact of the stockholder position goes well beyond its association with economist Milton Friedman. The entitlement theory represents a pivotal contrast to a utilitarian analysis of markets and ownership. The essential perspective is to look backward in time to the history of specific transactions and ask, Has the existing property scheme come about without violating anyone's rights? Let's develop this idea.

A History of Transactions

Have you ever considered that every single claim to ownership has a history? Take something that you own, such as the shirt on your back. Where did you get that shirt? Where did that person or company get that shirt? We can imagine how the shirt has physically changed hands from one person to the next. Eventually, we work our way through a history of transactions that includes the factory that made the shirt. Where did the factory get the materials to make that shirt?

Every owned item in this world has an *actual* history of transfers that runs back in time and eventually ends with an initial acquisition of some unowned material becoming an owned item. Allegorically, we can trace human economic transactions back to Adam and Eve in Western thought, to the time in the world when no one owned anything. At some point, people started making claims over the earth.

National Geographic News reports the following case:

> On July 20, 1969, astronauts stepped onto the moon and planted an American flag—not to claim the moon but simply to commemorate the U.S. role in the first moon landing. Forty years later a Nevada entrepreneur says he owns the moon and that he's interim president of the first known galactic government. Dennis Hope, head of the Lunar Embassy Corporation, has sold real estate on the moon and other planets to about 3.7 million people so far. (http://news.nationalgeographic.com/news/2009/07/090717-who-owns-moon-real-estate.html)

We may hope that not all initial acquisitions are so dubious. And that's the point for an entitlement theory of justice. Justice requires the non-violation of rights throughout

---

[3]The utilitarian response is to advocate property rights that maximize welfare. The utilitarian looks forward to the effects of an ownership scheme and judges markets and its property rights by virtue of its results. We first considered this idea in Chapter 3 Section 8 when we examined David Hume's defense of private property.

the entire chain of economic transactions, from the vast array of holdings around the world that go back in time to the conversion of the specific raw materials that created each product.

A **principle of justice in initial acquisition** specifies when a person who acquires an unowned item can be legitimately entitled to that item. When that occurs, a person who acquires this item in accordance with a **principle of justice in transfer** is also entitled to that item. No one is entitled to what he or she owns except by repeated application of this process through a chain of just acquisitions and transfers. These principles of acquisition and transfer specify people's rights in those contexts. This is the form of the entitlement theory: any moral evaluation of markets and business activity should assess whether markets and the resulting holdings conform to, or violate, principles of justice in initial acquisition and transfer.

In this view, ideal markets do not violate anyone's rights as long as the initial acquisitions are just. Presumably, the essence of trade is that people *consent* to the trade and consensual transactions do not violate people's rights. You can dispute the latter idea, of course, and then the argument is about articulating the principle of justice in transfer. In either case, we can draw on the previous chapter's discussion about consent and the island scenario of Chapter 6 to think about what must be true for markets to not violate your rights. For example, you might wonder whether the conditions of trade must have acceptable alternatives for establishing consent, or that there not be gross misrepresentation of the product. You might also argue that the trade not create any rights-infringing negative externalities. For the rights theorist, ideal market trading as represented in the island scenario should be an exercise about analyzing people's rights, not about what enhances buyers' and sellers' welfare or what increases the overall freedom of buyers and sellers.

The Wilt Chamberlain Example

Nozick reinforces these ideas through his famous Wilt Chamberlain example, named after a famous basketball player from decades ago. We could substitute LeBron James, Payton Manning, Tiger Woods, or whoever into the following story (See Figure 10.2).

Suppose that 50,000 people want to watch Wilt Chamberlain dunk basketballs. The ticket costs $50 a piece and the money goes directly to Chamberlain. Let's further suppose that D1 represents the distribution of what each person owns (Chamberlain is a1 and the spectators are b1, c1, and so forth) before they see Chamberlain play. Let's put aside all worries about injustices in D1 and presume that pregame D1 represents a just distribution of ownership on whatever theory of justice you endorse. Now it's game time. Everyone pays his or her $50 and watches Chamberlain dunk baskets. Let D2 represent what everyone owns after they see Chamberlain play,

FIGURE 10.2	**An Entitlement Theorist's View of Market Transactions**

Before Dunking		After Dunking
D1 $\longrightarrow$		D2
a1 $\longrightarrow$		a1 + $2.5 million
b1 $\longrightarrow$		b1 − $50
c1 $\longrightarrow$		c1 − $50
d1 $\longrightarrow$		d1 − $50
e1 $\longrightarrow$		e1 − $50
.	.	.
.	.	.
.	.	.

D1 = Total distribution of wealth in population before trade

D2 = Total distribution of wealth in population after trade

a1
b1 } = Wealth of person a, b, c, before trade
c1

a = The person getting paid to perform

b, c, d, . . . = the audience

which will be $50 less for each person plus $2,500,000 to Chamberlain for a sweet hour's work.

Were anyone's rights violated in this exchange? Where? (Nowhere, says Nozick.) For Nozick and his defenders, we have just reached an obvious but remarkable conclusion: markets, ideally conceived, preserve justice. There is no basis to criticize the resulting ownership distribution D2 as unjust if we start with justice and no one's rights were violated in a market trade. It does not matter that Chamberlain becomes exceptionally rich, that inequality has increased, and that each person has a little less. It does not matter how people's welfare was affected (presumably they liked the show, but who knows?). It does not matter if Chamberlain is a little more free for having more money and everyone else a little less free. As long as people consent to the trade, there is no basis to criticize the resulting distribution in terms of creating some injustice.

You buy a bicycle, go shopping, or open a bank account. You face conflict at work, wonder about the responsibilities of corporations, or encounter an ethical dilemma. As a matter of justice, the relevant perspective for proponents of this view is to figure out who has what rights, and act in a way that does not violate them.

As a practical matter of ethics, as long as we consent to our individual trades—and the history of transactions regarding that item is clean—then we have addressed everything that matters for the justice of markets.

But what about important social goals, such as raising standards of living, maximizing freedom, or promoting equality? What if we know that D2 is a distribution that does not achieve those important outcomes? Shouldn't government step in and redistribute monies through taxation and legislation to promote these important (democratically endorsed?) goals? No, says the Nozickian entitlement theorist. Redistributing *any* holdings, without *each person's individual* consent, would violate the rights of anyone who didn't consent to that tax. Without consent, the redistribution would be to treat people as tools to some further social end.

Thus, markets not only preserve justice, but any nonmarket redistributions in pursuit of other goals (for example, by government) typically create injustice because they would violate people's rights. "The general point illustrated by the Wilt Chamberlain example," writes Nozick ". . . is that no . . . distributional patterned principle of justice can be continuously realized without continuous interference with people's lives."[4] For Nozick, interferences without that person's consent violate the rights of that person.

Rectifying Injustice

Actual market transactions are not always clean of injustices, as advocates of this perspective recognize. If the initial transaction was unjust, or the item passed along a chain of transactions that included an unjust transfer, then the injustice carries through markets to the current ownership scheme. In this sense, markets not only can carry along justice, but given some wrong, they can carry along *injustice* from the past into the present, unless the wrong is corrected. The wrong must be rectified. If you purchase a car from someone who stole it, your purchase is tainted and the law will require you to return the car, even though *you* did not steal it. Likewise, a fully specified entitlement theory of justice must include a **principle of justice in rectification** that specifies how to correct and

---

[4]*Anarchy, State, and Utopia*, p. 163.

compensate for injustices that have occurred at any point along the ownership chain. One dramatic example is the looting that occurs during wars and conquests, which includes looted artwork and artifacts that end up in private collections and museums around the world. In the United States, slavery and the near annihilation of the Native American population are the most significant historical examples.

This closes the basic case for assessing the justice of capitalism, markets, and the business system according to an entitlement theory of justice. Justice answers two or three questions, as the case may be:

a. Was the holding acquired through a just transfer?

b. Was the initial acquisition just?

    If the answers are *yes*, then markets preserve justice. If the answer is *no* to either question, then markets perpetuate injustice, and now there is a need to answer one additional question:

c. Was an appropriate rectification given to the wronged parties?

    If the answer is *yes*, then justice is restored to markets. If *no*, then injustice persists and the situation requires rectification.

Applying the Entitlement Theory to Global Capitalism

How would an entitlement theorist assess our current capitalist system? Some entitlement theorists are staunch supporters of capitalism; others see much injustice. Let's consider one extended example of the entitlement approach, applied to the ethics and justice of contemporary global capitalism. There are two purposes for developing this example. First, it shows how the entitlement theory is remarkably relevant for understanding important current legal and social issues. Second, the example provides a provocative argument to invite a debate. Do you agree or disagree with the argument to follow. Why or why not?

In his article "Property Rights and the Resource Curse," philosopher Leif Wenar writes:

> Because of a major flaw in the system of international trade, consumers buy stolen goods every day. Consumers may buy stolen goods when they buy gasoline and magazines, clothing and cosmetics, cell phones and laptops, perfume and jewelry. The raw materials used to make many of these goods have been taken—sometimes by stealth, sometimes by force—from some of the poorest people in the world. . . . The plainest criticism of global commerce today is not that it violates some abstract distributive standard, but that it violates property rights.[5]

Economists and other social scientists have long noted that countries rich in natural resources often have very poor people. This terrible situation is sometimes called the **resource curse** or the *paradox of plenty*. These phrases refer to the fact that countries rich in natural resources are often among poorest in overall economic conditions. Have you ever wondered why a place like Nigeria, equatorial Guinea, or other developing countries could have so much wealth in oil reserves but its people are so desperately poor?

---

[5]Leif Wenar, "Property Rights and the Resource Curse," *Philosophy and Public Affairs* 36(1), p. 32.

Here is Wenar's argument.

1. "A people's right to its resources *is* a human right. Like a people's right to self-determination or a people's right against genocide, this is a human right proclaimed in primary documents of international law."[6]

2. The rightful owners of natural resources must consent to their sale.

3. Many governments and regimes that currently profit from selling oil to corporations do not have the consent of its people for making these sales.

4. Therefore, these sales violate people's rights.

Consider the third premise. The international community, including corporations and governments, currently accepts that whatever regime coercively controls the population has a legitimate power to sell that country's resources, including its oil reserves. According to the entitlement theory, however, the rightful owners must consent to the sale. What could it mean for a people to consent to the sale of their resources? At the very least, argues Wenar, who draws on legal precedents in other areas, people must be able to find out about the terms of sale, stop the transaction if they object to it, or not be extremely manipulated to make the sale. They must have freedom of the press to know the terms of the oil deals, the ability to voice dissent and stop the sales if they disagree with it; and a rule of law without fear of arrest or torture for voicing their dissent. "If these minimal conditions do not obtain in a country, then the silence of the people when a regime sells its resources cannot signal the people's consent."[7]

Based on his review of studies by Freedom House, an organization that measures political freedoms, Wenar concludes that many regimes that currently profit from selling oil to corporations do not have the consent of their people for making these sales.[8] These sales, thereby, violate the owners' rights. (And this claim isn't even saying anything about receiving a fair share of the profits.) Taking the sales of all these illegitimate regimes together,

> [I]nternational corporations illicitly transport into the United States over 600 million barrels of oil each year. This is 12.7 percent of U.S. oil imports: more than one barrel in eight. Most of this petroleum is refined into gasoline and diesel; the rest is used in making a vast range of consumer products from clothing, cosmetics, and medicines to toys, asphalt, and ink. . . . It is beyond doubt that there is a massive flow of stolen goods into the United States every year.[9]

Wenar concludes:

> Peoples have rights, and there are things no person or group may do to them (without violating their rights). Trafficking in a country's valuable natural resources without the people's consent certainly crosses that line. The priority in reforming global trade must be to enforce the rights that define the modern international order. The first step in improving the prospects of poor people is to enforce the rights they already have.[10]

---

[6]Leif Wenar, "Property Rights and the Resource Curse," *Philosophy and Public Affairs* 36(1), p. 15.

[7]Ibid., p. 21. You may wish to consider how the discussion of voluntary choice in Chapter 9 Section 3C applies to this discussion.

[8]http://www.freedomhouse.org/

[9]Wenar, "Property Rights and the Resource Curse," p. 25.

[10]Ibid., p. 32.

There is much to discuss about this argument. Do you think it is a good argument? Do the people of a country have a right to its natural resources? (If not, who does? a corrupt regime that holds onto power by force?) Is the right to natural resources an individual right or a group right?

The Interdependence of Ethics and Justice

This argument applies the entitlement theory of justice within the context of contemporary international law. We buy a toy at our local retailer to give as a gift to our nephew. But wait: we trace the history of transactions of that toy and we find that the acquisition of raw materials to produce the toy violated rights. A minor issue? An anomaly? According to the above argument, a simple application of the entitlement theory reveals *massive* violations of rights that travel through our entire economic system.

If you find the argument convincing, then what are the responsibilities of corporations that negotiate market contracts with corrupt regimes that are stealing oil from their people? What are your responsibilities as a consumer when you purchase these stolen goods? (Are these the right questions?)

These questions illustrate how the *ethics* of consumer purchases and debates about corporate responsibility can depend significantly on how you assess the *justice* of capitalism as it is currently practiced. If you lean toward a utilitarian perspective on justice, your analysis of global capitalism will raise different questions than an entitlement theory of justice, such as, "Will a more effective scheme of lawful commerce create improvements in overall welfare?"

These ideas illustrate a central theme of the book that was first presented in the Introduction and discussed in Chapters 4, 5, and 8. We often must connect (1) how we assess the system from an institutional point of view with (2) making decisions in the system from a personal point of view. Beliefs about justice and one's sense of ethics are tightly bound. Applying your sense of ethics in business and economic life is not separable from developing your beliefs about the proper roles of our political and economic institutions. This idea is at the heart of the model of ethics and values presented in the Introduction and explains why the book and the chapters are structured and organized as they are. The book is about *applying* ethics. But our success in doing so is possible only if we integrate ethics into a study of how business and economic institutions work, and what the roles and values of our leading institutions should be.

Remedies: Invisible Hand, Government Regulation, and Business Ethics Models

When an injustice occurs in the chain of transactions, what could be required to rectify this injustice? Ship back everything produced from tainted sales? Boycott items on an individual basis? Would these actions rectify the wrong? What would?

At the level of corporate responsibility, corporations could refuse to deal with corrupt regimes. But short of a law prohibiting such deals, would not some other corporation step in to make ready profits, and by so doing advance shareholder interests? How would stakeholders and stockholder proponents analyze this case? (How do you?)

In fact, Wenar de-emphasizes the potential for rectifying the injustice through individuals' and firms' ethical motives and actions. He suggests the use of law and government to right the wrong. Civil and criminal cases should be brought to U.S. courts on behalf of the wronged parties, he argues. The U.S. government should prohibit American corporations from dealing with corrupt regimes, as currently practiced against Sudan.

Governments should create a special fund to funnel import tariffs on tainted goods back to the poor people whose resources were stolen, he argues. All these proposals encounter practical difficulties but they serve to apply the law and regulation model in Chapter 8 for finding some means to rectify the original injustice.

As we've seen in Chapter 8, market problems can lead to calls for heightened ethics by market participants, new market incentives absent regulation, more law and regulation, or some combination of all three approaches. The first approach argues that we need to bring our *sense of ethics* into our market relationships, including personal commitments to avoid complicity in rights violations and to rectify any wrongs. The other approaches are impressed by the dominating role of self-interest, and so advocates lean on changing the rules so that self-interested incentives can produce the right results. The following excerpt demonstrates Wenar's view: "If the only way for ExxonMobil or China legally to get oil out of Equatorial Guinea is for there to be minimally decent governance in Equatorial Guinea, then there will be minimally decent governance in Equatorial Guinea, at least if there is any way at all for outsiders to help achieve this."[11]

This discussion of global capitalism is but one illustration for applying the conceptual framework of an entitlement theory of justice. We can examine many other intriguing cases of initial acquisition, transfer, and rectification to show the practical relevance of these ideas, both legally and ethically. Various cases can also test our thinking about what our rights should be in those contexts.

10.5   CRITICISMS OF NOZICK'S ENTITLEMENT THEORY OF JUSTICE

A. UNDESERVED INEQUALITIES

Not everyone is convinced by an *entitlement* perspective. Let's take a step back and reconsider the overall approach. Consider again the concept of a market trade, illustrated through the Wilt Chamberlain example. If we start with justice, so the example tells us, consensual trade that does not violate anyone's rights will always preserve justice.

Is that true? Let's iterate the process and imagine trade after trade in this ideal market world. Life goes on, people age, children are born, and market trade continues. Let's assume that every trade is by consent and no one's rights are violated in this world. Even so, not all trades work out the way people had hoped. Bad luck and poor decisions lead some people to become poor and others to become rich. Inequalities increase over time and some people find themselves in desperate exchanges (see Chapter 1 Section 4).

We might say, "These problems are the responsibility of those who make the trades. We are at liberty to be charitable but the inequalities created by markets create no injustice." But consider the children who are born into these desperate circumstances. *They* aren't responsible for their abject circumstances. Is it a just world when these children are born into a system when they did nothing to be responsible for such great inequalities and desperate circumstances?

Let's take all the one-year-olds who exist on earth today. Some were born into dire poverty, others into plenty, and the range of unequal starting points is so varied that it's

---

[11]Wenar, "Property Rights and the Resource Curse," p. 32.

hard to fully grasp the extremes. Even if we grant that no one's rights were violated to produce this unequal distribution of resources, we do know that many children suffer the consequences of their condition. Some will die for lack of simple medications that others would think criminal if they were not readily available.

Societies *could* organize their political and economic system to alleviate some of these inequalities. If they do not even try, would you say that these undeserved inequalities are an *injustice* to these children? A central role of our major institutions, many believe, is to correct for **undeserved inequalities** as a matter of social justice. *Underserved inequalities* refer to inequalities caused by factors that are not the responsibility of the individuals who are treated unequally.

A leading proponent of this perspective is political philosopher John Rawls. He writes:

> A primary function of major institutions, many believe, is to create conditions of social justice. One leading political philosopher, John Rawls, believes that this means correcting for *undeserved inequalities* that develop throughout society.

> This is an important though obvious point: When our social world is pervaded by duplicity and deceit we are tempted to think that law and government are necessary only because of the propensity of individuals to act unfairly. But, to the contrary, the tendency is rather for background justice to be eroded even when individuals act fairly: the overall result of separate and independent transactions is away from and not toward background justice. We might say: in this case the invisible hand guides things in the wrong direction. (p. 267)
>
> What the theory of justice must regulate is the inequalities in life prospects between citizens that arise from social starting positions, natural advantages, and historical contingencies.[12]

The essence of this critique is to say, Goals do matter for ethical reasoning. Undeserved inequalities are the predictable consequence of market transactions, even if no one's rights are violated through market trade. This form of argument is teleological (see box in Section 3). We specify a goal: to live in a world without undeserved inequalities. We should therefore adjust social and political institutions to achieve that goal. Were we utilitarian in our thinking, we would offer the same form of reasoning, but specify the goal as the maximization of welfare. In either case, we decide that it matters to evaluate the *outcomes* of market trade independent from the process that yields them.[13]

We could identify the goals as the pursuit of liberty, or equality, or welfare, and believe that our assessment of markets should be responsive to those values, interpreted as goals to be pursued. In fact, the highly influential criticism offered by John Rawls—that institutions ought to correct for *undeserved inequalities*—is not unique to Rawls, and this idea explains, in part, the sequential order of chapters: liberty (Chapter 9), rights (Chapter 10), equality (Chapter 11) and what people deserve (Chapter 12).

All of the arguments premised on the pursuit of social goals share a common judgment, that justice at one moment in time can yield injustice at another moment, even if no one's rights have been violated along the way. Critics of the entitlement theory argue

---

[12]John Rawls, *Political Liberalism* (Harvard, 1993), p. 271.

[13]This Rawlsian criticism of Nozick does not express or capture his own social contract theory about rights, which is introduced in Section 6 and elaborated on in Chapter 11 on equality.

that innocuous market trades *can* produce unjust outcomes without anyone intending this result, so a comprehensive ethical analysis requires more than reflections about rights.

Rights to Assistance

Critics of Nozick's entitlement theory of justice develop other responses as well. Section 2 introduced the distinction between positive and negative rights. Some argue that we must respect people's *positive* rights to treat people as ends in themselves. If people are, by nature, agents who make decisions, exert a will, and change the world in ways for which they are rightfully held responsible (see Chapter 9, on positive liberty), then what account of our rights best recognizes this conception of humanity? The idea of positive liberty is not about my circumstances of noninterference but about a *positive* characteristic about *me*.

Some rights theorists critique the entitlement theory by developing an account of positive rights. They argue, for example, that a right to vote, a right to satisfy basic needs, and rights for basic assistance are part of recognizing and protecting our capacities to be agents.

The intuition behind the Wilt Chamberlain example is premised on the idea that negative rights are the only rights we have. But proponents of positive rights argue that we need not accept the entitlement theory as the last word about the content of our rights.

IS THERE A PROLIFERATION OF RIGHTS?

Proliferation of rights refers to the accumulation of multiple claims about what people's *rights* are to the point that they are indistinguishable from claims about what people want. It's a criticism about rights-based approaches to ethics, to the extent to which these theories have difficulty specifying boundaries between what counts as a right and what doesn't. These debates often attempt to distinguish concepts of *rights*, *needs*, and *wants*. For example, I may need a lucky break without having a *right* to it. I may *want* an Ipad without *needing* it. And I may have a *right* to an inheritance without *needing* or *wanting* it. The challenge is how to identify the special class of rights without collapsing this idea into claims about what people need or want.

In this view, markets can violate our positive rights if they undermine our ability to have control over our lives. Market exchanges can preserve a sphere of noninterference but still entail duties to assist those in need—that is, those who have a positive right to this assistance. Note how this criticism stays within a deontological rights perspective, whereas the Rawlsian criticism attempts to undercut the entitlement theory by defending a goal-oriented approach to values.

This competing perspective about positive rights underscores the difficulty and lack of agreement about grounding and specifying how many rights we have. Some people worry about a **proliferation of rights** in society, particularly if they seem like nothing more than an assertion of what people want. How should we resolve conflicting claims about positive and negative rights? Questions about what should count as our substantive rights lead many theorists to reconsider their ultimate justification.

10.6   JUSTIFYING RIGHTS

This chapter began with a quarrel between Berlin and Mill's position about how to justify the importance of liberty. Mill supported a utilitarian justification while Berlin embraced a deontological justification, based on our status as persons. Similarly, rights theorists tend to fall into one of two groups. As elaborated in this chapter, some say that rights are deontological, identifying constraints on behavior independent from weighing consequences.

Locke and Nozick represent this tradition. Rights and utilitarianism become competing and incompatible ethical traditions on this view, a contrast first presented in the Introduction.

Other rights theorists merge consequentialist and rights traditions, however, such as John Stuart Mill and David Hume. They supported many laws that invest citizens with legally enforceable rights, but ultimately evaluated the justification for these rights in consequentialist terms. *Rule utilitarianism* (Chapter 7 Section 7) is the view that the legal rights (or rules) that a society recognizes should be those whose general conformity maximizes the people's welfare in that society. Rights are not natural or absolute in this view. They may justifiably vary across societies depending on what works for one people rather than another. Mill argued that having some scheme of legally recognized rights in one form or another is surely necessary to promote the general welfare. And many people endorse this idea today. Deontological rights theorists will say that the *point* of their theory is to reject utilitarianism. But for other rights theorists, the supposed conflict between these two traditions is misleading and their discussion is inseparable.

An interesting feature of rule utilitarianism is that ethics from a personal point of view need not be utilitarian. We have rights, they are defined by the convention of law, and we have a social duty to conform to those rights. Thus, for society to function effectively, we need to be motivated to respect people's (legal) rights; but we need not be motivated to advance utilitarian principles in our daily lives. If we want to know *why* we have those legal rights, the answer (for a utilitarian) is that they are justified on utilitarian grounds from an institutional point of view.

Not all utilitarians are comfortable with this separation between personal motives and institutional justifications, but for the rule utilitarian, the justification of our rights stands apart from claims about what should motivate people to act.

This conventional understanding of rights contrasts with Thomas Jefferson's account in the Declaration of Independence, where he asserts that we have *natural* rights that any government must protect and whose validity is explained by our nature as persons. The tradition of natural rights is often grounded religiously, but there are also accounts of pre-institutional human rights that are freestanding from religious grounding, such as the United Nations' Declaration of Human Rights of 1948. This document asserts that we have rights independent of the laws of our society, and these rights should guide what our legal rights should be. But this declaration offers little philosophical grounding to explain how and why we have these rights.

> See Chapter 3 Section 8 for more about the contrast between Hume's consequentialist and Locke's deontological grounding for rights. A contemporary defense of natural rights and law is provided by John Finnis in *Natural Law and Natural Rights* (Oxford University Press, 1997).

This debate raises a puzzle. Should we understand rights conventionally, as whatever a just legal system should protect based on considerations of welfare, equality, or other worthy goals? Or do we say that law ought to track the (natural) rights that we already have? This question reveals an enduring debate about the nature of rights. Philosopher Jeremy Bentham, an early proponent of utilitarianism, called natural rights *nonsense on stilts*. He believed that only by considering how rights function in society—and by weighing the benefits and costs of specific legal rules based on utilitarian analysis—can we offer a reasoned case to support the legal rights that a society ought to recognize. But Nozick's entitlement theory and Locke's account of rights are attempts to specify rights independently from institutional rules or the instrumental value of promoting some social goal.

This distinction between natural and conventional rights can bring new depth to Chapter 3 on property rights. In this chapter we discussed property rights as a precondition for market exchange and introduced the idea of consequentialist and deontological groundings for property rights. But we did not have the tools to fully assess the justice of the property rights that frame how markets develop. The debate on utilitarianism and rights theories in this chapter offers a more encompassing normative perspective for assessing the underlying property rights that shape capitalism. On the one hand, we can examine the claims, liberties, powers, and immunities that define our legal system as chess pieces to be carefully adjusted to create the best social results. We can understand the details of governmental regulation on utilitarian terms, or through a broader teleological perspective, based on goals for liberty, equality, or other values.

On the other hand, perhaps there are natural rights whose point of justification is to establish *side-constraints* on any teleological or consequentialist analysis. We would then say that various laws, such as antidiscrimination or equal opportunity laws, simply recognize the rights that are already ours, independent of the goals that those rights promote.

Regardless of this enduring foundational dispute, just about every rights theorist accepts that the language of rights function as a kind of *trump* over other values, placing duties on others not to violate those rights under normal circumstances, unless weighty reasons demand trade-offs, if such trade-offs can be ever permissible.[14]

In this section we developed the contrast between two broad justifications for rights: teleological and deontological. However, there is a third influential tradition that grounds rights in a *social contract*. In this view rights are whatever rules people would agree to under procedures of fair bargaining. The most famous contemporary proponent of this view is American philosopher John Rawls. We will develop this social contract tradition in the next chapter after introducing a discussion about the nature of equality (Chapter 11 Section 5).

Trade-offs among Values

Some believe that social choices always require trade-offs among values. For example, those who believe that trade-offs are inevitable will say that no society can have a maximum level of equality, liberty, fraternity, community, virtue, and whatever else we think important, all at the same time. At some point, more liberty means we will have less equality and vice versa. These are all distinct values, and if and when they conflict, we will need to choose which values matter more.

Philosopher Isaiah Berlin was sympathetic to this perspective and argued for **ethical pluralism**, the view that many values are important and they do not all reduce to or derive from some master value that can explain away all conflict. If pluralism is true, how do we make choices among values? Berlin had no answer to this question but offered this suggestion: societies should place a high premium on negative freedom to allow people the space to choose the values that matter most to them at a personal level. In the end, Berlin applied goal-oriented reasoning to his account of rights: the rights of a society should reflect the combination of values that a society decides make for the best trade-offs, including at least some minimum of liberty.

---

[14]Legal theorist and political philosopher Ronald Dworkin argued for rights as *trumps* in *Taking Rights Seriously* (Harvard University Press, 1977).

Alternatively, an account of rights need not be associated with advancing liberty or justice or balancing particular values. For Nozick, Locke, and other deontologists, the very idea of a right is to specify constraints that do not derive from any goal or custom, whether it's liberty, welfare, or other values. For these deontologists, respecting our rights should not be subject to *any* trade-offs in pursuit of potentially competing values.

10.7   SUMMARY

We all draw on a vocabulary to express our beliefs about ethics and justice. Some people emphasize liberty, others equality; some rights, others efficiency; and there are many others. How do these values influence our attitudes about markets, corporations, and government in society? How do they influence our motives and decision-making in business and economic life? We saw how efficiency is a value that some argue should lead us to support markets and capitalism; others argue that this same value should lead us to a critique. Discussions of liberty and rights produce the same range of opinions. Each chapter introduces distinctive methods of reasoning and normative tools that apply across many topics in business and economic life.

An entitlement theory considers the just conditions for initial acquisitions, transfers, and rectification of market activity. These ideas are currently integrated throughout domestic and international law. They also provide a framework for considering our ethical responsibilities within the market system. An historical account of justice offers an illuminating contrast to utilitarian and other goal-oriented perspectives. Some believe that property rights should be regarded as adaptable by law, custom, and as a means to support various moral goals; others believe that property rights are natural and create absolute side-constraints as a bulwark against the pursuit of those goals. Whether or not rights are best justified on deontological or consequentialist or other grounds, the analysis of rights plays an important role in our thinking about the ethics and values of business and economic life

KEY TERMS

legal rights	moral side-constraints	principle of justice in
natural rights	goal-oriented ethical reasoning	rectification
human rights	teleological theories of ethics	resource curse
negative rights	entitlement theory of justice	undeserved inequalities
positive rights	principle of justice in initial	proliferation of rights
individual rights	acquisition	ethical pluralism
group rights	principle of justice in transfer	

DISCUSSION QUESTIONS

1. Political philosopher Ronald Dworkin writes that "The concept of rights . . . has its most natural expression when a political society is divided, and appeals to cooperation or a common goal are pointless."[15] Is that true? Does that mean that applying an ethics of rights is already admitting to some type of failure?

2. Are patents and copyrights legitimate *rights*? Explain.

---

[15]Dworkin, *Taking Rights Seriously*, p. 185.

3. Can someone's rights be violated through no fault of others? Explain and give examples.

4. Suppose that an American museum is displaying a piece of artwork that was originally looted from a private home during the Holocaust. The museum discovers this fact only after it purchases the artwork and it has been on display at the museum for many years. No family members are living who can claim the artwork, except very distant cousins. What should the museum do? Apply both deontological and utilitarian perspectives for addressing this question.

5. A corporation downsizes and announces 8,000 layoffs as a means to increase its profits. Stock prices soar as a result of the announcement. The town where most of the employees live shudders (metaphorically speaking). Analyze the ethics of this action from rights-based and utilitarian perspectives.

6. Suppose that I buy clothes at a store with the intent to wear them to a party that night and then return them the next day. Is this unethical? Apply a rights-based and utilitarian reasoning to assess this situation.

7. Is health care a right? Is social security a right? If so, what are the bases for these rights? To what extent are corporations responsible for providing resources to support these rights, if there are such?

8. Select one specific economic right that interests you and that you support, such as workplace rights to due process and fair treatment, rights to a living wage, right to work, right to unionize, right to privacy, or corporate rights to free speech. What makes it a *right* in your view? On what basis is it justified?

9. If I need to earn income to survive, do I thereby have a right to work? Explain. If so, is this a negative or positive right? If there is no right to work, then does this mean that high unemployment implies no personal or societal obligations to help?

11

EQUALITY

11.1 INTRODUCTION

In 2011, Sandi Murphy made about $50,000 as an emergency room registered nurse, potentially saving people's lives on a daily basis. During that time, John Hammergren made about $131,000,000, most of which was from exercising stock options. (Hammergren is CEO of McKesson, Inc., a corporation that is a distributor of pharmaceuticals and IT health care systems.) Murphy will work for an entire year and make the same amount of money as Hammergren made in about a half a day.[1]

Consider the median income of a college graduate today who works full time with approximately two weeks' vacation—$50,000 per year. Let's say this is you, and you receive a 5 percent pay increase each year throughout your entire career, a hopeful estimate. If you work forty-five years, then the cumulative salary you'll earn is about $3,000,000. The average CEO of an S&P 500 company will make that amount in *three months* within a single year. Maybe you'll do very well and make a lot more than that, earning an initial salary that is two or three times the median income. Then your *lifetime* earnings will be what the average S&P 500 CEO makes in less than one year.[2]

Let's try one more comparison. According to World Bank statistics, the average salary of humans around the world is about $10,000 per year, and perhaps three billion people live off of less than $1,000 per year.[3] This means that billions of people, perhaps nearly half of the world's

WHEN YOU FINISH
STUDYING THIS CHAPTER,
YOU SHOULD BE ABLE TO:

1. Distinguish the idea of fundamental equality from the idea of being treated equally in the relevant respects.

2. Examine the implications of believing in equality from both institutional and personal points of view.

3. Understand and apply the concept of equal opportunity.

4. Describe the social contract tradition and apply it to debates in business and economic life.

---

[1] See *Parade* magazine's "What People Earn." Analysis: http://www.parade.com/what-people-earn/slideshows/real-people-2011.html#?slideindex=129. More recent data is available through 2013. The data on John Hammergren is from *Fortune* magazine: http://www.forbes.com/sites/christopherhelman/2011/10/12/americas-25-highest-paid-ceos/.

[2] This widely available data is based on information at http://money.cnn.com/2011/02/10/pf/college_graduates_salaries/index.htm, and http://www.forbes.com/sites/christopherhelman/2011/10/12/americas-25-highest-paid-ceos/.

[3] See http://data.worldbank.org/indicator/NY.GDP.PCAP.CD/countries?display=graph and http://www.oecd-ilibrary.org/content/book/factbook-2010-en.

population, can count their entire lifetime earnings, and they will probably make less money than *you* can expect to make as a college graduate in your first year out of college.

It's disorienting to fully comprehend these differences, putting aside our ethical judgments.

Yet judgment is part of the disorientation. What is your ethical judgment? Is there something wrong about a world where people experience these inequalities in income? If so, what is the wrong? Consequentialists approach these questions by examining the effects of these inequalities. For example, some people argue that great inequalities divide society, create social discord, reduce overall well-being, and undermine the basis for healthy democracies. By contrast, deontological rights theories such as Nozick's account presented in Chapter 10 examine how those inequalities came about: if people's rights were violated by the historical process that created those inequalities, then those inequalities are wrong; otherwise, they are not.

Neither of these perspectives fully captures the ethical intuitions of proponents of an approach analyzed in this chapter. The problem, they argue, is that vast income or other inequalities violate the equal value of all human beings. We ought to treat and be treated as equals in society because we *are* each other's equals. **Fundamental equality** refers to this basic belief in the equality of all persons.

We began with *income* inequality because critics of markets and capitalism often emphasize them. But we can be equal or unequal in many other respects as well. For example, we experience stark differences in vacation time, opportunities for advancement, risk of harm, and retirement benefits. What we can do with our income varies greatly too, in terms of access to buying goods and services, access to health care, educational, and cultural opportunities, and much else. We also experience a vast range of other types of inequalities: such as differing opportunities for employment, unequal freedoms, or inequalities in well-being. The subject of inequality may lead us to examine not merely economic inequalities but political and social inequalities as well.

People who call themselves **egalitarians** pursue a distinctive approach to ethics. They argue for greater equality in society on the premise that we are all each other's equals. Thus, the first step in the argument is to claim that we are fundamental equals to each other. The second step is to argue that in one or more specific respects, we should have greater social, political, or economic equalities than we do today. A voluminous egalitarian literature in philosophy and the social sciences characterizes different types of inequalities that people may experience in their lives, and then argues which we should care most about, given our fundamental nature as equals.

These ideas lead to two basic questions. First, What *is* the nature of the fundamental equality of persons? Second, What are the implications of this belief—both for the types of market and political institutions that we should support, and for how we should treat each other at a personal level?

In this chapter, we begin with a discussion of fundamental equality, especially as advocated by a leading proponent—political philosopher Thomas Nagel. We then examine implications of this view from institutional and personal points of view. To focus the discussion, the chapter emphasizes two types of inequalities that are especially relevant to discussions in business and economic life: (1) income and wealth inequality and (2) the concept of equal opportunity.

11.2 FUNDAMENTAL EQUALITY

"We are all equals," you hear proclaimed.

What does this mean? Historically, it hasn't been so. People have lived in slavery, caste systems, and rigid hierarchies. Even today, in the most democratic societies on earth, we could hardly spend one hour with our eyes open without seeing tremendous differences in the ways that people live and how they are treated. Even at the biological and physical level, we do not look the same and we do not occupy the same space. No person is identical to anyone else. So, how are we equals?

A commitment to fundamental equality is a normative idea about how we should value a person relative to other persons. It says: Strip away all the differentiations that any society or any biological condition could create among people as a descriptive natural and social fact and, at some level, we all have the same worth. We are all equally important. We all have the same human dignity. Different people express this idea in different ways, but whatever the expression, a belief in fundamental equality enables us to say, by being a person, you and I are equals.

THE COMMONALITIES AND SEPARATENESS OF PERSONS

Ethical language is a means to explore and interpret the world. Values of welfare, liberty, rights, equality, and others offer different vocabularies to express our moral perspectives.

They may also express different **metaphysical conceptions of the person**, which refer to differing views about whatever is ultimately real about being a person. For example, equality may express a commitment that whatever gives one person worth is also what gives the same worth to each other person. Equality invites a search to identify *commonalities* about being a person that all other persons share and that matter most for deciding how we should treat each other.

Other values may express a different commitment, however. For example, some theorists wish to emphasize that part of being a person is that we are morally *separate* from each other. An account of individual rights or respect may convey this idea, as might judgments about what people deserve, which can be an idea about how to treat someone for being *that* particular person (the subject of Chapter 13). These other values emphasize how particular persons are different and morally distinct from others. They provide ethical language for acknowledging the value of some person without comparison to others. For example, consider how

we love another because of who *that person* is, not because we perceive that this individual has some common trait shared by others. To take another example, people often believe that some particular person is deserving for what that person has done, without any comparison to others.

Ideas about human commonality and separateness need not compete with each other. For example, we may believe that persons are both moral equals and morally distinct. We may implicitly express this combination of beliefs by saying that we have *equal rights*, which expresses both the (1) *equal-ness* of our rights and that (2) particular persons have *individual rights* to be protected against all others. To probe the meaning of *equal rights*, consider this question: if we had to accept only one side of this expression, which would it be, equal-ness (of rights or whatever) or that some individual *has* rights?

In sum, ethical values can be interpreted, in part, as varied expressions to make sense of both sides of a metaphysical ledger: that we are morally separate from other and moral equals with other. Dualities such as these can be oversimplifying, but they have insight as well. The most fundamental point is that discussions of ethics and values can be understood partly as attempts to reason about what a person *is*.

Let's see how one egalitarian in particular discusses this idea of fundamental equality. Political philosopher Thomas Nagel describes how people have a special human capacity to live in both *personal* and *impartial* perspectives throughout life, no matter our cultural or religious backgrounds. We can interpret the world from different perspectives. From a personal perspective, we calculate what matters to us from our own point of view. This perspective, he points out, is not necessarily selfish because from within our own points of view we probably want to help others at times. But we also have a distinctive capacity to interpret the world from an impartial perspective. We recognize that there are other people who have perspectives that differ from our own. We can put ourselves in their shoes, one by one, and we can value what happens to them by the value they assign to their experience from their point of view.

Consider an example. From a personal perspective, if I'm let go from work, it matters a whole lot to me. I will be completely consumed by the experience and the repercussions. Let's say someone I have never met thirty miles away is also let go. I can certainly empathize with that person's plight if I find out about it, but I place a completely different value to that fact compared to the reality of *my* losing a job. This example illustrates how I care a great deal about many events that happen *to me* that I hardly give a thought to when they happen to others. For many events in life, when it happens to me, it's *very important*. When it happens to someone else: *not so important*. This is everyone's experience. It couldn't be otherwise—we occupy our own point of view.

But, says Nagel, we also have the capacity to assess situations by taking an impartial perspective. I can recognize that a job loss to someone else matters just as much to *that* person when it happens to *that* person as it does to me when it happens to me, and from an impartial perspective I can assign equal weight to that person's experiences as I do to mine. As Nagel writes, "This gives to each person's well-being very great importance, and from the impersonal standpoint everyone's primary importance, leaving aside his effect on the welfare of others, is the same."[4] I can recognize that my job loss from a cosmic or impartial perspective does not matter more *just because it happened to me*. To have this recognition is to perceive that human beings are fundamentally equal from this impartial perspective. In Nagel's words, our primary importance is the same, and we know that is true when we enter this perspective.

Egalitarians will often say that recognizing our fundamental equality is what it means to adopt an ethical point of view, in contrast to prudential, egoistic, or entirely self-referencing perspectives. This is why egalitarians will often emphasize the value of equality over any of the normative ideas so far discussed in the text—welfare, liberty, and rights. An egalitarian, for example, will explain why a complete narcissist or psychopath doesn't get ethics. The impartial perspective has absolutely no pull on such people and so they do not understand how to reason ethically as a guide to their personal conduct. By contrast, nearly all of us know how to *get outside of ourselves*, and that's to enter into, at least to some extent, an impartial perspective.

There are other ways to think about fundamental equality, including ideas from religious traditions that specify both what human beings essentially are, as well as regulative ideals about how we should regard each other. The most salient point is to consider that egalitarians endorse a claim about our fundamental equality, and this idea becomes the foundation for thinking through ethics at the personal and institutional levels, as depicted in Figure 11.1. We will turn to these topics in Sections 3 and 4.

---

[4]Thomas Nagel, *Equality and Partiality* (Oxford University Press, 1995), p. 65.

11.3 IMPLICATIONS FOR INSTITUTIONS

In this section we consider, first, why egalitarianism invites a focus on institutional analysis. Next, we examine two specific topics of economic inequality: income and wealth inequality, and equality of opportunity.

A. THE TILT TOWARD INSTITUTIONAL ANALYSIS

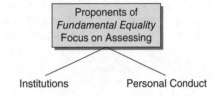

FIGURE 11.1 Pursuing Equality through Reforming Institutions or through Personal Action with a Given Institution

Egalitarians tend to emphasize the role of *institutions* for advancing equality, and it's revealing to consider why this is the case. The pressures of economic decision-making can be modeled as (a sometimes difficult-to-achieve) balance between our personal sense of ethics, the incentives we face, and the institutional constraints that shape our choices. For example, we considered in Chapter 8 how conflicts of interest represent an imbalance between ethics and personal incentives.

> Chapter 8 provides an extended discussion of the balancing act between ethics, incentives, and institutional arrangements.

Let's consider another potential imbalance between ethics and incentives especially relevant to egalitarians. If ethics as equality is too costly or remote from a personal point of view, then it is unlikely to translate into personal action, even if we recognize its demands from an impersonal point of view (see also Chapter 8 Section 6). This idea expresses a great puzzle for egalitarians: how is it possible to create an enduring egalitarian ethos in the face of a disconnect between the demands of equality and our personal daily incentives. The difficulty is this: we should give due regard to our fundamental equality (we know this from the impartial perspective) but, practically speaking, we live out our lives through our own personal perspective. We are only human. We recognize that everyone matters equally but we don't (and can't) live that way. So what should we do?

The solution egalitarians tend to embrace is to recognize a division of labor between ethics, incentives, and institutions, and focus on the role of institutions. The discussion about conflicts of interest is relevant here: when ethics and incentives conflict, one solution is to change the institutional rules to diffuse the conflict (like making a rule to prohibit a judge from hearing a case on a matter of personal interest) or at least lower the costs of ethical behavior (like creating a corporate culture where complaints can be heard without costly fallout). Similarly, if institutions uphold fundamental equality, then people can focus their daily lives elsewhere with assurance that institutions are doing their job. Nagel shares with most egalitarians this emphasis on institutional reform: "I believe," writes Nagel, "that impartiality emerges from an essential aspect of the human point of view, and that it naturally seeks expression through the *institutions* under which we live."[5] In the language of Chapter 8, egalitarians are mostly law and regulation theorists.

Let's contrast this position with a proponent of negative freedom who believes in negative rights. In this view, we ought to respect people's freedom by not violating their rights. What is the balance between ethics, incentives, and institutions in this normative framework? If our ethical injunction is to *not violate rights*, then I do not have to spend

---

[5]Nagel, *Equality and Partiality*, p. 64 (my italics).

every waking moment investigating calamities and inequalities unrelated to my personal actions. I can focus on my direct conduct and act so as not to violate others' rights.

This account suggests a contrasting account of the demands of ethics and individual incentives compared with the egalitarian. On the one hand, the burdens of justice are weighty because people's *personal sense of ethics* must include the injunction not to violate anyone's rights, even as they are focused on their own goals and lives. On the other hand, these ethical demands can be relatively weak compared to the egalitarian, because rights to noninterference do not address inequalities or imply obligations to remedy bad situations unrelated to what an individual causes. The general insight is this: as an account of ethics places more demands on the *individual*, these demands must be thin enough to be psychologically reasonable to follow from a personal perspective. Such are the ethics of rights of noninterference, claim its proponents, who argue that their approach shows how it's possible to align a reasonable account of a sense of ethics with our personal incentives. Unfortunately, humanity provides plenty of examples where even the most minimal standards of human rights seem to fall on deaf ears when they conflict with personal incentives.

Chapter 14 considers the importance of character and integrity in deciding how to balance our sense of ethics and personal incentives. Consider also the case study in Chapter 10, Section 4, which poses the challenge of whether to think about ethics primarily from institutional or personal perspectives.

For the egalitarian, the problem with this account is that it shortchanges what ethics really demands. It's not just the people with whom we directly interact that matter for ethics, it's everyone, because everyone matters. From this perspective, there is some child starving on the other side of the planet. Put yourself in the experience of that starving child, says the egalitarian. That child's experience matters because that person matters, in the same way that I matter. But what should I do with that insight from a personal point of view? Is it realistic to think that I can wake up every morning and pursue the substantive demands of fundamental equality? For egalitarians, we recognize demands of ethics that we are probably not psychologically ready or able to live by. And yet, that fact does not make the impartial perspective invalid, argues the egalitarian. Rather, it should focus our attention on the role of institutions for protecting and promoting our equality.[6] For these reasons egalitarians emphasize the role of *institutions* for advancing equality.

Should our ideals lead us to focus on *assessing institutions* or our *personal sense of ethics*? It's a recurring theme throughout this book. It may depend on which ideals we think are most important and how we view the capacities and limitations of human nature.

B. INCOME AND WEALTH INEQUALITY REVISITED

For proponents of egalitarianism, the long arc of social justice is about the movement toward greater equality in society. Perhaps the most basic political equality that we can experience is equality before the law: legal proceedings that treat us the same as anyone else would be treated in similar circumstances, no matter our connections to power and privilege. We live under a **rule of law** when we live by general laws that we can know, that apply equally, and that create stable expectations. Although there are many arguments on behalf of creating a

---

[6]Nagel (*Equality and Partiality*, p. 5), is not optimistic that society can successfully protect our human equality: "The problem of designing institutions that do justice to the equal importance of all persons, without making unacceptable demands on individuals, has not been solved—and that this is so partly because for our world the problem of the right relation between the personal and impersonal standpoints within each individual has not been solved."

rule of law, perhaps the most common is that a rule of law is necessary for people to respect each other as equals, which is why we also sometimes describe this notion as *equality before the law*. Beyond this most basic kind of equality, which no society has yet to perfectly achieve, *democratic* societies have developed many additional, wide-ranging political and civic equalities, including much greater racial, ethnic, and gender equality in law and social custom than in centuries past. The long and uneven historical march toward democratic government is often interpreted as a march to realize our fundamental equality. In other words, many people defend democracy through an egalitarian perspective, beginning from a belief about our fundamental equality to an investigation of the specific respects in which political and civic institutions ought to recognize our equal citizenship. Many historical and contemporary debates can be interpreted in these terms. Debates about the women's suffrage movement at the beginning of the twentieth century, the civil rights movement mid-century, and gay marriage today are all examples of arguments about what equal citizenship should mean in our society.

> A society establishes a *rule of law* when its legal principles state general precepts that citizens can know and that apply equally to any person in a similar situation. Societies that establish a rule of law create stable expectations that the law will treat people in nonarbitrary ways. See Chapter 3 Section 3 for a discussion of property rights and law.

Let's focus on claims about income and wealth inequalities. Some people believe that they provide an unsheathed display of the shortcomings and injustice of capitalism. Others do not. They believe instead that income inequalities are the inevitable outcome of a free society. Let's consider three views in this debate, focusing solely on whether income inequalities are compatible with—or undermine—the sense of our fundamental equality.

Here is a *first* view: as long as salary differences occur in a society that recognizes and protects its citizens' equal status, then there is nothing objectionable about patterns of income inequalities that result from market exchanges. Said again, political and civil equality matters a great deal, but not income inequality. We can tie this perspective to rights-based arguments from the previous chapter. A concern for people's rights can be interpreted as a concern for people's *equal* rights. We imagine a scheme of rights that define contracts and property rules, within a democratic society that protects various freedoms. These political and civil rights serve to capture the demands for fundamental equality, leaving income inequalities to vary based on market outcomes, without raising any special concerns about people's fundamental equality. In this view, there is no problem seeing each other as equals while recognizing that we make different amounts of money.

Let's return to the island scenario of Chapter 6, imagining two people engaged in a market trade. What must be true for the buyer and seller to make trades under conditions that respect their fundamental equality? Whatever the full answer, proponents of the first point of view deny that equal outcomes are even part of the answer. They argue that income inequality is the inevitable consequence of free trade. In this view, the invisible hand argument (Chapter 8) is fully compatible with political and civic equality.[7]

> This discussion suggests how the hypothetical island scenario of Chapter 6 is like a petri dish for analyzing what *free trade* could mean and what the requirements of *fundamental equality* could be in that context.

---

[7]If all of our valid rights are rights of noninterference, then there is an additional worry: If our earnings are redistributed without our consent as a means to achieve income equality, then government may be interfering with us. This libertarian argument is underdeveloped without a specific account of the content of our rights, but the general approach is to say, Fundamental equality matters in political and civic life, but is undermined when applied to regulating income inequalities through government redistribution.

A *second* view attacks the premise that vast income inequalities are compatible with political and civic equality. Significant income inequalities, some argue, are a sure symptom of political and civic *inequalities*. The ability of the rich to dominate politics, receive better education, receive better police protection and less severe prison terms, and many other noneconomic benefits, are the underlying wrongs of a society that permits money and capitalism as a dominating institution. Income inequalities may not undermine our fundamental equality per se, but it does so when wealth enables a person to dominate political and civic affairs.[8] In this view, market outcomes are problematic by undercutting our equal citizenship in political and civic life, which in turn undercuts our fundamental equality.

A *third* position is that income inequalities *directly* undercut our fundamental equality. Consider: Does a world that permits such huge gaps between rich and poor systematically convey the message that some people are more important than others, even if against a backdrop of political and civic equality? Consider rereading the first three paragraphs of this chapter. What do you think? If so, what should we do about that? Our views about the ethics and justice of capitalism depend significantly on how we think through these basic questions. The Occupy Wall Street movement, for example, expressed a range of grievances about capitalism, many of which are captured by the second and third views. These views correlate with the law and regulation model, which emphasizes the need for government to oversee market outcomes through its tax policies, property rights decisions, and business regulations.

EQUALITY AND HUNGER

People in some places in the world are so poor that they can't afford to acquire food through no fault of their own; what does that situation tell us about society's commitment to equality? Does that situation indicate a problem with markets or government (or both)? These questions relate to Sen's work on famines, discussed in Chapter 3 Section 6.

In sum, note first how we can evaluate income and wealth inequality through many ethical traditions and perspectives beyond the scope of this chapter. For example, we can assess the consequences of these outcomes through a utilitarian framework and debate incentive structures, or judge the motives and character of those who end up on top, or examine whether anyone's rights were violated in creating those inequalities. But in this section we applied a single idea: fundamental equality. Some argue that income inequalities that develop through capitalism can be compatible with our fundamental equality; others argue that economic inequalities undermine our political and civic equalities, and so indirectly undermine our fundamental equality; still others argue that the mere fact of income and wealth disparities directly undermine our fundamental equality.

C. EQUAL OPPORTUNITY

Among the many distinctions that egalitarians make, one stands out as particularly relevant for this discussion. We could focus our analysis on **equal outcomes** or **equal opportunity** for attaining outcomes. *Equal outcomes* refer to efforts to equalize the results of a process. *Equal opportunities* refer to efforts to equalize some of the conditions that shape the process, independent of its results. The discussion so far has analyzed income and wealth inequalities as an *outcome* of a market process. But others focus elsewhere. For example, recall the argument that economic inequalities are the inevitable outcome of a free society. In this view, some people apply themselves more effectively than others.

---

[8]Political philosopher Michael Walzer argues this position in *Spheres of Justice* (Basic Books, 1983).

A sole focus on equalizing outcomes undermines the sense that people are, at least in part, individually responsible for the outcomes that they create.

Many forms of egalitarianism accept this basic insight and seek to endorse egalitarian ideals without undermining an important role for individual responsibility. Thus, they often state their position as follows: from the standpoint of fundamental equality, we ought to correct for all (but only!) those economic inequalities for which people are *not* themselves responsible. We recognize our fundamental equality by supporting institutions that correct for all undeserved inequalities that set us apart through no fault of our own.

Based on this reasoning, many discussions of economic equality focus on the concept of *equality of opportunity*. This idea has tremendous impact in society today. In this view, focusing on income inequality as an outcome is to focus in the wrong place. Rather, fundamental equality in economic life demands a level playing field of opportunities, and then the rest becomes our own responsibility.

Equal opportunity is a central concept in business and economic life, including equal employment opportunity laws that ban discrimination in hiring practices based on age, disability, national origin, sex, religion, genetic information, pregnancy, and other types of discrimination (http://www.eeoc.gov/). Let's consider what equal opportunity means, not in a specific legal context, but as an ethical ideal for any society to achieve.[9]

The first insight is that equal opportunity expresses a formula about removing hindrances for achieving one or more specific goals. Opportunities indicate a relationship between people and their goals. If I have an opportunity, I have something less than a guarantee that I can achieve a goal, but I have something more than a remote possibility. As one theorist argues, opportunities occur when there is the absence of one or more obstacles for achieving my goal, under conditions where there are no remaining insurmountable obstacles. He writes, "Every opportunity is a chance of a specified agent or class of agents, X, to choose to attain a specified goal or set of goals, Y, without the hindrance of a specified obstacle or set of obstacles, Z."[10]

This formula can be very helpful for analyzing the concept of equal opportunity. For example, if people have equal opportunity to compete for a job, what does that mean? We need to fill in the details. For example, it can mean (and in part as a legal matter does mean) that men and women (X) can compete for jobs (Y) without any special preferences in the hiring process based on differences in persons' gender (Z).

An interesting upshot of this analysis is that *equal opportunity* does not refer to one single idea, and now we can see why. Equal opportunities are particularized to people, goals, and the hindrances that are to be removed. Understanding the relationship between people, goals, and hindrances helps to clarify what we are talking about when we discuss equal opportunity.

Equality in this context is about the absence of some specified obstacles for all those to whom the opportunity applies. This fact does not mean that people will not face unequal obstacles in other respects. For example, two job applicants can have equal opportunity for a job by not facing any discrimination based on age, sex, disability, and race, but one candidate may not own a car to get to the job interview, which can be an obstacle that another applicant does not face. More deeply, one applicant may not have the wherewithal or

---

[9]This discussion draws significantly from Peter Westen, "The Concept of Equality of Opportunity," *Ethics* 95 (1985), pp. 837–850.

[10]Ibid., p. 841.

imagination even to know that various opportunities exist. A lack of awareness about how to pursue opportunities can be one of the most powerful impediments, and so advocates of *equal opportunity* must identify the *specific obstacles* that they believe deserve special attention over others.

Let's consider a different point. Suppose that I own a business and want to hire people who are in my religion only. Should laws exist to prohibit this practice? (They do.) Why? The grounding for equal opportunity regardless of religion may or may not be based on a belief in fundamental equality. We could argue that this equal opportunity principle is justified because it creates a more productive workplace, increases civic peace, or is a demand of freedom. We can draw on a wide range of reasons from previous chapters or elsewhere to support or criticize this or any given principle. But equal opportunity principles could be—and often are—based on a belief in fundamental equality. This is why it makes sense to discuss equal opportunity in this chapter. But like many of the topics throughout the book, the reasons that justify any particular position can and often do draw on more than one ethical tradition or value. In a sense, this point conveys what this book is about: learning the nuances of these values and drawing on many of them for making decisions in business and economic life. Although the chapters focus on each value separately for clarity of presentation, the intent is to build an increasingly comprehensive perspective that allows for a full integration of these perspectives.

Consider one last interesting upshot of equal opportunity principles. They are not neutral. A law that prohibits employers from hiring based on religion is also denying the employers an equal opportunity—namely, the opportunity to hire on whatever criterion they want. This does not mean that we should not, thereby, prohibit discrimination based on religion. It's to emphasize that equal opportunity principles are not neutral in the world of opportunities. Laws that create some opportunities deny others opportunities, by preventing people from undercutting the opportunities that the law protects. Law professor Peter Westen concludes his discussion of equal opportunity by writing, "We do not really believe in equal opportunity as such. We believe in *particular* equal opportunities."[11] The question is which opportunities ought to be available in society, which denied, and what justifies that list. In particular, this chapter asks, Which equal opportunities are necessary for respecting our fundamental equality?

Read the Case Studies *Hiring Practices* and *Discriminatory Practices* only on MySearchLab

D. AN EQUAL OPPORTUNITY SOCIETY

We might identify a variety of specific equal opportunity laws—such as antidiscrimination laws mentioned above—as justified through a vision of creating an **equal opportunity society**. What could this mean as an aspirational ideal? Let's apply the analysis above to understand some puzzles in this area.

The relevant goal is not simply getting a job or having income but something broader and deeper, which helps explain why a job and wealth matter in the first place. Let's specify the goal as the pursuit of happiness, or reaching one's full potential as a person, or in the words of some writers, of achieving overall "life prospects."[12] An *equal opportunity society* refers to the aspiration that all persons within that society have the chance to reach their full potential against a backdrop of similar constraints and opportunities. But there

---

[11]Westen, "The Concept of Equality of Opportunity," p. 850 (my italics).

[12]John Rawls, *A Theory of Justice* (Harvard, 1971).

is much disagreement about which should be the relevant constraints and opportunities for developing this ideal. Two variations are **formal equality of opportunity** and **fair equality of opportunity**.

The trajectory of life prospects for someone born in a ghetto is far different from someone born in great wealth. Some will say that the most important point is that there be no laws or practices that formally discriminate against anyone—for example, based on birth, race, gender, or religious orientation. We can call this *formal equality of opportunity*, which refers to a society with laws and practices that ensure that positions are open to all applicants and are awarded to those with the most merits, as defined by the requirements of the position. Advocates of formal equality of opportunity argue that this vision respects our fundamental equality.

Others will say that these formal laws do not create real opportunity for many people because the remaining obstacles radically affect life prospects that the individual does not control. The role of our major institutions is not merely to recognize antidiscrimination laws, or create a viable rule of law, but to provide programs and structures that continually attempt to equalize the overall life prospects of everyone in society, such as providing for basic education and family assistance. Just consider the different life prospects of those who receive little education relative to those who experience extensive education. This point often starts by contrasting the sad state of an illiterate child, in war-ravaged nations with no opportunity for schooling, with the typical college graduate. But the point applies within developed countries as well.

Which opportunities should be equalized in this vision? The answer is: *all* opportunities that affect our life prospects and which result from factors that we should not be held responsible for. This vision is quite different from the more formal equality of opportunity discussed above. We might call this position *fair equality of opportunity*, which refers to a condition where people can pursue opportunities to enhance their life prospects without unequal impediments due to factors which are not their responsibility, such as inborn differences in social and economic class.

Much of the disagreement about interpreting this ideal depends on whether our political and economic institutions should correct for good and bad luck to properly recognize our fundamental equality. For advocates of formal equality before the law, people will absorb their own good and bad luck without our institutional structures compensating and without undermining our fundamental equality. Others ask, "How can we call each other equals and allow children to experience such unequal circumstances without any effort to improve the opportunities of those children who are worse off?"

Market and business life is often interpreted as a combination of both luck and skill. This idea leads some to argue that government should take an active role in correcting for the effects of bad luck in capitalism. Recall the Wilt Chamberlain example from Chapter 10. A series of seemingly innocuous market trades that violate no one's rights can still create massive inequalities based on good and bad luck. Inequalities can occur in outcomes, opportunities, and much else. Should concerns about fundamental equality include correcting for these inequalities? Which ones?

To summarize, this chapter focuses concerns about equality in relation to business and economic life. Many people criticize capitalism for its income and wealth inequalities; others do not. Some emphasize the important role of equal opportunity laws; others argue more broadly for an equal opportunity society. We can also distinguish the pursuit of political, legal, and social equality from arguments about economic equality. People disagree about all these ideas but, for many, they do so within a shared moral vision that sorting these differences should be grounded in the commitment that we are fundamentally equal.

11.4 PROFESSIONAL ETHICS AND THE PERSONAL POINT OF VIEW

Let's now consider other applications of fundamental equality from a personal point of view. Although egalitarianism typically focuses on institutional reform, we can also consider how belief in equality bears on personal motivations and a sense of professional ethics. In terms of Chapter 8, this section considers the professional ethics model interpreted through the value of equality, rather than through efficiency, liberty, or rights.

A. THE WORKPLACE: INTERNAL RELATIONSHIPS

Concerns about equal treatment are elemental. From an early age we are intensely sensitive to situations where we appear to be treated worse than others (especially if we have siblings). Parents are often looking for rules and procedures to handle this problem. For example, one way to divide a cake between two people is to have one person cut the cake and the other person choose which piece to take. It does not take much attention, when observing the interactions of children, to see that demands for equality (often *fairness*) can variously be interpreted as a high ethical principle or the simple result of envy.

If we fast-forward to the adult world, the psychology of equality has practical applications for living both in the workplace and beyond. Debates about economic inequality often focus at the macro level regarding income and wealth inequalities across society. But the hierarchy of the internal workplace identifies a different and no less important forum for thinking about equality. A work environment that flouts considerations of equality will probably find disgruntled employees. On the other hand, equal treatment can stifle an environment designed to reward creativity and excellence. The distinction introduced earlier between *fundamental equality* and *equality in the relevant respects* can be helpful here: making small efforts to recognize each other as fundamentally equal can counteract (to some degree) the meaning and significance of other workplace inequalities.

An organizational challenge is to create a culture of cooperation and respect among people whose conditions are considerably *unequal* in many respects. The point is both psychological and philosophical: if we believe in fundamental equality at a personal level, then we might ask ourselves how we can treat each other as equals against the backdrop of the rules, structures, benefits, and burdens that treat people unequally. One practical question (relevant to equality) to ask within any work environment is, "How can I confer respect on others in the face of those existing inequalities that I can do little about, or shouldn't do anything about?" For example, how do managers lead subordinates in a way that shows recognition of fundamental equality even in the face of a serious inequality in power?

Thinking about people as equals leads to such questions. A concern for equality can be examined on consequentialist grounds as well. For example, intractable disagreements often find solutions among people who perceive a climate where people are treated as equals. People more quickly find common ground with others, which often creates positive workplace externalities.

The basic point is that reflections about equality are not merely abstract or institutional. They relate practically to our personal outlooks and sense of ethics that we bring to the workplace.

B. OBLIGATIONS AND ASPIRATIONS

The distinction between *obligations* and *supererogatory* actions, first presented in the Introduction, matters across many debates in business and economic life and is especially relevant for discussions about equality.

For example, some egalitarians might distinguish that equality before the law is an *obligation* of justice, but caring for those less fortunate is ethically *admirable* without implying ethical or legal obligation. In the latter case, we might praise those who devote themselves to helping the less fortunate without criticizing or judging those who do not. Other egalitarians argue that economic inequalities directly create moral obligations. Notice how this debate is not about the badness of economic inequality (which both sides accept) but whether valuing equality identifies an *ethical obligation* or only an *admirable aspiration*.

This distinction is useful for Section 3. One way to consider the high demands of equality from a personal perspective—if you believe that there are such demands—is to shift those demands to institutions and then describe individual demands as discretionary rather than obligatory. *Given* the creation of institutions that promote equality, demands to be personally motivated to promote economic equality are less important than they otherwise would be, but admirable all the same. The emphasis on volunteer work through the non-profit world may illustrate this view, where non-profits identify a sphere where people live out moral aspirations that are not obligatory demands of justice. The competing interpretation of non-profits is that these services respond to our obligations of justice.

Within a work environment, you will need to decide not only whether you believe in fundamental equality and what that means, but the weight that you place on that belief—how your sense of ethics distinguishes what is obligatory from what is discretionary. Making this distinction is relevant for applying any of your values (see Figure 11.2).

Let's take one more example. Recall debates on corporate social responsibility. Some argue that corporations should have the discretion to donate earnings to charities without violating stockholders' rights to profits, justified in terms of the pursuit for equality. Deploying the distinction in this section, we could praise corporations that take up corporate social responsibility (and perhaps support them through our purchasing decisions) without conceiving of them as being ethically *obligated* to do so. At the same time, we could also argue that corporations do have obligations to respect people's human rights, no matter their decisions about charitable contributions. The point worth highlighting about this position is the ability to differentiate obligations from discretionary actions as part of the full expression of one's ethical perspective about corporate responsibility.

Someone may counterargue that corporations should be morally obligated to give to communities in need, such as relief efforts in Haiti, but should not be

FIGURE 11.2   Obligations and Aspirations

Liberty
Does it imply:

Obligations? Aspirations?

Equality
Does it imply:

Obligations? Aspirations?

Efficiency
Does it imply:

Obligations? Aspirations?

Other Values
Do they imply:

Obligations? Aspirations?

legally obligated to do so. Keeping all of these distinctions in mind can be important for not getting bogged down by confusions in these debates.

One interesting way that the law is sensitive to the distinction between obligations and recommendations is through the distinction between tax incentives that encourage specific corporate behaviors (e.g., for corporate donations) and laws that punish proscribed behavior (e.g., for polluting in a river). This distinction is akin to the difference between moral *claims* and moral *liberties* introduced in Chapter 2. Life may include many moral liberties. We often have a range of choices that are ethically acceptable without any duties at stake. Still, some choices may be more ethically admirable than others.

In sum, ethical disagreements may sometimes be less about the values at stake and more about whether some ethical value generates obligations or recommendations, and whether law should enforce the obligations or whether these obligations should be left to individual conscience. Further, the distinctions in this section highlight the complicated interplay between personal and institutional points of view. Whether a personal commitment to equality implies personal obligations or a discretionary recommendation can depend in part on whether institutions are succeeding or failing to uphold equality through their own rules and structures.

11.5   SOCIAL CONTRACT THEORY: LIBERTY AND EQUALITY JOINED

Eighteenth-century French philosopher Jean-Jacques Rousseau wrote, "If one inquires precisely into what the greatest good of all consists in, which ought to be the end of every system of legislation, one will find that it comes down to these two principal objects, *freedom* and *equality*."[13] An historical tradition called **social contract theory** attempts to combine the values of liberty and equality into a single conception of justice relevant for all the institutions of society, including business and economic life. This section offers a brief introduction to social contract theory as one influential approach for thinking about liberty, rights, and equality, taking the subjects of Chapters 9–11 as a whole.

Social contract theory refers to the view that the demands of ethics and justice derive from a contract among persons. The most important social contract theorist of the last century is philosopher John Rawls, whose *A Theory of Justice* has influenced many academic disciplines and policy debates. Most of this tradition, including Rawls's account, argues that these contracts are implicit or hypothetical, not actual historical contracts. For example, Rawls argues that, in order to derive principles of justice to regulate the major institutions of society, we should imagine what persons would agree to in a fair bargaining situation. He argues that persons should be situated under (what he calls) a "veil of ignorance" that requires them to abstract away from any knowledge about their own

Philosopher John Rawls believes that persons within a fair bargaining process would choose to live by *two principles of justice*. Most social contrast theorists, like Rawls, develop an account of justice through a hypothetical contract without claiming that societies were actually founded on contracts. However, one example of an actual contract at the foundation of society is the Mayflower Compact signed aboard ship as passengers arrived at Plymouth, Massachusetts, in 1620.

[13]Jean-Jacques Rousseau, *The Social Contract*, Book 2 Chapter 11. See, for example, http://www.constitution.org/jjr/socon.htm.

particular circumstances, such as their current social position, wealth, and skill levels. People then choose principles that serve to bind them in their actual social and natural condition and situation.

In the case of Rawls's theory, the argument is that persons within this fair bargaining process would choose to live by the following **two principles of justice**:

1. Each person is to have an equal right to the most extensive basic liberty compatible with a similar liberty for others.

2. Social and economic inequalities are to be arranged so that (1) they are to be of the greatest benefit to the least-advantaged members of society (the difference principle) and (2) offices and positions must be open to everyone under conditions of fair equality of opportunity.[14]

It's not the purpose of this section to analyze the full scope of these two principles of justice. In brief, the first principle specifies that all people should have equal rights to basic liberties, and the second principle specifies that economic inequalities are acceptable only if they benefit the least advantaged and employment is available under conditions of fair equality of opportunity (see Section 3C for further discussion of this concept). All major institutions of society should function in conformity to the demands of these principles.

Not only do Rawls's two principles of justice express a commitment to ideals of equality and liberty, but the contracting situation models these ideals as well. Each person affirms principles through his or her own distinct authority through a mutual agreement, not based on the authority of outsiders. We make this choice not as we are, but under a veil of ignorance that strips away our differences to emphasize our fundamental commonality (See Box "The Commonalities and Separateness of Persons", for further discussion of this idea). A social contract is a device that merges the ideals of equality and liberty and is often used to derive an account of rights as a result of mutual agreement. As suggested in the previous chapter, beyond deontological and consequentialist justifications, rights theorists sometimes ground their account of human rights by arguing that these are the rights that would be chosen by people from within a fair social contract.

A. BUSINESS AND THE SOCIAL CONTRACT

We can interpret normative relationships in society as deriving from an implicit social contract among citizens. As former U.S. president Theodore Roosevelt famously said, "We demand that big business give people a square deal; in return we must insist that when anyone engaged in big business honestly endeavors to do right, he shall himself be given a square deal." Roosevelt imaged an implicit contract between different sectors of society. The contract is a set of expectations that are neither legally enforced nor actually negotiated but the basis for creating moral understandings. Part of the appeal of this idea is that the obligation is the result of a relationship or tie, implicitly accepted as part of the ongoing terms of cooperation. It's not some abstract obligation unmotivated by circumstances. It's a relationship that should be accepted on the strength of the argument that all parties could reasonably agree to this arrangement for maintaining

---

[14]John Rawls, *A Theory of Justice* (Harvard, 1999), pp. 47, 53. Revised Edition.

those ties. This relationship can then be conceived as an implicit agreement among free equals.

B. PROFESSIONAL ETHICS AND THE SOCIAL CONTRACT

Although we will not develop the details of this rich and varied tradition, many practical insights have their underlying justifications within these reflections. When facing a difficult decision at work or elsewhere, you may think to ask, "How would others not directly involved look at this issue?" In essence, you are trying to strip away your own biases that might color your own interpretation of the situation, like the hypothetical contractor under a veil of ignorance. You are trying to imagine how others might decide or how they might perceive the decision from a more impartial perspective. You could ask the question this way: "How would an impartial spectator with no particular biases interpret what is going on?"[15] When we seek out others' opinions, build relationships and social networks, and trade ideas about the norms of an organization, we often seek to widen our narrow perspective, not merely for personal gain, but also to develop our sense of ethics. We adopt differing perspectives to be more like an impartial spectator who makes judgments from a moral point of view.

11.6   SUMMARY

Our sense of business and economic life depends in part on our beliefs about fundamental equality. If we are all equals, then in what respects should we be treated equally? This chapter considered a range of applications as they relate to judgments about our economic institutions and our personal and professional lives.

As noted especially in Section 3C, whatever equality demands, many people emphasize that only *undeserved* inequalities should raise concerns about justice or challenge the commitment to fundamental equality. This qualifying idea previews the topic of next chapter: an analysis of what people deserve.

KEY TERMS

fundamental equality	rule of law	formal equality of opportunity
egalitarians	equal outcomes	fair equality of opportunity
metaphysical conceptions of the person	equal opportunity	social contract theory
	equal opportunity society	Rawls's two principles of justice

DISCUSSION QUESTIONS

1. Consider this claim, "Every child in America should have an equal opportunity to graduate from high school." What could this mean? Do you believe in this principle? Why or why not?

2. Assess the following statement: If a society reallocated wealth and income so that it was equally distributed, the same inequalities would return within one or two generations.

---

[15]This question identifies Adam Smith's approach to morality in *A Theory of Moral Sentiments* (Prometheus, 2000).

3. If U.S. corporations participate in a society with growing inequalities, but they determine that they are violating no one's rights in their business activities, do they have a responsibility to use corporate resources to reduce these inequalities in some way?

4. Do rising income inequalities create obligations to redress this outcome? Apply utilitarian, rights-based, and egalitarian perspectives to answer this question. If your answer is "yes," who should bear these obligations?

5. Some egalitarians believe equality is so important that all values are really interpretations of equality. Welfare, liberty, rights, and whatever else we value are really an expression of treating people as equals in those respects: equality with respect to our welfare, our liberties, our rights, and so forth. One leading political philosopher writes that "the fundamental argument [about values] . . . is not whether to accept equality, but how to interpret it."[16] Do you agree that equality is the most fundamental value of all those studied in this book? Why or why not?

6. Political philosopher David Schmidtz writes, "When a [market] system's purpose is to enable people to cooperate for mutual advantage, or simply to prosper, it usually will be more to the point to be creating and improving opportunities rather than equalizing them. . . . Equal opportunity surely is part of the cluster concept we call justice, but it is a limited part."[17] What do you think?

7. How important is equality in the workplace? What could it mean to treat someone as your equal in hierarchical work relationships?

8. Imagine that you will be randomly placed in some existing social and economic circumstance that exists in the world today, and the probabilities of winding up within any particular situation match the current spread of social and economic arrangements as they exist today. How nervous would you be about your pending assignment? Does that thought experiment give you any insight about the current justice of our world and the nature of equality? How would a social contract theorist imagine the just and fair way to arrange social and economic circumstances so that you could willingly accept the results of that random placement? What are some other methods of ethical reasoning for assessing our social and economic circumstances?

9. Consider how John Rawls expresses the division of labor between the role of institutions in society and individual decision-making. In the excerpt below, *basic structure* refers to the major political, social, and economic institutions of a society:

> *What we look for, in effect, is an institutional division of labor between the basic structure and the rules applying directly to individuals and associations and to be followed by them in particular interactions. If this division of labor can be established, individuals and associations are then left free to advance their ends more effectively within the framework of the basic structure, secure in the knowledge that elsewhere in the social system the necessary corrections to preserve background justice are being made.[18]*

What does this division of labor imply about corporate social responsibility?

10. How do you characterize gender inequalities in the workplace? Using the analysis of this chapter, describe an equal opportunity principle that you believe should apply to regulate the workplace with respect to gender discrimination. Give examples to illustrate this principle.

---

[16]Will Kymlikca, *Contemporary Political Philosophy: An Introduction* (Oxford University Press, 1991), p. 5.

[17]David Schmidtz and Robert E. Goodin, *Social Welfare and Individual Responsibility* (Cambridge, 1998), pp. 84, 85.

[18]John Rawls, *Political Liberalism* (Columbia University Press, 1993), p. 269.

11. What is human dignity and how does this
    idea relate to the discussion of fundamental
    equality?

12. Explain what the civil rights movement was
    about, applying all the ideas discussed so far in
    this book.

13. The U.S. Declaration of Independence states,
    "All men are created equal." In the context of
    this document, what does this claim mean, in
    your view? Is it a mere rhetorical assertion or
    does this claim express something about the
    reality of persons, in your view?

12

WHAT PEOPLE DESERVE

12.1 INTRODUCTION

Just as you can enjoy a sunny day without paying for it, suppose that everything were free, including what others produce. Economists have long observed some problems that this surreal world would create: if we don't like the idea of paying for things, who, then, would have incentives to produce anything?

Incentives are at the core of any business and economic system. They describe our motivations, shaped by the institutions that surround us. Their study took center stage in the efficiency and welfare chapters (Chapters 6–8). But we also bring *our sense of ethics* to the market system, which we balance alongside the incentives and institutions that we face.

This sense of ethics may lead us to pose a question different from concerns about incentives. Suppose again that everything produced were free. Don't people *deserve* a wage for the work that they do? Wouldn't something be wrong if no one were compensated for their labor? Intuitions about what makes people *deserving*, sometimes called people's **just deserts**, are deeply ingrained in business and economic life. These judgments can motivate us to act one way or another, and they affect how we interpret our surroundings. Claims about our just deserts are an important part of our sense of ethics. They are about what people are due, based on who they are or what they have accomplished.

Consider these comments: "I deserve a promotion and pay increase for my hard work"; "No one deserves to be laid off for arbitrary reasons"; "The industrial worker who labored for thirty-five years didn't deserve to have his pension cut at retirement"; "I deserve basic respect in the workplace no matter my gender or race because I am a person like you"; "Gaping pay differences among people—that's not deserved"; "The holiday bonus that I received—well, that is very well-deserved."

Judgments about what people deserve are at the heart of many people's ethical perspective. They are part of the balance between ethics, incentives,

WHEN YOU FINISH STUDYING THIS CHAPTER, YOU SHOULD BE ABLE TO:

1. Characterize the concept of desert and distinguish the ideas of entitlements and just deserts.

2. Apply these ideas to debates about how or whether we deserve our wages, and other applied topics.

3. Consider institutional implications about the role of desert for supporting or criticizing capitalism.

4. Reflect on the very basic question of whether we deserve anything at all.

and the demands of institutions that frame many challenges that we face within the ethics of economic life.

These judgments can be pointed and emotive. They are also quite distinct from judgments based on other values. People may have rights, freedom, and equality, but in addition, we sometimes feel that people can be deserving. For example, I may admit that I have no *right* to a pay increase if I am denied one, but I may nonetheless believe that I deserve one. Further, if I am the manager, I may not be *free* to offer subordinates a pay increase even though I know they deserve it. To take another example, I may believe in the value of *equality* but also believe that paying people what they deserve is appropriate. But it's highly unlikely that everyone deserves the same income, so a principle of desert will probably lead to support for income inequality, not income equality. In all of these cases and others, judging what people deserve expresses its own value—sometimes complementing and sometimes conflicting with other values that define our ethical perspective.

In this chapter, we will examine the nature of desert and its relation to the ethics and values of business and economic life. First, we begin with the concept of desert and then apply these ideas to the case of deserved wages. Second, we will consider the important distinction between entitlements and just deserts, as well as other general puzzles about what people deserve. Third, we will examine institutional implications about the role of desert for supporting or criticizing capitalism. Finally, we will reflect on the very basic question of whether (and how) we deserve anything at all. The discussion questions at the end pose several applications of the discussions in the main text.

12.2   THE CONCEPT OF DESERT

Claims about what people deserve are so varied that they may seem to lack any common meaning. But most commentators perceive a shared conceptual structure that lies behind all of these expressions:

P deserves X in virtue of B, such that

P = one or more persons

X = specifies the thing deserved

B = the basis on which P is thought to deserve X.

The **desert basis**, B, explains the worthiness of a person or persons deserving something, based on some prior action of that person or some personal characteristic of that person.

Let's consider an example of someone who says, "American stock broker Bernie Madoff deserves punishment because he lied and defrauded investors of $65 billion through a Ponzi scheme." Bernie Madoff is P, the subject of the judgment, although presumably the point of expressing this belief is that *anyone* who defrauds investors deserves punishment. Punishment is X, which identifies the thing deserved, the object of desert. Depending on the example, someone could deserve punishment, as in the Madoff example; or a prize, as in the person who discovers the polio vaccine; or compensation, as in the person who performs work with an expectation of pay; or recognition, as in the person who is wrongly treated as less than human.

In fact, people can deserve all sorts of different **modes of treatment** as a fitting response to what they do and who they are, including punishment, rewards, prizes, compensation, or recognition. No matter how the object of desert, X is described, the basic idea is that someone believes that it is worthy for that person or persons to have X happen to them.

But on what basis is it worthy for a person to have that happen? In the example about Madoff, the desert basis, B, is designed to answer that question, and it is open to debate. Why did Madoff deserve to be punished? One answer: because he broke the law (in fact, he was convicted of eleven federal crimes and sentenced to 150 years in prison). Another answer: because he harmed others and committed a moral wrong. These are not the same answers. For example, let's say he was acquitted on a technicality. We could accept the legal result but continue to believe that he deserved punishment. He was lucky, we might say. As a result, we may also have conflicted intuitions about the law and feel critical about a legal system that fails to deliver just deserts, while also respecting the importance of due process.

This example illustrates two notable points about the concept of desert.

First, when someone says, "I deserve such-and-such," the first question to ask is, "Based on what?" If the person is going to sustain a claim about what he or she *deserves*, then the answer will point to something that this particular person did, or something about who the person is. (See Discussion Question 2 for more on the related concept of responsibility.) Contrast this point against the idea that someone is *entitled* to something, such as an inheritance. Claims about entitlements often differ from claims about desert. Compare:

P *deserves* X for B (the desert basis)

P *is entitled to* X for R (a rule or law)

In the latter formula, R stands for some rule or law. For example, a person is *entitled* to an inheritance because the law says so, but whether this person *deserves* it (or even could deserve it) is a whole other question. We typically appeal to some rule—legal or otherwise—to settle conflicts about entitlements. But settling conflicts about what people deserve requires a further justification, often more nuanced, about why the person is worthy to receive the thing deserved.

Second, even after identifying the structure of desert claims, we are still some distance from offering an argument or justification for these beliefs. Just studying the concept of desert, as presented above, does not answer the substantive question of what people actually deserve. That requires further argument. Like all the concepts studied so far, the point of *studying the concept* has a more limited, although practical, purpose. The values that we decide are most relevant for assessing a situation will frame the questions that we ask and the debates that will take place. For example, if a group of people decides that a situation calls for debate about what people *deserve*, we can then clarify two questions that focus the debate and contribute to a productive conversation:

1. *What* does someone deserve exactly? Is it a reward? compensation? punishment? something else? This question is about specifying the mode of treatment.

2. What is the *basis* for deserving this treatment? Is it based on the person's actions (which ones?), efforts, intentions, or something about who that person is? This question is about defending the desert basis.

Answering these two questions will go a long way in any debate about desert because they will clarify which are points of agreement and disagreement within any particular debate.

12.3   DESERVED WAGES

Taking this discussion as background, let's now examine several arguments about deserved wages. The topic is interesting on its own terms, and details of these arguments provide revealing complications. It also helps us consider the overall significance of reflections about desert within business and economic life.

In his book-length treatment about what people deserve, contemporary American philosopher George Sher argues that, among other reasons, the wages that you earn are justified as deserved compensation for subordinating your purposes to another's will, your employer.[1] In other words, wages compensate you for your loss of freedom, in the positive sense of freedom discussed in Chapter 9. You spend your time at work doing what your employer wants you to do for the purposes of the firm. In this sense, your working life is not explainable simply as an act of *your will*. You are *subordinating your will* when you'd rather spend more time with your family or sail around the world. Instead, when the alarm goes off, you act as an agent to advance your employer's will. What ought you to get in return? Enough compensation that allows you to live according to *your own* will, across your life as a whole. A wage is the practical means by which your employer can compensate you, by giving you an income that provides you with opportunities to do what you want with your life (that is, the part of life spent not working).

Have you ever thought about whether you deserve a wage and on what basis? This argument has some interesting premises. First, the argument does not deny or challenge the idea that you may be *entitled* to a wage as a function of your contract. That's a different point. Similarly, the argument also does not address whether the wage is justified for *utilitarian* reasons, such as creating good incentives for increasing the productivity of the firm. The point of the argument, rather, is to establish that there is a sense in which you also *deserve* that wage, independent from what you may be entitled to or what may yield good consequences. Second, the argument presumes that freedom—the sense of positive freedom discussed in Chapter 9—is valuable for persons to have. Note how this justification draws on a value outside the concept of desert and integrates it within a claim about what people deserve. Third, the argument may presume a certain kind of comparative equality: we may think it unfair to ask that I lose my freedom during one time period without compensating a gain in freedom during a later time period. (Is this correct?) Fourth, Sher argues that it is worthy for workers to receive wages as *compensation*, distinct from the idea of deserved wages as *rewards* or *prizes* or *recognition*.

What do you think of this argument? It has some resonance with a Marxian tradition that sees capitalism as a vehicle for exploiting, alienating, and subordinating people through their labor. However, unlike Marx, Sher believes that wages can provide a good remedy to selling one's labor, especially if the wage rate is high enough to satisfy workers' basic needs. The argument is interesting in part because it's not an obvious position about

---

[1]George Sher, *Desert* (Princeton University Press, 1989).

why we should receive wages, and yet it can resonate with the lived experiences of many people's working lives, trapped in a job but sticking with it because of the felt sense of compensated freedom that the income provides.

But the argument is puzzling too. If I love what I do and my work fully expresses my will rather than subordinates it, do I deserve a wage as compensation, according to this argument? The answer seems to be *no*. Under those circumstances, I am not subordinating my will, so there is nothing (about a loss of freedom) for the wage to compensate. That may seem like an odd conclusion, as it appears to imply that I deserve less wages the more that I identify with my work! In its defense, this conclusion is fully consistent with a person being properly *entitled* to a wage because of a contract, or for wages to be justified for other reasons. The implication, however, is that if we were to base our justification for wages *solely* on the criterion of deserved compensation for a loss of freedom, then we would need to track the degree to which workers are subordinating their wills to determine the proper wage.

This last point suggests that a *variety* of reasons may best explain why people should receive wages, and the argument need not reduce to only one idea. For example, perhaps we deserve wages not (or not only) as compensation for lost freedom but also as a reward and recognition for the effort that we put into our jobs. Consider the following scenario: we experience a reduced title change and significant pay cut, due to organizational restructuring and efficiency, but the demands of the job and our work efforts remain exactly the same, or even increase. Our sense of wrong, if we have that sense, could be grounded in a belief that compensation and recognition should be proportional with *work effort*, but in this case effort remains the same and pay and recognition decrease.

Let's consider another analysis. In economics, the theory of marginal productivity states that workers' wages are appropriately determined by the value added to the productive process. But why? Consider two distinct interpretations. First, some argue that firms should pay people no more and no less than their contribution to marginal product because that is what efficiency demands. The *marginal product of labor* is the additional product generated by an additional unit of workers' labor. This explanation expresses a consequentialist argument: a wage is justified as part of the process of creating efficiency gains. This argument depends on the weight and importance of efficiency as a goal. Consider now a second explanation for justifying a wage: people deserve a wage as a *reward* for creating that value. What's the difference between these arguments? The first justifies wages as a means to pursue an institutional goal: efficiency. The second justifies wages as rewards owed to individuals for doing something worthy (that they create value for others). This latter argument is just as controversial as Sher's ideas about subordinating our wills. For example, if the value of the benefit to others is defined by supply and demand conditions for the product, and if demand drops for reasons unrelated to the production process, is it correct to say that those workers now deserve less income just because of that drop in demand? If so, then workers' just deserts are determined by supply and demands conditions, which are controlled significantly by factors unrelated to the employees and what they have done. This conclusion is in tension with the intuition that people can only be deserving based on factors about *them*.

The purpose of this section is not to settle these debates, but to introduce challenges for offering one clean answer about whether and why we deserve wages for our work. Even after we separate the concept of desert from claims about entitlements or consequentialist arguments,

> Chapters 6 and 7 examine the value of efficiency.

the overall desert argument is still less clear than we may have first thought. In your view, is it true that we deserve our wages to some degree? If so, what is your own argument?

12.4   DESERT AND PROFESSIONAL ETHICS

Debates about desert apply across a range of topics, from the personal level about what individuals deserve in a working environment, such as hiring and promotion practices, to broader reflections at the institutional level about the role of desert for assessing the legitimacy of the capitalist system. The debate about deserved wages is one special application of this larger range of topics. Let's now highlight some general puzzles and features that apply across this range of these debates.

A. ENTITLEMENTS AND DESERT FROM A PERSONAL POINT OF VIEW

Ethical relationships in markets are often a mix of entitlements, expectations, and judgments about what people deserve. These contrasting values do not always reconcile with each other.

For example, in real estate transactions, buyer-agents are people who help buyers find a house to purchase. If the buyer does not sign a contract with the buyer-agent, however, then the buyer-agent may not be entitled to a commission if the buyer bails out of the relationship at the last moment and purchases the home without any involvement with that agent. But if the agent spent the last year working hour after hour to find houses for the buyer, including the one eventually purchased, then doesn't the agent deserve that commission?

This is a case where we leave the world of *legal entitlement* and recognize a sense of ethics in the language of desert. In fact, reflections about desert are often the area where we distinguish ethics—business ethics—from discussions about legal entitlements. In the case of the buyer-agent, if we believe that he deserves a commission as compensation or reward for his hard work, then our values will lead us to ignore legal loopholes (or wide gaps) that allow us to avoid paying that commission. These values become an ethical compass that help us decide how to act toward others, independent from what the rules and entitlements say. Claims about what we deserve often provide the language for expressing our ethical beliefs at a personal level so that we can distinguish these beliefs from facts about the incentives or rules of the system.

Intuitions about what people deserve and their actual legal entitlements in a market system can be likened to currents of water that separate or crisscross. We may compare people's entitlements against what they deserve and sometimes believe that they move in the same direction, more or less. But at other times we may think that they rush headlong into and against each other, and then we can be left with a sense that the entitlement system is in a state of dysfunction. For example, if most jobs in society were determined through discriminatory practices based on race, gender, and class, then intuitions about what people deserve will conflict with the entitlements that result in that society. Entitlements will still have legal force, but if they do not even approximate what people deserve, we can wonder where the justice is.

Thinking about what people deserve in business and economic life can have many practical applications for decision-making. For example, if managers take considerations of desert seriously, then they must consider not merely incentives and contract negotiations but also giving people what they really deserve—and deciding what that means. What factors should a merit increase take into account—innovative contributions, long work hours and overall commitment, years on the job? Consider another example. The financial crises that began in 2007 has led to much downsizing and has entailed large and painful lay-offs. Managers committed to ideas about what people deserve may be unable to avoid making those lay-offs, but they could still give thought to how to handle downsizing and what severance packages particular employees deserve, taking into account career contributions. Participants in an economic system can believe that, in many cases, supply and demand fail to track what people deserve but take notice how there can be some managerial discretion for applying a concept of desert in decision-making.

B. ENTITLEMENTS AND DESERT FROM AN INSTITUTIONAL POINT OF VIEW
Let's discuss a few notable examples of perceived recent conflicts at an institutional level.

1. *Bank bailouts.* The Federal Government's decision to bail out the banks settled the question of legal entitlements. But the Occupy Wall Street movement attested to the dissatisfaction that the bankers did not deserve that financial support.

2. *Income differentials.* Income differences are vast, as presented in Chapter 11. The average executive makes 250 times more than the average worker, which means that the executive in a few days' work can earn as much money as an entire year's work of the average worker.[2] We could analyze this data from the perspective of fundamental equality, from consequentialist analyses regarding the *effects* of income inequalities on social cohesion, and other ethical traditions covered in this book. But in the context of this chapter, we can consider an additional ethical perspective: what wages do people deserve? Some people argue that employees are the heart and soul of a company, so there is no way that an executive deserves that amount of compensation relative to the average worker. This idea was first presented as part of the stakeholder analysis in Chapter 5 Section 4. Some stakeholder advocates emphasize corporate responsibilities to employees, and they support shareholder proxies to cap executive pay relative to the pay of the average worker in the corporation. The argument is that the average worker adds a value that is deserving of compensation that has a closer spread with upper management's pay. The argument is about income differentials that fail any ethical test about a desert basis that could justify these differences.

   Recently, CEO compensation debates have included analyses of CEOs' lavish compensation packages despite poor corporate performance, further heightening the sense that corporate salary structures do not match what people deserve. Others disagree with this analysis, arguing that CEOs add tremendous value to the firm or that pay is appropriately determined by contracts and entitlements, not desert.

   In this last example, part of the argument is whether intuitions about what people deserve should become the compass for criticizing or advocating changes in the rules of the system: to either cap pay packages or adjust the scheme of corporate governance that leads boards to negotiate such lavish rewards. This is a lively debate in business ethics, with arguments coming from within corporations (through proxies on executive pay and discussions within corporate board), the media, and government (through legislative hearings and the work of the Securities and Exchange

Read the
Case Study
CEO Pay only on
MySearchLab

---

[2]See http://sociology.ucsc.edu/whorulesamerica/power/wealth.html.

Commission). We could extend these debates globally, to analyze income differentials across nations as well as within nations.

3. *Comparable worth and pay equity.* Economists, sociologists, and policy makers debate standards of **comparable worth**, sometimes called *pay equity*, which refers to the view that comparable jobs deserve comparable pay. The controversy arises from the fact that occupations that are historically dominated by men have higher pay than occupations historically dominated by women. More broadly, men on average make more money than women. What explains these differences? This question has generated a great deal of academic research. Although it's not the purpose of this section to analyze the complex data that are part of this debate, it is notable that what drives the debate is the belief that wages should, at least in part, track what people deserve and, if those differentials are explained through discrimination based on gender, then those undeserved income difference should be corrected. Economists and policy makers debate both (a) whether this data gives evidence for discrimination and (b) what, if anything, government should do to intervene in the market. But the debate itself presumes that the pay that people deserve is relevant for assessing market outcomes.

C. DESERT SOMETIMES SPURS ADVOCACY FOR REFORM, SOMETIMES NOT

The analysis so far suggests how arguments about what people deserve can offer an independent check for evaluating the entitlement rules of a system, both within a workplace environment and across the economy. Arguments about what people deserve may help identify some corruption or conflict of interest or institutional deficiency.

But now let's consider the opposite point: arguments about what people deserve do not always imply the need for institutional reform. Recall the case of Bernie Madoff. Suppose, contrary to the actual outcome, that he had been acquitted; and suppose that we continued to believe that he committed the crime despite the acquittal. We can both acknowledge that he deserves a punishment that the legal system is not providing but *also* believe that there is nothing particularly deficient or needing reform about the legal system. Perhaps the decisive evidence was tainted by mistake and thrown out of court, and this explains the decision. We could embrace other values that the legal proceedings uphold and, for that reason, grant that not every verdict can track desert. Consider another example: Suppose one football team clearly outplays another but a series of fluke events occur. A torrential downpour happens in the last five minutes, the refs make a few bad calls, a fan runs across the field at a bizarre moment. The other team wins. We can say: the first team really deserved to win that game—but that judgment doesn't imply that we should change the rules of football. Note, however, if the claim was that the first team was *entitled* to win the game rather than *deserved* to win, then this assertion, if true, does imply that someone—a league official or a commissioner—has a duty to change the score. For example, perhaps the "winning" field goal with no time left actually didn't go through the uprights and, on instant replay, the referees discover their mistake. The point now is not about desert. It's about the entitlement of the one team to have the number on the scoreboard change.

Let's summarize these ideas about entitlements and desert. Entitlements create duties on others to act in accordance with the demands of that entitlement. The study of rights (Chapters 2, 3, and 10) was significantly about entitlements and what justifies them. Ideas about what people deserve are different from ideas about entitlements. Just deserts express the worthiness of an outcome independent from the given entitlement. They can offer an ethical compass to evaluate and guide reform for any given entitlement system. Sometimes they express an ethical judgment without implying a deficiency of the system or duties to change the system. Whether claims about what people deserve should guide institutional reform or not depends, in part, on the values that we think should guide specific institutions. We will examine this point next.

12.5 CAPITALISM AND DEBATES ABOUT THE RELEVANCE OF DESERT

A. CHALLENGING THE RELEVANCE OF DESERT

The discussion of deserved wages reveals how people may be deserving for more than one reason. It may be that someone's wage is deserved as reward for high-quality work *and* as compensation for lost time. (By analogy, the arguments that we prepare to justify a salary increase to our boss may draw on many different types of reasons—reasons need not be exclusive.) This pluralism within desert matters for how we fine-tune our arguments. Although there is a common structure to all desert claims (as discussed above), specific arguments about what people deserve are diverse and seemingly without any one common normative foundation. The great strength of this analysis, some argue, is that interpreting this complexity is entirely fitting for recognizing the details of each person's special value. In this view, *ethics* as a study of how to live requires that we understand the *particulars of each person's life*, including our own, and only through the conceptual resources of this chapter is a full development of this sense of ethics possible.

Others see claims about what people deserve as a hodgepodge of intuitive (and somewhat arbitrary) judgments that are not well grounded and should derive from other values. These critics seek to diminish the role of desert within any ethical discussion about economic life. Let's consider the ideas driving this perspective more closely.

We live within a market system shaped by its rules of property and by a complex set of laws that regulate many aspects of economic life. These rules create legitimate expectations that people will follow these rules. Rather than develop an independent theory about *what people deserve*, we may instead believe that people should receive whatever results from the legitimate expectations of a just social system. We can express the point

THE SIGNIFICANCE OF PERSONS

We saw in a Box in Chapter 11 Section 2, "The Commonalities and Separateness of Persons," that different values express different ideas about the significance of being a person. Ideas about fundamental equality, for example, emphasize our value in terms of what is in common among human beings. Ideas about individual rights emphasize our separateness as persons. What do beliefs about what people deserve emphasize? Political philosopher George Sher says, "For how better to capture the moral importance of the differences between persons than to say that each person uniquely deserves things for precisely what he does, and for precisely what he is?"[3] Like rights, our beliefs about desert say something about how we are separate from others. The language of desert allows us to consider the full nuances of any person's particular situation. Perhaps as much as or more than any other value in this study, claims about what people deserve are *personal* assessments, and they are the area of professional ethics that most asks us to focus on the worthiness of any particular individual receiving some outcome. Section 6 adds to these ideas by discussing whether the reality of being human is compatible with deserving anything at all.

[3]George Sher, *Desert* (Princeton University Press, 1989), p. 211.

this way: we deserve the legitimate expectations of a system whose rules are justified on other grounds. There is no deep truth about *what people deserve* beyond these other justifications. Although it's still possible to use the language of desert to debate wages, hiring, compensation, or other matters, desert is a derivative concept, finding its justifications based on whatever creates legitimate expectations among people. (The contrasting interpretations of marginal productivity in Section 3 illustrate this point—wages are justified as a means to improve efficiency, which then derivatively becomes the norm for what a person deserves.) On this argument, it's our perception of expectations and the goals of an institution that primes our intuitions about desert, not the other way around.

One leading proponent of this view is political philosopher John Rawls, who articulates a position shared by other contemporary political theorists:

> There is a tendency for common sense to suppose that income and wealth, and the good things in life generally, should be distributed according to moral desert. . . . Now justice as fairness [Rawls's theory of justice] rejects this conception. . . . For in the way that one has a duty to uphold just arrangements, and an obligation to do one's part when one has accepted a position in them, so a person who has complied with the scheme and done his share has a right to be treated accordingly by others. They are bound to meet his legitimate expectations. Thus when just economic arrangements exist, the claims of individuals are properly settled by reference to the rules and precepts . . . which these practices take as relevant. . . . It is incorrect to say that just distributive shares reward individuals according to their moral worth. But what we can say is that, in the traditional phrase, a just scheme gives each person his due: that is, it allots to each what he is entitled to as defined by the scheme itself. The principles of justice for institutions and individuals establish that doing this is fair.[4]

We must justify property rights and markets on values *other* than desert, says Rawls—such as on the values of liberty and equality—and then the resulting system of entitlements derived from these values will define our legitimate expectations. What we deserve are these legitimate expectations of this just system. Theorists often call this view **institutional desert**, which derives or reduces some particular analysis of desert, or all accounts of desert, to the purposes and legitimate expectations of institutions, which, in turn, are justified through values other than desert.

Why would anyone advocate a derivative understanding of desert? Let's consider three answers.

1. Rather than criticize the way that market outcomes do not always match an intuitive sense of what people deserve, some people react by wishing to sever the ties between markets and desert. What would it mean to live in a system that used a principle of desert as the first principle for interpreting and shaping market outcomes? Apart from its impracticality, some object to the explicit moralisms: should we then believe that the rich would be understood to have their wealth because they are more worthy as individuals and the poor less worthy? Perhaps instead we should advocate an entitlement system for markets unrelated to claims about what people deserve, allowing people to live free from moralizing judgments about their worthiness based on market outcomes. For example, some commentators argue that it's offensive to think

[4]John Rawls, *Political Liberalism* (Harvard, 1993), pp. 310–313.

about people's compensation as a reflection of people's worthiness. In the words of philosopher Joel Feinberg:

> [D]istributing wages, profits, and salaries to whole classes of people as symbols of the recognition of superior talent seems inappropriate and, indeed, repugnant; for that would be to interpret the principle "better people deserve better things" in a manner wholly inconsistent with democratic and liberal ideas.[5]

On this view, a system that teaches us that our just deserts depend on market outcomes may led us to have illusions of self-worth or self-denial.

> In Chapter 14, we will develop the theme about the effect of market life on our character and identify.

2. Note how Feinberg, in the excerpt above, contrasts the value of a person's just deserts against *democratic and liberal ideas*, which refer to the values of liberty, rights, and equality studied in Chapters 9–11. His argument is that we should emphasize these latter values for thinking about business and economic life, which express the second reason to downplay the importance of desert: that other values matter more. For example, some argue that we should prefer a market system interpreted as *free contracts* without any further personal moral judgment about the resulting outcomes, which are in fact due to many undeserved factors. Or we may recall arguments from the chapter on equality. Our status as fundamentally equal people could be undermined, some may argue, if a society understood itself to be driven solely to distribute economic benefits and burdens on principles of desert. A welfare theorist will argue that the real issue is whether capitalism improves the overall welfare of society or not. A social contract theorist will argue that we should support whatever economic system would be chosen through a fair social contract. All of these ethical traditions and others provide counter-weights or skepticism of the relevance of desert for assessing market interactions.

3. Some people argue that disputes about what people deserve simply reflect **social constructs** that are too culturally or personally subjective to serve as an appropriate basis to justify or criticize market activities. *Social constructs* refer to ideas whose foundation and perceived validity derive solely from the context and contingencies of the social setting. For example, some people believe that the wealthy deserve and earn their place in society. Part of a Marxist critique is not merely to deny this claim, but to argue that many working class people are taught to believe this by a propaganda machine that is run by the wealthy elite. Intuitions about the incomes that we deserve, a Marxist will argue, reflect the beliefs of a capitalist culture rather than provide an independent moral point of view for assessing capitalism. Worse, they perpetuate a **false consciousness** among the lower classes through a system that distorts ideas to serve the interests of those who have the most power. *False consciousness* refers to the systemic distortion of ideas that serve the interests of those who have the most power rather than the truth about appropriate social relations. This criticism turns on its head the discussion in Section 3. That section emphasized how reflections about what people deserve provides a language for bringing out the nuances of our sense of ethics within particular contexts. But people who see these ideas as constructs argue that the results will simply reflect our cultural biases. They argue that intuitions about what people deserve lack any meaningful philosophical grounding.

---

[5]Joel Feinberg, *Doing and Deserving: Essays in the Theory of Responsibility* (Princeton, 1974), p. 91.

Ideas about social constructs and false consciousness relate to the discussion of cultural relativism in Chapter 3 Section 7.

In summary, these three points lead some people to think that desert is the wrong value for developing an assessment of markets and capitalism or to use as a personal guide for ethics.

B. THE STAYING POWER OF DESERT

Nonetheless, despite these objections, major political and ethical traditions still draw on the concept of what people deserve at some point in their reflections, even if they place most emphasize on other values.

For example, debates about the justice or injustice of capitalism have great historical force. On one side of this debate, Karl Marx develops an intuitive charge against capitalism that laborers deserve far more than they receive, and that capitalism, with its unjust entitlement system, systematically exploits the work that they do. Marx's critique of capitalism draws on many values and concepts, but the moral impulse that the system does not treat people as they deserve has exerted a lasting impact on those most critical of a market system.

Contemporary Marxist critiques of capitalism emphasize how the system reduces people to instruments for acquiring profits, rather than encouraging people to express their humanity through their work. We will develop this idea and other variations of this idea in Chapter 13 on the value of human relationships.

Alternatively, libertarians celebrate markets and capitalism, as discussed in Chapter 9 on liberty. Libertarians advocate unregulated capitalism. Provocatively, however, they both draw on a similar premise that people own themselves, and because of this fact, they deserve the product of their labor (see Chapter 3 Section 8 for an introduction to this idea). In the libertarian vision, this product entails expropriating private property from the commons with trade through free markets and commerce. In the Marxist vision, the system should require that workers not be exploited or alienated from the creations of their labor.

It's not the point here to develop these theories but to recognize that even traditions that de-emphasize claims about what people deserve typically draw on these claims at some point in the development of their theory. To give a few more brief examples: egalitarians and social contract theorists, as suggested in Chapter 11, often build their theories of justice from the basic intuition that many inequalities in society are undeserved and, thereby, should be subject to reform through a theory of justice. And welfare theorists in the economics discipline, who rely on efficiency analysis, typically introduce the idea of **entrepreneurial spirit**, which refers to the attitudes of creativity, risk-taking, and innovation as one of the factors of production for creating a successful business. Advocates of this concept often suggest that entrepreneurs deserve their profits for their creativity, risk-taking, and innovation.

In summary, some ethical traditions dismiss the relevance of desert and develop other values to think through the ethics and justice of business, such as efficiency, liberty, rights, and equality. Others balance multiple values and include desert as one ethical compass among others. Those who lean most heavily on ideas about what people deserve tend to apply those ideas for adjudicating workplace conflicts, or, at the broader institutional level, argue for greater government intervention in markets to correct for undeserved market outcomes. The invisible hand, law and government, and professional ethics models can all be interpreted from the point of view of what people deserve for guiding business and economic life. This analysis can create intriguing discussion, not only about what just deserts could mean, but also in defining its proper role for reflection within the ethics and values of business and economic life. See, for example, Discussion Questions 3, 4 and 8.

12.6 DESERVING ANYTHING AT ALL

So far, this chapter has introduced ideas about what people deserve as a *normative* value for guiding our political and economic decision-making, either at a personal level, such as thinking about wages and hiring within the workplace, or at the institutional level, such as assessing the justice of capitalism. But thinking about what people deserve can lead to some of our deepest reflections about the meaning of life. People often believe that they are deserving because they have free will and are responsible for their choices; but others wonder whether they can be deserving of anything at all. How far are we controlled by the whimsical or tragic realities of life? Are we fated to live one way rather than another? A performance of the Greek tragedies can generate great pathos regarding people who thought that they could control their lives, but in reality were fated to some tragic end. Thus, the topic of desert also raises *metaphysical* questions about the nature of persons apart from political and economic questions about how to assess a particular situation.

At one moment we believe we control our lives by our efforts, deliberate purposes, and ambitions. We are responsible for what we do and deserving of what we get. But where do our traits come from? We lucked into the upbringing we had, lucked into the time and place of our birth, lucked into the DNA we inherited (or not). We think we control ourselves, but our choices and constitution depend on so many forces about which we have no control. Wisdom, many believe, is the realization that we control precious little. Some of the skepticism about the centrality of desert for normative thought may derive from these reflections.[6] **Existentialism** is a late-nineteenth-and-early-twentieth-century philosophical movement that examines the human condition, especially the perception that life is absurd. Do we remain in delusion our whole lives, in absurd circumstances thinking that we pull the levers of life when we are pawns of external forces? What could ethics mean if we do not deserve anything at all? Long-standing debates about free will bring deep puzzles to each new generation in the face of advancing sciences that seemingly whittle away at the concept of pure choice—categorizing the biological, genetic, chemical, and evolutionary foundations of our consciousness. Various religious currents also challenge the probative force of being deserving, such as the Calvinist Christian doctrine that salvation comes from grace and many Eastern religions that make sense of humanity without any strong concept of personal responsibility or desert.

Theologian Reinhold Neibur is credited with coining the well-known serenity prayer that has roots in ancient traditions, as a partial response to these reflections, later adopted by Alcoholics Anonymous:

> God, grant me the serenity
>
> To accept the things I cannot change;
>
> Courage to change the things I can;
>
> And wisdom to know the difference.

---

[6]Political philosopher John Rawls casts these worries within his own rejection of desert as a basis for assessing institutions. He argues that even the factors that we think that we most control, such as our efforts and ambitions, are significantly the products of our upbringing or are part of our organic constitution, which we did nothing to deserve.

The assertion that we deserve nothing at all can derive from great humility, or skepticism about ethics, or skepticism about free will and responsibility, or a combination of these.

Yet the counterintuition does not fade easily: "I am responsible. I do deserve to be treated in certain ways based on what I do and who I am." Why believe this? Here's one answer: although we can reject free will from a far-off intellectual perspective, we cannot, in fact, live as though we do. From the inside of our own consciousness, we adopt a deliberative perspective and we base our actions on choices that we can only presume are ones made by our own free will. The argument is a bit paradoxical: we are free and responsible and deserving beings because we can't believe otherwise.

And so reflections about ethics and values challenges us to consider the metaphysics of what it means to be a person. Important arguments throughout the history of philosophy and religion are based on whether we (1) have free will, (2) can be held responsible for what we do, and (3) can be deserving based on our actions and who we are—and the interrelationship of all three ideas.

Some people try to separate these metaphysical issues from understanding desert as a value. Thus, we might distinguish *metaphysical* reflections from *normative* reflections about what people deserve in business and economic life. Ultimately, from a cosmic perspective, who knows what a person deserves or the extent to which people are really responsible for their lives? But we still can validly assert practical normative claims, such as "I deserve that reward based on what I did, if anyone does." In this view we can apply ethical intuitions about what people deserve without knowing the full reality of what it means to be human. But even if we do not need to probe the ultimate meanings of life to study the ethics and values of business, reflections about desert are an invitation to reflect on these deeper philosophical questions.

12.7   SUMMARY

What does our sense of ethics demand of us? To live in a system and to treat others in freedom and as equals, to advance the common welfare and respect the rights that are due each person? We can interpret these ideals to make individual decisions in the setting of professional ethics or by assessing political and economic institutions more broadly. But there is more, as we can ask what people deserve. This chapter introduced some competing perspectives to answer that question, including different views about the role of just deserts in our daily business lives and overall worldview. However we balance our values, we need to know what they are and reflect on the ethics, incentives, and institutions that we believe will realize those values.

KEY TERMS

just deserts	comparable worth	false consciousness
desert basis	institutional desert	entrepreneurial spirit
mode of treatment	social construct	existentialism

DISCUSSION QUESTIONS

1. Do CEOs deserve the compensation that they receive?

2. What people deserve may seem inseparable from the concept of responsibility. But on examination, the relationship between desert and responsibility is more complicated. For example, do I deserve to have my human rights protected? If so, is that protection due to anything that I'm responsible for? Don't I deserve some things (the most important things) just for who I am rather than what I'm responsible for doing? How do you understand the relationship between desert and responsibility?

3. Can corporations be deserving? After all, the law recognizes corporations as persons. Can they deserve to be punished? Can they deserve to be praised?

4. Stockholders receive corporate profits but do nothing to create those profits. The corporate structure systematically enforces an entitlement system that subverts our most basic intuitions about what people deserve. It's the people who do the work of a corporation who deserve the profits of that corporation. Assess the foregoing statements.

5. Suppose that we don't deserve anything. Would there be any point to ethics?

6. Is desert a social construct? What explains your perceptions about what people deserve? Are intuitions about what we deserve subjective in a way that the other values studied in this book are not?

7. How should we determine the compensation packages that public sector workers deserve—such as firefighters, teachers, and other government workers?

8. Suppose that the work of a manager seriously improves shareholder value. In your view, does that person deserve higher wages as a result? Why? Suppose this person increased shareholder value illegally; what is your judgment now? Why? Finally, suppose that you judge the product as harmful to society but legal, such as cigarette manufacturing. Does that judgment affect your evaluation of the wages that the person deserves? Why or why not?

9. Do celebrities deserve the compensation they receive? Do professional athletes deserve the pay that they receive? How about the owners of sports teams? What is the right way to analyze these questions?

10. Suppose that a committee is charged with hiring the most deserving person for some workplace position. Pick some specific position and answer the following questions: What should be the criteria for making the decision? Is *merit* a better word here and does it mean the same thing as *deserving*? Are affirmative action principles consistent or inconsistent with this charge? Describe one affirmative action principle that would be consistent with this charge and one principle that would be inconsistent. Finally, is the sole objective to select the most deserving candidate too narrow an objective for making hiring decisions, or is it just right?

11. Using the ideas from this chapter, what does it mean to say that a candidate is *overqualified*? Can an entire pool of candidates or large segments of the labor market be overqualified? If so, does this fact identify an institutional problem?

12. Most of the work in a society receives no pay at all: raising children. What do people deserve, if anything, for raising children? Apply the concept of desert as introduced in this chapter as a way to approach this question.

13

RELATIONSHIPS AND CHARACTER

WHEN YOU FINISH STUDYING THIS CHAPTER, YOU SHOULD BE ABLE TO:

1. Characterize debates about whether markets and capitalism foster or undermine good relationships and character.

2. Specify several ethical traditions that are closely linked to the arguments of this chapter.

3. Explain what a pragmatic perspective means for the study of ethics and how that connects with the themes of this chapter.

13.1   INTRODUCTION

What is ethics? We've examined many responses to this question throughout our study. Consider this answer: it's about the quality and character of human relationships. This idea can tie together many threads in this book. For example, we learned from the first several chapters that markets create special types of relationships—exchanges between buyers and sellers. Both parties are enmeshed in a system of property rights, which also express a normative web of human relationships of claims, liberties, powers, and immunities. Property relations are sometimes expressed through law and sometimes through more informal norms and expectations. The historical evolution of market and property relationships trace from the simple market trades of nomadic herdsmen in the last Ice Age to the complex interactions within global capitalism today.

We can understand the values introduced in Chapters 6–12 as normative tools to assess these relationships, including standards of welfare, freedom, rights, liberty, equality, and what people deserve. These values offer a diverse array of ideas for thinking about the ethics and principles of business and economic life. But these values are not the only way to reflect on relationships. Let's say we live in freedom, we are equals, our welfare improves, our rights are protected, and we get what we deserve. But do we lead good lives? Are they fulfilling and meaningful?

These questions mark something of a break from the preceding materials in the book. Rather than study ethics by applying specific values, let's consider our normative world from the interior of our lives: the sense in which markets and capitalism support or undermine our relationships and our character. This chapter examines the ethics and values of business and economic life from the most human point of view, our lived experience.

We begin with a discussion of friendship. We then examine arguments that first *criticize* and then *support* the institutions of capitalism based on how their incentive structures affect our personal relationships and character. In the course of this discussion, the chapter will elaborate on ethical traditions that closely connect with these perspectives, including virtue ethics, the ethics of care, and non-Western approaches to ethics.

13.2   RELATIONSHIPS

In Chapter 9 on liberty, we considered how ethics need not be about identifying rules external to us, but about how we express our will. No doubt ethics sometimes connotes a set of institutional rules or social pressures, but, more meaningfully, ethics is also about the attitudes that we bring to our relationships and how those relationships bear on our ability to live good and decent lives.

As a step into this topic, consider the following extended excerpt on the nature of friendship by contemporary philosopher Todd May.

> When I was 17 years old, I had the honor of being the youngest person in the history of New York Hospital to undergo surgery for a herniated disc. . . . The day after my surgery, I awoke to find a friend of mine sitting in a chair across from my bed. I don't remember much about his visit. I am sure I was too sedated to say much. But I will not forget that he visited me on that day, and sat there for I know not how long, while my humanity was in the care of a morphine drip. . . .
>
> The official discourses of our relations with one another do not have much to say about the afternoon my friend spent with me. Our age, what we might call the age of economics, is in thrall to two types of relationships which reflect the lives we are encouraged to lead. There are consumer relationships, those that we participate in for the pleasure they bring us. And there are entrepreneurial relationships, those that we invest in hoping they will bring us some return. . . .
>
> The encouragement toward relationships of consumption is nowhere more prominently on display than in reality television. Jon and Kate, the cast of "Real World," the Kardashians, and their kin across the spectrum conduct their lives for our entertainment. . . . Or, barring that, we can collect friends like shoes or baseball cards on Facebook. Entrepreneurial relationships have, in some sense, always been with us. Using people for one's ends is not a novel practice. . . . In our lives, however, few of us have entirely forgotten about . . . true friendship. Friendships follow a rhythm that is distinct from that of either consumer or entrepreneurial relationships. . . . Their rhythm lies not in what they bring to us, but rather in what we immerse ourselves in. To be a friend is to step into the stream of another's life. It is, while not neglecting my own life, to take pleasure in another's pleasure, and to share their pain as partly my own. The borders of my life, while not entirely erased, become less clear than they might be. . . .
>
> We might say of friendships that they are a matter not of diversion or of return but of meaning. They render us vulnerable, and in doing so they add dimensions of

significance to our lives that can only arise from being, in each case, friends with this or that particular individual, a party to this or that particular life.

It is precisely this non-economic character that is threatened in a society in which each of us is thrown upon his or her resources and offered only the bywords of ownership, shopping, competition, and growth. . . .

In a world often ruled by the dollar and what it can buy, friendship, like love, opens other vistas. The critic John Berger once said of one of his friendships, "We were not somewhere between success and failure; we were elsewhere." To be able to sit by the bed of another, watching him sleep, waiting for nothing else, is to understand where else we might be.[1]

This chapter has come full circle from the first reflections on markets in Chapter 1. At that early stage, the point was simply observational: what do we see in the relationship of market exchange? (Chapter 1 Section 3). We distinguished market exchanges from gifts and takings. Later chapters interpreted markets and corporations by introducing and applying a range of values and ethical perspectives. This chapter leaves the language of freedom, equality, rights, and what we deserve—and considers relationships through the language of friendships and betrayals, hopes and regrets, kindness and coldness. This language considers the fuller range of human emotions expressed, for example, through great art and literature across the ages. This is the territory of great novels that forage into the human condition, the joining of philosophy and literature, expressing the range of our own life experiences. What does this perspective tell us about business and economic life?

> This discussion of friendship relates to Michael Sandel's discussion of *market triumphalism* in Chapter 14 Section 4.

Political philosopher Todd May worries that the noneconomic character of friendships is threatened by a society too dominated by markets.

Is he correct?

Let's consider this criticism from a broader perspective.

13.3   CHARACTER: A CRITICISM OF CAPITALISM

How do you assess the quality of your relationships in a market system? Former fabric wholesaler president and CEO James H. Michelman spent a long and successful career in business and was so impressed and chagrined by his experience of the conflict between business and ethics that he wrote about it in great detail for the *Journal of Business Ethics*. Let's consider what Michelman says.[2]

No matter how much we want to be ethical, he writes, the bottom line is that business competition is *amoral*. He means that business decisions are based on rational calculations about what best maximizes returns for the firm, and morality is irrelevant for making those decisions. He is merely conveying his experience at this point in the argument, but he thinks it will be your experience, too.

---

[1]Todd May, "Friendship in an Age of Economics," *New York Times* (July 4, 2010); see http://opinionator.blogs. nytimes.com/2010/07/04/friendship-in-an-age-of-economics/.

[2]James Michelman, "Some Ethical Consequences of Economic Competition," *Journal of Business Ethics* 2 (1983), pp. 79–87.

What is the implication of this dismal fact about competition? "Consider our normal sense of what kind of persons we ought to be," Michelman asks. "We want to be kind, honest, compassionate, loyal, courageous. Whatever that list is, call it *our desired moral character*." He then asks, "What characteristics would we look for in the managers of a company in which we hold an important stake? Whatever this catalog turns out to be, call it the *desired business character*."[3]

The problem, Michelman says, is that—for most people, most of the time—these two sets of traits are far apart from each other.

> What is the manager's duty to himself? If the discharge of his corporate responsibilities requires him to run counter to his desired moral character and so to violate his own basic self, must he do so? The necessity of profit maximization provides the answer. If the firm is to survive, the manager's obligation must be to it, not to himself. It follows, then, that free enterprise can require the violation of the individual's most basic duties to himself.[4]

This argument is unsettling. He catalogues how business life commonly requires deception; wishing competitors ill; avoiding kindness, compassion, and sentimentality; cold calculations; the absence of mutual aid; and viewing the value of persons as tools to further profits. These attitudes constitute duties to the firm, precluding people from being who they morally want to be. Personal duties to help others, respect others, and be honest must be abandoned for hard-hearted attitudes, which are often marked, he writes, by "dislike and fear." He says, "Now I have not observed these statements to be always true, of course. But they hold as to primary tendencies" (p. 80).

The point of these reflections is not that we behave unethically on the terms of some external value system. The point is that we violate ourselves. Over time, we repeat behaviors that we commonly recognize as inappropriate from within our own value system. They eventually seep into our settled disposition, which we take wherever we go. So our private lives and more intimate relationships and friendships eventually become influenced by the business character that we are forced to accept.

This is not an encouraging picture. We sacrifice and violate our integrity, we live a stifled life through anemic and instrumental relationships, and we are forced to abandon the human traits of decency that we wish we could live by. He writes:

> Thus, the compartmentalization of our souls; the acceptance, but non-acknowledgement of hypocrisy, and so the impossibility of ever achieving a happy society. . . . And if only the ethically indifferent among us competed, ethical indifference would wholly define our economic universe. But most of us, vigorous competitors or not, are not ethically indifferent. Very few of us make always wholly rational competitive judgments, otherwise we would be monsters, not men. It is that dichotomy which finally represents the great flawed detail of free enterprise.[5]

What do you think? The argument is not merely or primarily a theoretical reflection. Michelman is conveying his lived experience, which he believes generalizes many

---

[3]Ibid, p. 82.

[4]Ibid.

[5]Michelman, "Some Ethical Consequences of Economic Competition," p. 86.

Moral integrity refers to the idea that our actions, emotions, and moral beliefs cohere and reinforce each other.

people's experiences. The point is not only to analyze the structure of his argument but to consider whether its premises *ring true* to your experience and perspective, or not.

There are actually two separate implications that we might consider, based on these reflections. The first is, as stated above, that life in competitive capitalism requires us to violate our **moral integrity**. Moral integrity refers to the idea that the actions, emotions, and moral beliefs of a person cohere and reinforce each other. In the excerpt above, Michelman suggests that competitive capitalism requires us to live with hypocrisy and contradictions.

A separable implication may be less about losing integrity and more about changing who we are. We may get caught up in the values of the corporation and adopt them as our own. Firms are teams and to motivate team play corporate values may become a higher morality for us. We can come to identify with the corporation, finding success and promotions along the way. We believe that all of our actions are good and right when they promote the interests of the firm. We can come to feel no contradictions in the decisions that we make. We simply become a different person over time. What some see as deception, wishing competitors ill, avoiding kindness, cold calculation, using people as tools—we may come to see as attitudes and actions that are all for the good.

This narrative can have many shades of interpretation. There is the employee who goes along unreflectively with the values required for business, never really endorsing or rejecting them—but living them nonetheless. For example, the firm asks you to transfer, which requires you to move your family and leave your relationships. You don't think twice or ever really question it. Of course you'll go. Without any reflection there is no contradiction; and reflection may come only years later. In another case a company executive may be highly reflective and deeply committed to the values of the corporation: my job comes first, above all.

There are many variations and subtleties to these descriptions that we could consider. If our beliefs and actions contradict each other we could describe the problem as a loss of moral integrity, as Michelman does, or as these latter examples suggest, simply the loss of who we are and a transformation into something else.

Let's consider one more criticism of market relationships. Economist Juliet Schor argues that markets lead to a work life that requires too much of our time.[6] We are overworked. We struggle to find a few hours here and there during the week to relax. We are so exhausted that we unwind by watching TV and shutting down. We take our two weeks of vacation (out of the entire year!) but it takes a week just to stop thinking about work. Our smart phone goes everywhere.

But what do good relationships most need? Time. And it's not only relationships. Being ethical requires time, as do most good things in life—time to reflect, to be sensitive and care about others' situations, to listen and respond to whatever a situation calls for. But a working life in a capitalist system squeezes our time. We start our careers with precious little time and the stresses only increase, until we retire fifty years later. Competitive capitalism makes us choose how we spend that next moment of thought and action, which will be spent largely for advancing the interests of a firm. Put aside existential concerns about moral integrity and hypocrisy. The most basic point for Schor is that we lack time in a competitive market economy.

---

[6]Juliet Schor, *The Overworked American: The Unexpected Decline of Leisure* (Basic, 1993).

But whatever the variations on these observations, they all are meant to express a common feature that relates to May's earlier reflections about the noneconomic character of friendship. In one form or another, a competitive capitalist economy undermines our ability to realize good relationships. We make compromised choices, and the workplace leads us to see relationships instrumentally. At best they are shallow; at worst, they are filled with dislike and fear. We also come to compromise and change our perspective on what life can be, for the worse, and we bring this compromised character to all of our experiences and relationships in life.

This section could develop further observations about these points of view. What are yours? Do you agree with these ideas?

We will next consider how these criticisms relate to some broader ethical and philosophical traditions. Integrating contemporary discussions, such as those outlined above, with traditions that in some instances date back thousands of years can add depth to your understanding of these arguments. These ethical perspectives do not directly imply criticisms of markets. They do so in the hands of the above critics, given their understanding of how markets affect our relationships and character. But others support and defend markets and capitalism through these same traditions, as we will see in Section 4.

A. VIRTUE ETHICS

These criticisms can be understood within an ethical and philosophical tradition called **virtue ethics**. This approach draws its inspiration from Greek philosopher Aristotle whose writings trace to around 300 B.C.E. We often think that ethics is about making the right choice or performing the right action. For virtue ethicists, choices and actions are only one part of ethics. The deeper subject matter is thinking about the whole person, and considering the nature of that person's **character**. A person's character refers to the emotions, qualities, beliefs, characteristics, and sensibilities that give shape to who that person is and explains the underlying reasons why people act as they do. In this view of ethics, we should judge not only *acts* as right or wrong but *people* as ethical or unethical based on having good or bad character. We can then interpret people's particular actions within the context of their whole life. For example, we could take the same action performed by two people, such as an instance of being insensitive or rude in the workplace. You know that one person has a kind disposition and the behavior is *out of character*. You learn that there has been a serious illness that just occurred in the family. On the other hand, the other person who was rude simply has a rude and uncaring disposition and the action is part of a long pattern of this sort of behavior. A distinctive contribution of virtue ethics is that we should judge actions by shifting our attention to people and their character. The name *virtue ethics* expresses the idea that ethics is about having **virtue**, which is the quality of having a good character. The flipside of virtue is having a **vice**, which is the quality of having a bad character.

The term **eudaimonistic ethics** refers to ethical approaches grounded in reflections about how to achieve the end of a well-lived life. The term *eudaimonia* is transliterated from a Greek term that contemporary ethicists use to recognize their deep affinity to the concept embedded in the ancient Greek philosophical tradition. The specific virtues identified by eudaimonistic theories depend on the

> This section elaborates on the ideas first presented in the Introduction, Section 4.

> Virtue *ethics* is the belief that ethics is about having *virtue*, which is about the quality of having a good *character*. Bad character traits identify people's vices. Virtue ethicists debate the qualities that define and differentiate virtuous and vicious characters.

> *Eudaimonistic ethics* refers to ethical approaches grounded in reflections about how to achieve the end of a well-lived life.

Aristotle's *doctrine of the golden mean* is part of Aristotle's theory of virtue ethics: that a virtuous disposition requires character traits that aim at the mean between two extremes. For example, courage is the virtue, of which cowardice and recklessness are the (vicious) extremes.

particular theory but they often include traits such as honesty, kindness, temperance, loyalty, courage, tolerance, and forgiveness. These theories typically specify vices to be avoided as well, such as greed, arrogance, self-centeredness, impatience, untrustworthiness, envy, disloyalty, or vanity. For Aristotle, a mark of virtue is to develop a disposition that is the mean between two extremes, which has come to be called the **doctrine of the golden mean**. For example, courage is the virtue, of which cowardice and recklessness are the (vicious) extremes. Character formation is about finding a disposition that appropriately balances competing psychological forces that can tilt too far in either direction. A good character is especially important, argues a virtue ethicist, for facing personal ethical challenges such as conflicts of interest (Chapter 8 Section 5).

A person's character is shaped over a long period of time. The ancient Greeks emphasized that it's the task of practical wisdom to be virtuous, which is learned from others in the community who share in this wisdom about right and wrong. While doing the right thing may be difficult initially, if we put in the effort and act morally, we create a habit for doing the right thing without thinking twice about it. Virtues then become habits of heart and mind that shape and determine our actions. The virtuous person finds virtuous behavior enjoyable—that's part of the significance of having virtue. The unfortunate flipside of these ideas is that a vicious disposition can also become a habit of heart and mind to make poor choices that become enjoyable. We may even lose the capacity to appreciate what virtue is—which is part of the damage done in having vices. The connection between knowing and doing is conjoined for the virtue ethicist and suggests another distinctive feature of this ethical perspective. Understanding right and wrong from only an intellectual point of view does not indicate that a person has moral knowledge, according to this ancient tradition. For character-based ethics, someone who is good at analyzing ethics but doesn't act on the conclusions is missing something—a good character. Knowing entails acting.

Character is relevant not only for action but for determining the quality of our relationships. Not by coincidence, Aristotle's writing on friendship remains a standard of analysis for considering the depth and meaning of that relationship, beyond his broader account of the virtues. It's remarkable to think that someone writing over 2,000 years ago could speak so eloquently about a personal topic that is as relevant today as it was then. Political philosopher Todd May references Aristotle at length in the more extended excerpt from which the earlier passage came. For the virtue ethicist, it's hard to overemphasize the importance of character development, because it shapes how we act and the quality of our personal relationships throughout life.

Let's contrast a virtue ethics approach with consequentialist and deontological approaches to ethics. Suppose that my purchasing decisions can be based on whether the firm selling those products has a record of corporate social responsibility (CSR). Should I? A consequentialist will be interested to know the overall *effects* of making decisions based on this information. A deontologist will want to know whether there are any duties or rules that require that I examine CSR in this way. The virtue ethicist will want to know whether living this way supports and expresses virtuous character traits, such as being charitable, benevolent, or just. This example summarizes three alternative approaches to ethics: we can analyze actions and institutions in terms of its *good or bad consequences*, in terms of *fulfilling specific duties* independent from consequences, or in terms of what leads to *a well-lived life*. All three approaches have their insights, although an advocate of one tradition or the other will emphasize one approach over the other.

With this background, let's consider several practical upshots of the eudaimonistic approach to ethics.

First, the most important ethical assessment of capitalism as an economic system is to examine whether or not the system corrodes people's character. Aristotle's ethics provides the background for understanding Michelman's ethical perspective.

Second, a proponent of this view emphasizes the training and circumstances that do or do not lead people to develop good characters, such as the quality of education, the values practiced at home, or the long-term effects of a work environment on character. If we conceive of ethics solely in terms of right and wrong action, we can miss the point that people have settled dispositions formed over a long period of time to act one way rather than another, so social policy should include thought about how institutions, such as markets, shape people's character over time.

Third, professional ethics is sometimes conceived as a specific code of rules for determining how to act in a given moment. For the virtue ethicist, the more fundamental point is to be surrounded by people who have good characters and good professional ethics will follow. For example, from the perspective of a business manager, one can develop a complicated set of rules to guide what people should do in situations or, as the virtue ethics approach recommends, invest in finding people of good character who have the wisdom to consult one another to discern the best response as situations arise, regardless of the ethical challenge. Michelman argues, however, that business success pulls against developing good character or being surrounded by those who have good character.

Fourth, life can become a pinball machine of decision-making that loses any larger perspective. A eudaimonistic approach to ethics recommends that we think through decisions, ethical or otherwise, from the vantage point of pursuing a well-lived life. This is to take the long view for making sense of the difficult choices of the moment.

B. THE ETHICS OF CARE

The market criticisms above can also be understood through a more recent feminist tradition called the **ethics of care**. Popularized and developed by psychologist Carol Gilligan, this tradition emphasizes how ethical reflection should focus on the quality of caring relationships. A leading feminist, Gilligan argued that the language of rights and justice did not accurately capture how women understand ethics in terms of relationships and responsibilities. Gilligan was especially critical of psychologist Lawrence Kohlberg's model of moral development that described universalist ethical principles as a more advanced morality than an ethics of caring. She argued that Kohlberg's stages of moral development represent a male bias and that women tend to speak with a different moral voice.

> The *ethics of care* refers to a feminist ethical viewpoint that emphasizes how ethics is importantly about assessing the quality of people's personal relationships and bringing caring attitudes into these relationships.

Ethics, she argued, requires relationships where people care about one another—where attitudes and motivations are the responsibility of both men and women but, more often, become minimized in men and emphasized in women. The ethics of care can be both a descriptive psychological theory (that men and women reason differently about morality) or a normative theory (that attitudes about caring within relationships offer an alternative or better approach for thinking about the demands of ethics than do abstract consequentialist or deontological approaches to ethics).

As a normative theory, many ethical problems in this view arise because people do not care about one another. Rather than conceive of ethics abstractly, in terms of rights, duties, or social contracts, we should pay attention to the particular context of a situation and apply powers of empathy to understand the other person's situation. Ethics is about the particularized relationships that we have with others.

How we interpret social interactions is crucial for an ethics of care, and we need to be reflective about how culture socializes us to behave in ways that reflect and perpetuate biases and prejudices. Those who develop an ethics of care tend to emphasize a culture of gender, racial, and ethnic equality in the context of caring relationships, an especially important objective in diverse domestic and international environments. Ethical theories that simply assess the rightness and wrongness of actions can miss the underlying reason why people's actions can be so awful: they can spring from unhealthy and unethical relationships, especially those between men and women premised on fundamental inequality. For an ethics of care, we should subject our judgments about rights, rules, and duties to critical scrutiny and ask whether we bring caring attitudes in service to fostering good relationships. Both the ethics of care and virtue ethics emphasize that analyzing *actions* identifies only the surface of ethics. We attain depth by understanding the underlying motives, outlooks, and character that leads to those actions.

This approach has a lineage to Scottish enlightenment philosopher David Hume, who argues that all of ethics springs from the psychological capacity for humans to feel sympathy toward others. Both eudaimonistic approaches to ethics and the ethics of care emphasize the psychological capacities required to be ethical in daily living. They are not identical approaches, however, as the former places special emphasis on relationships of caring whereas virtue ethicists offer a broader account of the range of virtues of a well-lived life. But these approaches can join one another among those who argue that a caring disposition is one of the leading virtues of a good life.[7]

Although the discussion of friendship and integrity that began this chapter is not directly about an ethics of care, adding this background can bring depth to the following question: what constitutes good relationships in business and economic life? Proponents of an ethics of care tend to take good relationships between family and friends as a model for thinking about good relationships in general. Good caring relationships should shape how we conduct and assess market relationships. Others challenge this approach, however. For example, writer Albert Carr defended the view that business should be conceived on the analogy of playing a game of poker. This idea relates to the *separation thesis*, as discussed in Chapter 8 Section 2. To be good at poker requires its own special sense of ethics. People who play expect deception (but not cheating) and they admire a good poker player. It's part of the game. Those attitudes applied to our relationships outside this game would be inappropriate. But within the game, they are just fine. Do you agree? Carr defends this point, and then argues that business, just like poker, includes special relationships that would be regarded as unethical in other contexts but are acceptable in the context of business.[8]

---

[7]Theorists writing in the tradition of the ethics of care include Professors Virginia Held, Nel Noddings, and Rosemarie Tong.

[8]Albert Carr defends this analogy in "Is Business Bluffing Ethical?" *Harvard Business Review* 46 (January–February 1968), pp. 143–153.

What do you think? It's interesting to examine this argument in light of the discussion developed in this chapter. (This poker analogy was also introduced in Chapter 8, Discussion Question 10.)

C. NON-WESTERN ETHICAL APPROACHES

Let's consider one additional set of ethical perspectives closely associated with the importance of relationships and character. Confucian, Buddhist, and other non-Western approaches to ethics often emphasize the value of interpersonal relationships and reflections about how to live a good life. Scholars in these areas emphasize that non-Western approaches often have much in common with Aristotle's eudaimonistic ethics by identifying virtues of a well-lived life, although they embed their account of virtues within a systematic philosophy typically different from Western philosophy.

Although it is difficult to offer general remarks about these rich and varied traditions, perhaps a central point of contrast is the perspective that ethics depends on our specific *role and responsibilities* and our *internal attitudes*, rather than on enlightenment values such as justice, individual rights, and democracy. For example, Confucian ethics conceives of the role of government in terms of a parent/child analogy (the government is parent and the subjects are the children), and the responsibilities of individuals in terms of their proper role within the larger group.[9] Buddhist author and monk Matthieu Ricard, who is also the translator for the Dalai Lama, particularly emphasizes the importance of our inner state of being and finding ways to bring altruism and pure motivations into daily living. He writes, "By happiness I mean here a deep sense of flourishing that arises from an exceptionally healthy mind. This is not a mere pleasurable feeling, a fleeting emotion, or a mood, but an optimal state of being."[10] Non-Western traditions, which are sometimes called *Eastern wisdom traditions*, tend to develop accounts of ethics within a much larger systematic philosophy about the nature of the world and our place within it, and they tend to emphasize the importance of spirituality as a process of inner reflection and purification.

As a result, most commentaries from these traditions are critical of market relationships based on motives of self-interest and individual pursuits. They argue that our internal motives should be responsive to the organic purposes of life as defined within their respective traditions. The material and individualist emphasis of capitalism undermines our abilities to develop this inner journey.[11] For these reasons, non-Western approaches tend to reject capitalism altogether or support a stakeholder perspective on the purposes of corporations, given the potential of this perspective to allow more altruistic motivations to influence market outcomes. Proponents of the Green movement sometimes draw support from within these non-Western traditions.[12]

---

[9]See Peter Nosco, "Confucian Perspective on Civil Society and Government," in *Civil Society and Government*, Nancy Rosemblum and Robert Post, eds. (Princeton University Press, 2002), pp. 334–359.

[10]See, for example, http://www.matthieuricard.org/en/

[11]American author and teacher Joseph Campbell summarized his work in comparative mythology and religion through the following expression: follow your bliss. For more on his views, see *The Hero with a Thousand Faces* (Princeton University Press, 1972) and the *Masks of God, Vols. 1–4* (Penguin, 1991). He is featured in *The Power of Myth*, a PBS documentary with Bill Moyers, aired a year after Campbell's death.

[12]See, for example, the work of Bill McKibben at http://www.billmckibben.com/

Although there are many fundamental distinctions among the different Western and non-Western cultural traditions, spiritual traditions, and religious traditions of the world, perhaps they all share the commonality of offering insights about the value of good relationships and character, as defined from within their respective views. To give one example, Christian theology typically includes an expression of a eudaimonistic approach to ethics, emphasizing Christian virtues of hope, faith, love, prudence, justice, restraint, and courage. Part of the study of comparative religions often includes differing accounts of religious ethics in terms of their vision of the good and their sense of proper relationships.

Cultural, spiritual, and religious traditions differ in many ways. However, this section emphasizes two commonalities that can offer a notable contrast to the discussions in previous chapters: (1) these holistic traditions embed their account of ethics within a larger systematic cultural, spiritual, or religious perspective about the meanings and purposes of life; (2) their accounts of ethics emphasize the importance of *our internal motivations*, how to conduct our *personal relationships*, and a *conception of a good life*.

Let's consider three practical upshots of these observations for business and economics.

First, when confronted with diverse cultural settings, especially in international business, ethical dialogue includes differing cultural perceptions of the virtues that make for good character and the quality of good relationships. In this context, an approach to business ethics that focuses on the rightness or wrongness of actions or rules separated from a discussion of cultural presuppositions may miss the practical point that we often embed our sense of ethics within these diverse traditions. Cross-cultural training is, in part, about learning different models and ways of speaking about good conduct and character. In this respect a study of different traditions helps motivate a culturally sensitive discussion of ethics. This practical point also leads to philosophical questions about ethics and cultural relativism (Chapter 3 Sections 3–7).

Second, these traditions ask us to think long and hard about our *motivations* and *emotional dispositions* in life. In this respect, they tend to reject or at least regard as incomplete consequentialist approaches to ethics that assess markets and capitalism in terms of the outcomes of decisions. Just as important—or more important—for these traditions is the inner state of people who live within a market and capitalist system. What is the lived experience? What is the effect of material pursuits on individual's well-being?

Third, non-Western approaches to ethics that develop accounts of good relationships and character prompt different questions than those typically prompted in previous chapters. For example, to what extent can a life in business manifest character traits and relationships that we admire? Consider people who are successful in whatever organization or business that you work. Do they display traits and have relationships that you admire? Asking these questions can offer compelling personal insight for your path ahead if you stay with that organization.

D. RELATING CHAPTERS 6–12 WITH DEBATES ABOUT RELATIONSHIPS AND CHARACTER

It's worth noting how Michelman's criticisms that began this chapter can be expressed through the terms of previous chapters without reference to relationships and character. For example, if Michelman is correct and competitive capitalism undermines our integrity, then free enterprise makes us less free by limiting our *positive liberty* (Chapter 9). Alternatively, we could say that capitalism reduces our *welfare*, making a happy society impossible to achieve because we are unable to balance our goals against the ethical constraints that we should live by (Chapter 10). These inner conflicts and compromised relationships make us worse off, revealing hidden layers of *inefficiency* that underlie many market exchanges (Chapters 6 and 7). Finally, we might draw on the concept of *desert*, and argue that markets require us to subordinate our wills to the firm to such a high degree that wages, no matter how high, do not compensate or restore what we have lost. What we actually deserve in compensation goes well beyond what a wage can provide (Chapter 12).

The point here is not to defend these critical arguments but to notice how the values in previous chapters can be relevant for developing the criticisms in this chapter. Interpreting our own or others' viewpoints through the lens of different values can offer valuable insights for expressing and elaborating these views. Which values create the dialogue depends, in part, on the audience at whom the ideas are aimed.

Those who most emphasize the values of Chapters 6–12 believe that these values provide the best dialogue for evaluating business and economic life. But advocates of the perspectives of this chapter argue that even if we can describe our views in terms of the values of previous chapters, we miss relevant insights without thinking about the quality of our lives over an entire life span and reflecting on its many moral and cultural nuances. For example, moral loss is not merely about one bad choice, or reducing overall welfare, or about a loss of freedom, or harming others, though all of this matters. From the perspective of this chapter, moral loss, if it occurs, is about the long-term erosion of integrity that can make life hollow, putting our relationships in peril, and squandering our deepest meanings.

And yet, we do not have to choose only one way to express our ethical perspective. Taken as a whole, the chapters of the book can create a conversation one with the other, each using different concepts to provide insights for directing our understandings and commitments about our ethics and values.

Additionally, this chapter suggests a path for introducing values beyond those studied in this book. For example, someone from a Buddhist tradition may emphasize the value of compassion; someone from a Roman Catholic tradition may emphasize the value of human dignity; and there are many other traditions and values. These illustrations are simplified at best, as all of these cultural and religious traditions emphasize many values that no short introduction or summary can do justice to. Whether or not you have an affinity with any cultural, spiritual, or religious traditions, you might consider making a list of the values that you think are most important for a study of business and economic life. You could then introduce these values into the conversation, adding them to the list that is part of Figure I.1 in the Introduction. The method of analysis in this book could be extended to those values, by asking, What sense of ethics, incentives, and institutional arrangements would best respect and promote those values?

E. Public Policy Implications from an Institutional Point of View

So far the chapter has developed criticisms of capitalism primarily from a personal point of view. We can also examine the *institutional implications* of these ideas. After noting his searing critique of capitalism, it's interesting to consider Michelman's conclusion:

> Now all this does not mean that a society necessarily is to reject free-enterprise in favor of some other economic scheme. For one thing, the system simply works. . . . Nevertheless, I do not think that the immoralities inherent in the economic competition can be overemphasized. For to admit the imperfectability of men and their

institutions is not to concede that they cannot be made better. But first we will have to have a clearer understanding of the nature of our current imperfections.[13]

Criticisms such as those above can be (and are) developed into many different kinds of critiques. Some advocate radical and wholesale rejection of capitalism as a form of economic organization. Others, like Michelman, acknowledge these imperfections but temper them with recognition that the system "works," which is to acknowledge and grant aspects of the stockholder position and efficiency arguments developed in Chapters 4 and 6. For Michelman, his point is not to condemn capitalism but to support it for what it does well, while recognizing the serious toll on relationships and character.

Let's briefly consider some public policy implications of the arguments so far presented in this chapter. Critics of capitalism may advocate prohibiting market activities that particularly degrade human relationships or devalue noneconomic spheres of life. For example, they are likely to support policies for maternity leave, religious holidays, vacation time, restricted work hours, retirement benefits, and other family-friendly legislation, interpreted as support for preserving quality relationships and developing human character from a more holistic perspective on life.

A key question for public policy from this point of view is, How can businesses and the economic system support people's efforts to seek a good life with friendships and character within a supportive public culture? The discussion of *blocked exchanges* in Chapter 1 Section 5 is especially relevant here. Recall that blocked exchanges refer to norms and policies that prohibit specific kinds of market activities. We could interpret laws that limit the reach of markets both in terms of the values discussed in Chapters 6–12 and in terms of the arguments in this chapter. For example, limiting the reach of competitive markets may help create space (physical, temporal, and conceptual) necessary for developing meaningful relationships untouched by metaphors of *consumer* and *investor* relationships. Stakeholder advocates may ground their position through the ethical perspectives surveyed in this chapter as well, placing special emphasis on more satisfying employer and employee relationships, or the viability of acting on ethical motivations in business, contrary to Michelman's argument. The arguments of this chapter can be supportive of more sweeping legal and social reforms as well, such as economic cooperatives and worker democracy.

In summary, this section has (1) introduced criticisms of capitalism based on how we assess relationships and character, (2) surveyed three ethical perspectives that most frequently ground these criticisms, and (3) considered how relationships and character can be a measuring stick for drafting policy and workplace initiatives that shape business and economic life.

13.4 RELATIONSHIPS AND CHARACTER: DEFENDING MARKETS AND CAPITALISM

Not everyone believes that reflections about relationships and character lead to negative assessments of markets and capitalism. Let's now consider this converse interpretation of economic life.

---

[13]Michelman, "Some Ethical Consequences of Economic Competition," p. 86.

Consider the character of someone who starts and runs a small business: disciplined, tenacious, wanting to do something to be proud of, overcoming adversity, building value for others in peaceful and cooperative ways, attention to detail, pursuing a vision, demonstrating great initiative, being responsible and willing to bear the consequences, building long-term honest relationships with consumers and suppliers, creating a good product, creating good jobs, creating wealth, and helping a community thrive.

Ask someone who runs a small business. See what the person says. This author recalls a conversation with a small restaurant owner in a thriving marketplace, proudly using local produce to help local farmers, talking about the people who visit and who appreciate his service, selling good food to benefit others, and making a living along the way. This person was proudly supporting the values of the Green movement, seeing himself as bringing *values into the market* and *building healthy relationships with others*. A proponent of this point of view asks: Isn't this story true millions of times over in a market system? Why can't relationships in markets be meaningful? They start as reciprocity, which is a healthy relationship to begin with, and then may develop into something more, as friendships, in the most noneconomic of senses. What precludes noninstrumental relationships as a pervasive feature of markets?

Next, recall the debate between stockholder and stakeholder proponents in Chapters 4 and 5. There is more at stake in the stakeholder view than what may have been apparent then. They argue that capitalism can include thriving relationships that support local communities, fair trade, philanthropy, and care for others and the environment. Wholefoods' CEO John Mackey was not merely asserting a philosophy of *doing good* by embracing the stakeholder point of view. In addition stakeholder advocates assert a philosophy of moral integrity, claiming that capitalism is compatible with a life of moral character, unlike the views of the critics in Section 3. Stakeholder advocates want to *live* their values through the market system. For many who believe in the stakeholder perspective and who are aware of the criticisms leveled in Section 3, insisting on the possibility for moral integrity within economic life may be the most important point about the stockholder and stakeholder debates. They fail to see how a thoroughgoing stockholder approach is compatible with their ethical beliefs, and so they bring a different vision to the market. It's interesting to note that in the context of Chapters 4 and 5, the stakeholder position is a type of critique of capitalism in relation to stockholder theory. But in the context of this chapter, stakeholder advocates are *champions* of capitalism in response to the criticisms in Section 3. They can be understood to recognize the potential problems raised above but argue that they have a way to address these problems within the system. Stockholder advocates most likely deny the problems identified in Section 3. A stockholder perspective, advocates will argue, need not entail personal ethical sacrifices as suggested by Michelman and others. Connecting the CSR debates of Chapters 4 and 5 with debates about how to live with integrity explains in part the potency and reach of these discussions about business and economic life.

But we need not become immersed in contemporary stockholder/stakeholder debates to find advocates for capitalism based on how it builds quality relationships and personal character. Consider a broader historical view. In a feudal economy, people of low status were often forced to sacrifice their dignity to an aristocratic class. Capitalism, some argue, eased those indignities by basing relationships on mutual self-interest. In this view, exchange relationships fostered equality of status and mutual respect. As one feminist commentator describes the historic shift toward capitalism:

> The ability of ordinary people to obtain credit with dignity reflects a larger transformation in the moral economy of social status made possible by capitalism. The aristocratic moral economy of debt was enmeshed in the logic of gift rather than commercial exchange. Credit was seen as a form of charity to the needy and dependent. . . . Honor redounds to whoever bestows such charity, setting the gift-giver on a higher social plane than the recipient. Recipients of unreciprocated gifts are obliged to honor and obey their benefactors. . . . By contrast, exchange on the basis of mutual self-interest can preserve the independence and dignity of both parties.[14]

The thesis of Anderson's essay is that capitalism—assessed solely on the quality of relationships—fares quite well when viewed through a historic lens. A market critic might respond: even so, can't we do better? Isn't some other economic model, such as communism, even better? In response to this line of questioning, consider the words of Somalia-born feminist writer and activist Ayaan Hirsi Ali:

> To appreciate just how effectively the free market strengthens moral character, it is helpful to glance at economic systems that undermine or openly reject it. Everywhere Communism has been tried, for instance, it has resulted not just in corruption and sub-standard products but also in fear, apathy, ignorance, oppression, and a general lack of trust. The Soviet Union and pre-reform China were morally as well as economically bankrupt.[15]

These remarks highlight how people's evaluation of markets and capitalism depends on what they are comparing those relationships against. Some people identify relationships better than what markets seem to deliver. They may experience these relationships in noneconomic life, within friendships, religion, or family. People's worldviews often depend on these deeper visions of human relationships, both in their possibilities and their limits. Markets critics may ground their criticisms in the experience of better relationships elsewhere or the experience of markets impeding relationships that they believe could be better.

But those who compare market relationships with worse alternatives will celebrate markets and capitalism for their freedom, recognition, respect, and equality of status. Market relationships can help people escape common oppressions and inequalities that define many people's private worlds—within abusive families, gang life, or dictatorial governments. To offer one example, the practice of microlending, touched on in Chapter 3 Section 3, is in part a story about women who find in market relationships the independence and dignity that their nonmarket life often did not offer. Many proponents of a market system observe how market relationships reward hard work and industry, creativity, and honesty.

Proponents of capitalism emphasize that many people find meaning, worth, and achievement in their jobs. Consider the results of a 2010 Gallup poll of U.S. workers. "The majority of U.S. workers," writes Lydia Saad of Gallup, "are completely satisfied with several aspects of their work environment, including their relations with coworkers, the flexibility

---

[14]Elizabeth Anderson, "Ethical Assumptions in Economic Theory: Some Lessons from the History of Credit and Bankruptcy," *Ethical Theory and Moral Practice*, 7(4) (2004), p. 352

[15]http://www.templeton.org/market/

of their hours, and the amount of work required of them."[16] These statistics, Gallup has found, have been steady throughout the last decade with high satisfaction, even in the face of the largest economic downturn since the Great Depression. Over 70 percent of workers, for example, are "completely satisfied" with their relationships with coworkers.[17]

Thus, the argument in this section is that a eudaimonistic approach to ethics and feminist reflections about an ethics of care do not necessarily imply criticisms of capitalism. To the contrary, many people with long careers in business emphasize how business success requires just the virtues that we most want to live by. For these supporters, capitalism allows us to live our values, if we choose to follow them.

Let's consider a second argument that proponents of capitalism and markets often develop, in relation to the discussion in this chapter. Suppose that we grant, contrary to the immediately preceding reflections, that relationships in economic life *do not* always express or embody the best or highest ideals of human association. What does this fact, if we grant it, imply about capitalism? Consider this response: even if economic life fails to capture everything that we want in human relationships, market supporters will often ask, "Is that such a bad result?" If markets are good for what they are—a system that "works" (in Michelman's words), raises standards of living, and is grounded in basic minimal values of reciprocity—then a capitalist system can leave the development of our most meaningful relationships to our more private spheres. Even if we grant limits and challenges to economic relationships, as long as markets perform their function without great harms, we can then develop the deep relationships we wish for—outside of economic life. As German playwright Bertolt Brecht wrote, "Food comes first, then morals."

In this view, wealth—even modest levels of wealth—creates unparalleled opportunities for meaning and advancement in creating a fulfilling life. A proponent of capitalism on this point will ask the following questions: Are you not free right now to develop meaningful relationships? If not, why not? Is it really the fault of markets and capitalism? Doesn't it have more to do with factors that apply or do not apply, no matter the nature of the economic system?

These questions prompt a final idea relevant to a defense of markets and capitalism responsive to the themes of this chapter. Perhaps the promise of an ethical economic life based on good relationships and character is overstated, that an analysis of relationships is not as important for assessing capitalism as its critics maintain. If our deepest relationships are sustained by choices outside of markets, then perhaps these critics overstate the impact of markets on the formation of relationships and character. A study of ethics for *all* of life rightly focuses on the issues of this chapter, but perhaps a study of the ethics of *economic* life should focus on values such as those presented in previous chapters: promoting efficiency, freedom, and equality; protecting rights; and providing people with what they deserve.

In sum, some proponents of markets and capitalism argue that market institutions encourage virtue and good character, drawing on the very ethical traditions that others use to criticize market relationships. Proponents and critics bring quite different observations about the quality of relationships made possible through markets and capitalism. Other proponents of capitalism challenge the role of these reflections for assessing economic life.

---

[16]http://www.gallup.com/poll/142715/job-stress-workers-biggest-complaint.aspx
[17]Ibid.

Even if the system requires personal sacrifices, this is life—and we ask too much if we demand that capitalism be the site for our deepest meanings. From this perspective, the values in the previous chapters offer the appropriate framework for analyzing ethical relationships in business, and the rest of the search for a well-lived life is up to us.

A TALE OF TWO CAPITALISMS AND THE PRAGMATIC POINT OF VIEW

Read the Case Study *Work-Life Balance* only on MySearchLab

We see markets through different lenses. Who has the better insights, the market critics discussed in Section 3 or the advocates of the values discussed in Section 4? Perhaps there is more than one answer, that relationships of economic life have many variations.

As the previous sections illustrate, discussion of relationships and character can be a basis to criticize or support business and economic arrangements. Their discussion can also structure debates across many areas of professional ethics. Consider the range of professional relationships that have their own dynamic: doctor–patient, lawyer–client, supervisor–employee, teacher–student, owner–contractor, therapist–patient, principal–agent, regulator–regulated, coach–athlete, religious leader–congregant, and others. This book offers a range of ideas to facilitate discussions that could be tailored to the ethics of more specialized professional relationships.

Even beyond professional ethics, this chapter prompts basic questions about pursuing a career: Is your future professional life one that will be filled with deep and meaningful relationships? Will your career support your character for living a good life? (And, just as importantly, How do you go about finding answers to these questions?)

Pragmatism refers to a philosophical tradition in the United States at the turn of the twentieth century that focuses on the way ideas connect with practical consequences.

These questions are about your ideals of a good life. More generally, a study of ethics and values can be interpreted as the practical pursuit of how best to make a good life for yourself. In this view, the value of an idea depends in part on what happens when those ideas are put into action. Do those ideas help life go better or not? **Pragmatism** is a distinctive approach and method for thinking about ethics. *Pragmatism* refers to a philosophical tradition in the United States at the turn of the twentieth century that focuses on the way that ideas have practical consequences.

For example, we observe markets not merely as detached observers, but we assess economic life normatively in relation to our own sense of ethics and values (Chapter 1). Each chapter has introduced ethical ideas that can guide our conduct and beliefs. What is the value of studying these ideas? There are many answers to consider. One answer is provided directly above: ideas matter and have meaning based on what happens when we put them into practice. This view of the subject was suggested in earlier discussions. For example, we considered how a person who incorporates the value of equality may experience the practical benefit of approaching conflicts by looking to find common ground with others (Chapter 11); or, someone who values efficiency may experience the practical benefits of building relationships as positive sum games rather than zero sum games (Chapter 6). A pragmatist always wants to know how an idea connects with what a person does, and assesses the idea on that basis.

The arguments in this chapter identify a pragmatic value for ethical reflection—that the ethics of economic life is not only about assessing markets and capitalism, or deciding about the right thing to do in a given situation, but it's also about the practical benefits of shaping your relationships, your character, and the sense of self that you want to have.

13.5 SUMMARY

The chapter introduced a debate: some see great virtue in the relationships and personal character that capitalism fosters; others see compromise, corrosion, and the loss of meaning. This chapter considered both sides of this debate. There is one pragmatic message that both sides seemingly share, however. For most people, relationships are what really matter in life and no matter where your professional ambitions and career successes take you, your happiness and well-being will depend on keeping sight of that simple truth.

KEY TERMS

moral integrity	virtue	doctrine of the golden mean
virtue ethics	vice	ethics of care
character	eudaimonistic ethics	pragmatism

DISCUSSION QUESTIONS

1. Does the free market corrode moral character? See http://www.templeton.org/market/ for a fascinating debate.

2. Do you think most employees enjoy their job or just endure them?

3. Have the most successful people in business achieved their status by being unethical? (Suppose that you are discussing this question with someone who disagrees with you. How do you gather evidence to support your position?)

4. When you meet someone for the first time, how often is one of your initial questions, "What do you do?" Does this (common practice) indicate that you strongly tie a person's identity with that person's line of work? How significantly should a career shape the formation of a self-identity?

5. When discussing individual ethics, it seems so much easier to judge someone else in a public setting than yourself or your closest friends. From the outside, we see conduct in others that violates some standard and we judge it to be unethical. But from the inside, when we are in similar situations, we are quick to perceive many valid reasons that justify or excuse our conduct. Is that true? Can you give an example? Should this fact lead us to be more empathetic and less judgmental toward those who violate ethical standards, or does this mean that we should more sharply judge ourselves and our friends? Is the ideal of ethical inquiry best conducted impersonally or from a particular and personal point of view? (Chapter 11 on equality contrasts these two perspectives.)

6. Suppose you work closely with someone who has done something unethical to you. But this person does not see any problem and there is no institutional mechanism to correct the problem. You need to continue working closely with this person. You think that this person is unethical and this person now dislikes you. How should you carry on your interactions with this person in an ethical fashion?

7. What explains the imperfections of capitalism, as Michelman describes them? Is it our human nature, or the rules of the free enterprise system? Is it an unwillingness to be ethical or our incapacity, given the system? What examples do you draw on to build your case?

8. Is there a distinction between *virtues* as they are defined for performing a specific role from *virtues* as they apply to all human beings? What is this distinction? How do we identify the relevant virtues in either case?

9. One of the most successful NFL football coach of all time is New England Patriots coach Bill Belichick. If you want to reflect on the ideas in this chapter in relation to pro football or his legacy, you might consider the article at http://www.nytimes.com/2010/12/07/sports/football/07rhoden.html?hp. How do you assess what it says?

10. Do virtual relationships in a digital age support or undermine the development of good relationships? What is the impact of online social networks and digital communications for experiencing a well-lived life? Compared to what?

11. What motives should we bring to our market interactions?

12. How can Aristotle's account of the golden mean be applied to assess people's attitudes about shopping and consuming? (We will discuss consumerism in the next chapter.)

13. Many ethical traditions, both Western and non-Western, place considerable weight on the value of loyalty. Should we have loyalty toward the corporation that we work for, apart from loyalty to particular individuals within the corporation? Why or why not?

14. How should we handle divided loyalties?

15. Which character traits are most important for successfully handling moral conflicts in the workplace? Can you offer examples to illustrate your position?

16. Recall the island scenario introduced in Chapter 6. We developed the image of two people trading in markets to determine the conditions under which the relationship would create an efficiency gain for both. We extended this scenario to consider whether or how market relationships foster liberty or equality. Apply the analysis of this chapter to the island scenario and evaluate markets from this point of view.

17. Consider the following statement: The problem with thinking about ethics in terms of good relationships and character is that it's easy to be ethical or virtuous when life is easy but not when faced with severe poverty, such as the need to steal food or medicines to survive. Similarly, it's easy to focus on developing good relationships for people who live middle-class lifestyles, but not so much for the working poor with no time and who must work a second job over the weekends. The ideas in this chapter are really aimed at the sensibilities of middle and upper classes, who have the time and resources to develop good relationships and character. Assess this reaction to the topics of this chapter.

18. Which is more important: (1) the *outcomes* of an action or (2) the *motives* and *character disposition* of the person performing the action?

19. How do your job experiences relate to the ideas of this chapter?

14

COMMUNITY AND THE COMMON GOOD

The life history of the individual is first and foremost an accommodation to the patterns and standards traditionally handed down in his [or her] community.
— Ruth Benedict, American anthropologist

WHEN YOU FINISH STUDYING THIS CHAPTER, YOU SHOULD BE ABLE TO:

1. *Characterize the tension between the forces of creative destruction and of community.*

2. *Analyze the motives that generate market relationships and whether they facilitate or undermine communities.*

3. *Distinguish different definitions of the common good.*

4. *Describe a communitarian ethical perspective.*

14.1 INTRODUCTION

From birth we are immersed in relationships that deeply influence our character and the trajectory of our lives. We examined this fundamental idea in Chapter 13, and yet that analysis may not seem to tell the full story behind the value of having good relationships. That chapter emphasized an individualist perspective—that relationships matter in relation to their effect on *me*. Anthropologist Ruth Benedict suggests a different connection: relationships express the social nature of human life. In this view, relationships are about the value of community and the nature of our shared existence (see Figure 14.1).

This chapter develops a series of observations and disagreements about community relevant for understanding the ethics of business and economic life. There is no single point of view about how to understand the value of community, and yet the divergent commentaries ahead attempt to answer the same question: to what extent does economic life create good communities? Many people consider this question to be the most important of all for the ethics of business and economic life.

FIGURE 14.1   **The Value of Relationships**

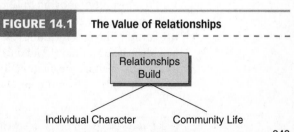

Relationships Build

Individual Character   Community Life

We begin with a debate about change and tradition as it relates to capitalism and business life. Next, we examine debates about the motives that support healthy communities. We then distinguish several meanings of the common good and introduce communitarianism as a distinctive ethical perspective.

14.2   CREATIVE DESTRUCTION AND COMMUNITY

Economist Joseph Schumpeter popularized the description of capitalism as the *perennial gale of creative destruction*. For Schumpeter and many others, to understand capitalism is to understand both sides of that concept: destroy and create. New forms of production and consumption replace old forms. People are hired, fired, replaced, and retrained. People adjust to constant turmoil and change. Success goes to those who adjust to the changes. Capitalism offers dazzling creativity as it destroys what came before. **Creative destruction** refers to this cyclical process in capitalism whereby old forms of capital and production are replaced by new forms of capital and production.

We study scenes of city life in grainy black and white photographs from a century before, with horse and buggies lining the streets. What was it like without the automobile? What happened to all those blacksmiths, buggy makers, and all those support industries that kept that form of transportation alive? We can fast-forward to any time period we like within industrial societies: the eight-track tape challenged vinyl records, followed by cassettes, CDs, and the iPad, which makes those previous mediums obsolete. Computers and the Internet continue to transform our economic lives, and the only certainty is that more technological change is on the way.

One striking illustration of this change is provided by a study of the Fortune 500, an annual listing of the top 500 U.S. companies as measured by revenues. Nearly half of the corporations listed in 1999 have disappeared from the list ten years later (destruction), which means that nearly half are new entrants (creation). Further, in bad times many new economic powerhouses are born. A study by the Kauffman Foundation found that "more than half of the companies on the 2009 Fortune 500 list were launched during a recession or bear market," another piece of evidence of creative destruction at work.[1]

But suppose you do not want change. You value the ways of life of your ancestors and your ancestors' ancestors. For you, community is the experience of stability across time, of unchanging values and comforts in an uncertain world. Community and tradition are your anchors. Change can take an enormous emotional toll. You do not want Walmart to close down the local hardware store that you've been visiting for the last forty years, with the bench out front for drinking a cup of coffee and talking with your friends. You do not want new roads gobbling up your bucolic fields (and your ancestors may have been right to resist the railroad coming to town as well). You also do not want to have to face the prospect of moving to find employment. You are established, you have worked hard, and now you are asked to pick up everything and leave? Societies that had persisted with limited changes for hundreds or thousands of years were turned upside down by the Industrial Revolution. And once markets and capitalism seep into society, the changes never stop—making the continually changing social landscape almost unrecognizable to inhabitants only a generation or two removed. The longer you live, the more you long for

---

[1]See http://www.kauffman.org/newsroom/the-economic-future-just-happened.aspx.

the good old days. How does creative destruction sound in that context? Not very good.

In summary capitalism and community can be seen as institutional opposites of one another. On the one hand there are institutions of change—markets and capitalism. On the other hand there are institutions of tradition—family, religion, and traditional cultural practices.

14.3 THE HUMAN PERSONALITY: SEEKING CHANGE AND TRADITION

These institutional tensions may express two contrasting aspects of the human personality. The churn of capitalism is the constant pursuit of improvement. Capitalism creates incentives to spur innovation. People with a **capitalist mindset** look at the margins of their activities and ask, How can that activity be improved? Is there a way to reorganize and do it better? With less cost? For more profit? How can some idea or resource be leveraged to create future production? The capitalist mind sees objects not for consumption but for their potential to leverage and create new growth. One thousand dollars may mean a whole lot of music downloads for some people (money for consumption), but for a capitalist mind that money also represents *potential to invest*—in a small business, for example—to create future production, growth, and change. This is money used to create capital. Some people see their higher education in terms of the immediate workload and tasks. Others see education as the building of personal capital to expand their possibilities for gaining future benefits. *Change agents* is a related expression, referring to people who are catalysts for changing an organization. Capitalism prizes youthful enthusiasm and risk; it rewards those who are ready to adjust to the changes taking place. Young people in every generation seek a different vocabulary, different music, different dress, different ways. They see what they have and they want change from what came before. Capitalism rewards this impulse for change in the young and in the young in spirit.

The idea of community taps into what we might call a **traditionalist mindset**, seeing value in continuing things as they are. Let's not always ask how to change, for in our rashness we will lose more than what we gain. It can take years to recognize why the traditional ways are best, and change can destroy options that later we will wish we had. Change has one permanence: it forever destroys the traditions and practices that came before, in part because their value depended on their continuity. Good communities create ways of life and then *resist* the constant efforts to change, absorb, destroy, and replace. Markets will always create new automations, new lay-offs, new forms of displacement and dislocation. In the winds of change, what difference does it make that someone has worked within that job and profession for the last twenty-five years? It could all be over in a week or a day. This is the reality of calls for efficiency.[2] Real value, rather, is found in our traditions.

The allegorical narratives of these first two sections express an important debate about the extent to which work and capitalism, as a matter of historical development,

> This contrast between change and tradition helps explain why the cultural, spiritual, and religious traditions mentioned in Chapter 13 Section 3 often express caution about the role of markets and capitalism in society. Traditions preserve community and, if capitalism causes change, the challenge is how those changes impact traditions.

---

[2]*Efficiency* here refers to what traditionalists regard as the underside of the capitalist mindset: single-mindedly doing whatever reaps profits, without regard to its effect on people and communities. This use of the word doesn't refer to Pareto optimality, the subject of Chapters 6 and 7, but rather refers to Huxley's usage in the opening excerpt in Chapter 6.

TRADITION AND CHANGE

The Tony award–winning Broadway hit *Fiddler on the Roof* is set in 1905 Russia, prior to the revolution. It begins with Tveya singing "Tradition," which sets up the humorous, poignant, and heartbreaking contrast between a family and culture that values tradition against the ambitions of youth and the larger society that seeks change.

PROPERTY RIGHTS AND COMMUNITY

This discussion extends the study of markets and property rights in Chapters 1–3. If markets symbolize change and community symbolizes tradition, consider how *property rights* mediate this tension. Sometimes property rights act as a bulwark against change, as in aristocratic traditions that pass wealth from one generation to the next or laws that prohibit or restrict market exchanges and other market developments (Chapter 1 Section 5). However, sometimes property rights foster change, as in patents, privatization efforts, and government subsidies that are designed to facilitate innovation and development. Cultural norms and government shape how a property system balances change and tradition within any society. The rationale behind many property rights can be interpreted through this dynamic.

Michael Sandel's idea about market triumphalism relates to Todd May's discussion of friendship in Chapter 13 Section 2.

undermines long-standing ways of life. It's also a reflection about competing aspects of the human personality, sometimes disposed to change and sometimes to tradition, threads deeply woven into the human perspective. Within a single life, we may often want or need both.

What kind of institutions do you want to have in society? What do you think about this debate?

14.4   MARKET TRIUMPHALISM VERSUS CONCERN FOR THE COMMON GOOD

The preceding contrasts relate to a debate about human motivations that drive market exchanges, the topic of the next two sections. Some commentators argue that capitalism rewards rampant individualism and glorifies material pursuits, and these motives of self-gain undermine community building.

Let's give two examples defended by proponents of this position.

First, political philosopher Michael Sandel worries about cultures that experience what he calls **market triumphalism**, which he describes as all-encompassing cultural norms that redefine social activities in terms of the language and values of market exchange.[3] We outsource war by private contract, we develop for-profit schools and prisons, we pay children for good grades, and we characterize relationships with metaphors of consumption and investment. Through a market culture, we come to reenvision *all* the goods of life in terms of a bargained exchange for mutual benefit.

Sandel cites a case study of day care providers frustrated by parents who picked up their children too late from day care. The care providers addressed the problem by instituting a fine for late pickups. The point, obviously, was to reduce the number of late pickups. The result? Late pickups showed a marked *increase* rather than the hoped-for decrease. It seemed that many parents were quite happy to pay the fine amount and pick up their children later. Sandel offers this insight: the new rules led each side of the parent/caretaker partnership to view the relationship through the terms of a bargained exchange rather than the terms of the common good of child care. And this perception further damaged that relationship. A better approach, in his analysis, would have been to bring together errant parents and day care providers in a conversation to reaffirm the common good of caring for the child that should be at the heart of their

---

[3]Michael Sandel, *What Money Can't Buy: The Moral Limits of Markets* (Farrar, Straus, and Giroux, 2012).

ongoing relationship, and the responsibilities that this implies for both parties.

A second study that draws a similar conclusion was offered in *The Gift Relationship*, a famous 1970 study by British social scientist Richard M. Titmuss.[4] Titmuss argued that a market in blood donations, where people are paid for their donated blood, actually reduced the quality and amount of blood for needy patients, compared to a system of donations. Market exchanges, he argued in this case, crowded out relationships that are better premised on advancing a common good of caring about the health of the members of a community. Titmuss's study spurred a massive literature about the limits of using markets to address social problems. Recall how we contrasted market exchanges from gift-giving in Chapter 1. We can now extend that discussion. For Titmuss and others, a society must include a culture of community giving—in terms of time, effort, and resources—distinct from markets and their incentives.

Let's clarify the argument: relationships viewed through the lens of markets can undermine our ability to foster a community outlook. It's an argument about the internal attitudes that foster community, and the extent to which market institutions undermine those attitudes.

WHAT CREATES COMMUNITY?

In *Better Together: Building the American Community*[5], Robert D. Putnam and Lewis M. Feldstein offer twelve case studies of people who worked together to solve social problems and in doing so created thriving communities. These authors emphasize that organizations have no magic formula for creating community, but they found some trends. Successful communities tend to include people who commit a great deal of time and effort to organizational efforts with a willingness to participate in many redundancies of contact and communication. Repeated communication may seem inefficient from a distance, but the authors found that people built trust and social capital through these repeated exchanges. The authors also observed the value of narratives and story-telling among those who build community—in terms of people couching their ideas and objectives within their own and others' personal stories. Personal stories allow people with varied backgrounds who initially may not know each other to build commonalities and shared purposes.

14.5   MARKETS THAT BUILD COMMUNITIES

Not everyone draws pessimistic conclusions. For example, don't we have many motives for what we do? Recall the idea of enlightened self-interest introduced in Chapter 8. It seems possible for people to seek individual gain but also want to promote a common good at the same time. In this interpretation, market relationships can be satisfying in part *just because* people who participate in them believe that they contribute to a system that promotes the good of community beyond their own private gain. Consider why people follow laws in their commercial dealings. Is advancement of their self-interests the full answer? The alternative view is that people endorse a shared purpose as part of the reason for abiding by those laws. What are the actual motives that drive markets and do they really undermine community life? Advocates of the invisible hand argument (Chapter 8) point to the positive externalities of rising living standards that allow people to use their wealth to preserve and protect the communities that they cherish.

---

[4]Richard Titmuss, *The Gift Relationship: From Human Blood to Social Policy*, Ann Oakley and John Ashton eds. (New Press, 1997).

[5]Simon and Schuster, 2004.

This wealth allows people to pursue the common good in ways that impoverished societies can only dream about. Consider what people do with the wealth that a market system creates. U.S. citizens donate more than $300 billion per year to foundations and charities. "Without a doubt," writes *New York Times'* Stephanie Strom, "the biggest event in philanthropy this year [2010] was the Giving Pledge, a commitment by 40 of the wealthiest Americans to give away at least half of their fortunes, about $600 billion."[6] Another article begins:

> At the top of the economic ladder, many Americans are generous with their wealth and time, supporting efforts to meet basic human needs, education, the arts, religion, the environment, animal welfare and more.
>
> More than 98 percent of the nation's richest households give. Those in the top 3.1 percent are responsible for 60 to 75 percent of the $360 billion given for charitable work last year, said Claire Costello, national foundation executive for philanthropic management at Bank of America Merrill Lynch.[7]

Supporters of this argument note that philanthropy has a long historical record in the United States with many charitable foundations and other philanthropic activity dating back centuries. The excerpts above are about the very rich, but proponents of this view point to widespread donations by local businesses in local communities as more convincing evidence. In sum, many people see in capitalism a thriving system with people motivated to support community values, who well understand that excessive self-interest should be tempered with a vision for the common good. Market critics are not so convinced. They point to tax breaks as the more plausible self-interested explanation for motives of giving. They also argue that while living standards are rising for some, they are decreasing for others, with increasing stratification and widespread evidence of community decay, unalleviated by the incentives of a capitalist system.

Read the Case Study *Life Choices* only on MySearchLab

Thus, it is a lively question for debate whether, on balance, market motivations foster or diminish attitudes for seeking a common good in community.

14.6   THE MEANING OF THE COMMON GOOD

These debates prompt two fundamental questions: what *is* the common good? And, what does it mean to be motivated to pursue the common good? Different people use the idea of the *common good* in different ways, and these differences are revealing for interpreting contrasting accounts of ethics in business and economic life. In general, the **common good** refers to an aspiration, expectation, or hope that people will support policies and be motivated to make decisions by considering the interests of the community as a whole. But this aspiration can have more than one meaning and application. Let's consider several competing definitions.

A. THE COMMON GOOD AS THE SHARED INTERESTS OF EACH PERSON

In its most simple sense, the common good may refer to support for specific *public goods*, as defined and examined in Chapters 6–8. Parks, clean air, safe streets, thriving

[6]See http://www.nytimes.com/2010/11/11/giving/11PLEDGE.html?_r=1&ref=giving.
[7]See http://www.nytimes.com/2010/11/11/giving/11CHOICE.html?ref=giving; for *The New York Times* special edition on giving, see http://www.nytimes.com/pages/giving/index.html?ref=business.

arts and education, and friendly neighborhoods may identify the shared interests in the community, on the supposition that each person benefits by their presence. According to this definition, the common good identifies the set of mutually beneficial shared interests within a given community, with the expectation that we should be motivated to place priority on realizing these shared interests. We may have local, regional, national, or global shared interests, such as parks (local), roadways (regional), defense (national), or clean air (global).

Consider why this aspirational ideal is thought to be so important. In Chapter 7, we studied how self-interested motives can lead to the under-provision or destruction of public goods and commons areas, which could make each of us worse off. Thus, aspiring for the common good is in part a plea to embrace more altruistic motives for overcoming collective action problems, which, in turn, makes each individual better off. From this perspective a community-minded spirit is for the good of each and for the good of all. In this view, the motive to pursue the common good can find its rationale *within* an individualist perspective. What matters are individual interests, but only through cooperation can we realize these interests. These arguments have an interesting twist, as explored in our study of public goods and commons problems: to advance our self-interests, we must be motivated beyond our self-interest.

B. THE COMMON GOOD AS THE AGGREGATED INTERESTS OF ALL PERSONS

Sometimes we may support a policy that works *against* our own individual interests in the name of the common good. For example, a farmer may support regulations about farm waste to protect a downstream watershed. Let's suppose that the farmer knows that this regulation will not offer material benefit to him. What then could motivate support for this regulation? In this context appeals to the common good may be a way to express motives distinct from perceptions of self-interest. Appeals to the common good are then contrasted against egoistic or prudential motivations (Introduction, Section 4). The common good would then refer to any ethical outlook that takes into account some aggregated understanding of others' interest beyond one's own. For example, utilitarians can describe their theory *as* a theory of the common good: we ought to support policies that offer the most benefits for the community overall by taking each individual interest as valid, and then aggregating those interests to create some overall judgment of community interest. Consider another example: democracy offers a procedure to aggregate individual interests through voting. These democratic outcomes can be interpreted as expressing the common good of a nation.

In *The Moral Landscape: How Science Can Determine Human Values* (Free Press, 2010) writer Sam Harris offers a provocative science-based defense for how to think about the well-being of the aggregated whole.

The relevant community may be local, national, or global. Regardless of its range of application, the essential idea is that we should be motivated to consider other people's interests and support policies that offer significant overall benefit. Ethics is in part about embracing these more altruistic motives, and, unlike the first account provided above, these motives can conflict with the pursuit of our individual interests.

C. THE COMMON GOOD OF COMMUNITY DERIVED
FROM THE SOCIAL NATURE OF PERSONS

Although many arguments about the common good fall under the descriptions in A and B, not all of them do. These accounts still presume that value is defined through and by the individual person. For many, these interpretations of the common good miss a deeper metaphysical meaning about the social nature of human existence.

For example, French philosopher Jacques Maritain, a prominent drafter of the United Nations' Universal Declaration of Human Rights, writes, "The common good is [not] the mere collection of private goods . . . it is the good human life of the multitude of persons; it is their communion in good living."[8]

In this context the reference to a common good can be a descriptive, spiritual, religious, or metaphysical claim about what it means to be a person. The idea is often conveyed in poetry, such as this well-known poem by John Donne:

No Man Is an Island

No man is an island, entire of itself;
every man is a piece of the continent, a part of the main;
if a clod be washed away by the sea,
Europe is the less, as well as if a promontory were,
as well as if a manner of thy friends or of thine own were;
any man's death diminishes me, because I am involved in mankind.
And therefore never send to know for whom the bell tolls
it tolls for thee.[9]

What are the claims in these passages? Our common good, the poem suggests, is a totality of circumstances that enable people to experience fulfillment. Fulfillment, in turn, entails recognition that our identity is wrapped into our close relationship with others, whether we realize this or not. A common good conviction in this respect conveys a metaphysical claim that the individual is a part of a larger whole. To evoke the common good, therefore, is often to draw on ideas that contrast *against* a utilitarian tradition that centers all value within the atomistic individual. Used in this way, the common good connects more readily with ancient Western and non-Western traditions that conceive of human life in terms of one's role within a larger society or organic unity, as embedded in many religious traditions today. These traditions often emphasize how recognition of a common good is necessary for attaining spiritual fulfillment.

These religious and philosophical traditions have no single approach for developing ideas about the common good. As mentioned in Chapter 13, these worldviews offer holistic understandings of the meanings and purposes of life, and they interpret the demands of ethics from within a comprehensive interpretation of reality. Although it is not possible to define one single common good conviction across all of these traditions, they typically share a vision of human reality that seeks concord among people, believing that at some deep level, everyone is connected to everyone else and that all people should live in harmony (in community or communion) with each other. These elevated reflections are often the subject of literature, poetry, and religion.

---

[8]Jacques Maritain, *The Person and the Common Good* (London: Geoffrey Bles, 1947). Maritain (1882–1973) was an influential proponent and interpreter of the thoughts of St. Thomas Aquinas. This quotation first came to my notice from Andrew M. Yuengart's essay "The Common Good for Economists," *Faith and Philosophy*, 38 (2001), pp. 1–9.

[9]John Donne (1572–1631) was an English poet, satirist, and lawyer. This poem is among his most famous. As a full disclosure, a reviewer of this book said that students studying ethical concepts in business and economics would never take poetry seriously, so keeping this poem is a poetic test case.

14.7 COMMUNITARIANISM

The debate about whether capitalism supports or undermines community is closely associated with a philosophical movement called **communitarianism**. Although the writings within this area are diverse, communitarian arguments tend to express one of the following three central claims about the relation of the individual to the community:

First, people's sense of ethics can develop only within some particular community or social context. This is a descriptive claim that moral beliefs form within communities.

Second, people are social by nature, which is a metaphysical claim about what it means to be a person. In previous chapters, we considered how values of freedom, equality, and desert are often interpreted as metaphysical claims about who we are. For example, a commitment to freedom may express a belief that by nature we are free; a commitment to equality may express the belief that by nature we are each other's equals. Similarly, communitarians say that we are, by nature, social creatures.

Third, communitarians argue that living in communities is valuable. This is a normative claim about the importance of protecting and fostering communities within any society.[10]

Let's illustrate a communitarian perspective by reevaluating the island scenario and efficiency arguments in Chapter 6. The island scenario describes a normative framework by presenting pre-community individuals who encounter each other on an island. For communitarians, this scenario is both descriptively and metaphysically inaccurate. Communities shape and determine people's sense of ethics, their sense of identity, and the meanings that they give to the world around them and to their relationships. For a communitarian, a study of ethics must start with concrete facts about how particular communities have influenced individual lives. The island scenario completely misses the first two communitarian claims described above. Anthropologist Ruth Benedicts expresses these descriptive and metaphysical claims in the excerpt that began this chapter.

Further, proponents of an efficiency perspective assess capitalism and markets in terms of whether it makes the *individual* better off. This normative perspective misses the third communitarian claim above. We should assess markets and capitalism in the communitarian view from the point of view of whether an economic system supports or undermines communities. Many communitarians worry that capitalism encourages rampant **individualism** and **materialism**, and these outlooks, sufficiently spread throughout society, undermine people's social orientation for seeking the common good in community. *Individualism* refers to theories or attitudes that express the commitment that the value and interests of the individual should take relative or absolute precedence over any other concern. *Materialism* refers to a cultural tendency in which material acquisition becomes the most important pursuit in life.[11] A closely related idea is *consumerism*, which refers to a culture that encourages a never-ending desire to purchase goods and services.

The point to emphasize in this section is how communitarianism represents a distinctive ethical perspective. Recall the first chapter on markets, when we asked, What do you see when you see markets (Chapter 1 Section 3)? We have considered ideas about welfare, freedom, equality, rights, and desert for observing and assessing capitalism, and

[10]See Daniel Bell, "Communitarianism," *Stanford Encyclopedia of Philosophy*, http://plato.stanford.edu/entries/communitarianism/.

[11]In philosophy, *materialism* also refers to other doctrines unrelated to this social and economic idea.

deciding how to make decisions in economic life. Suppose that we now form our sense of ethics within communities, and acknowledge that we are social by nature and that communities are essential for living a fulfilling life. As we have done for other values in preceding chapters, we can return to the model of ethics and values (see Figure I.1 in the Introduction), isolate on one particular value, such as the value of community in this chapter, and ask, "What is the best way to combine a sense of ethics, personal incentives, and institutions to promote and protect community?"

14.8 JUSTICE AND THE COMMON GOOD: COMPLEMENTARY OR CONFLICTING VALUES?

This section compares the ideas in this chapter against some of the approaches to ethics and values developed in Chapters 6–14.

A. A PROGRESSION OF IDEAS

Let's start by noticing three broad categories of thought developed in this book: *welfare analysis* (efficiency and utilitarianism: Chapters 6–8), *justice-based approaches* (freedom, rights, equality, and desert: Chapters 9–12), and *community-based approaches* (relationships, character, and community: Chapters 13 and 14). Although these divisions aren't always clear-cut, they reflect distinctive approaches to our subject as depicted in Figure 14.2.

FIGURE 14.2   **The Categories of Ethical and Institutional Analysis**

Three Categories of Ethical and Institutional Analysis

Justice-Based Approaches
Freedom
Rights
Equality
What People
Deserve
(Chapters 9–12)

Welfare-Based Approaches
Efficiency
Utilitarianism
(Chapters 6–8)

Community-Based Approaches
Relationships
Character
Community
(Chapters 13, 14)

Each perspective can be understood as responsive to a perceived incompleteness of the other perspective. For example, welfare approaches are consequentialist: they approach ethics by assessing outcomes. However insightful these theories, many people believe that assessing outcomes doesn't capture all of ethics, as emphasized by those within deontological traditions. Proponents of justice-based approaches often contrast their views against those of utilitarians, as seen in *A Theory of Justice* by American philosopher John Rawls. Many argue, for example, that we have *rights* that should constrain any utilitarian objective, or that we are free and equal as persons, which says something about who we are, not merely about the outcomes that we should achieve. In a similar vein, others argue that justice is about giving people their due, which prompts a focus on theories about what people deserve. Without returning to those details, we could summarize Chapters 6–12 by saying this: the ethics and values of economic life are both about what makes people better off (Chapters 6–8) and what conditions create justice (Chapters 9–12).

And yet, even these insights and arguments do not capture the fuller moral landscape, according to supporters of the views of the last two chapters. An economic and political system that improves the welfare of its citizens, protects rights, realizes liberty, secures equality, and gives people what they deserve is an inspiring ideal for a just society. These values also provide much insight for guiding our decisions in economic life. And yet, we can ask further questions about the culture of this society: do people experience valuable relationships, virtue, and well-lived lives? Do they experience community and a common good that provides meaning and fulfillment? We might describe this difference by saying that a prosperous and just society may lead to—but is not identical with—achieving a good community.

This summary proceeds at a high level of generality, and so it misses details and qualifications that we will not pursue here. But it does offer this insight for a study of business and economic life. We may tailor our interests about the ethics and values of business and economic life by focusing on conditions of *prosperity*, *justice*, or a *good community*, and this book provides ample materials to consider all three perspectives.

Those who place most emphasis on the value of a prosperous society will gravitate to the analysis in Chapters 6–8; on justice to Chapters 9–12; and on community to Chapters 13 and 14. A focus on prosperity will prompt conversation about how to make decisions and organize business and economic life to improve our own and others' *welfare*. A focus on justice will lead to conversation about the *freedoms, rights, equality, and just deserts* that ought to be part of our economic system. And a focus on community will lead to conversation about our *responsibilities* for pursuing the *common good* in support of community. Advocates of this last perspective may even begin their reflections about ethics through the ideas in Chapters 13 and 14, and then proceed backward through the other chapters, integrating ideas about justice and welfare within their holistic vision of life.

ETHICS AND VALUES

What are the values that you draw on to express your sense of ethics within markets and business? These need not presume the dominant values of the culture. You can apply the methods of this book for investigating those values and how they fit into an overall view of business and economic life. They may or may not focus on efficiency, liberty, equality, or the others presented here. But whatever they are, you will inevitably encounter your own questions about the sense of ethics that you should bring to your decisions, how your motives and beliefs cohere or conflict with the incentives of the system, and how to assess the institutions that surround you and affect your life.

B. The Relevance of Culture for Ethics and the Common Good

A second contrast across all the chapters is about the role of *culture* for ethics, a concept introduced in Chapter 3 on property rights. In the chapters that followed, we studied a range of ethics and values for assessing property rights, markets, and corporations. But what is the relevance of culture *for understanding ethics*? We considered consequentialist and deontological perspectives, as well as many values: welfare, freedom, equality, and others.

Some people argue that these values are abstract and universal—and they can be understood independently from any particular cultural setting and applied across cultures for offering guidance in business and economic life. Others, such as communitarians, argue that ethics is culturally embedded in the sense that the study of ethics cannot be separated from the study of particular cultures. For these proponents, ethics *is* the study of culture.

Thus, all of the values in this book could be interpreted as universal and abstract, or as cultural expressions of a particular time and place. It's also interesting to notice a related trend across the chapters: proponents of the values of liberty, rights, and equality (Chapters 9–11) tend toward a universal and abstract understanding of values. Those who focus on relationships, character, and community (Chapters 13 and 14) tend toward a culturally embedded understanding of values. The chapter on desert (Chapter 12) provides an interesting transition between these approaches. When people debate desert, they often blend universal and culturally specific understandings of ethics (see Figure 14.3).[12]

The progression of chapters from abstract to socially embedded values is a welcome progression for some, particularly for those who believe that ethics is primarily about social context and the nuances of particular situations. Others are less enthusiastic about particularizing ethics too much if it introduces cultural relativism, indeterminacy, and the biases of a culture that they hope considerations of ethics can counteract.

Consider how communitarian Daniel Bell characterizes and defends the importance of culture for the study of ethics:

> *The distinctive communitarian contribution has been to cast doubt on universal theories grounded exclusively in the liberal moralities of the Western world, on the grounds that cultural particularity should both make one sensitive to the possibility of justifiable areas of difference between the West and the rest and to the need for more cross-cultural dialogue for the purpose of improving the current thin human rights regime.*[13]

FIGURE 14.3   How Do You Interpret the Nature of Values?

Universal and   **Or**   Culturally and Historically
Abstract?   Embedded?

$\longleftrightarrow$

Efficiency, Liberty, Rights, Equality, Desert, Relationships, Character, Community

---

[12]For a good example of this blending, see George Sher, *Desert* (Princeton University Press, 1987).

[13]Daniel Bell, *Stanford Encyclopedia of Philosophy*, http://plato.stanford.edu/entries/communitarianism/.

His first point is to interpret the values of freedom, rights, and equality as liberal moralities of the West rather than timeless universal theories. His second point is to emphasize the advantages of taking a communitarian approach to ethics. If we understand values as culturally embedded, we are more likely to be sensitive to justifiable differences in values across cultures, and we are likely to be better at cross-cultural dialogue. (For this point, see also Chapter 13 Section 3.)

Given the communitarian emphasis that ethical ideas are highly influenced by culture, one practical implication is to be ready for international business relationships that might require great sensitivity to these cultural differences. Cultural experiences can lead to many different interpretations of what counts as prosperity, justice, and the common good. The role of culture has particular impact in current debates about human rights, given that claims about human rights are an attempt to devise a global ethics that is both universal in scope but sensitive to varied ethical traditions across all cultures.

> See Chapter 10 Section 2 for more discussion about the nature of human rights.

14.9   SUMMARY

This chapter examined the role of communal values in relation to the ethics of business and economic life. Is capitalism inherently individualistic in its orientation to value, expressing the triumph of efficiency over all other values? The discipline of economics, with its emphasis on efficiency and welfare, is so dominant that it may seem that markets can only be understood normatively in these terms, joining an explanatory study of markets with a commitment to individual welfare.

But we can separate the study of markets from these individualist underpinnings—in fact, this chapter attests to that possibility. For example, we can endorse communal values and then debate whether markets and capitalism support good communities. Some people will criticize capitalism based on these values, arguing that the system historically exaggerates values of individualism and materialism, undercutting the grounds for good community life. Others counter by identifying within capitalist societies thriving communities based on common good values. This chapter considers that intriguing debate.

KEY TERMS

creative destruction   market triumphalism   individualism
capitalist mindset   common good   materialism
traditionalist mindset   communitarianism

DISCUSSION QUESTIONS

1. How much charitable giving (in money or time) do you do, if any? If you have enough money to cover your personal expenses, do you feel any responsibility to provide charitable benefits to a larger community? which community? Why or why not? Do others have responsibilities in your view, such as corporations? government? Why them if not you?

2. Suppose workers could choose to receive lesser wages with an understanding that no one would be laid off due to a downturn in the economy. Would you agree to this? On what basis? Out of concern for a common good?

3. Communitarians often criticize global capitalism. Antiglobalization protests over the past decade range from zoning board battles over the creation of a local Walmart to indigenous peoples' traditions threatened by economic development. But not everyone believes that capitalism is so bad for tradition and culture. Economist Tyler Cowen argues that commerce and culture are allies, and that creative destruction and free exchange are the best things around (see his *Creative Destruction: How Globalization Is Changing the World's Cultures*).[14] What are your views about the relationship between capitalism, culture, and community?

4. Environmentalist Aldo Leopold advocated an expansive notion of the common good that embraced all living creatures. Environmental ethics, he believed, should follow the following principle: "A thing is right when it tends to preserve the integrity, stability, and beauty of the biotic community."[15] Is this ethic a promising *common good* approach for addressing environmental challenges that businesses face, in your view? What are some alternatives?

5. Identify a group that matters to you, such as your coworkers, your local community, or the citizens of your nation. List what you regard to be the shared interest of each. To what extent does business advance or impede those shared interests?

6. Can people in a work environment identify a common good? (Often, those who take a common good approach leave its definition incomplete, with the hope of bringing people into a conversation to find agreement. In this respect, the approach has some similarity to the social contract tradition introduced in Chapter 11

Section 5, which interprets ethics as whatever results from an agreement among persons. An important difference between these approaches is that, for common good proponents, the agreement itself does not ground its validity. The agreement simply helps identify what the common good is, which has independent validity.)

7. Is capitalist culture a corrupting influence on communities?

8. Do duties to oneself and duties to the common good ever conflict?

9. Is universal health care justified on a common good argument?

10. Suppose some automation process makes jobs redundant and displaces workers, such as automating turnpike payments via EZ-Pass lanes. Is this change an efficiency gain? How so? What is the best way to describe the costs? Costs in terms of what?

11. We introduced the concept of group rights in Chapter 10. Some people support the idea of group rights to preserve communities. Reconsider Wenar's argument about globalization in Chapter 10 through the approach described in this chapter. Do indigenous peoples have group rights over their traditional practices that should block the ability of pharmaceuticals to patent traditional medicinal treatments?

12. In what sense is the ideal of freedom in tension with, or supportive of, traditional values?

13. Why do we always talk about the *good old days*, even if we're not that old? Is this reflexive attitude unjustified nostalgia about days that probably weren't that good? Or is this our traditionalist mindset intuitively recognizing a lifetime of losses that we can barely understand?

14. Is it possible to establish a capitalist society that values community and the common good?

---

[14]Tyler Cowen, *Creative Destruction: How Globalization Is Changing the World's Cultures* (Princeton University Press, 2004).

[15]Aldo Leopold, *A Sand County Almanac* (Oxford University Press, 1949), pp. 224, 225.

15. If rising living standards come at the expense of environmental degradation, how should a common good approach analyze this conflict?

16. Do online forums create valuable sources of community? Explain.

17. Is there such a thing as a common good? Explain.

18. Nineteenth-century American poet Walt Whitman envisioned economic and social life in cooperative harmony, where each person's individuality is most fully expressed through life in community. Interpret and assess what the following poem conveys, by drawing on the range of values in this book.

I Hear America Singing

I hear America singing, the varied carols I hear,
Those of mechanics, each one singing his as it
   should be blithe and strong,
The carpenter singing his as he measures his
   plank or beam,
The mason singing his as he makes ready for
   work, or leaves off work,
The boatman singing what belongs to him in his
   boat, the deckhand singing on the steamboat
   deck,
The shoemaker singing as he sits on his bench,
   the hatter singing as he stands,
The wood-cutter's song, the ploughboy's on his
   way in the morning, or at noon intermission
   or at sundown,
The delicious singing of the mother, or of the
   young wife at work, or of the girl sewing or
   washing,
Each singing what belongs to him or her and to
   none else,
The day what belongs to the day—at night the
   party of young fellows, robust, friendly,
Singing with open mouths their strong melodi-
   ous songs.

19. How are technological advances affecting our notions of the common good and community? What are some examples?

GLOSSARY

act utilitarianism the view that an individual action is ethically right if it maximizes social utility.

altruism the view that people can be motivated to act to advance others' welfare without any reference to their own self-regarding desires.

arguments the process of giving underlying reasons to support a set of beliefs.

backward-looking reasons reasons to act based on constraints or principles that apply independently from assessing the consequences of that action.

benefit corporations for-profit corporations with a special legal status because they specify social responsibility as part of their core mission.

blocked exchanges the prohibition of a specific market exchange by law or custom.

board of directors elected by the shareholders, they oversee the activities and management of the corporation.

business and economic life the range of business, financial, and economic institutions that include interactions and decisions by consumers, managers, investors, employees, and owners.

business ethics a study of moral and social responsibility in relation to business practices.

capitalist mindset the outlook of taking existing resources and activities as leverage for future growth.

character refers to the dispositional qualities that give shape to who that person is and explain the underlying reasons for that person's actions.

civil society the voluntary associations of a society that are not government.

claim-rights/duties specify one type of property relationship that people may have with each other with respect to some thing.

collective action problems (or **social dilemmas**) choice situations where all the people involved would be made better off by some joint action and yet it's individually rational for each person to choose against this joint action. Also called Prisoner's Dilemmas.

common good an aspiration, expectation, or hope that people will support policies and be motivated to make decisions by considering the interests of the community as a whole.

communitarianism a philosophical movement defined by its reaction against liberal political theories that, according to these critics, devalue the importance of community.

comparable worth the view that comparable jobs deserve comparable pay.

commons any good whose benefits are nonexcludable and depletable.

communal property real or personal property owned by some collective whose members have broad liberty-rights to use that property.

conflict of interest occurs when some interest potentially or actually affects the ability of one or more persons to make an impartial judgment in a professional role when the expectation is that judgments in this area should not be influenced by that interest.

consequentialism an ethical theory that people should choose to do that which produces the best overall consequences.

consequentialist ethics for property rights assesses the property rights of a society by examining the consequences of these property rights among all those affected by those arrangements.

copyrights exclusive legal protections to copy, be credited with, and financially benefit from artistic or literary work.

corporate responsibility officers (CROs) managers who design and oversee the strategy of social and environmental responsibility of a corporation and who typically report to the chief executive officer (CEO).

corporate social responsibility (CSR) any social responsibilities of corporations that exist beyond making profits within the law.

corporate social responsibility movement the range of developments and arguments from the past several decades that convey a commitment to corporate actions beyond maximizing profits within the law.

corporation   a legal entity recognized by the state with rights and responsibilities apart from the persons running or working for the organization.

cost/benefit analysis   a decision-making process that weighs the total expected benefits of a decision against the total expected costs.

creative destruction   the cyclical process in capitalism whereby old forms of capital and production are replaced by new forms of capital and production.

CSR annual reports   public documents that showcase the nonfinancial performance of a corporation over the preceding year, including its responsiveness to stakeholder interests.

CSR rating agencies   organizations that rate corporations on their social and environmental performance beyond their financial performance.

CSR-related shareholder proposal   a resolution by a shareholder or group of shareholders that there be a vote that would require the corporation to take specific action related to socially responsible behavior.

cultural ethical relativist   an individual who believes that ethical standards are relative to a given culture. That is, right and wrong are defined by a given culture, and there is no further truth about what counts as right or wrong.

cultural norms   generally endorsed beliefs and behaviors of people within a given culture about what is appropriate or inappropriate.

culture   the shared norms, values, and practices that guide and shape some group or organization.

customary property rights   property rights regulated and authorized by custom.

democratic capitalism   a political, economic, and social system that combines a democratic political system with a capitalist economic system.

deontological ethics for property rights   assesses the property rights of a society in terms of ethical principles and rules that apply independently from analyzing the consequences of those property rights among all those affected by those arrangements. See also nonconsequentialist ethical theories.

descriptive (or **explanatory**) **analysis**   any study whose aim is to describe (or explain) how and why things happen.

desert basis   explains the worthiness of a person or persons deserving something, based on some prior action of that person or some personal characteristic.

desperate exchanges   trades of last resort that occur when and because one party to the exchange is in desperate circumstances.

doctrine of the golden mean   Aristotle's view that a virtuous disposition requires character traits that aim at the mean between two extreme dispositions. For example, courage is a virtue for Aristotle, which is defined as the mean between cowardice and recklessness, which are the corresponding vices as extremes.

domestic law   the law for citizens of a particular nation-state, with varying levels of local, state, and national jurisdiction.

duty (or **obligation**)   a requirement to do something.

economic system   the institutions and property arrangements that directly support and facilitate market activity.

egalitarians   individuals who argue for greater equality in society.

eminent domain   the Constitutional Fifth Amendment power of the government to take property from citizens if the taking is for a public use and includes just compensation.

entitlement theory of justice   a theory that specifies what must be true for private property holdings to be legitimate.

entrepreneurial spirit   an inclination toward creativity, risk-taking, and innovation that is a factor of production for creating a successful business.

epistemic device   any method or process that serves to increase knowledge about some subject area.

equal opportunity society   an aspiration that everyone within a given society has the chance to reach his or her full potential and pursue happiness against a backdrop of similar constraints and opportunities.

equal outcomes (or **equal opportunity**)   efforts to equalize the results of a process.

ethical absolutism   the view that some ethical beliefs apply absolutely across all cultures and beliefs in the sense that their validity is not relative to any particular cultural framework.

ethical egoism   the belief that people ought to do whatever is in their self-interests.

ethical objectivity   the view that ethical beliefs can express objective truths that are not merely a function of the subjective beliefs of each individual.

ethical pluralism   the view that many values are important and they do not all reduce to or derive from some common value that can explain away all conflict or trade-offs among values.

ethical relativism   the view that normative standards of evaluation are relative to the beliefs and practices of a group, culture, or individual.

ethical theory   an attempt to bring systematic order to ethical reflection. Ethical theories organize different ways to express our sense of ethics, and they convey a view about what ethics is really about.

ethical universalism   the view that at least some ethical beliefs have validity that applies universally across all individuals and cultures.

ethics and values of business and economic life   theories and beliefs about how people should make decisions and what is valuable both within and about business and economic life.

ethics of care   a feminist ethical theory that emphasizes the importance of bringing attitudes of sympathy and empathy to decision-making.

ethics of individual decision-making   the study of what choices people should make, how people should live, and how people should treat each other.

ethics tests   a quick-reference set of principles for helping people figure out ethical decision-making in any particular circumstance. See epistemic device.

eudaimonistic ethics   ethical theories grounded through reflections about how to live a good human life.

existentialism   a late-nineteenth-and-early-twentieth-century philosophical movement that pursues philosophy by examining the human condition, especially the perception that life is absurd.

fair equality of opportunity   a society with laws and practices that ensure that people can pursue opportunities to enhance their life prospects without unequal impediments caused by factors that are not their responsibility, such as in-born differences in social and economic class.

false consciousness   the systemic distortion of ideas that serve the interests of those who have the most power rather than the truth about appropriate social relations.

formal equality of opportunity   a society with laws and practices that ensure that people can pursue opportunities under conditions where positions are open to all applicants and are awarded to those with the most merits, as defined by the requirements of the position.

forward-looking reasons   reasons to act based on the consequences of that choice.

free-riding problem   occurs when those who enjoy the benefits of a good or service without paying the costs.

fundamental equality   the belief that all persons have the same worth.

gifts   goods or services offered without an exchange from the other as a condition of the offering.

global governance gaps   corporate activities subject to no effective law or regulation.

goal-oriented ethical reasoning   ethical decision-making that is based on or promotes an ethical value or goal.

Gross Domestic Product (GDP)   the final sales of all goods and services produced within a nation-state in a single year.

group rights   rights that apply to a group of individuals independent from the rights of the individuals who are part of the group.

human rights   rights that apply to all humans no matter their cultural or other differences.

ideal markets   idealized conditions of trade that imply the result that trade creates efficiency gains.

immunity/disability   a property relationship that people may have with each other with respect to some item.

incentive-compatible institutional design   institutions that produce good outcomes but depend only on people pursuing their self-interests rather than requiring some heightened sense of ethics to motivate action.

individual ethical relativist   an individual who believes that ethical standards are relative to what an individual thinks, with no further valid standard of ethical evaluation.

individual rights   rights that apply to individual persons.

individualism   theories or attitudes that the value and interests of the individual should take relative or absolute precedence over other ethical concerns.

inefficiencies   occur when people fail to take advantage of mutually beneficial gains, or when someone is made worse off by an interaction.

institutional desert   theories that define what people deserve based on the purposes and legitimate expectations of institutions, which are then justified through values other than desert.

institutional legitimacy   the conditions under which political, economic, and social institutions are acceptable and justified. Legitimacy can be understood descriptively in terms of a people's widespread perceptions that institutions are legitimate. It can also be defined normatively as whatever conditions ultimately justify those institutions.

institutional point of view   ethical analysis that assesses institutions rather than people's actions as the subject matter of ethical inquiry.

instrumental rationality   practical reasoning that allows agents to find effective ways to achieve some given end.

intellectual property   creations of the mind: inventions, literary and artistic works, and symbols, names, images, and designs used in commerce (http://www.wipo.int/about-ip/en/).

international law   rules and procedures that specify relations among states, individuals, businesses, and other international organizations.

invisible hand model   a framework of belief that markets combine with self-interested incentives to produce good results without anyone directly intending those good results, and without extended roles for ethical motivations and government in economic life.

just deserts   what people deserve or are due based on who they are or what they have accomplished.

law   a system of rules that function as the final coercive authority of a geographical region, usually enforced by a set of institutions, such as a government.

law and regulation model   framework of belief that government should exert a far more extensive role in markets, given the belief that self-interested incentives often lead to bad results from an ethical point of view.

legal property rights   property rights regulated by governments.

legal rights   rights recognized by some given legal system.

liberty-rights/no claim-right   specify one type of property relationship that people may have with each other with respect to some item.

market failure   occurs when seemingly rational people fail to achieve mutually beneficial exchanges when they could have or, even worse, when they make their lives worse by their market interactions.

market triumphalism   cultural norms that interpret all social activities in terms of the language and values of market exchange.

markets   willing buyers and sellers exchanging items that they value.

materialism   a cultural tendency in which material pursuits become what matters most in life. (In philosophy, materialism also refers to other doctrines distinct from this social and economic idea.) A closely related idea is *consumerism*, which refers to a culture that encourages a never-ending desire to purchase goods and services.

metaethics   an academic discipline that studies the nature and objectivity of ethics and addresses debates about relativism and truth.

metaphysical conceptions of the person   theories about what is ultimately real about being a person.

metaphysics   the study of reality.

microlending   loans to the very poor in situations where traditional banks would judge those applicants as non-creditworthy.

mode of treatment   the fitting type of treatment that a person deserves, depending on what a person does or who that person is, such as receiving a punishment, reward, prize, compensation, or recognition.

moral integrity   the idea that our actions, emotions, and moral beliefs cohere, integrate, and reinforce each other.

moral side-constraints   prohibitions on specific behaviors that are valid no matter the consequences that result from adhering to that prohibition.

natural rights   rights that human beings have by virtue of their nature as persons.

negative externalities   spillover effects on people outside a given transaction or activity that make third parties worse off.

negative liberty   freedom as a lack of interference in doing what we wish.

negative rights   rights of noninterference.

non-consequentialist ethical theories   theories that identify ethical reasons for action independently from weighing the consequences of a choice.

nongovernmental organizations (NGOs)   organizations that promote a social purpose that are not governmental organizations. The term was popularized by the United Nations. Within the United States, NGOs are often called *non-profits* or *civil society* organizations.

norm   any value or rule designed to influence our judgments or decision-making.

normative analysis   the study of what ought to be, how people should value and assess situations, and how people should act and live.

normative analysis of business and economic life   a study of the actions and assessments that people should make within and about business and economic life.

normative model   a representation of a normative system of thought and how the parts of the system relate to each other.

objectivist accounts of welfare   normative theories about welfare based on the central claim that a person's welfare is determined by factors that go beyond the subjects' own assessment of their welfare.

ownership   typically occurs when a person, business, government, or collective has *claim-rights* to exclusively possess, use, manage, and receive income with respect to that thing; *powers* to transfer, waive, exclude, and abandon that item; *liberties* to consume or destroy it; *immunities* from expropriation; *duties* not to use harmfully; and *liabilities* from court judgments.

pareto improvement (or **efficiency gain**)   when at least one person is made better off and no one is made worse off by moving from one situation to the next.

pareto optimality (or **fully efficient**)   when there is no feasible alternative state in which at least one person can be made better off without making someone else worse off.

patents   exclusive rights granted by government to an inventor that creates duties on others not to use or make a profit from a patented invention without the inventor's permission.

personal point of view   ethical analysis whose subject matter is about what personal decisions to make in any given situation.

personal property   tangible or intangible movable property.

personal rights   relationships among persons when the subject of these relationships is the persons themselves, not some other thing. For example, rights over our bodies are often called personal rights in contrast to rights over our car, which are called property rights.

political legitimacy   whatever conditions justify the government's use of coercive power.

positive liberty   freedom as people's ability to control their circumstances.

Positive rights   rights to assistance.

positive sum game   interactions where one person's gain is compatible with the other person gaining as well.

powers/liabilities   specify a type of property relationship that people may have with each other with respect to some item.

pragmatism   a philosophical tradition in the United States at the turn of the twentieth century that focuses on the way that ideas connect with practical consequences.

preferences   individuals' beliefs and attitudes that affect how those persons evaluate situations and make choices.

principle of justice in initial acquisition   specifies when a person who acquires an unowned item can be legitimately entitled to that item.

principle of justice in rectification   specifies how to correct and compensate for injustices that have occurred from violations of the principles of justice in initial acquisition and transfer.

principle of justice in transfer   specifies when a person can legitimately transfer an item to another person.

principle of limited liability   the principle that stockholders are typically immune from paying any debts of the corporation beyond their initial investment in purchasing the stock.

private goods   goods and services that are excludable and rival.

private property   real or personal property with an owner or owners who have claim-rights to exclude others from the use of that property.

professional ethics   ethics as it applies in professional settings.

professional ethics model   a framework of belief that no matter the interaction between markets and government, good societal outcomes can occur only if people within business and economic life bring their sense of ethics into their decision-making.

proliferation of rights   the multiplication of claims about people's rights to the extent that these claims become indistinguishable from claims about what people want.

property   owned things or relations among people with respect to things.

property relations   the ways that people relate to each other with respect to things.

property rights   property relations of ownership that the owner finds advantageous.

psychological egoism   the theory that people are, or can only be, motivated by their self-interests.

public goods   goods or services that are nonexcludable and nonrival.

public goods problems   whenever rational self-interest creates voluntary incentives for people to fail to produce a public good under conditions where all parties would be made better off if they had created the public good. These problems are a type of collective action problem.

public property   property usually owned by the government and often with broad liberty-rights for citizen use.

Rawls's two principles of justice   the principles that persons within a fair bargaining process would choose to live by when placed under a veil of ignorance. According to philosopher John Rawls, the two principles chosen would be that (1) each person has an equal right to the most extensive basic liberty compatible with a similar liberty for others; (2) social and economic inequalities are arranged so that (a) they are of the greatest benefit to the least-advantaged members of society (the difference principle) and (b) offices and positions are open to everyone under conditions of fair equality.

real property   real estate.

resource curse   countries rich in natural resources but are among the poorest in overall economic conditions.

rule of law   when a society has general, public, and understandable laws that apply equally to each citizen.

rule utilitarianism   the view that a rule is ethically right if the general adherence to the rule maximizes social utility.

self-interest   individuals pursuing the satisfaction of their own preferences, as developed in the context of the invisible hand model.

sense of ethics   the broad mix of ethical motives, sentiments, conscience, principles, and beliefs that influence people's actions.

separation thesis   the view that business and ethics are unrelated to each other.

social constructs   ideas whose foundation and perceived validity derive solely from the context and contingencies of the social setting.

social contract theory   any normative theory that derives the authority and content of ethics and justice as a result of a real or hypothetical contract among persons.

socially responsible investing (SRI)   investment strategies that place positive weight on the social performance of corporations beyond their financial performance.

stakeholder theory of corporations   a comprehensive theory of corporate responsibility that corporations ought to serve the interests of stakeholders.

stakeholders   all those who are significantly affected by corporate activities, including but not limited to stockholders, the community, customers, employees, suppliers, and those concerned about the environment.

stockholder theory of corporations   a comprehensive theory of corporate responsibility that corporations ought to serve the interests of stockholders, which is to maximize profits within the law.

stockholders   owners of the corporation who have stock in the company and typically retain claim-rights to sell their shares and receive returns on the profits of the corporation.

subjectivist accounts of welfare   normative theories about welfare based on the central claim that a person's welfare is determined solely by the subjects whose welfare is at stake.

supererogatory actions   good actions that are not morally required.

taking   an unwilling exchange or transfer.

teleological theories of ethics   ethical theories that specify a goal or end as the ultimate ethical good to achieve.

trademarks   signs that identify a distinctive source for the goods or services associated with those signs. The trademark enables its creator to file a lawsuit if someone is using that word, phrase, symbol, or design for purposes that are unauthorized by the creator of the trademark.

traditionalist mindset   the outlook of valuing existing ways of life and resources and finding ways to preserve those activities so that they remain the same over time.

transaction costs   costs associated with completing an exchange, including a transaction fee or the time and energy required to complete the transaction.

undeserved inequalities   inequalities due to factors that the affected individuals were not responsible for creating.

United Nations Global Compact   Founded in 2000 to specify stakeholder principles of social responsibility that all corporate signatories to the compact would voluntarily accept as constraints on pursuing profits.

utilitarianism   the ethical theory that the best actions and institutions are those that produce the consequence of maximizing the aggregate utiilty of everyone involved. Utilitarianism is a type of consequentialism.

values   refer to whatever standards we use to judge situations.

vices   refer to ethically objectionable character traits.

virtue ethics   an account of the qualities that define and differentiate good and bad character.

virtues   ethically admirable character traits.

voluntary choice   according to one writer discussed in Chapter 9, these are choices made when there are acceptable options, or if there is only one option, it is good enough that the choice is for reasons other than the fact that it's the only option.

voluntary exchanges   according to one writer discussed in Chapter 1, these are exchanges that either side to a trade can veto.

welfare (or well-being)   what is good for a person, group, organization, or society.

whistleblowing   the act of telling others outside the regular chain of command that some unethical or illegal activity is occurring within an organization.

INDEX

absolutism, ethical, 52
action(s)
  assessing the consequences of, 12–13
  supererogatory, 15
actus reus (law), 14
act utilitarianism, 130
Adelphia, 71
admirable aspirations, 203
The Affluent Society (Galbraith), 105
Alcoholics Anonymous, 221
Ali, Ayaan Hirsi, 238
All I Really Need to Know I Learned in
  Kindergarten (Fulghum), 1
altruism, 20, 71
Amazon, 104
Anderson, Sarah, 59
Angie's List (website), 104
Aquinas, St. Thomas, 30
argument(s)
  defined, 2, 3
  ethical, 66, 67, 82–83
  invisible hand, 8
  law and regulation, 8–9
  professional ethics, 9
Aristotle, 15, 30, 138, 229, 230, 231, 233
Arthur Anderson, 71
artists, rights of, 54
aspirations, 203–204
  admirable, 203
  moral, 203
  obligations and, 203–204
Athenian democracy, 164

backward-looking reasons, 14
bank bailouts, 215
Bell, Daniel, 254
Benedicts, Ruth, 243, 251
benefit corporations, 84
Bentham, Jeremy, 13, 130, 187
Berle, Adolf, 71
Berlin, Isaiah, 156–158, 169, 172, 173, 174, 188
Best Buy, 68
Better Together: Building the American
  Community (Putnam and Feldstein), 247
Bill of Rights, 163, 173
blocked exchanges, 24–25, 48, 236
board of directors, 58, 88
BP Gulf oil spill, 61, 107
Brecht, Bertolt, 239
British Journal of Medicine, 168
Brooks, David, 20
Buddhist economics, 83

business and economic life
  defined, 7
  deontological theories of ethics and,
    54–55
  equal opportunity, concept of, and, 199
  ethics and values of, 1–16
  invisible hand arguments, 8
  law and regulation arguments, 8–9
  normative analysis of, 5
  professional ethics arguments, 9
  social contract theory and, 204–206
  three competing perspectives about the
    role of ethics in, 8–9
business corporations. *See* corporation(s)
business ethics, 71, 116, 133, 140, 145–148,
  166, 183–184, 214. *See also* professional
  ethics
"Business Ethics in a Competitive Market"
  (Nelson), 125
"business judgment rule," 64

capitalism, 50, 55, 66, 79, 83, 96, 112, 141,
  148, 152, 160, 188
  applying the entitlement theory to
    global, 181–183
  character and, 226–240
  communitarianism and, 251–252
  competitive, 228
  and debates about the relevance of
    desert, 217–220
  democratic, 163–164
  markets and, 236–240
  Marx, Karl, on, 220
  as perennial gale of creative destruction,
    244
  philanthropy and, 248
  pragmatic point of view, 240
capitalist mindset, 245
care, ethics of, 231–233
Carnegie, Andrew, 149
Carr, Albert, 232
cause marketing, 128
Cavanaugh, John, 59
Center on Philanthropy (Indiana
  University), 20
Chamberlain, Wilt, 179–180
change agents, 245
character, 15–16
  capitalism and, 236–240
  criticism of capitalism, 226–236
  debates about relationships and, 234–235
  defined, 229

ethics of care, 231–233
  formation of, 230
  markets and, 236–240
  non-Western ethical approaches,
    233–234
  public policy implications from an
    institutional point of view, 235–236
  relationships and, 224–241
  virtue ethics, 229–231
character-based education, 16
character-based ethics, 230
Chicago Tribune, 128
China
  agricultural reform in, 44
  property relations in, 49
  Western ownership practices and, 49
  as world's third largest economic
    entity, 59
Christian theology, 234
Christian virtues, 234
Citizens United vs. Federal Election
  Commission, 91
civil rights, 197
civil society, 127–128, 149
claim-right, 31
claims, 49
Coase, Ronald, 142
Coasian theorem, 142
codes of professional ethics, 149
codetermination, 87
Cohen, Gerald, 160
collective action problems, 123, 126. *See*
  also public goods problems; social
  dilemmas
Committee to Encourage Corporate
  Philanthropy, 80
commonalities, of persons, 193
common good, 243–255
  as aggregated interests of all persons, 249
  appeals to, 249
  community and, 243–255
  of community derived from social
    nature of persons, 249–250
  defined, 248
  individualism and, 251
  justice and, 252–255
  market triumphalism *vs.* concern for,
    246–247
  materialism and, 251
  meaning of, 248–250
  relevance of culture for ethics and,
    254–255

religious and philosophical traditions and, 250
    as shared interests of each person, 248–249
communal property, 37, 48–49, 53
community, 243–255
    capitalism and, 244–245
    and common good, 243–255
    common good of community derived from the social nature of persons, 249–250
    communitarianism and, 251–252
    creation of, 247
    creative destruction and, 244–245
    intrinsic value of, 83
    markets that build, 247–248
    property rights and, 246
    traditionalist mindset and, 245–246
comparable worth, 216. See also pay equity
comparative equality, 212
compensation, 212–213
competitive capitalism, 228
conflicts of interest, 150–152
    ethics and, 151–152
    NYT ethics and, 151
    professional codes of ethics and, 151–152
    whistleblowing and, 151
consent, welfare and, 112–113
consequentialism, 13, 53, 175
    ethical, 13
    utilitarianism, 13
consequentialist ethics for property rights, 53
Constant, Benjamin, 164
constitutional rights, 91
consumer ethics, 153
consumerism, 251
Consumer Reports magazine, 104
consumer rights, 173
consumption philanthropy, 128
Container Store, 149
conventionalism, property rights, 52. See also cultural relativism
conventional relativism, 51
conventional rights, 188
cooperatives, 59
copyrights, 38
    application of, 38
    defined, 38
corporate charitable giving, 63
corporate citizenship, 84. See also corporate social responsibility (CSR)
corporate donations, 128
corporate ethics, 153
corporate giving, 20, 63, 80
corporate governance, 71
corporate law, 59
corporate personality, 91. See also corporate personhood
corporate personhood, 90–91
corporate purpose, 62–63, 78–82

corporate responsibility officers (CROs), 84
corporate rights, 40
corporate social responsibility (CSR), 67–69, 84, 127–129, 149, 230
    described, 67
    descriptive and normative interpretation of, 68
    interpreting from the stakeholder perspective, 84–85
    interpreting from the stockholder perspective, 67–69
    stakeholder theory of, 75–92
    stockholder view of, 10, 58–73
corporation(s), 58–59
    cooperatives, 59
    defined, 58
    and government, 85–87
    large, 59
    partnerships, 59
    personification of, 90–91
    profit maximization, 62–63
    purpose, 62–63
    small, 59
    social goals, 80
    sole proprietorships, 59
    stakeholder theory of, 60
    stockholder theory of, 60
cost/benefit analysis (CBA), 131
Craigslist (online trading system), 47
Create Jobs for USA program, 79
creative destruction
    capitalism as the perennial gale of, 244
    and community, 244–245
    defined, 244
cross-cultural training, 234
CSR. See corporate social responsibility (CSR)
CSR annual reports, 84
CSR rating agencies, 84
CSR-related shareholder proposals, 67, 84
cultural ethical relativist, 51
cultural norms, 11
    defined, 11
    recognizing, 11
cultural relativism, 52. See also conventionalism, property rights
culture
    defined, 48
    property relations and, 48
    property rights and, 48–49
    relevance for ethics, 254–255
customary property rights, 46–47
    fair trade, concept of, 47
    international business practices and, 47
    online trading systems and, 47
    regulation of, 46
    social networks and, 47

Dalai Lama, 233
Dancing with the Stars (television show), 25
d'Arge, Ralph, 144

Declaration of Human Rights (United Nations), 187
Declaration of Independence, 177, 187
Defoe, Daniel, 98
democracy, 162–163
    Athenian, 164
    and markets, 162–163
Democracy in America (De Toqueville), 139
democratic capitalism, 163–164
democratic socialism, 164
deontological theories of ethics, 14
    business and economic life and, 54–55
    for property rights, 53
descriptive or explanatory analysis, 26. See also positive analysis
desert basis, 210
desert(s)
    advocating reforms, 216–217
    from an institutional point of view, 215–216
    capitalism and debates about the relevance of, 217–220
    challenging the relevance of, 217–220
    concept of, 210–212
    institutional, 218
    from a personal point of view, 214–215
    and professional ethics, 214–217
    staying power of, 220
deserved wages, 212–214
De Soto, Hernando, 46, 49
desperate exchanges, 23
De Toqueville, Alexis, 138
dinner table test, 148
The Doctrine of Right (Kant), 34
doctrine of the golden mean (Aristotle), 230
Dodd-Frank Wall Street Reform and Consumer Protection Act (2010), 151
domestic law, 45
Donne, John, 250
duties, 14, 31. See also obligations

Eastern wisdom traditions, 233
eBay, 104
economic globalization, 49–50
economic systems, 49–50
    capitalism, 50
    socialism, 50
The Economist magazine, 68
education
    character-based, 16
    higher, 158
    public, 167
efficiency, 96–113
    as a basis for criticizing markets, 105–108
    complications about the meaning of, 109–113
    defined, 98
    ethics and, 96–113
    general features of debates regarding, 108–109
    Pareto improvement, 97
    preferences and, 110–112
    well-being and, 110–112

efficiency gain(s), 97, 110. *See also* Pareto improvements
  background conditions for trade to create, 102
  idealized markets creating, 98–100
efficiency standard, ethical and practical appeal of, 108–109
egalitarians, 192
  equality, value of, 194, 195
  institutions, role of, 194, 195
  liberal, 143
egoism, 13
  ethical, 13, 71, 88, 90
  psychological, 20, 70–71, 88, 145
Eikenberry, Angela, 128
eminent domain, 19–20, 40, 159
  defined, 19
  use of, 40
emotional dispositions, 234
employee rights, 173
employer rights, 173
Enlightenment, 162
Enron, 71
entitlements, 214–217
  legal, 214
entitlement theory of justice, 178
  applying to global capitalism, 181–183
  assistance, rights to, 186
  criticisms of, 184–186
  interdependence of ethics and justice, 183
  undeserved inequalities, 184–186
entrepreneurial loans, 46
entrepreneurial spirit, 220
Environmental Protection Agency, 69
epistemic device, defined, 103
Epistemology, 103
equal employment opportunity laws, 199
equality, 191–206
  civic, 197
  comparative, 212
  fundamental, 192
  and hunger, 198
  implications for institutions, 195–202
  before the law, 197
  political, 197
equality of opportunity, 201
  fair, 201
  formal, 201
equal opportunity, 198–200. *See also* equal outcomes
equal opportunity society, 200–202
equal outcomes, 198–200. *See also* equal opportunity
ethical absolutism, 52
ethical argument(s), 82–83
  structure of, 67
ethical consequentialism, 13
ethical egoism, 13, 71, 88, 90
ethical integrity, 148
ethical language, 193
ethical motives, 125–126
  and social norms, 125–126

ethical non-relativism, 52
ethical objectivity, 52
ethical obligations, 203
ethical pluralism, 188
ethical reasoning
  methods of, 16
  structure of, 67
ethical relativism, 51
ethical theories, 12–16
  assessing actions apart from their consequences, 13–14
  assessing the consequences of action, 12–13
  character and virtue in, 15–16
  character-based, 15–16
  deontological, 14
  ethical reasoning, methods of, 16
  ethics of care, 15
  feminist, 15
  importance of, 12–16
  nonconsequentialist, 14
  people's motives, importance of, 14–15
ethical universalism, 52
ethics
  Buddhist approach to, 233
  business, 145
  and business, 166–167
  character-based, 230
  conceptual link between freedom and, 167–169
  conflicts of interest and, 151–152
  Confucian approach to, 233
  disconnect between freedom and, 169
  efficiency and, 96–113
  eudaimonistic approach to, 231–232, 234, 239
  freedom and, 166–169
  general model of, 170
  incentives and, 152–153
  of individual decision-making, 4, 7, 10
  institutions and, 152–153
  law and, 12
  markets and, 87–89
  and morality, 11–12
  noninstitutional foundations for professional, 147–148
  non-Western approaches to, 233–234
  professional, 145
  relevance of culture for, 254–255
  self-interest and, 87–89
  sense of, 7, 136
  tests (*See* ethics tests)
  and values, 152–153, 253
ethics of care, 15. *See also* feminist ethical theory
  social interactions and, 232
ethics of individual decision-making, 4, 7, 10
ethics tests, 148
  dinner table test, 148
  golden rule test, 148
  gut test, 148
  New York Times (NYT) test, 148
eudaimonistic ethics, 229

existentialism, 221
externality(ies)
  negative, 102, 107, 111, 143, 166
  positive, 102
  workplace, 202
ExxonMobil, 184

fair equality of opportunity, 201
fair trade, concept of, 47
false consciousness, 219
FDA. *See* U.S. Food and Drug Administration (FDA)
Feldstein, Lewis M., 247
feminist ethical theory, 15. *See also* ethics of care
Fiddler on the Roof (drama), 246
Fifth Amendment, 19
First Amendment, 91, 173
Foner, Eric, 172
Ford Motor Company, 133
formal equality of opportunity, 201
formalized legal rights, 46
forum, 25
forward-looking reasons, 14
free contracts, 219
freedom
  ancient societies and, 164
  business ethics and, 166–167
  conceptual link between ethics and, 167–169
  defined, 158
  disconnect between ethics and, 169
  and ethics, 166–169
  institutional implications of negative, 159–162
  negative, 157–158
  positive, 158–159
Freedom House, 182
Freeman, R. Edward, 140
free markets, 161
free-rider, defined, 118
free-riding problem, 118
free speech rights, 24
French, Peter, 91
Friedman, Milton, 60–61, 62, 65, 67, 68, 72, 79, 89, 141, 145, 178
Fulghum, Robert, 1
fully efficient situation, 97. *See also* Pareto optimal situation
fundamental equality, 192, 193–194
  defined, 192
Fundamental Legal Conceptions (Hohfeld), 30

Galbraith, Kenneth, 105, 106
Gallup, 238–239
Gauthier, David, 139
Gawande, Atul A., 168
GDP. *See* gross domestic product (GDP)
gift-giving, 20–21
The Gift Relationship (Titmus), 247
Gilligan, Carol, 231
Giving Pledge, 248

Giving USA Foundation, 20
global capitalism, applying the entitlement
    theory to, 181–183
global governance gaps, 77
GNH. *See* gross national happiness (GNH)
    index
goal-oriented ethical reasoning, 175
goal-oriented ethical traditions, 175
goal-oriented morality, 175, 176
Godlee, Fione, 168
Golding, William, 19, 20
Goltz, Jay, 150
goods. *See also* services
    defined, 116
    private, 116–117
Google, 38
government, 6
    business role *vs.*, 69–70
    corporations and, 85–87
    eminent domain and, 19
    institutional point of view, role of, 141–142
    law and regulation model and, 143–144
    property rights and, 46–48
    regulation (*See* government regulation)
government regulation, 126–127
    and privatizing goods, 126–127
Grameen Bank, 46, 100
Gramm, Phil, 66, 67
Great Depression, 239
Green movement, 233, 237
gross domestic product (GDP), 59, 78, 112
gross national happiness (GNH) index, 112
group rights, 174, 183
gut test (ethics), 148

Hammergren, John, 191
happiness, 13, 53, 108–110, 112, 131, 132, 172,
    176. *See also* welfare; well-being
Hardin, Garret, 124, 126, 127
Harris, Sam, 249
higher education, 158
Hobbes, Thomas, 19, 20, 59–60, 61, 65, 142
Hohfeld, Wesley Newcomb, 30, 34
Hohfeld's four property relations, 31
    claim-right and duty relation, 31
    immunity and no power relation, 31
    liberty-right and no claim-right relation, 31
    power and liability relation, 31
homo economicus ("economic man"), 106
honesty, transparency and, 151
Honore, A. M., 36
Hugo, Victor, 1
human personality. *See* personality
human rights, 41, 76–82, 86, 107, 111,
    173–174, 182, 187, 196, 203, 205
Hume, David, 53, 54, 55, 187, 232
hunger, equality and, 198
Hunt, E. K., 144
Huxley, Aldus, 96, 97–98
hypocritical window-dressing, 68

Ice Age, 19
ideal market(s)

actual markets approximating, 103–105
    defined, 103
ideas, progression of, 252–253
immunity/ies, 31, 49
incentive-compatible institutional design, 139
incentives
    ethics and, 152–153
    and institutions, 152–153
income differentials, 215–216
income inequality, 196–198
individual ethical relativist, 51
individualism, 251
individual rights, 164, 174, 183, 193, 217
Industrial Revolution, 30
inequalities
    civic, 198
    effects of, 192
    income, 196–198
    political, 198
    undeserved, 184–186
    wealth, 196–198
    workplace, 202
informed consent, 166
injustice, rectifying, 180–181
institutional desert, 218
institutional legitimacy, 162
    consent and, 162
    defined, 162
institutional point of view, 4, 89–90, 106
    government and, 126–129, 141–142
    negative freedom and, 159–160
    positive freedom and, 162–163
    privatization of goods and, 126–129
institutions
    ethics and, 152–153
    implications for, 195–202
    incentives and, 152–153
    point of view, government and, 141–142
instrumental rationality, 101, 115
intangible goods. *See* intangible services
intangible services, 19, 30, 31
integrity, 87, 138, 148, 176
    moral (*See* moral integrity)
intellectual property, 38–39
    copyrights, 38
    patents, 38
    trademarks, 38
    WIPO definition of, 38
international business practices, 47
international law, 45
    characterization of, 46
invisible foot, 144
invisible hand, 136–153
    arguments, 8
    metaphor of, 8, 138–143
invisible hand model, 137
    adjusted, 142–143
    limited role for ethics from a personal
        point of view, 139–141
    limited role for government and law
        from the institutional point of view,
        141–142
    separation thesis, 140

James, LeBron, 179
Jefferson, Thomas, 177, 187
Journal of Business Ethics, 226
just deserts. *See* desert(s)
justice, 15
    and common good, 252–255
    principles of, 205

Kahneman, Daniel, 106
Kant, Immanuel, 14, 34, 169
Kantian duties, 89
Kauffman Foundation, 244
Kelo v New London, 19, 40, 132
Keynes, John Maynard, 157
Keys, Tracey, 59
Kohlberg, Lawrence, 231

law
    corporate, 59
    domestic, 45
    institutional point of view and,
        141–143
    international, 45
    property rights and, 45–48
    and regulation arguments, 8–9
    rule of (*See* rule of law)
law and regulation model, 137, 143–144
legal entitlement, 214, 215
legal property rights, 46–47
    regulation of, 46
legal rights, 35, 46, 65, 91, 173–174, 187
legitimacy, institutional, 162
Les Misérables (Hugo), 1
Leviathan (Hobbes), 19, 60
liability, 31
liberal egalitarians, 143
libertarians, 143
liberty, 49, 156–171
    two concepts of, 156–159
liberty-right, 31
Lincoln, Abraham, 162, 163
Locke, John, 53–55, 177, 178, 187, 189
Lord of the Flies (Golding), 19

Mackey, John, 60–61, 64, 67, 80, 83, 237
Madoff, Bernie, 71, 210–211, 216
Magna Charta of 1215, 173
Malnight, Thomas W., 59
managerial duties, 78–82
managerial liberty, 72
managerial responsibilities, 62
Manning, Payton, 179
Maritain, Jacques, 250
market exchanges, 19–21, 186
    blocked exchanges, 24–25
    defined, 19
    desperate exchanges, 23
    philanthropic contributions
        and, 20
    violent takings and, 19–20
    voluntary exchanges, 22
market failures, 116, 143, 152
market incentives, 153

market(s)
  background conditions to operate, 25
  building communities, 247–248
  character and, 236–240
  debates about defining, 22–24
  defined, 19
  democracy and, 162–163
  describing, 21
  desperate exchanges, 23
  efficiency as a basis for criticizing,
    105–108
  ethics and, 87–89
  exchanges, 19–21
  fair trade, concept of, and, 47
  freedom of, 160–161
  and noninterference, 161–162
  poverty and, 160–161
  property rights and, 25, 43–44, 159–161
  relationships and, 236–240
  scarcity and, 25
  self-interest and, 70–72, 87–89
  voluntary choice and, 161–162
  voluntary exchanges, 22
market triumphalism, 246–247
Marshall, John, 90
Marx, Karl, 30, 55, 141, 212, 220
materialism, 251
May, Todd, 225–226, 230
McKesson, Inc., 191
McMillan, John, 22, 44
Means, Gardiner, 71
mens rea (law), 15
metaethics, 52
Metallica (music group), 54
metaphysics, 91, 193
Michelman, James H., 226–228, 231, 234,
    236, 237
microcredit. See microlending
microlending, 46–47, 100
Mill, John Stuart, 13, 60, 130, 131, 172, 173,
    174, 187
The Modern Corporation and Private
    Property (Berle and Means), 71
monopoly rights, 35
Moore, Michael, 128
moral aspirations, 203
moral development, 231
  Lawrence Kohlberg's model of, 231
moral integrity, 228
morality
  ethics and, 11–12
  goal-oriented, 175, 176
The Moral Landscape: How Science Can
    Determine Human Values (Harris),
    249
moral liberties, 204
moral obligations, 203
moral rights, 173
moral side-constraints, 175
motivation(s), 20, 85, 88, 125–127, 141, 146,
    152, 170, 209, 234
  altruism and, 20, 233
  egoistic or prudential, 249

ethical, 125–126, 236
ethical egoism and, 88
internal, 234
psychological egoism and, 88
motives, outcome and, 85
Munzer, Stephen, 48
Murphy, Sandi, 191
mutual benefit as a personal value, 148–150

Nagel, Thomas, 192, 194, 195
Napster, 54
National Geographic News, 178
natural rights, 53, 174, 177, 187–188
nature, intrinsic value of, 83
negative externality(ies), 102, 107, 111, 143,
    166
  defined, 102
  rights-infringing, 179
negative freedom, 157–158
  institutional implications of, 159–162
  visions of a free society drawing on,
    164–166
negative liberty. See negative freedom
negative rights, 174, 186, 195
Neibur, Reinhold, 221
Nelson, Julianne, 125
Newman, Paul, 80
News of the Weird (syndicated newspaper
    column), 115
New York Times, 20, 38, 39, 66, 150, 248
New York Times Magazine, 61
New York Times (NYT) test, 148
no claim-right, 31
nonconsequentialist ethical theories, 14
non-consequentialist moralities, 175
nongovernmental organizations (NGOs),
    67, 85, 129
noninterference, 157–158, 161–162
  and markets, 161–162, 186
  positive freedom and, 163
  property rights of, 159–160
  voluntary choice and, 161–162
nonmarket environments
  takings, 19
  types of, 19
nonprofits, 129, 149
norm, defined, 26
normative analysis, defined, 26
normative analysis of business and
    economic life, 5
Nozick, Robert, 173, 175, 177, 178, 180, 186,
    187, 189, 192
Nussbaum, Martha, 110

objectivist account, of improving welfare, 110
objectivity, ethical, 52
obligations, 14, 203–204. See also duties
  and aspirations, 203–204
  defined, 14
  ethical, 203
  moral, 203
Occupy Wall Street movement, 79, 198, 215
Olsaretti, Serena, 161

On Liberty (Mill), 172
online trading systems, 47
outcome, motives and, 85
ownership, of property, 35–36, 48–49
  property rights and, 37

paradox of plenty, 181. See also resource
    curse
Pareto, Vilfredo, 97
Pareto efficiency, 108
  as an ethical ideal, 97–98
  limitations to, 129
  and trade, 99
Pareto improvements, 97, 108. See also
    efficiency gain
Pareto optimal situation, 97. See also fully
    efficient situation
partnerships, 59
patents, 35, 38
  application of, 38
  defined, 38
patient rights, 173
pay equity, 216. See also comparable worth
people's motives, importance of, 14–15
personality, 245–246
personal point of view, 4
personal property, 37
  intangible movable property, 37
  tangible movable property, 37
personal rights, 40, 49, 107
  property rights and, 40
philanthropy, 20, 248
Plato, 138, 158
pluralism, ethical, 188
political legitimacy, 69
political rights, 24, 197
positive analysis, 26. See also descriptive or
    explanatory analysis
positive freedom, 158–159
  consent and, 162
  democracy and, 163
  institutional implications of, 162–166
  noninterference and, 163
  visions of a free society drawing on,
    164–166
positive liberty. See positive freedom
positive rights, 174, 186
positive sum game, 100
poverty, 160–161
  markets and, 160–161
Poverty and Famines: An Essay on
    Entitlements and Deprivation (Sen), 50
pragmatism, 240
preferences
  defined, 110
  efficiency and, 110–112
  well-being and, 110–112
Premium Rush (film), 38
principle of justice in initial acquisition, 179
principle of justice in rectification, 180
principle of justice in transfer, 179
principle of limited liability, 58
prisoner's dilemma, 123

private goods, 116–117
private property, 37, 48, 53
private property rights, 48, 117, 166. *See also* ownership
privatization of goods, institutional point of view, 126–129
professional codes of ethics, 151–152
professional ethics, 145. *See also* business ethics
  within an efficiency framework, 145–147
  arguments, 9
  desert and, 214–217
  noninstitutional foundations for, 147–148
  and the personal point of view, 202–204
  social contract and, 206
professional ethics model, 137, 144–150
  mutual benefit as a personal value, 148–150
  noninstitutional foundations for professional ethics, 147–148
  professional ethics within an efficiency framework, 145–147
proliferation of rights, 186
property
  communal, 37
  defined, 30
  intellectual, 38–39
  nature of, 29–41
  ownership, 35–36
  personal, 37
  private, 37
  public, 37
  real, 37
  relations (*See* property relations)
  as relations among people, 29–30
property relations
  defined, 30
  Hohfeld's four property relations, 31
  tips for learning and applying, 33–34
property rights, 25, 29, 37, 50–51, 159–161
  as an intermediary between markets and government, 48
  application, 32, 35
  conceptual terrain of, 34
  consequentialist ethics for, 53
  conventionalism about, 52
  and culture, 48–49
  customary, 46
  deontological ethics for, 53
  Hohfeld's conception of, 30–32
  importance of, 50–51
  and law, 45–48
  legal, 46
  limits of, 39–41
  markets and, 43–44, 159–161
  non-consequentialist ethics for, 53
  of noninterference, 159–160
  normative theories of, 52–55
  ownership and, 37
  patents, 35
  personal rights and, 40
  of trade, 160
psychological egoism, 20, 70–71, 88, 145

public education, 167
public goods, 115–133, 248
  corporate responsibility, 127–129
  defined, 117
  ethical motives, 125–126
  government regulation, 126–127
  "The Tragedy of the Commons" (Hardin), 124–125
  two neighborhoods and a park problem, 118–124
public goods problems, 123. *See also* collective action problems; social dilemmas
  government regulation and, 127
  privatization and, 127
public property, 37
Putnam, Robert D., 247

Quirk, Joe, 38

Radford, R. A., 18, 140
Rand, Ayn, 71
rationality, instrumental, 101
Rawls, John, 185, 188, 204–205, 218, 253
real property, 37
reasoning
  consequentialism, 13
  ethical, 67
  goal-oriented ethical, 175
  utilitarian, 131, 133, 176
Reason magazine, 60
Reich, Robert, 70
relationships, 224–241
  capitalism and, 236–240
  and character, 224–241
  debates about character and, 234–235
  markets and, 236–240
  value of, 243
relativism, 51–52
  conventional, 51
  ethical, 51
  subjective, 52
representation, defined, 163
resource curse, 181. *See also* paradox of plenty
Ricard, Matthieu, 233
rights, 172–189
  of artists, 54
  to assistance, 186
  civil, 197
  constitutional, 91
  consumer, 173
  conventional, 188
  corporate, 40
  customary property, 46–47, 67, 174
  deontological tradition of, 177, 186, 192
  employee, 173
  employer, 173
  equal, 193, 197
  formalized legal, 46
  free speech, 24
  group, 174

  human, 41, 77, 79–81, 86, 111, 174, 187, 196, 203, 205
  individual, 174, 193, 217
  justifying, 186–189
  legal property, 46–47, 49–50, 174
  to life, 41
  and markets, 178–184
  monopoly, 35
  moral, 173
  natural, 174, 187–188
  negative, 174, 186, 195
  non-violation of, 178–179
  patient, 173
  personal, 40, 49, 107
  political, 24, 197
  positive, 174, 186
  private property, 48, 117, 166
  proliferation of, 186
  as side-constraints, 175–177
  stakeholder, 78–82
  stockholder, 58, 62, 63–65, 75, 203
  student, 173
  violation of, 111, 174, 176–177, 180–185, 195, 198, 201, 203
rights-infringing negative externalities, 179
Robinson Crusoe economy, 98
Roger and Me (documentary film), 128
Roosevelt, Theodore, 205
Rousseau, Jean-Jacques, 204
Royal Dutch Shell, 79
Ruggie, John, 76
Ruggie Report (United Nations), 76, 77, 79, 80
rule of law, 196–197
rule utilitarianism, 130, 133, 187

Saad, Lydia, 238
Sandel, Michael, 246
scarcity, 25
Schor, Juliet, 228
Schultz, Howard, 79
Schumacher, E. F., 83
Schumpeter, Joseph, 244
SEC. *See* Security and Exchange Commission (SEC)
Security and Exchange Commission (SEC), 71
self-interest, 7, 70–72, 87–89, 139
  ethics and, 87–89
  and markets, 70–72
  markets and, 87–89
Sen, Amartya, 50–51, 96, 160
sense of ethics, 5, 136
separateness, of persons, 193
separation thesis, 140, 232. *See also* invisible hand model
services, defined, 116. *See also* goods
shareholders. *See* stockholders
Sher, George, 212–213, 217
Singer, Peter, 131
Skinner, Quentin, 60
Smith, Adam, 101, 111, 138
Smith, Vernon, 99, 100, 101, 107–108

The Social Animal: The Hidden Sources of Love, Character, and Achievement (Brooks), 20
social constructs, 219
social contract
    business and, 205–206
    professional ethics and, 206
social contract theory, 204–206
    business and the social contract, 205–206
    professional ethics and the social contract, 206
social dilemmas, 123. *See also* collective action problems; public goods problems
social interactions, ethics of care and, 232
socialism, 50
socially responsible investing (SRI), 84
social networks, 47, 206
social norms, 125–126
    ethical motives and, 125–126
social performance, 84. *See also* corporate social responsibility (CSR)
social responsibility investing (SRI), 67
"The Social Responsibility of Business Is to Increase Its Profits" (Friedman), 67
Socrates, 130
sole proprietorships, 59
SRI. *See* social responsibility investing (SRI)
stakeholder rights, 78–82
stakeholders, 60, 75, 78, 100
stakeholder theory of corporations, 60
Starbucks, 79
Stevens, John Paul, 20
Stiglitz, Joseph, 144
stockholders, 58–59
    debates about rights of, 63–65
    property rights, 62
    rights, 58, 62, 63–65, 75, 203
    theory of corporations, 60
stockholder theory of corporations, 60
strict liability, defined, 15
Strom, Stephanie, 248
student rights, 173
subjective relativism, 52
subjectivist account of better-off, 110
Supercapitalism (Reich), 70
supererogatory actions, 15, 203
sustainability, 84. *See also* corporate social responsibility (CSR)

takings, 19–20
    defined, 19
    involuntary, 23
    violent, 19
    voluntary, 23
tangible goods, 19, 30, 31
teleological theories of ethics, 175
A Theory of Justice (Rawls), 204, 253
Thomason, Harry, 35

Tindall, Kip, 149
Titmus, Richard M., 247
trade
    Pareto efficiency and, 99
    testing the background assumptions of, 106
    transaction costs and, 101
    welfare effects of, 159
    welfare improving, 166
trademarks, 38, 39
    application of, 38
    defined, 38
trade-offs, among values, 188–189
traditionalist mindset, 245
"The Tragedy of the Commons" (Hardin), 124–125
transaction costs, 101, 104, 109, 112, 143
transactions, history of, 178–179
transparency, honesty and, 151
treatment, modes of, 211
triple bottom line (CSR), 84
Tucker, Albert, 123
Tversky, Amos, 106
"Two Concepts of Liberty" (Berlin), 172

Ubel, Peter, 105, 106
Ultimate Rush (Quirk), 38
undeserved inequalities, 184–186
    defined, 185
UN Global Compact. *See* United Nations Global Compact
Unical, 86
United Nations, 38, 41, 86
United Nations Global Compact, 81, 86
    goal of, 81
    ten principles of, 81
United Nations Human Rights Council, 76
United States Patent and Trademark Office (USPTO), 35
Universal Declaration of Human Rights, 15, 41, 81, 173, 250
universalism, ethical, 52
U.S. Food and Drug Administration (FDA), 24
USPTO. *See* United States Patent and Trademark Office (USPTO)
utilitarianism, 13, 176, 187, 188
    act, 130
    attraction and limitations to, 132–133
    problems with, 132–133
    rule, 130, 133, 187
    tradition of, 130–132
utility, 13, 130–131

values
    defined, 4
    ethics and, 152–153, 253
    general model of, 170
    interpreting the nature of, 254–255
    trade-offs among, 188–189

vegetarianism, 131
"veil of ignorance," 204
vice, defined, 229
virtue ethics, 16, 229–231
virtue(s), 15–16
    character and, 15–16
    defined, 229
    ethics, 16, 229–231
voluntary choice, 161–162
    markets and, 161–162
voluntary exchanges, 22

wages, deserved, 212–214
Wall Street (film), 71
Wall Street Journal, 79
Walmart, 59, 61, 104, 244
Walzer, Michael, 23, 24
Wangchuck, Jigme Singye, 112
wealth inequality, 196–198
The Wealth of Nations (Smith), 101
welfare, 108. *See also* happiness; well-being
    and consent, 112–113
    happiness and, 108
    individual, 108
    objectivist account of improving, 110
welfare-improving gains, 160
well-being, 108. *See also* happiness; welfare
    efficiency and, 110–112
    happiness and, 108
    individual, 108
Wenar, Leif, 181–184
whistleblowers, protection of, 151
whistleblowing, 151
    conflict of interest and, 151
    Dodd-Frank Wall Street Reform and Consumer Protection Act (2010) and, 151
    external, 151
    internal, 151
Whole Foods, 60, 61, 67
Wilt Chamberlain example, 179–180, 201
wisdom, defined, 221
women, ethics of care and, 231–232
Women and Human Development: The Capabilities Approach (Nussbaum), 110
women's suffrage movement, 197
Woods, Tiger, 179
workplace
    externalities, 202
    inequalities, 202
    internal relationships, 202–203
World Bank, 191
World Intellectual Property Organization, 38
    intellectual property, defined by, 38
World War II, 18, 156

Yunus, Muhammad, 46–47, 100

zero sum games, 100